Optimal experience

Psychological studies of flow in consciousness

Optimal experience

Psychological studies of flow in consciousness

Edited by
Mihaly Csikszentmihalyi
and
Isabella Selega Csikszentmihalyi

CAMBRIDGE
UNIVERSITY PRESS

Published by the Press Syndicate of the University of Cambridge
The Pitt Building, Trumpington Street, Cambridge CB2 1RP
40 West 20th Street, New York, NY 10011-4211, USA
10 Stamford Road, Oakleigh, Victoria 3166, Australia

First published 1988
First paperback edition 1992

Printed in the United States of America

Library of Congress Cataloging-in-Publication Data
Optimal experience.
Bibliography: p.
Includes index.
1. Consciousness.   2. Consciousness – Cross cultural
studies   I. Csikszentmihalyi, Mihaly.
II. Csikszentmihalyi, Isabella Selega.   [DNLM:
1. Consciousness.   2. Cross Cultural Comparison.
BF 311 062]
BF311.063   1988   153   87-24289

British Library Cataloguing in Publication Data
Optimal experience : studies of flow
in consciousness.
1. Consciousness – Religious aspects
2. Psychology and religion
I. Csikszentmihalyi, Mihaly.
II. Csikszentmihalyi, Isabella Selega.
291.2'2   BL53

ISBN 0-521-34288-0 hardback
ISBN 0-521-43809-8 paperback

For Mark and Christopher

Contents

Acknowledgments

In the years since we first started studying flow so many people have helped with ideas, moral support, and financial funding, that it is not humanly possible to give each of them the credit due. Nevertheless, it is a pleasure to remember here those persons who have left a particular mark on the development of the research reported in this volume. No one will ever know how important their encouragement and support have been in furthering these difficult investigations. This token of thanks should not, however, place any responsibility on their shoulders for any weaknesses in our work.

The first studies on the flow experience were funded by the Applied Research Branch of the National Institute of Mental Health. The more recent developments have been supported by the Spencer Foundation, whose Board has exercised over the years a very beneficial influence on innovative research in the behavioral sciences. We should like to thank personally the former president, Thomas James, and the executive director, Marion Faldet, for their patience and understanding.

At the University of Chicago the friendship and encouragement of Bernice Neugarten and Jacob W. Getzels have always been very dear to us. Norman Bradburn, Robert Butler, Donald Fiske, John MacAloon, and Salvatore Maddi all have done work in areas related to this volume, and with their scholarship they have helped the development of our ideas. Donald Levine and Edward Laumann have provided moral support with their interest on numerous occasions.

Of scholars at other universities Donald Campbell of Lehigh has been a model of how psychologists could apply their thoughts rigorously to areas outside their immediate field. Jerome Singer of Yale and M. Brewster Smith of Santa Cruz have been attentive and judicious critics of our work. With Howard Gardner of Harvard and David Feldman of Tufts we have had many pleasant and stimulating exchanges through the

xii *Acknowledgments*

years. Jean Hamilton, now in private medical practice in Washington, D.C., was an early friend and collaborator who has continued to work in this area. Of the many colleagues whose influence is evident in this volume we should like to single out Richard deCharms of Washington University in St. Louis; Edward Deci and Michael Ryan of Rochester; Edward Diener, Jack Kelly, and Douglas Kleiber at the University of Illinois, Urbana; Mark Lepper of Stanford; and Brian Sutton-Smith of the University of Pennsylvania. Three journal editors have been particularly helpful in disseminating the research on flow: Thomas Greening of *The Journal of Humanistic Psychology*; Ladd Wheeler of the *Review of Personality and Social Psychology*, and John Broughton of *New Ideas in Psychology*. The interest and encouragement of Ralph Burhoe, founder of the Institute on Religion in an Age of Science, and of Philip Hefner, its current president, have also been important. Of those who have presented the ideas contained in this volume to a wider public we should mention Daniel Goleman, now with *The New York Times*, Robert Cross of the *Chicago Tribune*, John McCormick of *Newsweek*, and Michael Dibb, who produced documentaries for the BBC.

Among colleagues abroad we wish to acknowledge Professors Hans Aebli at the University of Berne in Switzerland; Michael Argyle at Oxford University, England; Hermann Brandstetter at the University of Linz, Austria; James Crook, of Bristol University, England; Marten De Vries at Limburgh University in Maastricht, Holland; Heinz Heckhausen of the Max-Planck Institute in Munich, Germany; Hiroaki Imamura at Chiba University, Japan; Elisabeth Noelle-Neumann at the University of Mainz, Germany; Ivàn Vitànyi at the Center for Research in Culture in Budapest, Hungary; and in Canada Roger Mannell and Jiri Zuzanèk at Waterloo University; Len Wankel at the University of Alberta; and Gerald Kenyon at the University of Lethbridge.

Of those who have at one time or another contributed to the research included in this volume we wish to thank Ronald Graef, who was among the first collaborators in the study of flow; Edward Donner, Tom Figurski, Susan Gianinno, Marlin Hoover, Suzanne Prescott, Barbara Rubinstein, and Carolyn Schneider.

Finally we should like to thank Susan Milmoe of Cambridge University Press for her helpful and astute editorial leadership.

Contributors

Maria T. Allison, Department of Leisure Studies, Arizona State University.

Massimo Carli, Institute of Psychology, University of Milan Medical School, Milan, Italy.

Isabella Selega Csikszentmihalyi, Editor and Writer, Chicago.

Mihaly Csikszentmihalyi, Committee on Human Development, Department of Behavioral Sciences, University of Chicago.

Margaret Carlisle Duncan, Department of Leisure Studies, University of Wisconsin, Milwaukee.

Antonella Delle Fave, Institute of Psychology, University of Milan Medical School, Milan, Italy.

Seongyeul Han, Department of Psychology, University of Seoul, Korea.

Reed Larson, Department of Child Development, University of Illinois, Urbana.

Judith LeFevre, Committee on Human Development, University of Chicago.

Richard D. Logan, Department of Human Development, University of Wisconsin, Green Bay.

Jim Macbeth, School of Social Sciences, Murdoch University, Western Australia.

Fausto Massimini, Institute of Psychology, University of Milan Medical School, Milan, Italy.

Richard G. Mitchell, Jr., Department of Sociology, Oregon State University.

Jeanne Nakamura, Committee on Human Development, University of Chicago.

Kevin Rathunde, Committee on Human Development, University of Chicago.

Ikuya Sato, Research Institute for Japanese Culture, Tohoku University, Sandai, Japan.

Anne J. Wells, School of Nursing, University of Illinois, Chicago.

I. A theoretical model of optimal experience

1. Introduction

MIHALY CSIKSZENTMIHALYI

Some ten years ago the first publications reporting studies of what we have called the "flow experience" appeared in print, beginning with an article in the *Journal of Humanistic Psychology* and then the book *Beyond Boredom and Anxiety* (Csikszentmihalyi 1975a, 1975b). In the relatively short span of time since those unheralded beginnings, scholars in a variety of disciplines have found the concept of an optimal state of experience theoretically useful. A great amount of research has accumulated during the decade, and some of the results are now being applied in educational, clinical, and commercial settings. *Flow* has become a technical term in the field of intrinsic motivation. This introduction briefly reviews the events related to the development of this concept, and the rest of the volume presents some of the most representative and important contributions to the study of the flow experience during these crucial initial years.

The prehistory of the flow concept: before 1975

I was led to investigate the range of experiences that eventually became known as *flow* by certain observations I had made in the course of my doctoral research with a group of male artists (Csikszentmihalyi 1965; Getzels & Csikszentmihalyi 1976). The artists I studied spent hour after hour each day painting or sculpting with great concentration. They obviously enjoyed their work immensely, and thought it was the most important thing in the world. Yet it was quite typical for an artist to lose all interest in the painting he had spent so much time and effort working on as soon as it was finished. As long as he was at work on a canvas, the artist was completely immersed in the painting. It filled his thoughts for twenty-four hours a day. Yet as soon as the paint was dry, he usually

3

stacked the canvas in a distant corner of the studio against a wall and promptly forgot it.

Few artists expected any of their paintings to make them rich or famous. Why, then, did they work so hard at the easel – as hard as any executive hoping for a raise or a promotion? None of the extrinsic rewards that usually motivate behavior seemed to be present. Money and recognition appeared to play a minimal part. The object itself – the finished work of art – held few attractions once it was finished. So what accounted for the deep fascination that painting had for the artists?

The deterministic metaphysics underlying modern science suggested that there must be an answer (Popper 1965, p. 61). Regularities in human behavior don't just happen by chance. They are either caused or they have reasons. In psychology, the most widely held causal explanation for why artists paint is some variant of the notion of "sublimation." They enjoy painting, according to this explanation, because it is the closest socially acceptable symbolic expression of the artists' true desires, which are repressed instinctual cravings. But if one observes artists at work for any length of time, the sublimation hypothesis wears thin fairly soon. There is just too much genuine excitement and involvement with the emerging forms and colors to explain it all in terms of a substitution for something else. And why does the artist typically keep seeking ever more complex challenges, why does he constantly perfect his skills if the whole point is to experience vicariously the simple forbidden pleasures of his sexual programming? Up to a certain point sublimation as a cause might be a useful proposition. A few of the artists seemed to have begun painting partly to resolve an Oedipal tangle, or even earlier repressions. But whatever the original cause might have been, it was obvious that the activity of painting produced its own autonomous positive rewards.

Nor were these rewards something that artists expected to achieve after the activity was completed. The usual reason for actions that are not driven by causes is the expectation of reaching a goal-state that acts as a reward for the action. But the reason for painting did not seem to be the usual desire to achieve external goals. That suggested that the reasons might be within the activity: that the rewards of painting came from painting itself.

In the mid-sixties, when these observations were being made, few psychologists were as yet interested in intrinsic motivation; the ruling paradigm was still exclusively focused on explaining behavior in terms of extrinsic rewards. One of the few exceptions was Abraham Maslow.

His distinction between *process* and *product* orientations in creative behavior, which led him to identify "peak experiences," was the conceptual framework closest to the phenomena I was trying to understand (Maslow 1965, 1968). He described people who behaved like the artists in my study: people who worked hard not in order to get conventional rewards, but because the work itself was rewarding. Maslow ascribed the motivation to a desire for "self-actualization," a need to discover one's potentialities and limitations through intense activity and experience.

Maslow's explanation was compelling, but it left many questions unanswered. For example, could any kind of process – or activity – give intrinsic rewards, or only a few chosen ones, like the making of art? Did all intrinsically rewarding experiences *feel* the same; were the intrinsic rewards from art the same as those one gets from sports, or from writing poetry? Did all people have the same propensity to be intrinsically motivated, or did one have to be born an artist to enjoy the making of art? Maslow's pioneering work, primarily idiographic and reflective in nature, did not explore very far the empirical implications of these ideas.

Still intrigued by the question of intrinsic motivation, I turned to the literature on play in the hope of finding an explanation. A substantial body of thought had been developing about the play of children (Piaget 1951; Sutton-Smith 1971) and of adults (Huizinga [1939] 1970; Caillois 1958; Sutton-Smith & Roberts 1963). Play is clearly intrinsically motivated. Whatever its evolutionary significance and adaptive value might be (Beach 1945; Bekoff 1972, 1978; Fagen 1981; Smith 1982), people play because it is enjoyable. My contribution to this literature in the late sixties was an article describing the historical changes in the way rock climbing has been practiced and experienced (Csikszentmihalyi 1969), and an embryonic model of the flow experience developed with H. Stith Bennett, who at that time was a student at Lake Forest College (Csikszentmihalyi & Bennett 1971).

By the early seventies, research on intrinsic motivation was gathering momentum at a few universities. The theoretical justification for this movement can be traced in part to D. O. Hebb's (1955, 1966) "optimal arousal hypothesis" that was extensively studied by Daniel Berlyne and J. McV. Hunt, among others (Hunt 1965; Berlyne 1960, 1966; Day, Berlyne, & Hunt 1971). This hypothesis was a way to account for laboratory experiments showing that even rats did not work exclusively to get food or to avoid shocks, but were also motivated by novelty, curiosity, and competence "drives" (Harlow 1953; Butler & Alexander 1955; White

1959). If any new stimulus could start complex exploratory behavior on the part of a monkey or a rat, this meant that the days when a few basic drives could account for everything an animal did were over. Among the influential statements that have supported this position were the volume edited by Fiske and Maddi (1961), the theoretical article by Dember (1974), and the review by deCharms and Muir (1978).

The first generation of researchers to focus directly on intrinsic motivation included Richard deCharms (1968, 1976), who earlier had investigated the achievement motive with David McClelland. His review of the literature on social motivation almost a decade ago (deCharms & Muir 1978) helped put the concept of intrinsic motivation on the intellectual agenda of psychologists. In his research, deCharms found striking differences among schoolchildren in terms of whether they did or did not feel in control of their lives. He called the first type "origins," because they believed that what they did was what they wanted to do; and he called the second type "pawns," because they felt that they were just being pushed around by outside forces. An important characteristic of the "origins" was their intrinsic motivation: Since they felt they owned their behavior, they took it more seriously and enjoyed it regardless of outside recognition. Indeed, deCharms hypothesized that in contrast to what drive theories might predict, if people were rewarded for doing things they had initially chosen spontaneously, their intrinsic motivation to do them would decrease.

At the University of Rochester, Edward Deci tested deCharms's prediction (1971, 1972, 1975). He found that if people were given money for doing things they enjoyed, they lost interest in those things faster than when they were not rewarded. Deci agreed with deCharms that under such conditions people came to see their involvement in the activity as being instrumental, controlled by external forces rather than freely chosen. Recognition of the reality of intrinsic motivation led Deci and his colleagues by an inevitable logic to investigations of autonomy and self-determination (Deci & Ryan 1985).

Mark Lepper's team of researchers at Stanford University discovered intrinsic motivation at about the same time. They were influenced by the social psychology of Heider (1958) and Kelley (1967, 1973), which ascribed greater importance to causal attributions than earlier cognitive theories of motivation had, and by the self-perception theory of Bem (1967, 1972), which assigns a similar autonomous power to the self construct. Studying children engaged in play activities, Lepper's team replicated and refined the overjustification findings, specifying the conditions under which rewards interfere with behavior, and thus clarifying the dynamics of intrinsic motivation (Lepper, Greene, & Nisbett 1973; Greene & Lepper 1974; Lepper & Greene 1975). The literature on this topic was summarized in a volume appropriately entitled *The Hidden Costs of Reward* (Lepper & Greene 1978).

Thus by the early seventies there seemed to be enough of a theoretical rationale for believing that people were motivated to act by a much wider range of rewards than traditional psychology had suspected, and that many of these rewards were not based on prewired consummatory or homeostatic principles, like eating, having sex, or avoiding pain. But demonstrations of the importance of intrinsic rewards were still based on rather restricted laboratory settings, in which the behavior of small children was observed according to a few fixed experimental paradigms. Very little was known about intrinsic motivation in natural settings. No one knew whether the deep involvement artists experienced at their easels was a common occurrence among adults in other walks of life, and whether that involvement was the manifestation of an underlying experience so enjoyable as to be a reward in its own right.

The slowly cumulating research on intrinsic motivation differed from my own interests in another important respect. Lepper, Deci, deCharms and the other researchers in the field were interested primarily in intrinsically motivated *behavior* – in what made it happen and what its consequences were. They were inducing intrinsically motivated performance in laboratories, but they were not concerned about how the person so motivated was feeling. They were prepared to accept the existence of intrinsically motivated experience without wishing to know what it was; what they wanted to know was how it affected the subjects' task persistence or creativity. Although I, too, was interested in these issues, my first concern was about *the quality of subjective experience* that made a behavior intrinsically rewarding. How did intrinsic rewards *feel*? Why were they rewarding?

In order to answer these questions, I and my students, first at Lake Forest College and then at the University of Chicago, interviewed in depth over two hundred people who presumably would be familiar with intrinsic rewards. These were individuals who spent great amounts of time in strenuous activities for which they got no money and little recognition. They included amateur athletes, chess masters, rock climbers, dancers, high school basketball players, and composers of music. Basically what we wanted to find out was how such people described the activity when it was going particularly well.

The results of those studies constitute the first coherent statement about flow (Csikszentmihalyi 1974, 1975a, 1975b). They will not be summarized here, since a more systematic presentation of the flow model will be given in the next chapter. Their major contribution was to identify, across the widely diverse activities, a common experience that the respondents felt was *autotelic*, or rewarding in and of itself. Eventually we came to call this experience *flow*. The term had been used as a metaphor by some respondents to describe their feelings while involved in their favorite activities, and the short Anglo-Saxon word seemed preferable to the more clumsy, if more precise, term, *autotelic experience*.

After describing how it felt to be in a situation that was intrinsically motivating, we went on to explore the characteristics of those activities that provided intrinsic rewards. Again, despite the obvious difference between such endeavors as climbing rocks and writing music, a common set of structural characteristics was found to distinguish those patterns of action that produced flow from the rest of everyday life. The major implication of this aspect of the study was that not only play, leisure, or creative pursuits such as painting make flow happen. Intrinsic rewards can be built into any activity, including work.

The second decade: after 1975

The publication of *Beyond Boredom and Anxiety* did not attract much attention at the time, but the ideas contained in it slowly worked their way into a wide variety of academic and practical settings. The book has been reprinted three times so far, and it has been translated into Japanese (1979) and German (1985).

The most immediate impact was on those scholars who study the psychological and sociological implications of free time – on the literatures of play, sports, leisure, and recreation (e.g., Widmeyer 1978; Pearson 1979; Sutton-Smith 1979; Iso-Ahola 1980; Kleiber 1980, 1981, 1985, 1986; Kleiber & Barnett 1980; Egger 1981; Neulinger 1981a,b; Kelly 1982, 1986; Ingham 1986; Samdahl 1986). Several dissertations tested the concept and applied it to different populations. For instance, Gray (1977) developed a flow questionnaire and found it useful with a sample of older retired persons; Progen (1978) developed a questionnaire to be used in a variety of sports, as did Begly (1979) and Adair (1982).

To these fields the flow concept contributed one important insight: From the perspective of subjective experience, work and play are not necessarily opposites. In order to define leisure, the quality of the experience might be a more valid guide than the nature of the activity. Many people derive greater rewards from their jobs than they do from free time. For them the traditional distinction between "work" and "leisure" makes little sense. If a person enjoys selling cars more than bowling, which activity is work for that person, and which leisure?

Cultural anthropology is another field to which the concept of flow turned out to be relevant. Here it was Victor Turner (1974b) who saw the similarity between the flow experience and a series of phenomena he had been studying for years, the so-called liminal situations. In a great variety of cultures, Turner found, normal social roles are occasionally suspended or even reversed in well-defined ritual situations. Some examples are rites of passage, pilgrimages, or more secular institutions like the carnival or the Christmas office party. The reason for having these reversals, according to Turner, is that while they last they provide participants with a feeling of *communitas*, an emotionally rewarding closeness comparatively free from the constraints of social roles and responsibilities. This feeling of participation in turn helps to cement the bonds of social solidarity after the episode ends.

Following Turner's lead, the flow concept became an influential idea in the anthropology of play (Cheska 1981; Harris & Park 1983). For instance, at the 1987 meeting of The Anthropological Association for the Study of Play held in Montreal, a symposium dedicated to flow dealt with the following subjects: the miniature world of chess in Washington Square Park in New York City (Francis 1987), a study of the emotional consequences of risk and competition (Hilliard 1987), a comparison of the flow theory with the Taoist philosophy of Chuang-tzu (Sun 1987), and an analysis of flow in television reporting (Zelizer 1987).

The similarity of flow to experiences reported in mystical and other religious contexts was also apparent (Carrington 1977). Therefore Mircea Eliade, who had accepted the task of editing a new *Encyclopedia of Religion* for the publishing house of Macmillan, commissioned for it an article on the flow experience (Csikszentmihalyi 1987a).

Early criticism of the concept had focused on its supposedly Western bias. Although its development had been influenced by Eastern sources such as the *Bhagavad Gita* and Zen, some critics felt that flow was too active and goal-directed a process to represent a panhuman, species-specific trait. In response to this criticism, the argument in favor of the universality of flow is that the specific *content of the activities* producing flow vary from culture to culture; in the West, flow activities might indeed be on the whole more active, competitive, and controlling than in other parts of the world. But the *dynamics of the experience* that make enjoyment possible are presumably the same regardless of the culture. Several of the chapters in this volume support this argument. The studies of Sato with Japanese teenagers, of Han with Korean elderly, and of Massimini and his group with various European and Asiatic populations illustrate quite conclusively that the parameters of enjoyment are the same the world over.

Because flow occurs within the privacy of a person's consciousness, its implications for the discipline of sociology have been largely ignored. In an early review, Murray Davis (1977) compared the studies on flow with the work of the great sociologist of everyday life Erwing Goffman (calling both of us mystics; but, the reviewer observed, whereas Goffman is a *pessi*mystic, I am an *opti*mystic). One sustained application of the flow concept to sociology was Richard Mitchell's book on mountain climbers (Mitchell 1983), a section of which appears as Chapter 3 in this volume. As Mitchell's work suggests, despite its subjectivity, flow might contribute to the understanding of many problems central to sociology. After all, alienation and anomie, two of the conceptual pillars of that discipline, are also subjective phenomena.

In the field of psychology, where the flow concept seems to belong more naturally, the impact has been proportionately greater. A fair amount has been written on flow as a useful idea, as an interesting phenomenon, and as a potentially important aspect of human life. One of the fields in which the impact of the concept has been substantial is the recently evolved literature on happiness or subjective well-being. In this line of investigation, the flow model is usually seen as the leading activity-based theory of happiness, often traced back to Aristotle's views (Diener 1984; Diener, Horwitz, & Emmons 1985; Argyle 1987). In comparison with the conceptual impact, the yield of empirical studies has thus far been rather meager. There have been exceptions, of course; some of the most noteworthy ones are included in the present volume.

As one would expect, researchers working in the field of intrinsic motivation became interested in the studies of flow primarily because for the first time the phenomenon was being looked at in natural settings (deCharms & Muir 1978; Amabile 1983; Deci & Ryan 1985). In the realm of more general psychological theory, Eckblad (1981) has tried to integrate flow with other motivational and cognitive models in a systematic fashion. In Germany Heinz Heckhausen has investigated the relationship between achievement and intrinsic motives, with special reference to flow (see Aebli 1985).

Examples of laboratory studies influenced by the flow concept are the neurological investigations of Jean Hamilton, who found intriguing attentional patterns associated with the intensity of flow experiences (Hamilton 1976, 1981; Hamilton, Holcomb, & De la Pena 1977). Mannell (1979; Mannell & Bradley 1986) has conducted social-psychological experiments focusing on flow and other motivational concepts.

In our own laboratory at the University of Chicago, research on flow has become an integral part of every investigation being conducted. Thus the study of how urban Americans create a symbolic environment in their homes, reported in the volume *The Meaning of Things* (Csikszentmihalyi & Rochberg-Halton 1981), includes a chapter on flow. So do the study of teenage experience reported in *Being Adolescent* (Csikszentmihalyi & Larson 1984) and the study of television-viewing patterns contained in *Mirror of the Mind* (Kubey & Csikszentmihalyi, in press).

Perhaps the most interesting conceptual implication of flow has been in terms of a theory of sociocultural evolution. The link between a psychological selective mechanism, obeying its intrinsically motivated goal-seeking tendency, and cultural change was first perceived by Professor Fausto Massimini of the University of Milan. Our first article on the subject (Csikszentmihalyi & Massimini 1985) stimulated a vigorous debate that occupied much of three consecutive issues of the journal *New Ideas in Psychology* (1985, vol. 3, no. 2, 3; 1986, vol. 4, no. 1). Even earlier, J. Crook, the British ethologist, had perceived the evolutionary significance of flow in the concluding chapter of his *Evolution of Consciousness* (Crook 1980). Implications of the flow model for creativity and cultural evolution were more systematically explored in Csikszentmihalyi (1986, 1987b). A fuller treatment of this link may be found in Chapter 4.

Practical applications. The flow concept was developed as a result of sheer curiosity. It was the fruit of "pure" research, motivated only by the desire to solve an intriguing puzzle in the mechanism of human behavior. And, as many early critics were to point out, it was very ethereal, bordering on the mystical. It lacked the hard, concrete objectivity that a pragmatic psychological concept should have. Considering all this, it is in many ways astonishing that so many practical applications have been found for it.

One of the first arenas in which flow was seen to be potentially useful was education. Mayers (1978) had shown that the degree to which high school students enjoyed a given course predicted their final grades better than previous measures of scholastic achievement or aptitude did. Looking at the problem from the other end, Plihal (1982) has shown that the amount of enjoyment teachers get from teaching is related to the amount of attention students show in class. In the Indianapolis public school system, a group of dedicated teachers at the "Key School" have implemented a K–6 curriculum based in part on the flow theory. There is certainly much that could be done to improve the educational process by increasing the enjoyment it potentially contains, but is so rarely part of the school experience (Csikszentmihalyi 1982b,c; Csikszentmihalyi & McCormack 1986). In the present volume, a number of chapters explore the contributions of the flow model to educational issues. Larson shows how boredom, anxiety, and enjoyment affect students' involvement in written research projects. Chapters by Carli et. al. and by Nakamura in Part IV illustrate the difference that flow makes in the scholastic achievement of Italian and American students.

The flow model is not only relevant to education in general, but also to various forms of special education. At Oklahoma State University, for example, the flow model has helped the faculty to develop a textbook and a summer course designed to train teachers of physically handicapped children to enjoy themselves despite their handicaps. Occupational therapy is another field where the model has had an impact and has informed the emerging field of "occupational science." At the other end of the continuum of special education, gifted children are being studied to see under which conditions they most enjoy using personal computers. Some implications of the flow model for learning and enjoying personal computers were explored by Malone (1980) and Turkle (1984).

In *Beyond Boredom and Anxiety* it was claimed that the most urgent applications of the flow model were in schools and on the job, where most people spend most of their lives – often in boredom or in states of uneasy anxiety. Therefore educational and occupational uses of the model seem to be the most urgent ones. In a series of studies on industrial accidents among factory workers in Hungary, I. Vitanyi and M. Sagi (personal communication) found that bored workers tended to take unreasonable risks and those who felt anxious complained of imaginary illnesses, whereas those who were able to derive enjoyment from the job were not only personally more satisfied but contributed much more to the productive goals of the factory. These researchers also related the tendency to enjoy one's work to a variety of background factors, especially to patterns of family life and the uses of free time. Others have explored the potential of "flow management" by specifying the characteristics that would make an executive enjoy his or her job, as well as motivate the work force to enjoy theirs. For example, at the Institute of Organization and Social Studies of the University of West London, Gillian Stamp has applied the flow model to leadership development. Several management seminars in the United States now take the phenomenon into account in their curricula. The implications of optimal experience for consumer behavior have also been explored (Bloch & Bruce 1984; Bloch 1986).

In this volume, the enjoyment of work – or the lack of it – is a central theme of several chapters. It appears in Chapter 3, where Mitchell explores the sociological implications of anomie and alienation; in Chapter 7 by Allison and Duncan, which deals with working women; in Chapter 12 by Delle Fave and Massimini, who report on work and leisure in traditional societies; and in LeFevre's study (Chapter 18) of flow in the urban American work environment.

The most obvious – if perhaps in the long run not the most generative – applications of flow are in the context of play and leisure. In the late 1970s and early 1980s several groups experimenting with adult play therapies used the model in their activities. Bernard De Koven, a "game designer and play facilitator," integrated the flow model in the seminars he ran from his Game Preserve in Pennsylvania, and so did the New Games Foundation that had been started by Stewart Brand on the West Coast. Policy for recreational planning and the management of public parks has also been influenced by the concept (Berger & Schreyer 1986).

That psychotherapy could benefit from the flow perspective is something a few clinicians are beginning to entertain. Instead of focusing exclusively on past causes of malaise, this perspective would try to identify and to develop those actions and situations that provide the best subjective experiences. In this sense, flow provides to clinical psychology a standard of positive psychic functioning, analogous to the standard that physiology provides to pathology in the field of medicine (Massimini, Csikszentmihalyi, & Carli 1987). A similar idea informs the application of flow to a statewide antidrug campaign: The idea is to present youth with examples of "natural highs," of complex, involving experiences in productive contexts. An early paper on school crime and juvenile delinquency (Csikszentmihalyi & Larson 1978) had already suggested that much crime and vandalism are the result of boredom. Efforts at various forms of rehabilitation appear to benefit from this view, and from the concrete features of the flow model that point at possible means of improvement. The first nationwide study of juvenile crime in Saudi Arabia, directed by Dr. Sharif Malik (1985), and the subsequent policies deriving from the study were informed by flow theory. In this volume, the chapter by Sato represents one of the applications of the flow model to the study of deviance.

Other applications have ranged from advertising research to the design and redesign of museums. Ken Davis (1988) has written a book in which the flow model is used to help audiences become involved with the theater. Whenever the quality of human experience is at issue, flow becomes relevant. It helps explain why people enjoy their work and their leisure; it also helps explain why in some circumstances people are bored and frustrated. When boredom becomes a major part of life, it helps explain the alienation and apathy underlying much of personal pathology and some of the societal forms as well.

The pages that follow present some of the most stimulating conceptual extensions of the original flow model together with a selection from the research that in the past decade has rounded out our understanding of the conditions that make an enjoyable life possible. The chapters cover a broad range of human experience from work to play to deviant behavior and include studies of men and women, young and old, and Western and Eastern samples. They illustrate the enjoyment – or lack of it – reported by cleaning women in their humble jobs and by sailors cruising their yachts on the South Seas. Despite its breadth, this volume represents only the barest beginning in a field of research and application that eventually will, we hope, grow much larger. The flow model opens up a new perspective on some of the most exciting aspects of human experience. The challenge lies in exploring this fascinating view in order to make life more worthwhile. We hope that at least a few readers will put down this book with a resolution to take up that challenge.

2. The flow experience and its significance for human psychology

MIHALY CSIKSZENTMIHALYI

In the ordinary course of events, psychologists observe human action either in clinical settings, where the "patient" is seeking therapeutic redress for some impairment, or in experimental settings, where the confines of the laboratory and the parameters of the experimental design allow only a tiny fraction of potential responses to be manifested. The theoretical models of human action that psychologists have constructed in the past half century reflect this poverty of observational data: They tend to be mechanistic, reductive, and biased in favor of pathology.

To provide a more complete view of what human behavior and experience entail, it is necessary to begin observing what people do and what happens to them when they are not confined to the couch or the laboratory, but are involved in their normal lives in real ecological settings. In particular, it is important to observe them in those moments when their lives reach peaks of involvement that produce intense feelings of enjoyment and creativity. Without accounting for these aspects of experience, models of human behavior will remain one-sided and incomplete. The studies of the flow experience included in this volume attempt to provide evidence on which a more realistic model of human behavior can be built.

The major psychological trends of this century – including drive theories, psychoanalysis, behaviorism, cognitive psychology, and the contemporary atheoretical neuropharmacological approaches – all share a common epistemology. In an attempt to be as scientific as possible, they have developed reductionistic accounts of human action, discounting or ignoring the most obvious aspect of the human phenomenon, namely, the existence of a conscious self. To explain away reflective awareness, with all its implications, might have seemed like a wise strategic move. By ignoring the self as an agent in its own right it seemed possible to develop a psychology as concretely based on impersonal processes as mechanics and physics.

The "billiard ball" metaphor of behavior is the standard view of human motivation underlying these approaches. A person's actions are explained entirely in terms of the vector sum of discrete forces external to the individual self. Given condition X, one expects behavior Y. The Xs specified by each theory are different: They might include psychopharmacological conditions, internal drive states like hunger, or they might consist of external rewards, or of interactive concepts like libidinal repression. But in each case, the effort of modern psychology has been to specify the Xs that are independent of the subjective states of the experiencing organism. Only by holding to the notion of external agents (hormones, drives, instincts, learning schedules, and so on) that act invariably in a predictable direction with a minimum of interference from the subject who is the object of their agencies, did the project of a scientific psychology seem tenable.

To a certain extent, this reductionistic project makes sense. After all, it is in general true that men and women begin to search for food when the sugar level in their blood falls below a certain point. It is true that they will quickly learn to perform acts for which they are rewarded, and that they tend to desist from those actions that bring punishment in their wake. The power of sexual drives, and of their repression, is equally beyond doubt.

Yet, despite the preponderant evidence in its favor, reductionist psychology fails as an accurate theory of human behavior because it ignores the phenomenon of the self. Thus it cannot account for those rare but extremely significant instances in which people decide to contradict those "forces" that in ordinary circumstances appear to determine their behavior. It does not explain, except by convoluted ad hoc arguments that end up begging the question, why people fast and occasionally starve themselves to death, why they sometimes lead celibate lives, and why they often do exactly the opposite of what they have always learned and been rewarded for.

The fact is that people do what they want to do, and what they want to do does not depend directly on outside forces, but it depends on priorities established by the needs of the self. Thus motivation cannot be reduced to causes at a lower – or different – order of organization than the self of the subject. The reason it appears that so much about human behavior can be accounted for by simpler mechanisms – such as drives, stimulus–response sequences, and the like – is that people *want* to act in terms of the instructions such mechanisms convey. In general, people *want* to eat when they are hungry; they *want* to work hard if they are rewarded for it, and so on. But it is an excessive simplification to deduce from these regularities that humans simply follow the instructions contained in their genes or in the conditioning they receive. It is more accurate to say that these lower-order mechanisms determine the organization of the self, but once the self is operational, it becomes an independent causal agent, taking over from drives or stimulus–response links the direction of human behavior.

The human organism cannot survive as a bundle of neural reflexes, or even of stimulus–response learning pathways. In order to perform within the infinitely complex ecosystem to which it became adapted, it needed to establish autonomy from the genetically determined instructions that had shaped its behavior through the long eons of its evolution.

The system that has evolved to provide this autonomy is the self. The function of the self is to mediate between the genetic instructions that manifest themselves as "instinctual drives" and the cultural instructions that appear as norms and rules. The self must prioritize between these various behavioral instructions and select among them the ones it wants to endorse.

The structure of consciousness

In order for the self to mediate between these often conflicting instructions, the human organism had to develop another feature, an informational system that could differentiate among a great variety of stimuli, that could choose certain stimuli and focus selectively on them, and that could store and retrieve the information in a usable way. This feature, based on the biological evolution of the central nervous system, we call *consciousness*. It is composed of three functional subsystems: attention, which takes notice of information available; awareness, which interprets the information; and memory, which stores the information (Broadbent 1958; Pope & Singer 1978). The content of consciousness is experience, that is, the sum of all the information that enters it, and its interpretation by awareness (James 1890).

Attention is the medium that makes information appear in consciousness. The human organism is limited to discriminating a maximum of about seven bits – or chunks – of information per unit of time (Miller 1956). Orme (1969), on the basis of von Uexkull's (1957) computations, estimates the duration of such an "attentional unit" to be on the order of 1/18th per second; in other words, we can become aware of 18 × 7 bits of information, or 126 bits, in the space of a second. Thus a person can process at most in the neighborhood of 7,560 bits of information each minute. In a lifetime of 70 years, and assuming a waking day of 16 hours, this amounts to about 185 billion bits of information. This number defines the limit of individual experience. Out of it must come every perception, thought, feeling, memory, or action that a person will ever have. It seems like a large number, but in actuality most people find it tragically insufficient.

To get a sense of how little we can actually accomplish with the amount of attention at our disposal, we might consider how much attention it takes to follow an ordinary conversation. It is claimed that to extract phonemic information from speech signals would take 40,000 bits of information per second if each bit had to be attended to separately; fortunately, our species-specific genetic programming allows us to chunk speech into phonemes automatically, thereby reducing the load to 40 bits per second – or approximately one-third of the total processing capacity of attention (Liberman, Mattingly, & Turvey 1972; Nusbaum & Schwab 1986). This is why we cannot follow a conversation and at the same time do any other involving mental task, like writing a letter, playing chess, or playing tennis. Just decoding what other people are saying, even though apparently an effortless and automated process, interferes with any other task that requires one's full attention.

Finitude is one of the most important characteristics of attention. In reviewing Kahneman's (1973) pioneering book on the subject, Norman (1976, p. 71) writes:

> The limit on attentional capacity appears to be a general limit on resources.... The completion of a mental activity requires two types of input to the corresponding structure: an information input specific to that structure, and a non-specific input which may be variously labeled "effort," "capacity," or "attention." To explain man's limited ability to carry out multiple activities at the same time, a capacity theory assumes that the total amount of attention which can be deployed at any time is limited.

Similarly, Hasher and Zacks (1979, p. 363) write: "Consistent with a capacity view of attention, we think of attention as a nonspecific resource for cognitive processing. This resource is necessary for the carrying out of mental operations, but its supply is limited." And Eysenck (1982, p. 28) states: "The original notion of attention has been replaced by a conceptualization in which attention is regarded as a limited power supply. The basic idea is that attention represents a general purpose limited capacity that can be flexibly allocated in many different ways in response to task demands."

Because attention is the medium that makes events occur in consciousness, it is useful to think of it as "psychic energy" (Kahneman 1973; Csikszentmihalyi 1978a; Hoffman, Nelson, & Houck 1983). Any nonreflex action takes up a certain fraction of this energy. Just listening to an ordinary conversation closely enough to understand what is being said takes up one-third of our psychic energy at any given time. Stirring a cup of coffee, reaching for a newspaper, trying to remember a telephone number – all require information-processing space out of that limited total. Of course individuals vary widely in terms of how much of their psychic energy they actually use (i.e., how many bits of information they process), and in terms of how they invest the energy they do use.

We shall use "awareness" to designate all those processes that take place in consciousness after a bit of information is attended to. It includes such steps as recognizing the stimulus, categorizing it in terms of previous information, and disposing of it either by preserving it in memory or by forgetting it. Some of the most important processes of awarenesss are thought or cognition, feeling or emotion, and conation or volition (Hilgard 1980). Cognition refers to the various steps by which bits of information are recognized and related to each other. Emotion defines the attitude that consciousness takes toward the information it is processsing, basically in terms of an "I like it" to "I do not like it" axis. Volition is the process by which attention remains focused on a certain range of stimuli, instead of moving on to other targets (M. Csikszentmihalyi 1986). All of these processes of awareness require attention for their implementation, and thus they are also "information" in consciousness, subject to the same limitations of information processing already discussed (Neisser 1967; Treisman & Gelade 1980; Treisman & Schmidt 1982; Hoffman, Nelson, & Houck 1983). In other words, one cannot think, feel, and will in relation to more than a few stimuli at the same time.

The memory subsystem stores information that has passed through consciousness, and that can be again recalled. It provides consciousness with access to far more than the 126 bits of information per second that the limits of attention restrict it to. Yet storing and recalling information also make demands on attention, so memory has its own limits (Atkinson & Shiffrin 1968; Shiffrin 1976; Hasher & Zacks 1979; Neisser, Hirst, & Spelke 1981; Nusbaum & Schwab 1986).

These three subsystems – attention, awareness, and memory – allow consciousness to act as a buffer between genetic and cultural instructions on the one hand, and behavior on the other. By transforming physiological processes into subjective experiences, consciousness makes it possible to gain control over the anonymous instinctual forces.

At a certain point in ontogenesis, each individual begins to realize his or her own powers to direct attention, to think, to feel, to will, and to remember. At that point, a new agency develops within awareness. This is the *self*. The self is simply an epiphenomenon of conscious processes, the result of consciousness becoming aware of itself. The structure of the self gains shape as information related to one's body, one's past memories, and future goals. Eventually the scope of the self extends to cover the entirety of consciousnesss. At that point, the self becomes the symbol that stands for the full range of the individual's conscious processes – including those unconscious contents that occasionally surface in awareness.

Like every system, the main function of the self, once it is established, becomes to maintain itself, and possibly to grow and to replicate. Once the human nervous system evolved consciousness it made the development of the self inevitable. And as soon as the self evolved in its turn, the control that genetic instructions had on man was broken (Dawkins 1976; Crook 1980; Csikszentmihalyi & Massimini 1985). The self could now choose to act in ways that went against the millenial wisdom that natural selection had built into the biological fabric of the species. The self could be selfish or selfless, regardless of the wishes of the selfish genes that made its existence possible.

For example, if I were to feel hunger, and I had no consciousness, I would immediately be directed by a loop in my nervous system to begin searching for food. Most psychological theories assume that this more or less is what happens with humans. But what actually happens is that, as the pangs of hunger enter consciousness, I evaluate the information, give it a name (e.g., "Gee, I feel hungry"), and then decide what to do about it. Nine times out of ten, I will start seeking food, just as if I had no consciousness and genetic instructions regarding hunger had a direct control over my behavior. On the other hand, if my self had become organized around the goal of becoming slimmer, I might decide to skip a meal in order to lose some weight; or, if my self had become identified with the goal of being a traditional Catholic and it was Friday, I might decide to fast; or I might decide not to eat so as to save money, or for any of a hundred reasons that at that moment are more congruent with the goals of the self and thus take precedence over the biological instructions contained in my genes.

Consciousness provides the same buffering function between cultural instructions and behavioral outcomes. In every society, social controls provide a network of rewards and punishments that are expected to force individual behavior in conformity with the norms that ensure the continued survival of the system. Here again, nine times out of ten one can predict that behavior will follow relevant norms. But here also each individual has the potential to override socialization because consciousness transforms cultural instructions into experience, and as such it can deal with experience in the same detached way that it can with genetic drives. Consciousness frees the organism from its dependence on the forces that created it, and provides a certain control – however feeble and precarious it is – over our behavior. Whatever can be represented in consciousness can potentially be controlled through the investment of attention, or psychic energy.

From an evolutionary standpoint, the self is a very chancy mutation. Its advantages are clear: By acting as a clutch between programmed instructions and adaptive behaviors, it enormously increases the possibilities of a fit between the two. There is no longer any need to develop laborious genetic links between certain types of stimuli and certain desirable responses; consciousness can fill in the linkages symbolically. We do not need, for example, thousands of separate warning systems specialized for every environmental danger; a generalized "instinct" for *self*-preservation can do most of the job. Control over experience brought with it control over thought, emotion, and will; eventually it made mankind one of the most powerful natural forces on the planet.

Clearly, there is also a negative side. In operating as a clutch, consciousness has disengaged us from the forces that have guided evolution up to this point. We are no longer forced to act blindly, but it is by no means certain that the choice and control we have wrested will serve us better than the blind instructions of our genes used to do. In fact, it is very possible that the self, drunk with its sense of self-importance, will end up destroying the environment that brought it about and thereby end life on earth.

The teleonomy of the self

Once the self becomes established in consciousness, its main goal is to ensure its own survival. To this effect, attention, awareness, and memory are directed to replicate those states of consciousness that are congenial to the self, and to eliminate those that threaten its existence.

The self represents its own interests as *goals*. Each self develops its own hierarchy of goals, which become, in effect, the structure of that self. Whenever a new experience enters consciousness it is evaluated in terms of the goals that reflect the self, and it is dealt with accordingly. A bit of information that fits these goals strengthens the structure of the self, whereas one that conflicts with them creates disorder in consciousness and threatens the integrity of the self. We receive most goals from the genetic instructions of our biological inheritance, or from the cultural instructions embodied in societal values. But here, too, consciousness allows our choices a certain autonomy and independence.

We use the term *psychic entropy* to refer to those states that produce disorder by conflicting with individual goals (Csikszentmihalyi 1978a; 1985a). Psychic entropy is a condition in which there is "noise" in the information-processing system. It is experienced as fear, boredom, apathy, anxiety, confusion, jealousy, and a hundred other nuances, depending on the nature of the information and the kinds of goals the information is in conflict with. For example, the sight of a thunderstorm on a morning I planned a picnic produces a mild frustration commensurate to the amount of psychic energy I had invested in the goal of having the picnic. The same sight might produce panic in a farmer who had a great deal of money and energy invested in a harvest that is threatened by the storm.

Psychic entropy not only causes disorder in consciousness, but it impairs its efficiency as well. Attention is withdrawn from other tasks to deal with the conflicting information. Intense physical pain, for example, prevents us from thinking about anything else. But so does any threat to the self, even of a symbolic nature. An imagined slight, a breach of protocol can have equally paralyzing effects.

The state of mind described here as psychic entropy is of course well known both to common sense and to psychology, but its nature has not been clearly understood, for lack of a viable theory of self. It is true that in the past few decades a number of psychologists have conducted extensive studies of basic emotions or primary affects such as anger, distress, sadness, fear, shame, contempt, and disgust (Tomkins 1962, 1963; Ekman 1972; Izard 1977; Izard, Kagan, & Zajonc 1984; Frijda 1986). But these investigators generally assume that each emotion is separately "wired in" as a response to a specific set of stimuli, instead of being an integrated response of the self system. As a result we know a great deal about negative emotions, but the information has little theoretical coherence. A partial exception is the work of Bandura (1977, 1978) and Bandura and Schunk (1981), whose concept of "self-efficacy" provides a possible model for a more unified understanding of negative as well as positive experience.

In clinical psychology and psychiatry "disphoric moods" are recognized as markers of depression and other pathological mental states (Beck 1967, 1976; Blumberg & Izard 1985). That negative moods interfere with concentration, ease of concentration, and a sense of control has often been reported (Hamilton 1982). However, the extensive clinical literature on the subject is generally interested in dysphoria as a personal trait that differentiates normal from ill people, rather than as a condition that affects everybody under certain conditions. Current explanations include the "activity theory," according to which people suffer from negative moods because they engage in fewer pleasant activities (Lewinsohn & Libet 1972) and because they perceive activities as potentially less pleasurable (MacPhillamy & Lewinsohn 1974); and the "learned helplessness" (Seligman 1975) or "attributional" theories, according to which people prone to depression blame themselves for the occurrence of unpleasant events (Seligman et al. 1984). Finally, a number of psychopharmacological approaches have attempted to ameliorate the symptoms of depression and dysphoria through chemical means (e.g., Murphy, Simons, Wetzel, & Lustman 1984). None of these perspectives, however, views the person who experiences bad moods as a total system, a self that is actively trying to establish order in the contents of consciousness.

In social psychology, Festinger (1954) and others have described conflict in the information being processed by persons, and thus they are potentially closer to a systemic description of what we have termed "psychic entropy." But their analysis also leaves out the concept of self, and the dissonance they talk about ends up being one-dimensional, confined only to cognitive aspects. Cognitive scientists and students of artificial intelligence, who also study the dynamics of information in consciousness, are even more focused on the rational aspects of information and thus leave out the dimensions of affect and motivation, which are central to the operations of the self (Mandler 1975; Piaget 1981; Zajonc 1984).

Even less is known about the state of consciousness that is at the opposite end of the pole from the negative one just described (Leeper 1965; Izard 1971; Singer 1984). This is the condition we have called psychic negentropy, optimal experience, or *flow* (Csikszentmihalyi 1975b). It obtains when all the contents of consciousness are in harmony with each other, and with the goals that define the person's self. These are the subjective conditions we call pleasure, happiness, satisfaction, enjoyment. Because the tendency of the self is to reproduce itself, and because the self is most congruent with its own goal-directed structure during these episodes of optimal experience, to keep on experiencing flow becomes one of the central goals of the self.

This is the *teleonomy of the self*, that is, the goal-seeking tendency that shapes the choices we make among alternatives. It is the third set of rules that affects the course of human action, the others being the genetic teleonomy, or the tendency of biological patterns to replicate their kind across time, and cultural teleonomy, which tends to impose social norms and values on human behavior in order to replicate itself across generations (Massimini & Calegari 1979; Csikszentmihalyi & Massimini 1985; Massimini & Inghilleri 1986).

Genetic and cultural teleonomies are well known to social science, and their effects on behavior have been extensively studied. Very little is known, on the other hand, about the teleonomy of the self. What is it that people do to fulfill their being? This is the question that the present volume addresses.

Pleasure and the genetic teleonomy. Of all the ways to build a self around a hierarchy of goals, the most "natural," and hence philogenetically the most primitive, is to endorse consciously the genetic teleonomy. This means, very simply, that the person identifies his or her goals with the genetic instructions programmed in his or her organism. The person's ultimate goals will center around eating well and being comfortable, healthy, and sexually satisfied.

It is important to note, however, that, when these "drives" become goals, they cannot be satisfied any longer by restoring physiological homeostasis. A person will keep eating even after he or she is no longer hungry, because food is required not just to keep the body in fuel, but also to keep the self in an ordered state. Thus the satisfaction of biological needs becomes necessary for the continuity of the self.

Although genetic instructions form the basis for all human goal hierarchies, the exclusive pursuit of pleasure cannot lead to evolutionary development, and it is detrimental to any form of social order. Most religious and ethical systems warn against building selves on purely genetic goals. The Christian "sins," such as gluttony, lechery, greed, and intemperance, describe selves built primarily around genetically programmed pleasure.

Habits leading to substance addiction follow the same pattern. If experiencing pleasure is the only way to maintain the order of the self, then drugs and alcohol become perfectly appropriate means for doing so. Thus a self originally organized around the pleasure principle might end up by working against the genetic teleonomy whose cause it had originally espoused. Excessive sexual indulgence does not lead necessarily to procreation, and gluttony can soon become unhealthy. When a physiological need becomes a goal, it ceases to be under the exclusive control of its original genetic instructions and begins to follow the teleonomy of the self.

Power and cultural teleonomy. In addition to endorsing the genetic teleonomy, the self can also be organized around cultural instructions. Every human group, no matter how small and simple, has a set of goals aimed at ensuring its own continuity. These are the norms or rules without which the social system would lose its identity and decay into a crowd engaged in a "war of all against all." A central feature of every social organization is a hierarchy that differentiates power relationships among people in different statuses.

Social differentiation is itself genetically based. Social insects are anatomically differentiated to faciliate the performance of their specialized functional roles (Wilson 1975). Dominance–submission hierarchies seem to be present in all socially living primates. Already during the first year of life, human infants placed in a playpen begin to show differential access to toys, and thus create spontaneously the rudiments of social stratification, with the familiar Marxist differentiation between those who control resources and those who do not. By six years of age quite stable and generally accepted rankings in "toughness" develop among boys (Freedman 1979, 1984; Omark, Strayer, & Freedman 1980).

The more complex the social system – the more statuses and roles it contains – the more markers of differentation it will have to use (Davis

& Moore 1945). Eventually the social hierarchy becomes relatively autonomous of biological instructions and starts to motivate people to act
in terms of its own mechanisms of social control, by offering rewards
and punishments to those who abide by its norms.

What we know of present preliterate societies suggests that through
the evolution of social systems persons who achieved higher positions
in the hierarchy usually had above-average organizational or economic
skills, and they were given a proportionately greater share of power and
respect in their communities. In turn, they were expected to use their
skills to benefit the group. The leader of the hunt had to give from his
greater share to the hungry; the richest landowners had to save their
surplus for times of famine and then open their storehouses to the
community; the wise shaman had to be available for consultation when
a member of the tribe needed the help of magic.

With time, it seems that social recognition has become programmed
as a reward in the human nervous system. Men and women find it
pleasant when others recognize their selves by paying attention to them.
On the other hand, solitude is for most people a painful state to be
avoided at all cost (Fortune 1963; Bowen 1954; Peplau & Perlman 1982).

It is not our task here to debate whether social differentiations are
actually functional. The fact is that they exist among the headhunters
of New Guinea and in the Soviet Union as well as in capitalist societies.
What is relevant in this context is that people consciously internalize
the social hierarchy and make it their own. Thus a person, having enjoyed attention and respect from others, will try to replicate the internal
harmony of the self by reproducing the conditions conducive to it. After
a certain time, the self of this person will require continuous inputs of
social recognition in order to maintain its integrity.

What form this seeking for recognition will take depends on several
things, especially on the normative structure of the social system. In a
community of warriors, a person might have to display increasing violence to be recognized, whereas in a community of monks recognition
will come to the most peaceful. In New Guinea respect and power go
to the man who owns most pigs and yams. In our society the principle
is more or less the same, although among us money acts as a mediator
of possession.

As with the endorsement of biological drives, a teleonomy of self based
on social instructions can easily get out of hand. When it is power that
keeps the self in a negentropic state, a new "fix" is needed constantly,
regardless of the requirements of the community. Thus the individual's

hunger for recognition often conflicts with the harmony of the social order.

Another way to build a self in relation to instructions endorsed by the social system involves becoming part of the social order rather than controlling it. Instead of moving up the social hierarchy, the goal here is to merge one's being with that of a greater force. The self loses its autonomy in the process, but in exchange gains identification with a larger, more powerful entity.

The "oceanic feeling" of infancy (Freud 1961; Winnicott 1951) is a pleasurable state that persists in adulthood as the "collective effervescence" that takes over in ritualized social situations (Durkheim [1912] 1967), or as the sense of "communitas" that is so enjoyable when social roles are temporarily suspended (Turner 1969). To replicate such negentropic experiences, the self may direct consciousness to seek out conditions of this type again and again.

Thus the teleonomy of the self might be constructed primarily around goals that involve participation. These could range all the way from becoming a communist believer to becoming a Hindu mystic; although vastly different in many respects, both choices involve abnegation of other goals in order to experience belonging with a powerful transpersonal system. The faithful employee, the patriotic citizen, the religious zealot, the sports fan, the intellectual snob are other manifestations of the same solution.

Again, it is important to remember that such sacrifices of individuality are not necessarily what they appear to be. The behavior of the person who takes such a course of action is not under the control of the transpersonal system. It still follows the teleonomy of the self, even when it appears to be entirely selfless. The hero who is willing to die for his country may not be primarily concerned with the best interests of the majority of his compatriots; his primary concern may be to keep his self in greatest harmony. Hence it is perfectly possible that some of the most "selfless" participants in a given system will actually help to destroy it, since their need to replicate a sense of belonging takes precedence over the system's needs.

Flow: the emergent teleonomy of the self. Pleasure, power, and participation are some of the basic models on which a self can be built. It is probably the case that each person uses all three of these kinds of goals, in various combinations, and in various degrees of intensity, to shape consciousness.

But if these were the only sources of motivation, human behavior would remain the same over time. Yet consciousness evolves. Over the course of centuries, attention has become focused on more and more differentiated stimuli. Individuals today may not be able to process more discrete bits of information than their ancestors did a million years ago. But they certainly have access to a great deal more information than their ancestors had, because the extrasomatic memory system of the species – such as books, museums, laboratories, and computer files – has expanded dramatically.

Systems for knowing have also evolved. Entirely new epistemologies, techniques, and intellectual disciplines have arisen over time, and their cumulative algorhithms have made the manipulation of information more complex than it has ever been.

The same is true for the development of noncognitive skills. Perhaps an average Cro-Magnon man was able to adapt to more aspects of his environment than an average urban American can. It could be argued that he had to know how to use his body, his mind, and his hands in more complex ways. But there is no question that the cumulative adaptations of contemporary technology are immeasurably more complex than they were even a few decades ago.

It is equally clear that emotions and feelings have evolved with time. Again, it might not be true that a randomly chosen person from a large modern city would have a broader repertoire of feelings or would display a more complex emotional response than a Renaissance citizen, or a Medieval peasant, or a Phoenician trader, or a Paleolithic hunter. But the variety of sensibilities available to us is again unprecedented in any prior age. Each of us can choose and combine the emotional responses of Zen monks and of the Marquis de Sade, of vegetarians, of aesthetes, of utter materialists, and of the most refined idealists.

To explain how consciousness has evolved through time, in addition to the models considered earlier, it is necessary to recognize an emergent teleonomic principle of the self. Pleasure, power, and participation are not enough to account for the dazzling variety of new goals that people constantly adopt and pursue. The motivation to go beyond established patterns of behavior is due to an organizing principle of a different kind.

In our everyday activities, either by chance or by design, we come in contact with experiences that we have never been exposed to before. Occasionally the experience is one that was previously never had by a human being. For instance, when the Montgolfier brothers first left the earth in a balloon, or when the first swimmer with an oxygen tank started exploring a coral reef, a whole new range of experiences became available. The same is true of when the laws of arithmetic or geometry were invented, or when the music of strings sounded for the first time.

Of these unprecedented experiences, for which neither genetic nor cultural instructions exist, most will be either neutral or negative, and will be promptly forgotten. Some of them, however, will be negentropic – that is, they will increase the order of the self because they will be congruent with already established goals. Therefore they will produce a sense of exhilaration, energy, and fulfillment that is more enjoyable than what people feel in the normal course of life. When this occurs, a person will tend to replicate this state of being in preference to others. The activity that produced the experience will be sought out again and again. To the extent that this is done, the self will be built on the model of emergent goals.

The evolution of consciousness – and hence, the evolution of culture and ultimately the evolution of the human species – hinges on our capacity to invest psychic energy in goals that are not modeled exclusively on the teleonomy of genes or cultures. When we step beyond motivations based on pleasure, power, and participation, we open up consciousness to experience new opportunites for being that lead to emergent structures of the self. This is autotelic motivation, because its goal is primarily the experience itself, rather than any future reward or advantage it may bring. Paradoxically, however, new ideas, artifacts, and technologies of great usefulness are often discovered in activities that had no practical goals in view, but were engaged in exclusively for the enjoyment they provided (Huizinga [1939] 1970; Caillois 1958). The flow experience is the prototype of such intrinsically motivated states of consciousness.

The structure of flow. The autotelic experience is described in very similar terms regardless of its context (Csikszentmihalyi 1975b; Csikszentmihalyi & Robinson 1986). Artists, athletes, composers, dancers, scientists, and people from all walks of life, when they describe how it feels when they are doing something that is worth doing for its own sake, use terms that are interchangeable in their minutest details. This unanimity suggests that order in consciousness produces a very specific experiential state, so desirable that one wishes to replicate it as often as possible. To this state we have given the name of "flow," using a term that many respondents used in their interviews to explain what the optimal experience felt like.

Challenges and skills. The universal precondition for flow is that a person should perceive that there is something for him or her to do, and that he or she is capable of doing it. In other words, optimal experience requires a balance between the challenges perceived in a given situation and the skills a person brings to it. The "challenge" includes any opportunity for action that humans are able to respond to: the vastness of the sea, the possibility of rhyming words, concluding a successful business deal, or winning the friendship of another person are all classic challenges that set many flow experiences in motion. But any possibility for action to which a skill corresponds can produce an autotelic experience.

It is this feature that makes flow such a dynamic force in evolution. For every activity might engender it, but at the same time no activity can sustain it for long unless both the challenges and the skills become more complex (Csikszentmihalyi 1982a). For example, a tennis player who enjoys the game will want to reproduce the state of enjoyment by playing as much as possible. But the more such individuals play, the more their skills improve. Now if they continue to play against opponents of the same level as before, they will be bored. This always happens when skills surpass challenges. To return in flow and replicate the enjoyment they desire, they will have to find stronger opposition.

To remain in flow, one must increase the complexity of the activity by developing new skills and taking on new challenges. This holds just as true for enjoying business, for playing the piano, or for enjoying one's marriage, as for the game of tennis. Heraclitus's dictum about not being able to step in the same stream twice holds especially true for flow. This inner dynamic of the optimal experience is what drives the self to higher and higher levels of complexity. It is because of this spiraling complexity that people describe flow as a process of "discovering something new," whether they are shepherds telling how they enjoy caring for their flocks, mothers telling how they enjoy playing with their children, or artists describing the enjoyment of painting. Flow forces people to stretch themselves, to always take on another challenge, to improve on their abilities.

Flow activities. In everyday life, challenges and skills are rarely balanced. Either there are too many things to do, clamoring for attention, in which case we tend to be worried or anxious; or there seems to be nothing to do, in which case we end up feeling bored. This is why flow typically occurs in clearly structured activities in which the level of challenges and skills can be varied and controlled, such as ritual events, games, sports, or artistic performances. Occasionally, however, an entire culture, a whole way of life becomes so coherently structured that everything in it provides flow – including work and all the routine, obligatory aspects of everyday life.

It is useful to keep the name "flow activities" for those sequences of action that make it easy for people to achieve optimal experiences. Of course, no activity guarantees the occurrence of flow, because it can only provide challenges, and whether a person will enjoy that or not depends also on one's skills. Spelunking is a highly involving flow activity, but only for those who can tolerate long periods of darkness in cold, wet, and dangerous enclosed spaces.

The complexity of a flow activity depends on the gradient of challenges it can provide, and consequently on the difficulty of the skills it requires. Tic-tac-toe is a game of extremely low complexity, hence one gets bored with it fast. The challenges of chess, on the other hand, are almost impossible to exhaust. Surgeons who repeatedly perform the same operations, such as appendectomies, quickly become bored with their work. Academic surgeons who do state-of-the-art operations report experiencing flow as intense as any artist or sportsman.

The autotelic personality. But it is not only the objective structure of the activity that will determine whether flow will occur or not. Just as it is the person who must recognize the challenges in a situation, in the last analysis it is that person who will determine whether the activity produces flow rather than anxiety or boredom. A football player may be so worried that he won't enjoy a minute of the game. An assembly-line worker may discover in the boring routine of the job a set of challenges that keep the worker as involved as if it were an exciting game.

The ability to experience flow may be due to individual differences that are in part inborn, but it certainly can be learned. Many techniques of meditation or spiritual discipline attempt to develop control over consciousness. For instance, the various yoga traditions train the ability to concentrate attention, to control memory, and to limit awareness to specific goals. When a person learns such skills, it becomes much easier to achieve the necessary balancing of challenges and skills.

In our studies of mathematically talented high school students, for instance, we found that some youngsters were bored most of the time when doing math homework, whereas others enjoyed doing it. Not surprisingly, the first group was on the way to giving up on mathematics, even though their ability appeared to be at least as high as that of the group that was still involved with it (Csikszentmihalyi & Nakamura 1986). Why is the same homework boring to some and enjoyable to others? The objective challenges of the task do not account for the differences. Nor does the objective level of skills. They must be looked for in the personality of the students, in their ability to recognize challenges at a level commensurate with their skill, where others only see tiresome obstacles.

Dimensions of the flow experience. When a person's skill is just right to cope with the demands of a situation – and when compared to the entirety of everyday life the demands are above average – the quality of experience improves noticeably. It does not matter whether one originally wanted to do the activity, whether one expected to enjoy it or not. Even a frustrating job may suddenly become exciting if one hits upon the right balance.

For this to happen, however, the activity must have relatively clear goals and provide rather quick and unambiguous feedback. It is difficult to become immersed in an activity in which one does not know what needs to be done, or how well one is doing. A game without rules, without a way to assess performance, would be impossible to play. Surgeons unanimously claim that the reason their craft is so enjoyable is that they always know what must be done – to cut out a specific tumor, to reset a given bone – and second by second they are getting information about how the operation is proceeding (Csikszentmihalyi 1975b, 1986). Blood in the cavity during an operation, for example, may mean that the scalpel has slipped. Because of this availability of immediate feedback, surgeons say, their work is much more enjoyable and exciting than the work of internists or psychiatrists. (Internists and psychiatrists, however, enjoy their work because they pay attention to a set of challenges, goals, and feedback that, although less concrete than those surgeons attend to, is nevertheless just as real to them.)

In addition to an equilibrium of challenges and skills, clear goals, and immediate feedback, the flow experience reported by people involved in enjoyable activities shares other common characteristics. Perhaps the most universal of these is the focused concentration people report whenever an activity is deeply enjoyable. Because flow produces harmony within the self, attention can be invested totally in the activity at hand. This produces that "merging of activity and awareness" so typical of enjoyable activities. One simply does not have enough attention left to think about anything else. A consequence of this state of affairs is that the usual preoccupations of everyday life no longer intrude to cause psychic entropy in consciousness. "The court – that's all that matters," says a young basketball player. "Sometimes on court I think of a problem, like fighting with my steady girl, and I think that's nothing compared to the game. You can think about a problem all day, but as soon as you get in the game, the hell with it!"

Then there is the sense that the outcomes of the activity are, in principle, under the person's own control. Rock climbers, for example, insist that their hair-raising exploits are safer than crossing a busy street in Chicago, because on the rock face they can foresee exactly every eventuality, whereas when crossing the street they are at the mercy of fate.

Another common feature of flow experiences is a "distorted" sense of time. When consciousness is fully active and ordered, hours seem to pass by in minutes, and occasionally a few seconds stretch out into what seems to be an infinity. The clock no longer serves as a good analog of the temporal quality of experience.

Because of the deep concentration on the activity at hand, the person in flow not only forgets his or her problems, but loses temporarily the awareness of self that in normal life often intrudes in consciousness, and causes psychic energy to be diverted from what needs to be done. In the terms that George Herbert Mead introduced ([1934] 1970), the "me" disappears during flow, and the "I" takes over (Csikszentmihalyi & Bennett 1971). When the self is conscious of itself, not only does it become less efficient, but the experience is usually painful (Wicklund 1975; Carver & Scheier 1981; Csikszentmihalyi & Figurski 1982). In flow the self is fully functioning, but not aware of itself doing it, and it can use all the attention for the task at hand. At the most challenging levels, people actually report experiencing a *transcendence* of self, caused by the unusually high involvement with a system of action so much more complex than what one usually encounters in everyday life. The climber feels at one with the mountain, the clouds, the rays of the sun, and the tiny bugs moving in and out of the shadow of the fingers holding to the rock; the surgeon feels at one with the movements of the operating team, sharing the beauty and the power of a harmonious transpersonal system.

When all these elements are present, consciousness is in harmony, and the self – invisible during the flow episode – emerges strengthened. The negentropic quality of the flow experience makes it *autotelic*, or intrinsically rewarding. The mountaineer does not climb in order to reach the top of the mountain, but tries to reach the summit in order to climb.

The goal is really just an excuse to make the experience possible. Even surgeons admit that what fascinates them about their job is not so much the ability to cure the patient, or the money, or the prestige, but rather the exhilaration of the difficult task that they are called to perform (Csikszentmihalyi 1975b, 1986).

The implications of the flow experience. When goals are clear, when above-average challenges are matched to skills, and when accurate feedback is forthcoming, a person becomes involved in the activity. At this point, concentration focuses on what needs to be done. Climbers, concentrating on their progress and the potential holds on the rock face, have no attention left over for anything else. Violinists must invest all their psychic energy in feeling the strings and the bow with their fingers, following the notes on the score and the notes in the air, and at the same time feel the emotional content of the piece of music as a whole. Irrelevant thoughts, worries, distractions no longer have a chance to appear in consciousness. There is simply not enough room for them. Self-consciousness, or the worry we so often have about how we appear in the eyes of others, also disappears for the same reason. Because the activity forces us to concentrate on a limited field of stimuli, there is a great inner clarity, awareness is logically coherent and purposeful.

This is the ordered, negentropic state of consciousness we have called flow. It stands out in its integrity from the formless, confusing, and often frustrating conditions of normal, everyday life. Because it reaffirms the order of the self and is so enjoyable, people will attempt to replicate it whenever possible. This tendency to repeat the flow experience is the emergent teleonomy of the self.

And this repetition leads to a selective process: Those activities and experiences that are most enjoyable will have a greater chance of being remembered and of being built into the memory-storage of the culture. Thus enjoyment, which is to the teleonomy of the self what pleasure is to the teleonomy of the physical organism – a mechanism for maintaining order – is the cutting edge of sociocultural evolution. Flow is a sense that humans have developed in order to recognize patterns of action that are worth preserving and transmitting over time. This was Huizinga's ([1939] 1970) great insight: that the "serious" institutions that constitute society – science, the law, the arts, religion, and even the armed forces – all started out as games, as contexts in which people could play and experience the enjoyment of goal-directed action. Science, for instance, Huizinga claimed, has spontaneously evolved in every culture

as games of riddling in which individuals test their memory, their knowledge of facts and relationships, in a public contest against other riddlers
– a perhaps primitive, but highly enjoyable, display of knowledge.

The flow experience is important to understand because it provides
a key for understanding the strivings of the self and the quality of
individual well-being (Inghilleri 1986). It also helps explain which institutions increase order and which produce disorder in consciousness,
and hence gives us a clue to the direction of sociocultural evolution. The
chapters that follow develop these themes, moving from very broad
speculative issues to increasingly detailed and systematic analyses.

3. Sociological implications of the flow experience

RICHARD G. MITCHELL, JR.

The social structure of certainty and uncertainty

Flow, for the most part, takes place in avocational rather than vocational activities. Although it would be ideal to enjoy one's work, and in a few fortunate societies this might indeed be the case, it is generally true in our society that most people do not find deep involvement and enjoyment in their productive work, but seek it instead in leisure activities. Csikszentmihalyi (1975b) points out that artists, scientists, surgeons, and members of a few other occupations may experience flow while working, but they constitute exceptions. Most people, most of the time, find their lives made up of predominantly nonflow situations. But what sort of experience is "nonflow"?

Flow occurs in an existential middle ground. We experience it when a balance is achieved between abilities and responsibilities, when the skills we possess are roughly commensurate with the challenges we face, when our talents are neither underused nor overtaxed. Flow emerges in circumstances that are perceived as both problematic and soluble.

Beyond flow are two conditions. Both represent a state of imbalance between challenge and skill. When this imbalance is brief, temporary, or task-specific, we refer to the ensuing responses as boredom or anxiety. The impact of this short-term imbalance is minimal. But when imbalance is persistent and pervasive across many social roles and occasions, when the world typically and in general presents challenges significantly greater than or less than one's perceived skills, when one is no longer free to choose, or when uncertainty spreads beyond a limited stimulus

This chapter is adapted from Richard G. Mitchell, Jr., *Mountain Experience: The Psychology and Sociology of Adventure* (Chicago: University of Chicago Press, 1983), pp. 170–91, 207–25.

field, then social life itself takes on a predominantly certain or uncertain quality, coloring definitions of both self and society.

For some people, daily routines involve only slight and infrequent variety or challenge. They perceive the network of role relationships in which they are enmeshed as both comprehensive and constraining. For them the social world is a nonnegotiable fact. The outcome of social encounters is readily predicted on the basis of interactants' roles in an inflexible social structure. Independent volitional action is neither required nor encouraged. Goals are subjugated to a tyranny of permissible means. Most personal skills and resources are superfluous.

For other people, daily routines frequently pose urgent and difficult problems. Capacities are routinely overstressed in attempts to perform necessary tasks. The social world is more mystery than concrete entity. Social encounters produce confusing and contradictory outcomes seemingly unrelated to efforts to predict or control them. Existing skill and personal resources are inadequate, the means for meeting basic needs unclear.

The key and common feature in both of these extremes is the degree of certainty or uncertainty with which the results of action in one's social world can be predicted. The terms *alienation* and *anomie* may be used to represent the polar states of certainty and uncertainty concerning these predictions.

Alienation and anomie

Alienation is one of the oldest concepts in the social sciences, derived from yet earlier notions of original sin. This longevity, however, has not contributed in any significant way to a simple definition of the term. Anomie, more recently arrived on the sociological scene, nonetheless shares with alienation a considerable diversity of interpretations.

Efforts to organize the melange of meanings applied to alienation and anomie have been made. Seeman in an early article (1959) catalogues alienation according to five usages in the literature: powerlessness, meaninglessness, normlessness, isolation, and self-estrangement. Feuer (1963, p. 137), in a more structural view, divides alienation into six types: (1) the alienation of class society, (2) the alienation of competitive societies, (3) the alienation of industrial society, (4) the alienation of mass society, (5) the alienation of race, and (6) the alienation of generations.

Scott (1965) describes alienation in regard to its sources as four kinds of inadequacies of social control: lack of commitment to values, absence of conformity to norms, loss of responsibility in role performance, and deficiency in control of resources. Barakat (1969, p. 134) divides alienation into three sequential stages: "(1) sources of alienation at the level of social and normative structures; (2) alienation as a psychological property of the individual; (3) behavioral consequences of alienation." Johnson (1973, pp. 370–80) distinguishes five types of alienation according to level of association: segmental encounters, primary relationships, institutional relationships, mass associations, and reified (projected) relationships.

These schemes, while stimulating, have themselves been fraught with confusion. Classifications overlap and are paralleled by other categories. This is not to demean the work that has been done. The confusion in these terms must in large part be attributed to their extremely broad, and often casual, application rather than to inadequacies in the schemes that propose to organize them. I suggest another way in which alienation and anomie may be understood and related, one that integrates a part of Marx's and Durkheim's work.

Marx is often credited with focusing the concept of alienation on the individual's position in the economic order. He saw workers in a capitalist system, for example, as being forced to sell their labor to those who own the means of production. In so doing they are stripped of any meaningful relationship to the goods they produce and become alienated from their labor. Marx's concept of labor is similar to the idea of meaningful work that offers the opportunity for creative self-expression. Production, labor, is a vital process of self-actualization.

> Production, for Marx, is "the direct activity of individuality." Through the production of objects the individual "reproduces himself . . . actively and in a real sense, and he sees his own reflection in a world which he has construed." This "reproduction of himself" constitutes an actualization of his otherwise implicit "self" or personality in the realm of objectivity. . . . In other words, the kind of production considered by Marx to be man's "life activity" is motivated by nothing more than the need to create, to express oneself, to give oneself extended embodiment. (Schacht 1970, pp. 85–6)

Alienation, according to Marx, is the experience of work without opportunity for self-directed creativity, work for some end exterior to the work itself. Such employment no longer has intrinsic value but becomes a burden, a noxious but necessary drudgery.

> In what does this alienation of labor consist? First, that the work is *external* to the worker, that it is not part of his nature, that

consequently he does not fulfill himself in his work but denies himself, has a feeling of misery, not well-being, does not develop freely a physical and mental energy, but is physically exhausted and mentally debased. The worker therefore feels himself at home only during his leisure, whereas at work he feels homeless. His work is not voluntary but imposed. . . . It is not the satisfaction of a need, but only a *means* for satisfying other needs. (Marx [1844] 1956, p. 169)

For Marx, the antithesis of alienation was gratifying and meaningful work through which creative self-expression is possible. Hegel used "alienation" in two ways (Schacht 1970). Marx focused on the first of these when he wrote of alienation as "surrender" to alienating work, and a giving up of one's time and effort in order to obtain some future remuneration – be that a paycheck or spiritual salvation. For Hegel, this "surrender" was also the solution to a more unendurable condition. Alienation is, in Hegel's second sense, a "separation" from the social substance, suggestive of what Durkheim ([1897] 1951) referred to as anomie.

For Durkheim, the cause of anomie lay not in repressive or unrewarding work but in a breakdown of normative constraints concerning economic aspirations. It is not a lack of creative opportunity but a disturbance in the social order that leads to anomie and anomic suicide. This is not necessarily because objective conditions worsen. "Every disturbance of equilibrium, even though it achieves greater comfort and a heightening of general vitality, is an impulse to voluntary death. Whenever serious readjustments take place in the social order, whether or not due to a sudden growth or unexpected catastrophe, men are more inclined to self-destruction" (Durkheim [1897] 1951, p. 246).

When persons are no longer constrained by a stable economic order, "human activity naturally aspires beyond assignable limits and sets itself unattainable goals" (Durkheim [1897] 1951, pp. 247–8). Uncertainty about the appropriateness of desires leads to disorientation, confusion, a sense of normlessness that some resolve through suicide. Although Durkheim was aware of a condition in direct opposition to anomie, in which "excessive regulation" and "oppressive discipline" overly restrict individual action, he granted this circumstance little importance. It receives mention only in a footnote followed by the qualification that "it has so little contemporary importance and examples are so hard to find . . . that it seems useless to dwell upon it" (Durkheim [1897] 1951, p. 276).

Anomie	Flow	Alienation
Prevailing uncertainty		Prevailing certainty
Ability < Responsibility		Ability > Responsibility
	Ability ≈ Responsibility	
Subjective experience	*Subjective experience*	*Subjective experience*
Confusion-disorientation	Competence	Frustration-repression
Normlessness	Self-as-cause	Powerlessness
Isolation	Action and awareness merge	Self-estrangement
Motive for action		*Motive for action*
Social and economic		Personal freedom,
Security, stability,		Creative self-expression,
certainty		challenge
Comprehension, control		Recognition, creativity

Figure 3.1. Relationship between anomie, flow, and alienation

My use of alienation borrows from Marx, and that of anomie from Durkheim. Unlike either of these authors, however, I see alienation and anomie as the opposite poles of a continuum from certainty to uncertainty in experiencing social life. Figure 3.1 illustrates these relationships. The idea that alienation and anomie fall at polar extremes of a continuum of certainty or uncertainty is not entirely new. Cooley (1912), for example, discussed two opposed extremes of experience that he called "formalism" and "disorganization," which correspond roughly to my uses of "alienation" and "anomie." Formalism he identified as "mechanism supreme," disorganization as "mechanism going to pieces."

> The effect of formalism upon personality is to starve its higher life and leave it the prey of apathy [and] self-complacency.... Disorganization, on the other hand, appears in the individual as a mind without cogent and abiding allegiance to a whole and without the larger principles of conduct that flow from such allegiances. (Cooley 1912, p. 343)

Formalism or alienation leads to the stifling of creativity and apathetic acceptance, while disorganization or anomie leaves people confused, without direction, uncertain.

Parsons conceptualized anomie as the opposite of "full institutionalization."

The polar antithesis of full institutionalization is . . . *anomie*, the absence of structured complementarity of the interaction process or, what is the same thing, the complete breakdown of normative order. . . . Just as there are degrees of institutionalization so are there also degrees of *anomie*. The one is the obverse of the other. (Parsons 1951, p. 39)

Others have suggested pairings of similar concepts. Coburn (1975, p. 214), in discussing the relationship between work conditions and health, identifies three possible "demands–individual ability" conditions: demands exceed capabilities; demands and capabilities match or are congruent; capabilities exceed demands. He labels the first "work pressure" and the third "worker underobligation" and argues that both of these types of job–worker incongruences have negative consequences for mental health.

French and Kahn (1962) describe the condition in which abilities exceed demands as frustration; the situation in which abilities and demands are congruent as self-actualization; and that in which work demands are greater than capacity as role overload.

Barakat (1969), while recognizing, but not incorporating, anomie in his framework, divides the term *alienation* into conditions of overcontrol, powerlessness or undercontrol, and normlessness. He subsumes anomie under his own definition of alienation, arguing that alienation arises from two sources, which he identifies as states of overcontrol and undercontrol in social structures.

Overcontrol is defined here as a state of over-integration or great emphasis on moulding individuals into the society and/or the social systems of which they are members. . . . Thus among instances of overcontrol are: (1) states of powerlessness; (2) depersonalized relationships; and (3) demand for conformity. . . . Simply, undercontrol refers to states of disintegration, permissiveness, and lack of restraints . . . normlessness and disintegration in interpersonal relations. (Barakat 1969, pp. 4–5)

In using the terms *alienation* and *anomie*, I refer to subjective states experienced by individual social actors. Although it may be possible to speak stereotypically of categories of persons as being alienated or anomic, as in "blacks are alienated" or "workers are anomic," it is more accurate to focus on the individual's perception of his or her social circumstances. Only if persons link their races, occupations, genders, and so on to the quality of their social relationships is it of interest here. For me, alienation and anomie are conscious states. I reject the idea that individuals may be alienated or anomic from some standpoint of which they are not aware (see Schacht 1970, pp. 154–9). Perceptions are realities for purposes of understanding social relationships. "If men define situations as real, they are real in their consequences" (Thomas & Thomas 1928, p. 572). Reality does not precede its defining.

Anomie

Anomie is experienced when uncertainty about behavioral outcomes extends to the greater part of social interactions met by the individual. When new social encounters are largely unrelated to previous social experience, unpredictable by known rules, and unstructured and foreign, when the behavior of others in the interaction and the effect of one's own acts upon those others remain uncertain, the individual experiences anomie. The social world appears fleeting, irregular, insubstantial. In the world of work the lives of confidence-game artists, secret agents, and racecar drivers provide a high degree of uncertainty about behavioral outcomes, but uncertainty may be engendered also in more conventional roles that lack clear responsibilities, such as those of the salesman, the broker, or the manager whose company operates in a rapidly changing environment. Anomie expresses itself in three ways.

When the world becomes too uncertain, a sense of normlessness, meaninglessness, or isolation may obtain. One experiences normlessness when known rules for social behavior are inapplicable or ineffective, meaninglessness when understandable purposes for action are absent, isolation when social support from one's fellows is inadequate or undependable. The anomic individual finds himself or herself unsupported by significant others, free to choose from meaningless alternatives, without direction or purpose, bound by no constraint, guided by no faith, comforted by no hope. The uncertainty of outcomes elevates the taken-for-granted to the problematic, the routine to the traumatic, the normal task to the major test.

Anomie motivates a search for social stability, security, and certainty. The goal of anomic persons is the restoration of stable interaction, escape from pervasive uncertainty, reintegration into an understandable and predictable social order. In response to anomie people seek a state in which the demands placed upon them to achieve are in rough equilibrium with their capacities. Using the limited case of economic achievement, Merton (1938, 1957) explains several types of deviance in terms of people's efforts to adapt to anomie, to alter their life experience in the direction of increased predictability and control. Not everyone, however, is in want of security, stability, and certainty.

Alienation

When people can predict their own behaviors on the basis of the social order in which they are situated, when they perceive their world as constrained by social forces, bound over by rule and regulation at every turn to the extent that personal creativity and spontaneity are stifled, when they know what they will and must do in a given situation regardless of their own interests, they experience alienation. The alienating social world is omnipresent and repressive. Meaningful mobility is forlorn, the stability of relationships renders self-directed change elusive; security, stability, and certainty are no longer desirable or even tolerable. Life in the concentration camp, in prison, or on the assembly line provides a high degree of certainty about behavioral outcomes. It may also be alienating. This alienation expresses itself in two ways.

When the social world becomes too certain, the individual feels powerless and self-estranged. Powerlessness is sensed as one's own behavior proves insufficient to bring about outcomes sought in the social world. Action produces an inadequate effect. Self-estrangement grows from a social life lacking rewards in the here and now. Action is without autotelic character. Social tasks are undertaken and performed for rewards outside those activities themselves. The certainty of outcome reduces interaction from challenge to drudgery, from a novelty to a necessity.

In sum, the lives of social actors can be described in terms of their perceptions of the predictability of social outcomes. This dimension is bounded by alienating certainty at one extreme and anomic uncertainty at the other. In between is a common and desirable condition sought by alienated and anomic persons alike.

Competence

The goals of the alienated individual are both different from and similar to those of anomic persons. They differ in that alienated individuals, in searching for occasions to utilize their perceived abilities, may purposely seek out problematic and puzzling circumstances, or actively encourage continued instability in some areas of their social lives.

More important than the differences, however, are the similarities. Both alienated and anomic social actors are seeking ways of bringing into balance their perceived abilities and the responsibilities confronting them. Both endeavor to match the challenges they face with the resources they possess. Both attempt to move toward a state of equilibrium between what they perceive themselves capable of doing and what they are allowed or required to do as a result of their position in the social structure. Achievement of this balance renders activity intrinsically rewarding, enjoyable, "fun." It becomes leisure in the classic sense (de Grazia 1962, pp.11–25).

In neuropsychological terms, organisms are motivated to alter environmental inputs, reducing stimulus variability when too much is present, increasing variablity when stimulation falls below some optimal level (Hebb 1955; Berlyne 1960; Hunt 1965). Social-psychologically, role expectations are met with appropriate and adequate role performances. Persons are motivated to achieve what White (1955) refers to as competence, a sense of personal worth, self-as-cause, efficacy in interaction with others. Sociologically, normatively prescribed goals are articulated with socially legitimated means.

Competence grows from the process of recognizing one's abilities and applying them meaningfully and completely. Competence means assessing oneself as qualified, capable, fit, sufficient, adequate. Competence emerges when a person's talent, skills, and resources find useful application in meeting a commensurate challenge, problem, or difficulty. In sum, the competent individuals' perceived abilities are roughly equal to their perceived responsibilities.

A sense of competence is a prerequisite to flow. Flow is found in using a full measure of commitment, innovation, and individual investment to perform real and meaningful tasks that are self-chosen, limited in scope, and rewarding in their own right. Flow is the "opposite" of both alienation and anomie. In terms of social actors, motivations, and aspirations, flow is not some stressless lacuna but a balanced, dynamic tension.

Avocations as means of avoiding alienation and anomie

How the everyday social world is experienced affects the selection of avocational pursuits. Feelings of overstress or underutilization of skills, perceptions of life as going on within a rigid structure or a tenuously constructed subjective reality, experiences of prevailing alienation or anomie, lead to different kinds of recreational activities. Generally, avocations contrast with and sometimes complement routine affairs. They do not duplicate them. Although it need not be the case, for most persons an essential feature of their recreation is its separation from everyday life, discontinuity from normal action-frames (Ball 1972, pp. 124–5). As Goffman notes, adventures are not to be found within but beyond common routines. "Ordinarily, action will not be found during the weekday work routine at home or on the job. For here choice-takings tend to be organized and such as remain are not obviously voluntary" (Goffman 1967, pp. 194–5).

If daily routines are threatening, uncertain, if existence in the world is insecure, then recreation will be sought in another realm – in situations where outcomes are not influenced by the players' efforts, where actors are largely freed from the necessity of choice. In this sort of recreation, strategy and skill are inapplicable. All that is required or desired in play is the passive acceptance of variability in fateful circumstances. Such people fulfill the prediction of Dostoyevsky's Grand Inquisitor: "I tell thee that man is tormented by no greater anxiety than to find someone quickly to whom he can hand over that gift of freedom with which the ill-fated creature is born" (Dostoyevsky 1957, p. 234).

When everyday activity is constraining, routinized, invariant, overly structured, when experience of the world is one of excessive regulation and oppressive discipline, then people seek variety and personal challenge in their recreation. They search out occasions for creative self-expression, more puzzling problems, and difficult tests. They yearn for freedom of choice, for situations where outcomes hinge on the volitional control of players. Resources are purposely limited to decrease the probability of success and ensure that the uncertainty of these outcomes is maximized.

In short, those who experience a surplus of certainty in their daily lives, that is, those who are alienated, will seek uncertainty in play. On the other hand, those who view the world as mainly uncertain, that is, anomic persons, will seek certainty in recreation.

Donald Ball (1972) supports these arguments, noting that recreational activity falls along a continuum of action in which participants have greater or lesser degrees of control over their play. In some action situations, such as mountain climbing, players are "control oriented." By virtue of their skills and strategies, they exercise considerable influence over outcomes. In other situations such as "fair" dice games, participants have little control, are more "acceptance oriented." Ball argues that the type of action sought by players depends on the amount of perceived risk or uncertainty experienced by them in everyday nonplay affairs:

"*Control oriented* action is positively associated with sociocultural units where regularly perceived risk is low . . . [and] *acceptance oriented* action is positively associated with sociocultural units where the regularly perceived risk is high" (Ball 1972, p. 126).

To test these hypotheses, Ball used ethnographic data from Murdock (1967) and Textor (1967). He identified seven indicators of potential risk, including scarcity of food supply, degree of urbanization, and several measures of political integration, leadership, and organizational complexity. These indicators were compared, in four hundred cultures indexed by Textor, to the games most popular and prevalent, dichotomized as control-oriented versus acceptance-oriented. In general, the data supported his hypotheses and he concluded that the "type of action is a function of risk, and more specifically, that deliberate risk-taking [control orientation] is associated with the absence of perceived risk in everyday life. Action is searched for where and when it is not likely to be found; when it is extraordinary rather than ordinary" (Ball 1972, p. 134).

Ball's argument can be applied to persons within a given sociocultural unit. It is true that Americans climb mountains, but which Americans? Certainly the majority do not. Control- and acceptance-oriented avocations are both readily available in this country. Los Angeles residents can reach the peaks of the Sierra Nevada and the gaming tables of Las Vegas with similar ease. Why do some choose the mountains and others the gambling casinos?

In modern, highly industrialized societies such as the United States, risk will be perceived differentially. Some will find their circumstances routinely more threatening and tenuous than others. Who would be likely to face such regular risk and uncertainty? Those persons who have hazardous, low-prestige occupations, insecure employment, less education; the politically disenfranchised; minorities and other stigmatized groups that have less than average control over their own life space and experience. This is the segment of the population that would be expected, following Ball's hypothesis, to seek high-certainty recreational activity in contrast to the unpredictability of their daily affairs.

If Ball is correct, mountaineers will be found in obverse circumstances where certainty and security are normal, risk and uncertainty improbable. The climber's everyday life should be characterized by stability and permanence in both interpersonal relations and institutional position.

Surveys of mountaineers in California (Mitchell 1983, pp. 184–86), Alberta, Canada (Bratton, Kinnear, & Koroluk 1979, pp. 55–7), and data from the early membership records of the British Alpine Club (Lunn 1957, pp. 43–4) substantiate these anticipations. In each sample, white, middle-class, married males with graduate-level education and secure, remunerative, and prestigious employment predominated. Ball's contention that those in social environments characterized by relative certainty will seek control-oriented uncertainty in their recreational activities would seem to be correct. Those with minimal likelihood of experiencing uncertainty in their daily affairs – men with stable personal lives and established and respected careers – are also those found pursuing moutaineering and similar avocational activities.

The reader may feel a commonsensical contradiction beginning to emerge here. If the notion is accepted that alienation, especially in the world of work, motivates a search for control-oriented risk, then why is it that engineers, technicians, and other professionals climb mountains? Surely assembly line workers, keypunch and telephone-switchboard operators, theater ticket takers, mail sorters, and a whole range of other clerical personnel must also find their work alienating, confining, bereft of opportunity for creative self-expression, to an equal or greater extent than scientists, technicians, and the like. In fact, are not today's engineers and technicians, for example, viewed as special sorts of skilled and respected craftspersons? Are they not the elite who, guided by the principles of science, wield the powerful and sophisticated tools of technology in creating a better world for all humankind? Is their work not inherently purposeful, meaningful, and challenging? So many people believe.

The problem lies not in the absolute but in the relative deprivation experienced by scientists, engineers, technicians, and similar others. Although clerks, laborers, and assembly line workers may encounter few opportunities for creativity and self-expression, they seldom expect more. Many of these workers have already abandoned the quest for personal creativity as a capacity beyond them or inevitably denied them and leave it at that. A job is a job, they say; what matters is the pay and security. "The average manual worker and many white collar employees may be satisfied with fairly steady jobs which are largely instrumental and non-involving, because they have not the need for responsibility and self-expression in work. They are relatively content with work which is simply a means to the larger end of providing the pay checks" (Blauner 1970, p. 96).

But not everyone abandons the search for creativity. Some, in fact, are given little choice in the matter. It is expected that scientists and their pragmatic helpers, the engineers and technicians along with some other skilled professionals, will actively seek creative self-expression in their work. Whereas the assembly line laborer may abandon this elusive hope, the scientist or successful businessperson may not. They are driven to succeed in this search, not only by their own unrealistic training but by the opinions of others regarding the proper enactment of their role.

The scientist, engineer, and technician again provide clear examples. Throughout their training these professionals are inculcated with the idea that their chosen work in life will be contributory, creative, and meaningful. They come to believe that science, through the rational study and manipulation of a physical universe, presumably governed by predictable and immutable laws, will advance humankind toward a better understanding and control of the world. But the realities they encounter in the world of work do much to undermine this positivistic hope. They soon discover that much of what they are called upon to do on the job is less than helpful and more than a little dull, particularly for the applied scientist, technician, or other professional. These persons in particular experience a considerable schism between their academic preparation and actual work experience. Their training consists in learning broad theoretical principles, but that knowledge is often put to use in narrow, pragmatic circumstances.

One structural engineer-climber reported dreaming of building great bridges or skyscrapers. He now designs cabanas for beach homes and golf courses. A research chemist who hoped to find alternatives to fossil fuel energy now monitors production equipment at an oil refinery. The work of corporate science and technology is frequently limited to the development and refinement of products designed to exploit markets while placating government inspectors and consumer advocates, not the solution of larger social, technical, or conceptual problems. Even work presumably as creative as the symphony musician's may be institutionally constrained. Musicians learn that technical accuracy, punctuality, and obedience are more stringent requirements for continued membership than individual creative expression in star solo performances.

These realities of the scientists', technicians', and other professionals' lives are often obscured from persons outside. As far as such persons are concerned, the scientist or professional still is and must be a creator, and they act toward him or her accordingly. Scientific and professional work must be meaningful, even if theirs is not; the scientist must be engrossed, fascinated, inspired. Thus, scientists and similar others experience recurring social encounters in which they are expected to take their work seriously; to act, at least outwardly, as if it were rewarding and purposeful. They are not allowed the luxury of self-indulgent bitterness toward their disappointing jobs. Rather, they are continually reminded of what their work ideally entails and are called upon to demonstrate enthusiasm for these ideals.

Instead of finding creative self-expression in work, and because that work stimulates others to remind them constantly of what that work could, should, and ought to be, applied scientists and related professionals are alienated to a greater extent than others. In that alienation lies a motive for searching out avocations that offer challenging opportunities for action, such as mountaineering. The mountains offer an alternative arena to the world of work and other routine life experiences, an arena in which meaningful and creative self-expression may realistically be found. Mountaineering offers the anithesis of alienation; it offers the potential for flow.

Barbara Zeller, a Colorado mountaineer, describes the relationship between perceived social conditions and climbing in this way:

> Most people today are secure, financially and socially. . . . We have all the conveniences and comforts, but it's like living in an elaborately decorated cell. . . . There is nothing mystical about the way we are controlled and over-governed by rules and systems. Others control you. You are like a puppet; you don't make your own moves. . . . Sure, [climbing] is an escape, but it's escape from the control of others. . . . If it is escape, it's escape from others back to yourself. You get yourself back again for awhile. (Zeller, in Jenkins 1979, p. 20).

The effects of rationalization on flow in everyday life

The key concept, the desirable condition, the sought-after goal of climbing is the social-psychological condition of flow. The mechanisms of flow (see Chapter 2) are obvious in the mountaineering setting, but what of other less exotic social action? Is it possible to find or create the climber's enthusiasm and gratification in more common encounters?

The answer is a tentative yes. Csikszentmihalyi (1975b, pp. 140–60) argues that it is possible to conceive of flow and its contradictions as microphenomena sprinkled throughout daily routines and encounters. Conversation, for example, is sometimes embarrassed and halting when the roles of participants are unclear or the definition of the situation is unresolved. At other times, talk may be stifled by rules of order or other proprietary considerations so that only a vestige of one's ideas is communicated (Lyman & Scott 1970, p. 132). There are also times when conversation progresses comfortably, when ideas are exchanged directly, emotions are shared, and participants feel both that they understand and that they are understood.

If flow is presumably available in a wide range of action, especially in leisure, why is it not a more frequent experience? After all, a seemingly sensible notion of many social scientists and lay people alike is that ordinary lives lack even the remotest parallel with experiences like climbing a mountain. This notion is only partly correct; it is more descriptive than prescriptive. Flow is possible in everyday events. However, there are cultural factors that discourage the discovery of flow and diminish the range and frequency of interactions with high flow potential, especially in conventional leisure and sport. The process of rationalization is at the heart of these factors.

Viewed from a historical perspective, Western civilization is now in the throes of a great realignment of social and economic patterning. Max Weber called this process of change "rationalization," the infusion of scientific method, technological improvement, and rational management into all areas of human endeavor. It is manifested in the West through the religious ethic of Protestantism (Giddens 1971, p. 169) and the economic form of capitalism. Rationalization connotes more than guidelines for the organization of production or the generation of practical knowledge; it reflects an underlying value, urging the injection of calculation and method in meaning patterns at all points in life (Schlucter 1979, pp. 14–15). Rationalized society is characterized by the increasing capacity to predict and control natural phenomena in the external world. It is also accompanied by a rejection of the impractical and spontaneous in favor of the measured and purposeful. Rational life is not merely utilitarian and sensible, it is desirable and proper.

Rationalization has left in its wake three sorts of deficiencies in social experience: linguistic restrictions on the expression of leisured states, a separation of basic functions of life, and disenchantment at the loss of unifying myth.

Linguistic restrictions. Why is flow not a more frequent experience? One partly correct answer is that actually it does occur more often than conventional wisdom suggests, but is simply overlooked. Csikszentmihalyi (1981a) argues that many social scientists are so convinced of the supremacy of extrinsic rewards in motivating human behavior that flowlike experience is ignored or regarded as insignificant. Flow may be hard to find simply because so few are looking for it or are prepared to identify and discuss it once found.

Robert N. Wilson elaborates this idea. In an eloquent essay (Wilson 1981), he argues that our language itself works against a full grasp of the flow concept. Rephrasing the Whorf hypothesis, Wilson reminds us that it is only possible to perceive and take action toward those objects and processes that can be expressed through available linguistic frames. Like a window latticework, the structure of language provides sharp clarity and definition to parts of the experiential universe while obscuring or occluding others. According to Wilson, our language is dominated by what Suzanne Langer calls discursive symbolism; this is the language of scientific and technical reports, textbooks, and instruction manuals. Discursive language is more useful in getting things done. It is deliberate, analytic, purposeful; if you will, left-hemisphere–dominated. "It is instrumental in the double sense that it assists in . . . shaping our mundane actions and also that it is predominantly a means to an end, a pointer or reference to objects and events outside itself" (Wilson 1981, p. 292).

Other means of expression, what Langer calls presentational language, are needed to articulate the flow phenomenon. Such means are hard to find. Caught as we are in a "rational linguistic trap" (Wilson 1981, p. 289), we find these presentational elements often unfamiliar or inaccessible. Presentational language is reserved for infrequent efforts to express the soft, fragile subjectivism of artistic appreciation, mystical wonder, religious spirituality, and other elusive sentiments. These are neither common nor comfortable topics for many people. Trapped in a restrictive language frame, flow searchers are like artists off to capture the sunset with hammer and nails, compose songs for pulleys and levers, choreograph a chemical reaction. Flow seems rare and ephemeral to those half-blinded by incomplete perception, slow to emerge into full consciousness as a significant component of daily life. Rationalization creates other effects that separate flow from routine experience and that lead some to seek compensation in an isolated and distinct leisure pursuit.

Separation of the functions of life. A key social-structural component of rationalization is progressive differentiation. Adam Smith ([1776] 1980) and Durkheim ([1893] 1947) called this process the division of labor, the development of new roles and units or organization in society, each devoted with greater intensity to the performance of some narrower function than those it replaced (Glaser 1978, pp. 16–17). Differentiation produces a separation in the spheres of life. Functions formerly served by the primordial institution, the family, are now performed by a variety of specialized organizations: the school, factory, church, and so on. Within each of these institutions, individuals enact varied roles and hold different statuses to which they attach variable importance.

The differentiated organization of labor segments work and leisure, allotting separate times and places for each. In the name of efficient production, workers are discouraged from singing, laughter, or other playful behavior on the job. Such nonwork activity in the employment setting is considered deviant, "goofing off." The opportunity for play is institutionalized in the form of paid vacations and holidays, and persons are expected to use these "life spaces" (Parker 1971, p. 25) in their designated ways, for leisure (Biggart 1980, p. 34). This is a key proposition of the "compensatory hypothesis" proposed by Wilensky (1960) and refined by Kando and Summers (1971), wherein leisure behavior is linked directly to negative or positive attributes of work.

When work is perceived as overly regimented and routine and aspirations for creative expression are unabated, some workers turn to nonwork pursuits such as climbing in search of a direct, uncompromising challenge to the full spectrum of their abilities. On the mountain, rationalization is held in abeyance. Alone or in small groups the climber ventures to awkward and demanding places where competence in the tasks at hand is mandatory, differentiation is minimal.

Yet climbers and those with like avocations are a minority. Others in rationalized society respond to the confining circumstances with greater emphasis on the tasks at hand in the hope that increased effort will somehow produce greater and more abundant satisfactions than the paltry ones now available. That faith is ill founded.

Disenchantment. The ultimate disappointment in rationalization is not its shrinkage of complex and commanding tasks to be done, but a more fundamental malaise. What is missing from rationalized society is not action but purpose, a sense of belonging to a unified, animated, spiritually encompassing world.

Weber was fond of Friedrich Schiller's phrase the "disenchantment of the world" (Gerth & Mills 1946, p. 51). According to Weber, disenchantment was the inevitable, if lamentable, negative by-product of rationalization. The rationalized world increasingly becomes an artificial product of mechanical manipulation, estranged and separated from conquered nature. Modern science replaces primitive superstition, but with new ways of knowing comes a vast new unknown. The pantheon of ancient gods, the mysterious animation of ever-present spirits and sprites have vanished. The sacred grove has been logged and sold, the enchanted pool pumped dry. Likewise, the reassurances of religious myth – an omnipotent deity, the heavenly host, a sky filled with angels – all are gone. Astronomers and astronauts reach out into the expanding universe and discover humanity's insignificance and solitude. Instead of the surety of God's grace there remains only the ability to reject null hypotheses, to reduce the probability of error. Knowledge of material things is gained, but holistic, spiritually encompassing understanding of life is lost.

The metamorphosis of leisure

Rationalization strips life of spiritual vitality, creates linguistic limits and structural barriers to the experience of flow in ordinary events. But what of these segmented activities specifically set aside for play? Even these are influenced by rationalization, and thus flow potential is further restricted. Leisure in a rationalized world has special qualities. As society is permeated by the perceived need for ever-increasing scientific guidelines and calculated control, the form and content of play is profoundly affected.

Guttmann, mincing no words, has described the European criticism of rationalized sport:

> Sport is not an escape from the world of work but rather an exact structural and functional parallel to the world of work. Sport does not offer compensation for the frustrations of alienated labor. . . . It seduces the luckless athlete and spectator into a second world of work more authoritarian and repressive and less meaningful than the economic sphere itself. (Guttmann 1978, p. 69)

What causes this mutation of institutionalized leisure from the joyful spontaneity of flow toward less desirable states? A reexamination of the constituents of flow reveals a variety of rationalization effects, each distorting or diminishing flow potential in leisure.

Flow is made up of a limited number of essential elements. For flow to occur outcomes must be significant and determined by individual volitional action; the act must be intrinsically rewarding, occasioned by a merging of action and awareness, an absence of self-consciousness;

54   Richard G. Mitchell, Jr.

and action must take place in a limited stimulus field (Csikszentmihalyi 1974, 1975b). Rationalization aids achievement of only the last condition. Each of the other components is variously diminished or eliminated to the extent that leisure is rationalized. Commercialized leisure provides useful examples of these effects, although certainly not all such activities are bereft of flow potential.

Flow is possible only when real, meaningful, fateful outcomes are dependent upon the volitional action of participants. Activities that are trivial in substance or beyond the control of actors do not facilitate flow. Grappling with raging rivers, hunting wild carnivores in the bush, and going on moutain pack-train expeditions would seem to offer much fateful experience, but as these activities are rationalized, outcomes are no longer personally controlled. Outdoor adventure enthusiasts on commercial white water raft journeys, big game hunts and the like, find that much of the significant action is prescribed by the professional staff and that they are often relegated to the role of largely helpless incompetents, of glorified baggage. For example, on some river raft trips in Colorado, no more is required of customers than a willingness to get wet and some effort to remain in a boat. Planning, logistics, scouting, route selection, boat management, camp setup, cooking, and fireside entertainment are provided by guide service personnel. Outings such as these are clearly fateful encounters, but the participants have little to do with the outcomes.

Lasch echoes Huizinga's concern that as games are rationalized and lose their sacred ritual qualities they deteriorate into trivial recreation and crude sensationalism (Lasch 1978, p.109). Such is the case in other commercial leisure activities in which actors retain control but the significance of play results is sharply reduced.

Hockey, baseball, basketball, football, tennis, and a host of other games have been miniaturized and simplified so they can be played with electronic images that are projected on a video screen and are controlled by subtle wrist and finger motions. The experiences of torpedoing enemy ships, destroying alien invaders, Grand Prix auto racing, even intergalactic war and other improbable activities are available for a small sum at nearby amusement arcades or through home video equipment. These ersatz games disregard the energy, skill, and determination required for their full-scale counterparts. The violence, brutality, injury, even death that actual participants would face are trivialized into machine-made light flashes and noises. To a large extent actors determine outcomes in these games but the results are hardly fateful.

For an event to offer the potential for flow experience it must be perceived by actors as intrinsically rewarding, satisfying in its own right. Rationalization occasions a shift in many forms of play from the achievement of immediate enjoyment to the earning of ultimate success, from means to ends. Competition becomes the dominant form of play and winning the preeminent goal. Intrinsic gratifications are replaced by the extrinsic rewards of prestige and profit. This shift, in turn, alters other components of flow.

In flow experiences, self-consciousness is eliminated. Action and awareness are tightly and reflexively intertwined, merging together. It is this quality that provides the concept with its strongest sociological roots. It is possible to locate this blending of action and awareness in what Mead ([1934] 1970, pp. 273–381) identified as the fusion of the *I* and the *me*. When the impulsive, spontaneous, nondirectional *I* urges behavior in correspondence with the expectations, definitions, and guidelines of the incorporated other, the *me*, flow may occur.

Thus the social act, as Mead (1938, pp. 3–25) defined it, is abbreviated in flow. Initiating impulses give rise directly to consummatory action without the need for focused perception or constructed manipulation. In flow, conscious mediation between the individual and society is unnecessary. In the special circumstances of flow, behavior is at once personally satisfying and socially appropriate yet requires neither rehearsal nor correction. In Caillois's terms, ludus encompasses paidia but does not constrain it. Flow is a condition without deviance. Action and attention are focused exclusively in the present. Actors neither apprehend their deeds nor reflect upon them; they lack both fear of the future and guilt for the past.

In contrast, rationalized play is eminently self-conscious and fraught with potential deviance. As concern shifts from playing to winning, as games become more competitive and especially as external rewards grow in importance – when scholarships, prizes, bonuses, and political advantage ride in the balance – the temptation to rule deviation grows. "Transposed to reality, the only goal of *agon* [competition] is success. The rules of courteous rivalry are forgotten and scorned. They seem merely irksome and hypocritical conventions. Implacable competition becomes the rule. Winning even justifies foul blows" (Caillois 1961, p. 54). Cheating must be minimized. Making decisions about the conduct of play becomes too critical to remain in the hands of players themselves. Although participants might be fair judges of their own enjoyment, this is a matter of diminished significance. Other theoretically unbiased specialists emerge who are charged with the duty of detecting rule transgressions, noting legitimate accomplishments, and assigning appropriate rewards and punishments: judges, referees, umpires. Overall, regulation of games becomes the duty of boards and commissioners who evaluate the impact of new developments and who structure rules to ensure that technical or strategic innovations do not disproportionately favor some players or groups over others.

Finally, rationalized specialization extends beyond play to participants themselves. As players are subdivided and the rules of interaction refined, certain activity-specific qualities grow in importance. Persons who possess or develop those attributes are selectively recruited into these games. Players within each activity come to approximate each other but are increasingly differentiated from the general population. Physically adapted and temperamentally suited players are chosen and trained to be best at a single game. Their talents are not usually transferable to other kinds of play.

As a result, those leisure activities with the strongest cultural mandate, the most rationalized sports, have the least potential for flow. Rationalization drives people from the field of play altogether. Self-consciousness grows extreme. The stakes have gotten too high. Winning is of such importance, competition is so keen, players are so specialized, the chances of an average individual performing adequately are so remote and the chances of being criticized are so likely that it is no longer worth the risk. Losing imparts a stigma, becomes a sign of inferiority, irrationality, lack of commitment. It becomes easier to join the bystander-analysts than to continue a halting and unappreciated participation. Actual play is abandoned in favor of discussion and comparison of others' performances. Finally, the last vestige of volitional control is given up. For some, sport undergoes a last transformation into a game of chance, a gamble, in which onlookers in no way influence the action but wager on outcomes in the office football pool or at the local bookie.

The metamorphosis nears completion. Through the process of rationalization, play is transformed. Ludus replaces paidia. Rules expand. Impulsiveness, individual creativity, are discouraged; regimentation, precise execution, and routine are demanded. The purpose of play shifts from the achievement of immediate enjoyment to the earning of ultimate success, from means to ends. Self-consciousness is heightened, action and awareness divided. In an urgent effort to regain some valued but intangible aspect of life, the disenchanted ones search for flow experience in less than encompassing ways. They look where other people structure the action, make decisions, take risks for them. Partial commitment offers only partial fulfillment. Others are drawn to the shallow, frantic allure of synthetic play in which they may find endless electronic distraction but little lasting satisfaction. Flow continues to elude them.

Conclusion

The elusiveness of flow should be taken seriously. As Csikszentmihalyi (1981a) points out, the significance of enjoyment is not trivial. It is vital to the survival of society. In the long run a boring system cannot last. An essential quality of any social order is the way opportunities for expressive experience are institutionalized.

> Are they segmented into leisure activities that eventually preclude enjoyment because they become ruled by instrumental goals? Are intrinsic rewards available in adult roles – in jobs, in the family, in schools, in communities? These are the questions that disclose the essential structure of a social system. It is important to know how a society produces its means of subsistence, but it might be more important to know what pleasures it can give its members. (Csikszentmihalyi 1981a, p. 339)

Society without play grows stilted and stunted. When members are discouraged from spontaneous expressivity in play, they may overlook other possibilities. Elemental play and scientific curiosity stem from a common source, a generous hospitality toward newness, puzzlement, the untried difficulty, the emerging unknown. Creative acts of whatever order, in play or art or scientific inquiry, call for a willingness to follow the flight of hazardous processes, to surrender the self to forces beyond one's control. Creative life, which is to say a vitally experienced and satisfying life, cannot be led easily or safely (Wilson 1981, p. 302). It is demanding, challenging, stressful.

Stress is a key term. Stress may be defined as a social-psychological condition of perceived urgency, importance, or significance associated with some set of persons or events. A stressful situation is one that matters, one that is real, meaningful, and commanding. Stress is simply and essentially stimulation. Genuine leisure – flow, that is – is not possible without it.

Leisure is sometimes conceptualized commonsensically as the antithesis of stress, as a respite from the burdens of demanding work, home life, and other responsibilities. This notion of leisure as being stress-free is problematic. It is predicated on assumptions about social life that are only partly tenable in modern industrialized countries.

Gone are the days of rugged individuals eking out a subsistence on the wild frontier. In the name of rational efficiency, work activity is stripped of complexity and novelty, streamlined, standardized, routinized. Following the ghost of Frederick Taylor (1923), the occupation has been simplified to a set of logically related tasks, the individual reduced to an assortment of roles and statuses. This process is not limited to clerical or assembly line jobs but is beginning to influence all categories of work. Engineers, chemists, computer programmers, and other professionals are likewise affected. Far from increasing stress, these organizations at all levels function to isolate people from sensation and varied experience, minimize their decision-making domain, limit options, cloister and confine.

Numerous psychological experiments have demonstrated that humans and animals alike seek out and are rewarded by moderate complexity, uncertainty, novelty in their environments (see Fiske & Maddi 1961; Harris 1972). Maximum motivation is reached and gratification for accomplishments potentiated when a balance is achieved between our abilities and our responsibilities, when the skills we possess are roughly commensurate with the challenges we face, when our talents are neither underused nor overtaxed. But for many persons enmeshed professionally in modern large-scale organizations, this relationship between task and talent, between ability and responsibility is woefully skewed. Many in our society feel this imbalance and curtailment in their range of actions and creative potential. Some are willing to forgo intrinsic rewards in exchange for material plenty and economic security. Mountaineers, and others, are not. In what they perceive as a homogenized, sterilized, rationalized, and rule-governed social world, climbers and their ilk seek a raw encounter with an environment that can be met only with a full measure of personal commitment, innovation, and investment.

To be without stress is to be eddied in the stream of life experiences, cut off from stimuli, noxious or otherwise. Less is required of the person and less is possible. The opposite of stress is not celebration, satisfaction, or tranquillity. It is a state of reduced awareness and diminished capacity, of torpid disinterest as found in drug-induced stupor and, when logically extended, in coma and quintessentially in death. Only by the distortions of Orwellian doublethink can such stresslessness be judged a desirable leisure goal.

Civilization protects us not just from real dangers but sometimes from the full possibilities of our humanity. Science and technology provide facts and leverage but offer no global understanding or inclusive moral order. They strip life of mystery and spirituality. Rationalized play loses its iconic meaning and autotelic reward. But there are solutions. We are not shut up forever within the iron cage; it is of human design and we can escape.

The transition is not complete. Play and other enjoyable actions are not all rationalized away. The immense possibilities of human spirit are not yet flattened to the dehumanized outline of two-dimensional men and women. Although the vital reaffirmation of self in flow comes only from stressful engagement, we are capable of that effort. Flow is to be found in the climbing of mountains. But for some the mountains may be far away or otherwise unreachable.

Invisible mountains surround us all. They are hidden in stamp collection albums, in paints and brushes, in the well-written lines of a letter to a dear friend or an irritating politician, in making a fine soufflé, in delivering a convincing speech, or in performing delicate surgery. Flow is not reserved for leisure in the limited sense of sport or recreation, but is possible whenever commitment, energy, and will find meaningful and effective application in the world of social experience.

4. Flow and biocultural evolution

FAUSTO MASSIMINI, MIHALY CSIKSZENTMIHALYI,
AND ANTONELLA DELLE FAVE

This chapter is about the role of the flow experience in the construction and complexification of the self, and, in a broader sense, its role in biological and cultural evolution. Some of the theoretical assumptions underlying this relationship have already been developed elsewhere (e.g., Massimini & Calegari 1979; Massimini 1982; Csikszentmihalyi & Massimini 1985; Csikszentmihalyi 1987b). The main contention is that people tend to replicate optimal experiences more often relative to other experiences in order to maintain an ordered state of consciousness.

The characteristics that make the flow experience a negentropic state of consciousness – high concentration and involvement, clarity of goals and feedback, and intrinsic motivation, all made possible by a balance between perceived challenges and personal skills – have already been described theoretically and confirmed empirically (Csikszentmihalyi 1975b, 1982a; Csikszentmihalyi & Graef 1979). One of the purposes of this chapter is to show the underlying sameness in the phenomenology of this experience by reporting examples from interviews with individuals in very different cultures.

In addition, by considering which activities produce flow and the number of people in each sample who find flow in various activities, it is possible to begin estimating how this experience might influence biological and cultural evolution. For example, when a person learns to experience flow in the context of a religious vocation, as in one of the samples considered in the following pages, the replication of cultural instructions having to do with prayer, meditation, and ritual

The authors wish to express their gratitude to the teachers and administrators at the Navajo Community College in Tsaile, Arizona, and at the Mahidol University in Bangkok, Thailand, who have helped collect the data reported in this chapter.

60

ceremonies may take precedence even over the replication of that person's biological instructions.

Enjoyment and cultural evolution

Cultural evolution refers to the differential transmission of information contained in artifacts – that is, objects, symbol systems, activities, and other behavior patterns that owe their existence to human intentionality. Although artifacts are human products, they in turn shape human consciousness (Berger & Luckmann 1967; Csikszentmihalyi & Rochberg-Halton 1981). Artifacts contain behavioral instructions in that they define the reality in which the physical organism is to operate. Often they also contain explicit directions for action – such as norms, regulations, and laws. In this sense artifacts parallel the function of genetic instructions that direct the biological behavior of the organism. Whereas genetic instructions are coded chemically in the organism's chromosomes, the information contained in artifacts is coded and stored extrasomatically – in the action potential inherent in objects, in drawings, in texts, or in the behavior patterns of other individuals with whom one interacts. We might use the term "meme" coined by Dawkins (1976) for the replicating unit of cultural information.

One of the most distinctive peculiarities of sociocultural evolution is that although its material content is extrasomatic, its dynamics are entirely within human consciousness. The three phases common to all evolutionary processes – variation, selection, and transmission – are mediated by the mind. Cultural variation begins when new memes arise as ideas, actions, or perceptions of outside events. Selection among variant memes – and retention of the selected ones – also involves a more or less conscious evaluation and investment of attention. And so does the transmission of the retained meme: Unless people invest psychic energy in the new variant, it will not survive long enough for the next generation to be aware of its existence.

Perhaps the most universal qualification of positively selected artifacts is that they improve the quality of human experience. Whenever a new cultural form promises pleasure or enjoyment, it will find a receptive niche in consciousness (for the role of pleasure in evolution see Cabanac 1971; Burhoe 1982). This combination of reasons for the adoption of a new artifact is well expressed by the Greek poet who saluted the introduction of the water mill into the

Roman Empire: "Spare your hands, which have been long familiar with the millstone, you maidens who used to crush the grain. Henceforth you shall sleep long, oblivious to the crowing cocks who greet the dawn" (quoted in Bloch 1967, p. 145). Compared to the millstone, the water mill offered women smoother hands, less physical effort, and more disposable time – presumably adding up to an overall improvement in the quality of experience.

Clearly, enjoyment is the main reason for the selection and retention of most artistic cultural forms. Painting, music, drama, and even the mere ability to write are symbolic skills adopted because they produce positive states of consciousness. Such positive states are also provided by books of fiction and television sets, which appear to "waste" psychic energy, but they do so while providing a certain type of pleasurable feedback to the investment of attention.

But some of the most utilitarian artifacts also survived because they provided enjoyment to those who used them. In discussing the introduction of the first metal objects at the end of the stone ages, Colin Renfrew writes:

> In several areas of the world it has been noted, in the case of metallurgical innovations in particular, that the development of bronze and other metals as *useful* commodities was a much later phenomenon than their first utilization as new and attractive materials, employed in contexts of display. . . . In most cases early metallurgy appears to have been practiced primarily because the products had novel properties that made them attractive to use as symbols and as personal adornments and ornaments, in a manner that, by focusing attention, could attract or enhance prestige. (Renfrew 1986, pp. 144, 146)

Products with novel properties continued to attract attention regardless of utilitarian considerations. Interest in automobiles started not because of their usefulness, but because they made possible various stunts and races that captured people's imagination.

According to Huizinga ([1939] 1970), human institutions originally arise as games that provide enjoyment to the players and the spectators; only later do they become serious elements of social structure. At first, the thoughts and actions that these institutions require are freely accepted; later they become the taken-for-granted elements of social reality. Thus science starts as riddling contests, religion as joyful collective celebrations; military institutions start as ceremonial combat; the legal system has its origins in ritualized debates; and economic systems often begin as festive reciprocal exchanges. Those forms that provide the most enjoyment are selected and transmitted down the generations.

But once a set of memes, for whatever reason, finds a niche in consciousness, it can go on reproducing without reference to the enjoyment of its hosts. Coins were first minted to enhance the prestige and the economic power of kings, and to facilitate trade. When the exchange of necessary products became dependent on a monetary system rather than barter, however, people were unable to resist its spread and had to adapt to it whether they liked it or not. Or, as Max Weber noted in relation to the history of capitalism, what began as an adventurous game of entrepreneurs eventually became an all-embracing economic system similar to an "iron cage" from which it is very difficult to escape (Weber 1930).

If it is true that artifacts exploit enjoyment as the medium for their survival, any account of cultural evolution must give consideration to what people enjoy doing. People enjoy experiences in which they are faced with opportunities for action – or challenges – that are matched with an appropriate level of personal skills. The simple formula for enjoyment, Challenges/Skills = 1, was originally developed in the context of empirical studies with urban American adults (Csikszentmihalyi 1975b). Since then it has been confirmed by studies of adolescents in the United States (Csikszentmihalyi & Larson 1984), in Italy (Carli 1986), and in a variety of rural European and Asian samples (Massimini, Csikszentmihalyi, & Delle Fave 1986). The one modification that later studies have brought to the original formulation is that, in order for the experience to be enjoyable, it is not enough for the challenges and the skills to be in balance; in addition, both dimensions have to be above average or higher (Carli 1986).

Because of this relationship, people tend to overreproduce memes that raise the level of existing challenges, provided that at the same time they can raise the level of their own skills (Csikszentmihalyi 1982a). The process by which states of consciousness seek increasingly greater opportunities for action is essentially a process of *complexification*. This principle accounts for both the generation of new artifacts, and to a lesser extent for their subsequent acceptance and transmission.

The relationship between complexification and enjoyment does not mean that people are constantly motivated to seek out higher challenges. In fact, the opposite is true. When free to use time at their discretion, most people most of the time prefer to relax, to find pleasure in low-intensity interactions like sitting with a bottle of beer in front of a television set. "Pleasure" is a homeostatic principle that drives people to save energy and to derive rewards from genetically programmed actions that are necessary for the survival of the species, such as eating and sexuality. Enjoyment, which requires the use of skills to meet increasing levels of challenge, is a relatively rare experience, yet one that seems to be universally recognized and prized. Thus, although pleasure is generally a conservative principle involved in the selection and transmission of already existing artifacts, enjoyment leading to complexification is more often responsible for the generation of new cultural forms.

At the most general level, then, it can be said that the process of complexification, which is experienced as enjoyable, defines the interface of the symbiotic relationship between the evolution of human beings and the evolution of culture. Cultural forms that offer the possibility of increasing enjoyment will survive by attracting attention, and people who invest attention in such forms develop a more complex consciousness.

Psychological selection of bio-cultural instructions

Behavioral instructions carried by either biological or cultural memory are inoperative unless and until they are decoded and acted upon in consciousness. Hunger or sexual needs affect behavior only because they produce a subjective psychological state that can be recognized as "hunger" or "desire." Once we are aware of hunger, we can plan and choose the behavioral sequences most appropriate to carry out the biological instructions. This symbolic representation of biological instructions in consciousness allows for the enormous flexibility of human behavior. Similarly, cultural instructions must be decoded to affect the phenotype, and therefore to reproduce themselves. It is not enough for a language to survive in a written form, if no one is able any longer to match letters with meaning, the signifier with the signified. Like Etruscan, it then becomes a dead language. An artifact, like a stone bridge, theoretically contains within itself the secret of its structure. But unless someone has recorded the principles of architecture and the sequence of steps required to build it – the cultural instructions – in a language accessible to future generations, the knowledge of how to build bridges would die out.

The necessity of psychological selection follows from the fact that attention – which is necessary to encode, decode, and follow instructions

– is a finite quantity. At the individual level, attentional capacity seems to be limited to processing about five to seven "bits" or "chunks" of information at a time (Simon 1969; Craik & Lockhart 1972). Hence one must constantly *choose* what to attend to, what to store in memory, what to recall, which course of action to embark on, when to stop. Economists have begun to compute the financial costs of acquiring information and memory storage (Linder 1970; Becker 1976). But the allocation of attention is an even broader problem as it determines how people will express the potential information contained in their genes, and which memes they will select, preserve and transmit (James 1890; Csikszentmihalyi 1978a; Hamilton 1981).

The limits of attention in individual consciousness determine the necessity for a constant, ongoing selection among genetic and mimetic instructions. In this sense attention can be seen as psychic energy, which keeps information in an ordered state. Whenever attention is withdrawn, entropic processes begin to curtail the ability of the instructions to preserve and transmit their form. As they are forgotten, languages, religions, and technical skills lose their shape, their ability to affect behavior predictably. Many scholars have doubted that the selective paradigm can be applied to cultural information, because there are no segregating particles underlying culture as there are physical genes responsible for carrying on chemically coded information (e.g., Daly 1982, p. 402). There is, of course, no reason to expect information to be coded in similar material media. A clay tablet and a radio wave can carry the same information, although their material structure is very different. The "segregating particle" at the stage of psychological selection is *a subjective experience*.

Psychological selection takes place in consciousness when information is activated through attention. The allocation of attention obeys its own goals: Consciousness tends to maintain order in experience. The basic principle of psychological order is pleasure, or the symbolic representation of biological homeostasis in consciousness (Csikszentmihalyi & Rochberg-Halton 1981; Csikszentmihalyi 1982a). Pleasure alone, however, could not account for evolutionary changes in psychological selection. These changes are due to another process, developed from the first – the autotelic principle of enjoyment, or flow.

The state of flow is induced when a good fit results from the interaction between two lists of instructions: those contained in the rules of a cultural "game" (e.g., a tennis match, a religious ritual, a professional activity) and the list of intrasomatic instructions – based on biological predis-

66   F. Massimini, M. Csikszentmihalyi, A. Delle Fave

positions – which constitute the actor's skills. From an evolutionary perspective, flow is the function of a specific relation between extrasomatic and intrasomatic memory: When chunks from the two reach a balance (i.e., challenges = skills), a state of inner order or coherence results. This third type of negentropic system – the first being the result of the ordering of biological information, the second of cultural information – is the state of flow. This interaction between internal and external instructions unlocks a specific mode of being characterized by an autotelic principle. A person in flow wishes to do what he or she is doing for the sake of the activity itself, independently of external consequences. Evolution seems to have built into humans a predisposition to enjoy the integration of the two great negentropic systems of culture and biology into a third system – that of the self, or information in consciousness.

Outline of the report

In view of these theoretical assumptions, we shall try to answer the following two questions: How do people from very different cultures describe the flow experience in terms of its onset, its continuation, and how it feels while it lasts? What kinds of activities make the experience of flow possible, and what do they suggest about the replication of biological and cultural instructions?

Samples. Over the course of the past 3 years, a total of 636 persons belonging to 12 different samples have been given questionnaires and interviews. These samples were purposefully chosen to cover as disparate cultures and subcultures as possible. They included 255 males and 381 females from 14 to 86 years of age, and from varied socioeconomic backgrounds. In terms of biological inheritance, 533 were Caucasian and 103 Oriental. In terms of cultural inheritance, they included four different samples of traditional alpine communities around the Val d'Aosta region of northern Italy (N = 166); white-collar workers (N = 64) and students (N = 107) in the city of Turin (northern Italy); cave explorers (N = 64), dancers (N = 60), former drug addicts (N = 61), nuns, and lay religious people who were blind (N = 10), all from northern Italy; students from the Navajo Community College in Arizona (N = 77); and students from Mahidol University in Bangkok, Thailand (N = 26).

Procedures. The main source of data was the Flow Questionnaire (Flow Q). This instrument consists of three quotations describing the flow experience that were taken from the original flow interviews (e.g., "My mind isn't wandering. I am not thinking of something else. I am totally involved in what I am doing." For the rest of the quotations, see Chapter 8). The respondent was asked to read each of the three quotations, and to indicate if he or she ever experienced something similar. If the answer was yes, the respondent was asked to indicate what activity provided such an experience, and how often. Over 500 activities were identified as providing experiences similar to the ones reported in the quotations.

If the respondent identified one or more flow activities, a number of further questions were asked about the nature of the experience. Of these we consider the following three: How does the experience get started? What keeps it going, once it starts? and How does it feel? (see Csikszentmihalyi 1974, pp. 325–7).

The open-ended answers to the questionnaire were coded into several dozen subcategories, depending on the focus of the answer; these were later grouped into nine major categories that seemed to best reflect relationships between the subcategories. For example, the three subcategories Being Able to Reach a Goal, Satisfaction in the Use of Skills, and Being Skilled in the Activity were combined in the major category *Skills*.

Of the nine major categories the one labeled *Environment* is the only one that was not explicitly identified previously as an element of the flow experience, although its importance is implicit in the requisite structures for the centering of attention on the activity. The Environment code included the following subcategories: Absence of Distractions, Having the Right Amount of Time, the Right Environment, and the Interpersonal Atmosphere. Although not specifically singled out as important dimensions of the flow experience, these elements are clearly in line with previous descriptions of flow.

The structure of the flow experience

The answer to the first two questions – How does the flow experience start? and What keeps it going? – will be illustrated with examples drawn from five of the samples that show some of the largest differences: the college students from Turin, the Navajo students, members of the Walse community from the Alpine region of northern Italy (N = 33), a group of former drug addicts living in a halfway house, and the sample of blind religious persons.

When these diverse individuals describe the experiences that approach most closely the flow state in their own words, they use terms that are very similar to each other and that match closely expectations derived from the flow theory. We shall begin by seeing how the respondents described the beginning of the optimal experience in those activities that they singled out as being most similar to the quotations describing the flow experience.

How the activity starts. In all five samples, the most frequent answer to this question (given by 40% of the 288 respondents) involved the category *The Activity Itself*. In other words, the performance of the activity was enough to trigger the experience. This is not surprising since the flow activity is, by definition, the context for the autotelic experience. Whenever a person learns to experience flow in a given activity, just by starting to get involved in that activity will start providing the optimal experience:

I don't have to do anything to get this sensation started. All I have to do is get into the water and start moving. (Turin student – swimming)
It starts when the ceremony begins. It can happen anytime, anywhere. (Navajo – participating in traditional ceremony)
It starts spontaneously, and it keeps on as long as I keep reading. (Walse – reading)
This feeling starts all by itself, very naturally . . . It can start anywhere, it is not restricted by time or space. (Ex-addict – studying)
The feeling begins as soon as I start praying. (Blind nun – praying)

The second most frequent modality for entering flow, mentioned by 13% of the respondents, related to the category *Concentration*, which refers to the focusing of attention, to the avoidance of distractions necessary for optimal experience. Here are some of the answers coded in this category:

This way of feeling arises when I am really concentrating. (Turin student – studying)
I have to concentrate and get involved. (Navajo – reading)
I immediately immerse myself in the reading, and the problems I usually worry about disappear. (Walse – reading newspapers)
This kind of feeling starts when I get my attention focused on what I am doing. (Ex-addict – studying)
It starts the moment when . . . I only think of God, of my love. (Blind nun – praying)

Another mode of entry into the flow experience is provided by the perception of *Challenges*, which in turn require concentration and involvement. About 9% of all the responses fell into this category. Some of the examples follow:

> To make this feeling come, I have to be very involved. . . . It can begin only after I have invested and made sacrifices to the demands of the activity. (Turin student – studying)
> Well, it comes when the trophy-sized buck steps out into view, say about a good 15 yards away, and then I notch an arrow which I will send into his vitals. (Navajo – bow hunting)
> I try to do my acting as well as possible. (Walse – taking part in a traditional Walse dramatic performance)
> All it takes is for something to hit you that you want to get a picture of. Even an old can could be a valid subject. (Ex-addict – taking photographs)
> I put everything into it, so it will come out right. (Blind woman – knitting)

Intrinsic Motivation was coded when the respondents mentioned a special interest, a particular attraction for the autotelic aspects of the activity. A total of 9% of the responses fell into this category:

> It starts as soon as something attracts my attention particularly, something that interests me. (Turin student – reading)
> I just want to do it, and I do it. (Navajo – silversmithing)
> Whenever I work with greater strength and will. (86-year-old Walse – working in the fields)
> It can start at any moment, as long as I have the intention of studying. (Ex-addict – studying)

Positive Moods and *Environment* were each mentioned by 7% of the respondents. It is not necessary to give examples of positive moods, since these are fairly obvious: They describe the enjoyment, the excitement, the happiness one feels when the experience is optimal. A favorable environment seems important especially for activities that could be easily interrupted by outside distractions, such as intellectual endeavors like reading or studying.

> The place is the most important stimulus: for instance when I am in a train, alone in the compartment. . . . I will automatically tune out and start thinking. The train is one example, and the most frequent one, but an empty waiting room will do as well. (Turin student – thinking)
> It usually happens when I am in a quiet place. (Navajo – studying)
> This feeling happens often, and always when I am up there, away from the noise, the crush of the crowd. (Walse – mountain climbing)
> It can start wherever there is a chance to read undisturbed. (Ex-addict – reading)

After the facilitating effects of the environment, the next most frequently mentioned category involved the use of *Skills* (6%). Matching personal abilities with the opportunities in the environment was an important source of satisfaction:

> This feeling is surely a consequence of my ability to do well the exercises I am involved with. (Turin student – doing aerobics)

It starts by helping other people. (Navajo – taking part in traditional curing
ceremonies that require the therapeutic participation of the audience)
I tell myself: "I've been able to do it again." (75-year-old Walse – working in
the fields)
This kind of feeling starts when you begin to see the results. (Ex-addict – model
building)

Feedback is an important part of the flow experience, because it keeps
concentration on the activity by providing information about how well
or how poorly a person is doing. Positive feedback, mentioned in 3%
of the responses, seems to be especially important at the beginning of
the experience:

The feeling begins as the activity unfolds. As you draw you cannot judge in
terms of some final goal; it is the moment-by-moment rightness that makes
you feel good. (Turin student – drawing)
When I put together the pieces I have laid out, and I see that what I have
planned is taking shape. (Walse – doing carpentry)
When the thing is taking shape. (Ex-addict – carving)
When I see that things are going well. (76-year-old blind nun – book binding)

The last category coded for helping start the flow experience was
Growth in the Complexity of the Self. Although only 2% of the responses
mentioned this as one of the triggers of the experience, as we shall see
later this is one of the most important dimensions of flow. It refers to
a person's awareness that by confronting higher challenges, his or her
skills are also increasing, and thus a more complex order is developing
in consciousness.

I reach this feeling when I am able to achieve harmony. (Turin student – rock
climbing)
It starts when I feel like I am constructive and creative, when I am about to
create a new product. (Navajo – silversmithing)
I feel serious and involved in confronting new complexities and hoping to be
successful. (Walse – playing the clarinet or saxophone)
The only thing I do is study . . . I compare what I've learned with reality, and
see how it works. (Ex-addict – studying)

How the experience proceeds. The same nine categories that accounted for
how the flow experience started lent themselves also for coding the
reasons for what kept it going. The frequency of the various categories,
however, was slightly different. Again the *Activity Itself* was mentioned
as the most frequent reason, in 25% of the cases. But, for the continuation
of the activity, the next most often invoked reason was *Growth in Complexity* (13%), which was mentioned over six times as often for the continuation of the activity as it was for its beginning. The comparison of
the frequencies with which the various categories were mentioned as

Table 4.1. *Answers to the Flow Questionnaire concerning the onset and the continuation of the flow experience*
(N = 636)

How does it start?	Percentage of answers	What keeps it going?	Percentage of answers
The activity itself	41	The activity itself	26
Concentration	13	Growth of complexity	13
Challenges	9	Intrinsic motivation	12
Intrinsic motivation	9	Environment	11
Positive mood	7	Positive mood	11
Environment	7	Skills	10
Skills	6	Concentration	6
Positive feedback	3	Challenges	4
Other	3	Positive feedback	4
Growth of complexity	2	Other	3
	100		100

being important for the onset and for the continuation of the flow experience are listed in Table 4.1.

Three components seem less important to sustain the experience after it has started: the activity itself, the concentration on the activity, and challenges. In contrast, the other components are more important to sustain the experience than they were to getting it started: especially the growth in complexity, intrinsic motivation, the favorable environment, positive moods, and the use of skill, each of which was mentioned in 10% of the responses or more as elements that kept the experience going once it got started.

The phenomenology of flow

One of the questions of the Flow Q asked respondents to describe how they felt when the activity they had identified as similar to the quotations was going well. In some ways a questionnaire is not a very good instrument for collecting phenomenological data; most people are not used to putting the contents of their consciousness into words, and thus the answers tend to be short and stereotyped. Nevertheless, this method makes it possible to get a preliminary idea of how flow is experienced by a great number of respondents from extremely varied sociocultural backgrounds. The results again suggest, as they did with the conditions that made the insurgence and the maintenance of flow possible, that the quality of the experience is remarkably similar across samples.

Positive Mood. Most answers (50%) were simply coded "Positive Mood" because they only described a generalized sense of well-being, positive affect, or ordered consciousness. The samples varied from a low of 31% for the Turin students to a high of 68% for the Occitan farmers, in terms of how many of their responses fell into this category. Here are some typical answers that were coded as positive mood:

I am serene, extroverted . . . I feel at ease with myself and with others. (Turin student – skiing)
I enjoy it. (Navajo – silversmithing)
I am cheerful: I smile and feel more sociable. (Walse – teaching cross-country skiing)
One feels well, quiet, peaceful. (Ex-addict – reading)
I feel happy. (Blind nun – writing articles for religious journal)

The second most often mentioned dimension of experience concerned the use of *Skills*. About 20% of the responses focused on this element, ranging from a low of 5% for the Navajo students to a high of 35% for the Walse mountaineers. In general, all the traditional alpine communities were quite a bit above the average in stressing skills, and so were the blind religious people (31% of their responses were coded in this category). Apparently when the challenges for survival are high, the successful use of one's skills becomes particularly enjoyable.

I feel satisfied. I love beautiful things and if I am able to create them I feel I am all right; I like to get a sense of what I can do. (Turin student – painting)
I feel I have made an accomplishment. (Navajo – studying)
I feel proud of what I can do. (67-year-old Walse – tending flowers)
One gets to feel rather satisfied. (Ex-addict – studying)
I feel satisfied, occasionally I tell myself, "You are doing fine." (Blind woman – knitting)

A total of 10% of the responses were coded in terms of *Concentration*, which was also the second most important factor in the insurgence of the flow experience. Interestingly, this dimension was almost never mentioned by the traditional alpine farmers, but it was high on the list of the young urban respondents (21% of the Turin students' answers fell into this category). Perhaps the focusing of attention is so easy and automatic in the traditional cultural environment that it is barely noticed, while its rarity in the cities makes it particularly enjoyable. Some of these quotations also suggest that one of the enjoyable results of deep concentration is forgetting the self, and feeling part of a larger transpersonal system.

I feel as if I belonged completely in the situation described in the book. (Turin student – reading)

I identify with the characters, and take part in what I am reading. (Walse – reading)

My mind gets entirely involved, I don't think about anything else, because I must think about focusing, about the lens, about the light. (Ex-addict – taking photographs)

I felt we were one, that we were united. She was a creature to be loved. (Blind woman – caring for a gravely ill friend)

Theoretically, perhaps, the most important dimension of the flow experience is the enjoyment derived from *Complexification* of the self. This is what accounts for the evolutionary potential of the experience. After a flow episode, a person reflecting back on it realizes that he or she was able to confront high challenges successfully. As a result, the self in consciousness becomes transformed into a more complex entity. The person is now aware of having greater skills and is ready to face higher challenges in the future.

Of the total responses, 7% were coded in this category. The sample of dancers (15%), of students from Thailand (10%), and some of the alpine communities mentioned this dimension more frequently. It seems clear, however, that even when not mentioned directly, this aspect of the experience is salient in the mind of many of the respondents (it is in fact often implicit in the responses coded for "Skills"). This is how growth of complexity as a source of enjoyment was described by some of the respondents:

It is a feeling of pleasant reaction to an effort that has mobilized my attention to grapple with previously inchoate thoughts, which now have become grasped in what I think is their true meaning, and have been more or less logically arranged. (Turin student – following own thoughts)

I feel like I have the book stored in my mind. (Navajo – reading)

I feel rewarded for having been successful after all the effort. (72-year-old Walse – learning to read and write German)

It is a feeling of completion. More aware and stronger. (Ex-addict – studying)

Some of the answers focus on *Intrinsic Motivation*, or the pure enjoyment derived from repeating the activity over and over again. Four percent of the total answers were coded for this response, the highest frequency being among the Walse mountain farmers (7%) and two of the other alpine groups.

Perhaps the best part of it is that I feel as if I could go on doing it until I am completely exhausted physically and mentally. (Turin student – playing soccer and volleyball)

It is like you can do it again and again. (Navajo – studying math)

I get this wish to keep on going. (Walse – collecting historical data about the Walse culture)

One feels like one is pressed to go on. (Ex-addict – carving wood)

These categories fill in the broad outlines of how people describe the flow experience. In addition, 1% of the responses mentioned the enjoyment of getting *Feedback*, ½% that of having *Control* of the activity, and 8% of the answers were so idiosyncratic as to be coded *Other*. It is not so much the exact proportion of these responses that counts, as their essential similarity to each other and to the flow model of optimal experience. If a different coding method were to be used and if the labels used to name the categories were changed, the conclusions derived from the data would also change. But however one might translate this experience into a written description, the basic parameters of the optimal state of consciousness are clear.

The description includes a sense of inner harmony – happiness, satisfaction, serenity – which is the result of the full use of personal abilities, of the concentrated investment of psychic energy, leading to a sense of inner growth through intrinsically rewarding interaction with some aspect of the outer or inner environment. These few dimensions account for over 90% of the responses given by over 600 individuals from Arizona to the Alps and to Bangkok.

Flow activities and biocultural selection

Having summarized the descriptions our respondents gave for the onset and the phenomenology of optimal experience, we now turn to review the range of activities that people mentioned as conducive to flow. In doing so it will be possible to obtain a glimpse of the psychological processes that differentially select among biological and cultural alternatives the ones that provide the most enjoyment. These are the ones that should be preferentially preserved and transmitted down the generations. We proceed by first giving an overall view of the major categories into which the 500 activities mentioned can be grouped, and then by examining in closer detail how in each of the five samples respondents focus preferentially on certain activities and develop more or less unique strategies for optimizing experience. These strategies, in turn, have repercussions for the kind of genes and memes that will be differentially replicated.

Table 4.2 presents a summary of the eight main categories into which the first and most important flow activity mentioned by our respondents was coded. The first two categories – Work and Studying – can be considered "productive," in that they are generally considered socially useful and are extrinsically rewarded. It is perhaps surprising that such

Table 4.2. *Activities mentioned as providing flow experiences by five samples interviewed with the Flow Questionnaire*

	Percentage mentioning activity				
Activities	Turin students (N = 107)	Walse farmers (N = 33)	Navajo students (N = 77)	Ex-addicts (N = 61)	Blind religious (N = 10)
Work	3	46	—	23	22
Studying	19	—	29	16	—
Reading	30	20	18	7	45[a]
Prayer, meditation, and religious ceremonies	—	—	12	12	27
Sport, hobby	22	30	24	7	—
Music, media	6	—	—	7	—
Friends, family	—	—	5	7	—
Other and none	20	4	12	12	6
	100	100	100	100	100

Note: Only the first activity mentioned by each person is included. Empty cells mean that the activity in question was not reported as the primary source of flow in that sample.

[a]Reading in braille.

a large number of responses, ranging from 22% among the Turin students and the blind to a high of 46% among the Walse mountaineers, referred to a productive activity. If Reading – which is also in part a productive activity, at least for students preparing for an intellectual career – is added to this total, the percentage goes up as far as 67% for the blind (who derive a great amount of enjoyment from reading in braille) and 66% for the Walse.

For the younger groups, and also for the Walse, active sports and hobbies are a reliable source of flow, ranging from a high of 30% to nothing among the blind. In some of these samples, religious activities also provide enjoyable interactions, thus allowing for the reproduction of rituals that preserve and transmit certain cultural values.

On the whole, Table 4.2 shows a counterintuitive pattern. Contrary to expectations, it is not leisure and mass entertainment that produce the most frequent and intense optimal experiences. It is not the fabled free-time activities that our culture is so proud of having developed, such as television, travel, and the myriad expensive amusements; it is more often the everyday work activities, the hard concentration of reading and studying, and the self-effacing discipline of religious rituals that make people feel good about their lives. Of course the samples in Table 4.2 are far from being "typical" of any particular culture – although the Turin students begin to be representative of northern Italian college students. The point is not so much to demonstrate what *is*, but rather to intimate what *can be*. In other words, these patterns begin to illustrate the flexibility of human adaptation by showing the range of activities that can produce optimal experiences, and thus also the range of possible cultural instructions that it is possible to endorse and to transmit over time.

The college students. This sample included 107 students from the Teachers' College of the University of Turin. Their ages ranged from 18 to 55 years, the gender distribution was 15% males and 85% females, and they represented every socioeconomic background. The flow experience as described in the quotations of the Flow Questionnaire was recognized by 97% (or 104 respondents) of this group. As can be seen in Table 4.2, the most frequently mentioned flow activities were reading, sports and hobbies, and studying. The frequency with which reading and studying were mentioned reflects the process of cultural replication that is the specific function of this group. Given the fact that these students are preparing themselves for a teaching career, their ability to experience flow in such activities facilitates their learning cultural instructions, which later they will have the task of transmitting to their own students.

In looking at how these students become involved in the flow experience, it is noteworthy that they emphasize the importance of Concentration, the use of Skills, and of Intrinsic Motivation. Perhaps these dimensions are especially important for those who are specializing in intellectual activities. Concern for intrinsic motivation is an important trait for future teachers to pass on to their students as it facilitates the replication and transmission of culture (Csikszentmihalyi 1982 b,c; 1986).

The Walse community. This sample included 33 respondents belonging to a traditional German ethnic group that lives in isolated mountain communities in northwestern Italy. The respondents were 13 men and 20 women between 20 and 86 years of age. Every one of them identified with the flow experience as described in the Flow Q. As shown in Table 4.2, the activities they associated most often with such experiences were work, sports and hobbies, and reading. By work they generally meant traditional productive activities such as needlepoint, gardening, and working in the fields. Their sports and hobbies included activities related mainly to the mountains, such as hiking, climbing, skiing, and teaching to ski. Much of their reading involved texts that dealt with the history and traditions of their community, because several respondents were actively involved in the gathering and diffusion of information about the Walse culture.

This group provides a good example of a culture that remains alive only because of the constant involvement of its members, who have linked the flow experience to the activities that are characteristic of that culture. Thus the tendency to preferentially replicate certain states of consciousness helps the survival of an entire way of life that otherwise would be slated for oblivion under the pressure of modernization. It is interesting to note that, contrary to what happens in many other traditional settings that are becoming extinct owing to the disinterest of the youngest generation in the way of their elders, young Walse are also actively participating in maintaining and transmitting their culture through the linkage between the flow experience and such activities as mountain climbing and traditional crafts.

In their description of the structure of the flow experience, the Walse stand out among the 12 samples as emphasizing more than any other the satisfaction derived from the use of Skills, both as one of the conditions for starting the experience and as a major dimension of the optimal experience itself. This pattern makes sense considering that most of the respondents lead a very exhausting life in a natural environment that presents unusually high challenges and requires constant physical effort. The ability to respond to such demands with appropriate personal skills thus becomes a deeply satisfying part of the experience. Several respondents hold the equivalent of two jobs; for example, they may work in an office but also tend their orchard or work as carpenters in their free time. This means that each day they must integrate instructions that derive from two different culturotypes. This continuous process of integration presumably leads to increased complexity of consciousness. The bicultural evolutionary process is even more strongly evident in the the Navjo sample.

The Navajo students. The Navajo sample was collected at the Navajo Community College (NCC) located in Tsaile, Arizona. The 77 respondents were between 18 and 47 years of age, and 27 were male and 50 female. The NCC aims to provide a bicultural education to its students by transmitting Western cultural instructions (e.g., mathematics, physics and biology) at the same time as transmitting memes from the traditional Navajo culture (healing ceremonies, traditional medicine, native philosophy, religion, and crafts).

As shown in Table 4.2, the Navajo students experience flow primarily in their studies, in sports and hobbies, in reading, and in traditional religious ceremonies. The specific activities indicate that the flow experience helps the replication of instructions belonging to both cultural systems: the traditional one through activities such as weaving rugs, working silver, and participating in native rituals; and the modern one through sports and such hobbies as working with cars. Moreover, it is important to note that the linkage between flow and study in the NCC leads to the replication of instructions from both cultures.

This situation explains why the Navajos were the most likely of the 12 groups to mention Concentration as a condition for the starting of the flow experience and were also one of the sample that mentioned it most often as a component of the optimal experience. In addition, the Navajo students were also more likely than most other groups to mention the Growth of Complexity as an essential component of flow. As in the Walse sample, the Navajos must integrate two streams of cultural information in their daily life. This requires a reordering of consciousness conducive to increasingly higher levels of complexity.

The former addicts. This group included 61 people between 14 and 40 years of age, 47 of whom were male and 14 female. They lived in rehabilitation communities or were outpatients of drug treatment centers in the province of Piedmont, Italy. They belonged to the full range of social class levels and had been drug dependent, mostly on heroin, for periods ranging from 2 to 14 years. During the period of dependence, the most frequent ways of earning money to pay for the habit were prostitution for the women and burglary or drug dealing for the males. Pending rehabilitation, the most frequently mentioned flow activity had to do with work (usually involving the production of crafts), studying, and prayer.

Considering the particularly difficult path these respondents have to pass through in order to detach themselves from toxic dependence, the ability to find enjoyment in an ordered state of consciousness may become a determining factor in the outcome of their rehabilitation. If they are able to link such an experience to complex and constructive activities, their slow improvement should become surer. By replicating the flow state in such contexts they have a chance to recover their biological potential as they restructure their attention to activities outside the attractive field of the drug, the use of which endangers their survival and their biological reproduction. Similarly, they have a chance to recover their potential for cultural transmission because the new activities that are providing flow help to ease them back into the mainstream of culture. Moreover, some of the respondents are now actively involved in the negative selection of instructions concerning the use of mind-altering substances by participating in rehabilitation efforts in the community.

One of the most striking facts about how members of this group describe the flow experience is that they rarely mentioned Challenges, Skills, or clear Feedback, either as conditions for the onset of flow or as a component of the optimal experience itself. Instead, for them the flow experience relies almost exclusively on the Activity Itself, on Intrinsic Motivation, and on Concentration. This particular pattern seems to describe well the condition of these young people who have to relearn, after a period of passivity and disorder, how to use their abilities within a lifestyle structured in terms of complex goals. It is not surprising, then, that what helps them to achieve flow is the structure of the activity itself, their wish for the activity, and the concentration necessary to sustain it.

The blind sample. This very small sample of 10 respondents was composed of 5 nuns and 5 lay persons (1 man and 4 women) ranging in age from 31 to 76 years. They suffer from a biological deficit that affects survival as well as biological reproduction, and also limits their ability to select and transmit cultural instructions. Despite such heavy handicaps, 9 of the 10 respondents claimed to recognize the flow experience. The most numerous responses involved reading in braille, praying and meditating, and working. Reading allows them to maintain a linkage with cultural instructions, despite the biological deficit. By linking this activity with the flow experience they actively help replicate memes: One of the women, by writing articles in a religious journal, also helps the selective transmission of cultural instructions. Prayer and meditation are independent of the ability to see and thus are particularly useful vehicles of flow for members of this sample. Especially in the case of the five nuns, this kind of flow activity helps compensate for having given up biological reproduction in order to replicate the religious memes.

Work is also an important source of flow for this group. The respondents teach, work as telephone operators, bind old books, and do knitting. These are complex activities and represent very high levels of challenges. In fact, in describing the onset of the flow experience, this sample was the second highest of the 12 in mentioning the importance of Challenges, and they were by far the highest in mentioning the importance of Positive Feedback. It is clear that without being able to monitor moment by moment the outcome of their actions, it would be difficult for them to enter flow. As a result, when they describe how the experience feels, these respondents are among those most likely to mention the use of Skills as an important component of the optimal experience.

Conclusions

After reading brief accounts of the flow experience originally given by urban Americans, respondents from very different cultural backgrounds, ranging from Thailand to Arizona to the Alps, were able to recognize and to identify that state of mind. The overwhelming majority claimed to have had similar experiences quite often. When asked to describe how they started on and how they felt during the flow experience, the respondents spontaneously reconstructed the flow model by mentioning dimensions stressed by the theory: the activity itself, concentration of attention, the balance of challenges and skills leading to increased complexity, clear feedback, and intrinsic motivation.

It seems clear that the state of consciousness described by the model is a panhuman characteristic prized equally highly by all sorts of people – young and old, healthy and handicapped, traditional and modern. They all find in such experiences a rare fulfillment that they try to recapture as often as possible. The question then becomes, What must one do to find this harmonious state of mind?

For some people, flow is available in the daily productive activities that help increase the material complexity of the environment. Working, taking care of fields and gardens, helping those in need of help become sources of enjoyment. Others find it in leisure, or in reading books that offer alternative subjective realities. Some find it in the ordered harmony of religious ritual, and still others might search for it through the byways of chemical "trips."

What a person learns to enjoy doing has important consequences. In the short run, it will influence the specific nature of the experience: how much concentration it requires, how many challenges it provides, and hence what degree of complex growth it makes possible. The nature of the activity also determines the content of consciousness while the flow experience lasts. Someone who learns to enjoy killing animals for sport will be processing different information from what occupies the consciousness of a person who enjoys cultivating flowers. Therefore the activity that becomes linked to flow will help shape the kind of self that the person develops.

In the long run, what activities are chosen as vehicles for the experience might determine the shape of the culture itself. For instance, when productive work cannot provide it, and people turn more and more to pastimes for bringing order to consciousness, the social system is bound to be very different from that in a culture where everyday activities are enjoyed. Patterns of action, whether controlled by genes or by memes, have a greater chance of being replicated if they are also enjoyable. For this reason, the implications of flow extend far beyond the momentary experience.

II. Varieties of the flow experience

5. Introduction to Part II

MIHALY AND ISABELLA CSIKSZENTMIHALYI

Flow can happen anywhere, at any time, provided that the person's capacities and the opportunities for action in the environment are well matched. This optimal interaction is most typical of conditions when people voluntarily become involved in activities designed to be enjoyable, such as sports, games, spectacles, and artistic or religious performances. But one of the contributions of the flow concept has been to remind us that activity and experience are ultimately independent of each other. The most lavish entertainment can be boring, and the most routine job enjoyable. It is impossible to explain the quality of the experience by reference to the objective conditions of the environment, or by reference to the person alone; only the interaction between the two yields the answer.

The practical consequence of this perspective is to open up the possibility of improving the quality of experience in situations that previously were seen to be naturally boring or stressful, such as work or study. If it is true that in principle any activity can be made enjoyable, there is no excuse for resigning oneself to a boring life.

The chapters that follow show the enormous variety of conditions that can produce flow, from the ritual swarming of Japanese motorcycle gangs to the solitary ordeals of polar explorers. In each case, however, the experience becomes enjoyable only when personal skills and the challenges of the situation are in harmony, and when the other conditions of the flow experience – concentrated attention, clear goals, feedback, lack of distractions, and so on – are made possible.

Beneath the wide differences in the situations reported in these chapters there runs a common theme: Regardless of gender, age, ethnic or cultural origin, enjoyment is the same everywhere, and it is made possible by the same configuration of subjective and objective conditions.

In Chapter 6 Ikuya Sato describes in painstaking detail the phenomenology of Japanese motorcycle gangs. The *bosozoku*, or "speed tribe," are a modern manifestation of an ageless pattern of rebellious adolescent display. Both social scientists and the popular press have seen their antics as symptoms of psychic frustration and of social unrest. Sato shows us that these pathogenic "interpretations" miss an important point: For the *bosozoku* youth, the rituals of the "run" are deeply exciting and enjoyable.

This fact does not invalidate the previous explanations based on compensatory mechanisms, but it adds a new perspective to their conclusions. For it could be argued that any accomplishment, from the most beautiful poem to the most satisfying religious ceremony, is motivated by feelings of frustration with the limits of the human condition. This is in fact what Freud, among others, implied in the notion of sublimation. So to say that motorcycle gangs are a form of rebellion against the powerlessness of youth is not telling much. The question is, What do they get from their rebellious activity? Is the positive experience they gain worth the effort and the danger? One contribution of the flow theory has been to switch the attention of investigators from issues of causality to issues of consequence. The point is not so much to understand what accounts for a given behavior, but rather to know what psychic rewards it brings about.

The enjoyment of motorcycle "runs" turns out to hinge on the same conditions made familiar by earlier studies of flow. East and West meet on this ground; the balance of challenges and skills and the rest of the dynamic connections necessary for the flow experience suggest that, as far as enjoyment is concerned, the psychic unity of mankind is vindicated.

But with these Japanese youth we also encounter a form of *group flow* never previously studied in any detail. As Sato notes, in addition to the skillful use of body and machine, the cyclists involved in a run experience two other important and perhaps disquieting inputs into their awareness. One is the sense of belonging to a social organism that Emile Durkheim called "collective effervescence," and Victor Turner called "communitas." In the words of one youngster, the throbbing line of motorcycles becomes a "dinosaur . . . a tide of headlights devouring the city." The other is *medatsu*, or the awareness of being seen, of looking conspicuous. For most of the cyclists, this is one of the main purposes and greatest rewards of the run. It is easy to see that the sense of communitas and of *medatsu* would be particularly rewarding to individuals who feel isolated, powerless, and inconspicuous. Although this is true, one might suggest that every person, hemmed in by the limits of individual traits and circumstance, must feel to a certain degree isolated, powerless, and inconspicuous. Thus enjoying a sense of belonging and of recognition are not necessarily pathological symptoms, but understandable aspects of being human.

To what extent do social-structural characteristics such as gender and social class influence the opportunities to experience flow? This question reflects one of the most basic issues of political philosophy. The entire Marxist perspective hinges on the theses developed in the early *Economic and Political Manuscripts* and in *The German Ideology*, according to which unequal control of property is inhuman because it deprives people who do not own the means of their subsistence from exercising control over their actions. As a result, men without property end up exploited not only in material terms, but, most important, in terms of their essential human nature: They are no longer masters over the psychic energy that goes into work; and work being the most complex activity in their lives, they lose control of their own experiences.

Given the fundamental importance of this thesis, it is remarkable how little we still know about the experiential concomitants of social class. To what extent is it true that class differences correspond to differences in the quality of experience? In Chapter 7, Maria Allison and Margaret Duncan report on a pilot study of working women, some involved in privileged professional occupations, others holding blue-collar jobs in the service and manufacturing industries. The question Allison and Duncan ask is, Do the optimal experiences of these two groups of women differ?

The results, even though they are based on a very small sample, are suggestive. In both groups, women feel best for the same reasons – that is, whenever the characteristic flow conditions are present. But there is a clear difference between the two groups: For the professionals, the flow conditions are built into their jobs, whereas for the manual workers, they are not. For both groups, interaction with people, and especially with children in growth-producing situations, are occasions for flow.

Allison and Duncan also introduce a new term, implicit in previous discussions. They call the extreme experiences of boredom or anxiety "antiflow," and show that these are more common for the blue-collar workers on the job, and for both groups of workers in the routine housekeeping activities.

These findings suggest that every person tries to maximize the intensity and frequency of flow. If the work environment is conducive to flow, people will invest attention in the job and increase their involvement in it. If the work environment only provides "antiflow," employees will develop a strategy of minimal involvement with the job and save their attention for those activities that make flow more likely, such as family interactions and leisure. The overall quality of experience, the total amount of flow a person has, may not be influenced by social class; but the context in which flow is experienced may be heavily influenced.

Another contribution of Chapter 7 is that it provides a glimpse of the strategies women use to turn boring or anxiety-producing situations into settings for flow. This theme will be repeated in the last two chapters of this section, in which Reed Larson and Richard Logan reflect more systematically on the qualities necessary to engender flow in neutral, or sometimes even desperate, situations.

In the meantime, however, we turn to another set of germane issues. We have seen so far that Japanese youth and American working women describe their optimal experiences in terms that agree with the original flow model. These findings are important because one of the earliest criticisms of the flow theory has been that it describes a Western psychic phenomenon, and that it is more applicable to the experiences of men than of women.

Nevertheless, it might be objected that Japanese youth are already Westernized in their outlook, and that a study of working women taps the worker's ethos rather than some peculiarly female quality of experience, and therefore also fails to prove the cross-gender applicability of the model. Thus the importance of Seongyeul Han's findings reported in Chapter 8.

Han interviewed elderly Korean men and women who had only recently emigrated to the United States. His respondents were thoroughly imbued in Korean culture and few of them spoke any English. Han translated descriptions of the flow experience into Korean and asked the respondents whether they ever had comparable feelings, and if yes, how often and in what situations.

It was clear from the interviews that all the respondents immediately recognized the experience and attributed to it enjoyable characteristics. The one cultural difference, which might also have interacted with age since Han's respondents were all 60 years of age or older, was that the elderly Koreans reported fewer flow experiences than did American adults. The reason for this might have been that they perhaps took the descriptions of flow too literally. In several cases, when asked if they ever became so engrossed in whatever they were doing that they wouldn't notice if "the phone rang, the house was burning," they answered that no, if the house was burning down, they would notice it. Otherwise the Koreans appeared to understand the flow experience in the same terms as our Western and Japanese samples did.

Of course, the context of activities in which the experiences occurred was different and reflected the cultural background of the respondents. Meditation practices and the reading of sacred texts were mentioned relatively often. The game of *go* was a flow activity for several men, but the most frequent activities that yielded optimal experiences for men were productive ones such as arranging business deals or working at a craft. For women also, traditional female productive activities like weaving, gardening, and cooking were mentioned more often than typical leisure activities.

Perhaps the most important contribution of Han's study is the link to be found between the reported frequency of flow experiences on the one hand, and life satisfaction on the other. Although this finding is not unexpected, it does provide a welcome confirmation of how necessary flow experiences are to the quality of life. What was unexpected in Han's findings is that the link is much stronger for women than for men. For these elderly Korean males, life satisfaction was more strongly related to financial success and economic independence than to the reported frequency of flow. For the women, however, the reverse was true. This trend suggests that men are socialized more rigidly than women to find satisfaction in material accomplishments. But another interpretation is possible: Since for these men flow most often occurs in the midst of economic activities, material accomplishments for them might be a form of feedback that keeps concentration on the activity.

In any case, Han's study strongly supports the generality of the flow model of optimal experience already discussed in Chapter 4. It is not only male Western elites who respond to the motivational properties of flow; young and old, male and female, Easterner and Westerner describe the best moments of their lives in similar terms. That flow is not an ephemeral state but contributes to the overall quality of life is also an important finding.

As Larson shows in Chapter 9, in addition to being a reward in itself, optimal experience also helps bring about more conventional extrinsic rewards. Larson studied a group of high school students who were involved in a major writing assignment over a period of several weeks. He interviewed each student repeatedly during the course of the assignment, and collected writing samples that were later analyzed and rated blind by experienced English teachers.

Regardless of their ability and preparation, the students' cognitive performance was constantly under the influence of their emotional states. Many of these affective states had their origins outside the school, but their effect on the assignment was nevertheless substantial. The assignment itself produced its own emotional energy: Some loved their topic, others hated it or were bored by it, and these feelings changed at different points in the course of the assignment.

The important point Larson makes is that the essays written by students who were bored were boring to read; the essays written by students who were overwhelmed by the assignment were fragmented and disorganized. The essays that the readers found enjoyable to read were those that the students had enjoyed writing.

Again, the smallness of the sample makes these findings more suggestive than conclusive, yet their implications are substantial, for they suggest that enjoyment is not only good in itself, but brings about desirable outcomes. Paradoxically, it is when one stops worrying about success and forgets oneself in the enjoyment of the activity that one produces the best work, the work that will be rewarded and appreciated. At least this seems to be true for student compositions. Amabile (1983), Deci and Ryan (1985), and others have made the same claim for creative activities in general. How widespread is the case that the best chances for success come to those who are not guided by it, but are motivated instead by involvement with the activity?

In describing how students struggle to research and write a good paper, Larson presents some of the strategies they use to achieve concentration and facilitate flow. He illustrates the type of cognitive restructuring that people use to turn boring or overwhelming situations into enjoyable ones.

This is the theme that Richard Logan takes up, on a very grand scale, in the last chapter of this section (Chapter 10). He takes the least promising situations, such as concentration camps or the frozen emptiness of Antarctica, and shows that even the worst conditions will yield enjoyable experiences if one performs the right kind of cognitive restructuring. Essentially this involves taking control over the information reaching consciousness. The lone polar explorer, the prisoner of the Gulag cannot change the objective conditions of their surround. But such persons can change the focus of their attention, and interact with a stimulus field of their own choosing. As a result, the inhuman situation changes into a tolerable, sometimes actually an enjoyable, one.

Drawing on the accounts of such people as Alexander Solzhenitsyn, Admiral Byrd, Victor Frankl, Bruno Bettelheim, and Charles Lindbergh, Logan shows how such a restructuring of consciousness can make the difference between life and death. The steps these people use to snatch flow from the jaws of adversity are in principle the same ones employed by the working women described by Allison and Duncan, and by the high school writers studied by Larson.

But, Logan argues, some people are better equipped than others for turning an ordeal into a flow experience. What makes some people able to do it? Logan provides some interesting pointers: They are people who have developed a habit of observing their surroundings – processors of information. They are people used to being in control of their actions, who have achieved self-discipline. They are people who are seeking the limits of their own selves without being self-seeking, or even self-conscious. If he is right, this list contains important signposts for what we should try to achieve in the rearing of our children.

Part II provides a bird's-eye view of some contexts in which flow can be achieved, ranging from the fairly predictable, such as the rituals of motorcycle gangs, to the most extreme ordeals. This view is not intended to be systematic, but rather examplary. By showing some of the most disparate contexts of flow, it tries to give an idea of all the many possibilities that lie in between. The next section takes up where this one leaves off, by examining instances in which people, not satisfied with separate flow activities, organize their entire lives as one single flow process.

6. *Bosozoku*: flow in Japanese motorcycle gangs

IKUYA SATO

A recurrent feature of most societies is tension between the generations, a tension that often finds expression in more or less open, more or less ritualized conflict between youth and their elders. This conflict has been said to be directly proportional to the rapidity of social change and to the amount of new information unavailable to their elders that each new generation must assimilate (Davis 1940). Japan is no exception to this trend. At least since the end of World War II, youth movements of various sorts have expressed, in various forms of ritually organized behavior, a departure from the goals and norms of adult Japanese society.

Perhaps one of the most visible of such forms has been juvenile motorcycle gangs, particularly the *bosozoku* groups, which include mainly young men between 15 and 21 years of age. The term *bosozoku* means "violent-driving tribe" or "out-of-control tribe," and the name implies the character image that both group members and outsiders assign to participants in the so-called runs that are the most important activity of the groups. The number of individuals associated with *bosozoku* gangs rose from about 12,500 in 1973 to about 39,000 members with some 24,000 vehicles in 1983 (Keisatsucho 1981; Homusho 1983). During the same period the number of arrests associated with their activities increased from 28,000 to 54,819 cases, which included 48,278 traffic and 6,541 criminal citations (Keisatsucho 1981, 1983, 1984).

The considerable risks taken have led people to impute abnormality

Research for this chapter was supported by the Toyota Foundation, the Center for Far Eastern Studies and the Committee on Japanese Studies at the University of Chicago, the Japanese Society for the Promotion of Science, and the Japanese Association of Psychology. I gratefully acknowledge the helpful comments and encouragement of Professors Mihaly Csikszentmihalyi, Gerald Suttles, Hary Harootunian, Gary Fine, and Takekatsu Kikuchi.

to *bosozoku* members and to view a run as an acting out of psychological strains. My own experience as a participant observer in Kyoto over a period of several years made such reductionistic explanations less and less convincing. The riders' accounts suggested that runs were very enjoyable, and that they were ordered by a set of rules. They did not simply provide thrills, but also offered an opportunity to experience a heightened state of consciousness and a strenghtened sense of self.

Reductionistic explanations of motorcycle gangs

Why do young Japanese join in a *bosozoku* run? This question usually presupposes an irrational answer and implies the further question: Why do they join in a run when the risks are high and there is little material reward? Two types of answers are usually provided.

One is based on the ulterior motives "behind" the run: The run is said to satisfy a pressing need to overcome frustration or inferiority. The other answer is that *bosozoku* youths are simply "driven" to express frustration or inferiority. The run becomes an "outlet," or an enactment rather than an evasion of such emotions. We find many instances of each viewpoint in both the mass media and in scholarly treatments of *bosozoku*. An example is a June 12, 1978, editorial in the *Mainichi* (a major Japanese newspaper):

> What would be the causal relationship between the onset of the rainy season and the stirring up of *bosozoku*? Many scholars point out that the proliferation of *bosozoku* is caused by "frustration" and "desire to show off." Is it because people's frustrations accumulate before and after the onset of the rainy season, when it is so muggy?

Kaneto (1981), a psychologist and the chief social investigator of the Family Court of Toyama, is more explicit on this point. After mentioning five categories of pathology leading to *bosozoku* activity (pathology of adolescence, family, school, workplace, and society as a whole), he says, "They are self-conscious as dropouts and try to satisfy the desires for self-assertion and recognition by the run, which are not satisfied in school or the workplace. Even their attachment to cars seems abnormal to me" (Kaneto 1981, p. 212).

Similar arguments have been put forth by scholars (e.g., Chiba 1975; Tamura & Mugishima 1975; Kikuchi 1981). However, neither the mass media nor the academic studies have substantiated these arguments with empirical investigations. Most of the studies take the existence of frustration for granted and merely guess about the characteristics of the *bosozoku* run without the support of empirical data.

The results of preliminary interviews with my informants as well as a review of the literature on *bosozoku* suggest that the second category of answers is more plausible than the first one. In this case, the run is treated as *asobi* (play), that is, an intrinsically enjoyable activity. Whereas the irrationality of the actor is focused on in the first category of answers, *non* rationality becomes crucial in the second. Two words, *spiido* (speed) and *suriru* (thrills), frequently appear in these accounts. For example, Tamura and Mugishima (1975) included "speed and thrills" as a possible answer to a questionnaire item that asks for "reasons for participation in *bosozoku*." This questionnaire was administered to 1,224 *bosozoku* youths under correctional treatment. "Speed and thrills" was the most frequently chosen reason given for participation. (For similar results, see Nagayama et al. 1981, pp. 29–30.) "Speed" and "thrills" also frequently appear in interviews reported in popular books. Whereas "frustration" and "inferiority complex" are motives that are inferred or imputed by outside observers, "speed" and "thrills" are "native categories."

It is unfortunate that neither academic nor journalistic accounts have tried to explore more thoroughly the implications of these native categories. Although some academic studies do see the run as an instance of play or "vertigo" (e.g., Tamura & Mugishima 1975, p. 70; Taniguchi 1982, p. 128), they mention speed and thrills in passing as "only" the youths' own words, and there is no further curiosity about the conditions that produce "vertigo" or of its phenomenological characteristics.

We cannot, of course, expect much from journalistic accounts as they report interviews unsystematically. They seek, essentially, to attract readers by accounts full of vivid expressions and instances of bravado (e.g., Nakabe 1979; Ueno 1980a, 1980b, 1980c).

Run and flow: a constructivist explanation

Instead of providing explanations that reduce the phenomenon to determining conditions, we consider explanations that account for it in terms of its consequences. This "constructivist" approach would stress the positive outcomes that motorcycle gang members try to achieve through participation in the run, rather than stressing the frustrations that might drive them to it.

Flow

One particularly appropriate concept for exploring the motivation involved in "speed and thrills" is "flow." Csikszentmihalyi and his associates (1974, 1975b) have described the common structure and characteristics of autotelic (intrinsically enjoyable) activities by means of intensive interviews and questionnaires. Csikszentmihalyi's analysis of diverse autotelic activities (e.g., chess, rock climbing, surgery, rock dance) indicates that those who engage in these activities often experience a peculiar dynamic state, which he calls "flow" and defines as "the holistic sensation that people feel when they act with total involvement" (Csikszentmihalyi 1975b, p. 36). He continues,

> In the flow state, action follows upon action according to an internal logic that seems to need no conscious intervention by the actor. He experiences it as a unified flowing from one moment to the next, in which he is in control of actions, and in which there is little distinction between self and environment, between stimulus and response, or between past, present, and future.

Preliminary interviews with my informants suggested that the speed and thrills of a run can indeed be characterized as an experience of flow. A later more systematic investigation supports this interpretation and makes it possible to compare *bosozoku* runs with other flow activities.

Method. Accounts of informants' experiences and motives for joining *bosozoku* runs were obtained primarily through semistructured interviews and a questionnaire. In addition, some direct observations were made of *bosozoku* runs.

Questions about flow during a run were asked in interview sessions in which group members were also asked about the history and structure of the group and their personal background. All of the interview sessions were tape-recorded and transcribed verbatim. Of the 33 interviews, 30 were usable. The mean age of the 30 informants was 17.9, with a range from 15 to 21. Six were female; 24 were male.

The second source of information consisted of questionnaires filled out by informants at a year-end party of the *bosozoku* group or during interview sessions. Sixty-six of the 70 questionnaires were usable. The mean age of all respondents was 17.3, with a range from 15 to 24. Ten were female; 56 were male. After the results of the questionnaires were computed, more narrowly focused interviews were conducted with 20 additional male informants. Casual conversations and discussions with informants during weekly meetings and other more informal occasions were further sources of information.

Direct observation of *bosozoku* runs provided further information. During my field research nine runs took place. I observed four of them. In addition, I was a passenger when some of my informants raced each other on city streets. These were not considered runs, but they did involve some acrobatic driving techniques. Although I did not participate in a run as such, these experiences gave me some personal sense of it.

Outline of the run. A run starts from a previously agreed upon assembly point, usually a city park or parking lot. Members of one or several groups come together before an appointed time usually arranged at the last run or at a conference of leaders held especially for that purpose. Although they make every effort to conceal the arrangements from the police, the information often leaks out so that new plans must be made The number of participants in a run varies from 10 to 100 or more. Quite often the size of a run expands in the course of the night by absorbing the vehicles of observers.

A run consists of several sessions of high-risk races broken by intermissions. The length of each session varies from one to two hours. The speed of a run depends on several factors such as density of traffic and condition of the road. Speeds will usually vary from 70 to 100 km/h (44 to 63 mph) on city roads where the speed limit is usually 40 or 50 km/h. Although the course of a run is decided and transmitted to the participants beforehand, it is frequently changed depending on contingencies, such as an unexpected number of police cars or exceptional density of traffic. Changes in the course are indicated by the *sento-sha* (front vehicle). The leader of the group fills this role, or when several groups join in a run, the leader of the group that sponsors the run. A group flag flying from a motorcycle or a car indicates the name of the host group. The member who holds the flag is called *hatamochi* (flag holder).

Several measures are taken to prevent the band from becoming disorganized and in order to cope with certain risks in a run. First, although the participants are free to race each other, no one is allowed to pass the front vehicle. Second, a few automobiles are in charge of *shingo heisa* (intersection blocking): that is, they block the traffic intersecting the course of the run by making loud exhaust noises and sounding their horns. Automobiles in the front part of the band also clear out the course of the run by intimidating ordinary motorists with their exhaust noises and horns. Motorcycles in the rear position of the band may be engaged in *ketsumakuri* (tail wagging) to hinder chase by police cars. When the police cars reach the tail of the band, the motorcycles slow down and zigzag until the band gains sufficient distance on the police.

If there is no emergency, riders exhibit several types of improvised performances of acrobatic driving techniques to their fellows, passers-by, or curiosity seekers. The techniques include *vonshasen kama* (zigzag-ing across four lanes), *hanabi* (firework; making sparks by striking asphalt pavement with the kickstand of the motorcycle), and *raidaa chenji* (rider change; interchanging riding positions while driving a vehicle).

Intermissions are necessary because a run requires a high degree of concentration and tension. Although resting places are agreed upon beforehand, they are frequently changed according to contingencies. At the resting place, the leaders and executive members collect information about traffic accidents and arrests that have occurred during the pre-ceding part of the run. The other members just rest and chat. Meanwhile, those who have fallen behind the band catch up with it. (Even if the resting place is changed, they can easily catch up because several specific places are routinely used as alternative resting places.) When most par-ticipants have assembled at the resting place and after necessary infor-mation has been checked, the leader of each group takes a roll call and announces the opening of the next session of the run.

At the end of a run, participants reassemble in a designated place. When the run includes several groups, the groups reassemble in dif-ferent places in their respective territories. Not all participants get to the reassembly points. Some may have gone home early and some may have been arrested during the run. Among those who have come to the reassembly point, some fall asleep as soon as they get there, and some continue to engage in acrobatic performances or drag races. In the mean-time, the leader of the group announces the breakup. The youths go home in the light of dawn.

Characteristics of experience in the run. According to Csikszentmihalyi (1975b, pp. 38–48), the flow experience has the following six phenom-enological characteristics:

1. merging of action and awareness
2. centering of attention on limited stimulus field
3. loss of ego (or transcendence of ego)
4. feeling of competence and control
5. unambiguous goals and immediate feedback
6. autotelic nature.

The results of interviews and questionnaires show that the *bosozoku* run includes opportunities for experience that are characterized by these six features. But the run also has some additional characteristics when compared to other flow activities.

Centering of attention

During a run, *bosozoku* youths enter into a context of activity that is clearly bracketed off from everyday life. Numerous components of the run help to create this separate context: a definite timing, the sudden start of loud noises of motorcycles with remodeled mufflers, sounds of horns, sudden beams of headlights crossing each other in the darkness of night, and the spectacular massed presence of a great number of vehicles. Informants use the the words *(o)matsuri* (festival) or *kaanibal* (carnival) to describe the atmosphere. The carnival atmosphere (Bakhtin 1968) seems to contribute to the engrossment in the run. Informants use many onomatopoeic and mimetic expressions to describe the excitement of such an atmosphere. It seems that onomatopoeic expression is a convenient tool to describe action-type activities that by nature tend to defy reconstruction in articulate verbal form. Onomatopoeic expressions are also frequently used in the informants' daily conversations, when they recount and dramatize their experiences in action-type activities (e.g. run, gang fight). The close connection between action-type behaviors and their reconstruction in terms of onomatopoeic and mimetic expressions suggests the possibility that the expressions themselves become a factor that programs future action-type behavior (see Matza 1964; Hannerz 1969; Leary 1977, pp. 66–7). In addition to using vivid phrases, informants were frequently frustrated by their inability to express their experience precisely. "How can I say it?" or "What shall I say?" was often repeated in the interview. This is in marked contrast to the reconstruction of flow experiences in sophisticated words and expressions by many informants in Csikszentmihalyi's study (1975b). This difference is probably based on the youths' action-oriented lifestyle and their unfamiliarity with articulate verbal expression.

> My heart makes a sound like "Don-don! Don-don!" It's pounding. It's almost painful. [I say to myself,] "Oh! We've come here again!" So many cars! So many people! My heart sounds like "Ban-ban! Been! Doki-Doki!" Like being stricken with polio. . . . I cannot say it in words, by mouth. I just cry, "Evaooo!"

The darkness of night reduces peripheral visual distraction. Uniforms, headbands with the mark of a rising sun, and group flags can be seen directly ahead with the headlights of vehicles. These are important props that dramatize the scene and create a rather clear-cut theatrical "frame" (Goffman 1974). Before starting, some participants inhale paint thinner, apparently to limit their field of awareness. But it is, above all, the loud sounds that engross the youths in the frame of a run. At least, this is what they most frequently report. In addition to making exhaust noises and honking horns, those who are in cars play their stereos at full volume. Windows stay open even in winter to let in the surrounding "noise." While outsiders may regard these sounds as random noise, *bosozoku* youths report that they resemble music with a consistent beat. As we shall see later, they say that "listening to good music" is very similar to how it feels to take part in the run.

Feeling of competence and control

Considerable physical danger is involved in runs. In 1983, a total of 6,711 *bosozoku* were arrested for "collective dangerous behavior" (Keisatsucho 1984, p. 205). A 1981 police report lists 89 youths accidentally killed during runs in Japan in 1980, and 87 youths in 1981; the number injured was 1,097 in 1980 and 841 in 1981 (Keisatsucho 1981, p. 30). At least three members of the group I studied were killed in accidents during runs over a period of three years. (The number varies depending on how one defines the group boundary. Some informants mentioned five deaths, others only three.) Many of my informants had been injured and some were crippled.

Nevertheless, physical danger is one of the important factors that seems to focus the youths' attention on the immediate situation. They increase risks on purpose by acrobatic driving. Their costume also appears to indicate a readiness to expose themselves to danger. The riders rarely use protective gear such as leather gloves, boots, or helmets. (Willis 1978, pp. 54–6, offers a similar observation about British "bike boys.") Even those who have just left the hospital and are still wearing plaster casts ride on motorcycles without protection.

This willingness to take risks seems irrational and pathological. And, indeed, *bosozoku* youths themselves often actively present themselves as danger-loving daredevils. Conversation among informants also contains much boasting about close calls. At the same time, measures are taken to avoid particular dangers: for example, intersection blocking to avoid cross traffic, and tail wagging to avoid arrests. Informants almost uni-

formly say that danger itself is not enjoyable. Danger is not pursued for
its own sake but is regarded as something that should be overcome by
one's own skills and used to produce a jolt of "thrills" (see Balint 1959).
Risk is necessary to provide a challenge to one's skill, but this challenge
should be one that can be overcome. Insurmountable challenges or risks
that might not allow one to demonstrate skill (such as easy arrest) are
to be avoided. During a run, feelings of competence and control overcome the awareness of danger. The following is a typical answer about
this aspect of run experience:

> No, I don't think it's dangerous. I rather think about going ahead
> as far as I can.

Awareness of danger, however, does rise to the surface of consciousness shortly before the beginning of a run or when one reflects upon
the run afterwards:

> Sometimes, shortly before we start, I think that it may be danger-
> ous. . . . Sometimes, I get nervous before the start. But once we
> start, I forget [the danger]. . . .

> And after getting back, I say to myself, "What did I do at that
> moment!" I get scared when I think back on it. . . . I think "How
> could I do that!" after a run. But once we start. . . .

Being pursued by the police in squad cars means not only physical
danger but also running the risk of arrest and detention. The police are
thus a persistent challenge that is not easily overcome. The outwitting
of the police, however, leads to feelings of competence and control:

> Once we start, it's fun to be chased by police cars.

> It's so delightful to be chased by patrol cars.

> Well, the most exciting thing is to get away from the pursuing
> police cars.

Police cars also seem to symbolize the general power and authority
of the Japanese police, and perhaps the authority of the generalized
"other," the powerful adult society as a whole. While they are overwhelming and unchallenged in everyday life, its members can be beaten
and mocked within the bracketed context of a run:

> Another thing is defiance. How should I say this? The thrills of
> defying the police, or the fun of matching them. It's really fun.

The feeling of control is derived also from the recognition that one
has transformed a city into one's playground. The ex-leader of a group
writes in his manuscript:

> We start a run by putting the bike party at the tail of the band.

Hoon! Guaan! [onomatopoeic expression of exhaust noise] Seventy to one hundred vehicles start their engines all at once. We can hear nothing but the exhaust noises. Nobody can, even the police cannot, stop us. . . . The moment the engines are started, the disorderly crowd becomes a dinosaur. It's really overwhelming. We speed down the middle of the road. Who cares for police cars !? When I see the band from my front position, it's like a tide of headlights devouring the city. (Sato 1984, p. 33)

Kawaramachi Avenue is the main street of Kyoto. This street is (or has to be) almost always included in the course of a run, not only because a large audience is to be found there but also because the street is a major symbol of the city.

"Let's go and beat Kawaramachi!" . . . Well, we say "go and beat" (*iwasu*) when we play around and make lots of noise there.

Well, I feel that "This [Kawaramachi] is my street" [during a run].

You know, we go up and down Kawaramachi [Avenue] again and again. At such a time, I feel that Kawaramachi is the place for *bosozoku*.

The significance of overcoming physical dangers is not unlike that in rock climbing, reported by Csikszentmihalyi (1975b) and Mitchell (1983). But the risks taken in the *bosozoku* run are far more unpredictable and unmanageable than those of rock climbing. In fact, some rock climbers regard driving a car or walking down the street as more dangerous than rock climbing (Csikszentmihalyi 1975b, pp. 83–4). *Bosozoku* would not say this about the run. It is also said that many professional racers regard driving a car on the street as more dangerous than racing on a racetrack. Whereas the danger of a mountain and of a racetrack might be calculated beforehand and carefully matched to one's skills to a considerable extent, a run includes many uncontrollable contingencies. Even those youths who do intersection blocking run the risk of some cars rushing into the intersection without noticing them. Moreover none can predict exactly the number of police cars or their movement.

One of the important characteristics of a flow activity is that it contains ordered rules that make action and the evaluation of action automatic and unproblematic (Csikszentmihalyi 1975b, p. 47). Actors predict and cope with events on the basis of the implicit rules. There seems to be such a set of rules in the run as well, which is assumed to regulate events in it. For example, the *bosozoku* youths assume that police cars will not cut into the band if they do tail wagging. They also assume that ordinary cars will not rush into an intersection once they hear the exhaust noises at the cross street. These assumptions are, of course, "rules" only for the *bosozoku*. Occasionally, police cars cut into the band or ordinary cars rush into the crossing. Even if policemen and ordinary cars move in ways that are anticipated by the rules, it is not because they share the rules as normative regulations, but because they have to do so for the sake of their own safety. The rules are imposed upon policemen and ordinary cars. Although an informant characterized the run as a "game in which life is at stake," it is a rule-ordered "game" only for *bosozoku* youths. Many informants have actually experienced situations in which their lives were at stake.

These unpredictable and uncontrollable factors sometimes disrupt the feeling of competence and control:

> Even if I get high on a run, I feel somehow scared. Yeah, I definitely think so. I often think, "Will I go home alive?"

> Oh, it's dangerous. But it [the chance of having an accident during a run] depends wholly on luck.

We shall see later how this aspect delimits the quality of flow.

Unambiguous goals and immediate feedback

In the clearly bracketed context of the run, means–ends relationships are simplified. One clearly knows what is right and what is wrong. High speed and extreme physical danger are prerequisites for unambiguous and immediate feedback. To fall behind in the parade or to encounter pressing danger are clear signs that one did something wrong.

Facial expressions, gestures, and moves of fellow participants also serve as important forms of feedback. They not only confirm and maintain the frame of a run but they heighten the participants' excitement and involvement:

> Any difference between solo driving and driving in a group? Of course! They're totally different. Because there's no mirror [in the case of solo driving]. How can I say this? Is it awkward to say, "I can feel people's eyes?"

> There are some guys who get really high. They race engines with a really loud roar, like *hohohohohohoon!* If I see such a guy, I think in my mind, "I have to do it, too. I have to keep up with that guy!"

In other words, fellow participants become amplifiers as well as "mirrors" for the feedback. But the mirror or amplifier is sometimes defective and gives dampening feedback:

> Well, I think the [reaction of a] partner on the pillion seat is crucial. . . . If he's a stupid novice, it's so miserable. . . . Such a guy says nothing [to stir me up]. If he's a smart guy and says, "Oh, K! You're great!" or "Let's go! K! Let's make fun of the police car!" I'll be really excited.

Passers-by and curiosity seekers also provide important feedback, especially in busy areas like Kawaramachi Avenue. *Medatsu* (being seen, looking conspicuous) is the word that is almost always used to describe the importance of the feedback from an audience:

> Because, you know, because Kawaramachi is the main street of Kyoto. That's why we always went there. . . . If we could not be seen (*medatsu*) in Kawaramachi, we should have driven somewhere else. Kawaramachi is so narrow. Who would go to Kawaramachi, if there were not a lot of people there?

The notion of *medatsu* is crucial in understanding the enjoyment derived from this particular flow activity. I elaborate the implications of this concept in detail later.

Merging of action and awareness – loss of self-consciousness

When an actor is completely involved in the immediate demands of action, he loses awareness of his self as a separate "observer." One's "ego," which may intervene between self and environment, disappears temporarily in the flow state (Csikszentmihalyi 1975b, pp. 42–4; see Mead [1934] 1970, pp. 273–81). The physical dangers of the run, and the rapid sequence of perceptions, decisions, operations, and movements seem to lead to this loss of ego. The participants forget themselves and feel as if their bodies move automatically:

> Instinct. My body moves instinctively. It moves without any thought. I forget myself.

> I think about nothing. Really. I think about nothing but my driving.

> On a run I forget everything. I feel I am running with all my heart and mind and strength.

Closely related to the loss of ego is the feeling of being merged with the world of the run. At its apex, youths feel that they get totally "tuned into" the rhythm of the run. Informants frequently use *moetekuru* (burning like a fire), *shibireru* (being paralyzed), and *nottekuru* (getting high) in describing this feeling. When one becomes fully engrossed, even subtle cues are enough to "burn one like fire":

E.:   I lose myself completely when I hear exhaust noise.
M.:   We can be burning like fire just because of the exhaust noise.

Some who are in automobiles start moving their bodies in order to get tuned into the rhythm:

> Steering wheel. When I am burning, it appears in my handling of the steering wheel [he moves his body rhythmically]. . . . I get myself tuned into the rhythm. Yeah, anyone who is skillful at driving does this.

When one loses self-consciousness, the usual sense of time is lost. The temporal framework in the run is different from that in ordinary life:

> How can I know that [lapse of time]? I say, "Really? It's time already?" I say to myself, "Really?" It will be dawn in a moment.

> Time passes so fast. . . . Well, no. I forget time. I say, "Really? Is it time to go already?" or "Oh! I didn't notice that!" I don't mind at all about such a matter as [lapse of] time. The only thing we have to keep in mind is the assembly time.

In the state of psychological flow, one loses track of "time" in the usual sense of the word. Reflecting afterward, one cannot grasp it by means of the time sense and memory for time used in everyday life. The feeling of "collective effervescence" (Durkheim [1912] 1967) typical of the run is also related to the loss of ego. (This is discussed later.)

The autotelic nature of the run

Like other activities that are usually called "play" or a "game," the major enjoyment of the run is found in the activity itself. In this regard, a run is qualitatively different from those activities that are carried out mainly for the sake of extrinsic rewards such as money or fame, although the latter does figure into the broader range of bosozoku activities. As Csikszentmihalyi (1974, 1975b) has shown in detail, autotelic activities differ somewhat from each other with regard to the type of intrinsic rewards and the quality of the flow experience they provide. Questionnaire responses and interviews indicate that the run has its own peculiar characteristics as an autotelic activity.

The questionnaire included a rating scale that required respondents to evaluate the relative importance of nine reasons for enjoying runs.

Eight of the nine reasons were adopted from the questionnaire used by Csikszentmihalyi. The eight reasons have been found to "represent exhaustive and nonredundant incentives for participating in activities which lack conventional rewards" (Csikszentmihalyi 1975b, p. 14). The other reason, that is, *medatsu-koto* (being seen, looking conspicuous), was added to the questionnaire because the preliminary interviews had suggested that public display constitutes an important component in the enjoyment of the motorcycle run.

Table 6.1 shows the ranking of the reasons that *bosozoku* respondents gave for enjoying the activity; the responses of 21 informants were excluded from the computations, since most of them had not taken part in a run for over 6 months at the time the questionnaire was administered. The responses are compared with those of Csikszentmihalyi. All other groups except high school basketball players rank "enjoyment of the experience and the use of skills" and "the activity itself" highest, whereas *bosozoku* youths rank these two reasons third and fourth. The total autotelic rank in the bottom line of the table indicates the relative importance of intrinsic rewards for the various groups. The equation for computing "autotelic scores" (Csikszentmihalyi 1975b, p. 19) consists in adding the score on "enjoyment of the experience" to the score on "the activity itself," and subtracting the score on "competition" and the score on "prestige." Aside from high school basketball players, *bosozoku* youths rank the autotelic component lowest of all the other groups studied, even though their ratings are still relatively high. Throughout this chapter it is assumed that differences in rating patterns of groups are based on differences in qualities of activities and not on cross-cultural differences. These results presumably indicate internal differences among autotelic activities. They support the notion that the run is motivated primarily by intrinsic rewards, but suggest that, compared to other activities like chess or rock climbing, the intrinsic rewards are relatively less salient. It should also be kept in mind that the interview records strongly indicate that the youngsters do see the activity itself as enjoyable.

Follow-up interviews also show that different types of enjoyment come into play at different phases of a run. On broad avenues like Gojo or Horikawa streets, where traffic is light at midnight and the youths can speed at will, "the enjoyment of the experience" (i.e., enjoyment of the experience of speeding) and "the activity itself" become the primary gratification. On the other hand, on Kawaramachi Avenue, where there is a large audience, the enjoyment of public display (namely, the

Table 6.1. *Ranking of mean scores given for reasons for enjoying activity, by groups*

Reason	Rock climbers (N = 26)	Composers (N = 22)	Dancers (N = 27)	Male chess (N = 28)	Female chess (N = 20)	Basketball (N = 35)	Bosozoku (N = 45)	
1. Enjoyment of the experience and use of skills	1	1.5	1.5	1	1.0	5	4.0	5.0[a]
2. The activity itself	2	1.5	1.5	2	2.0	4	3.0	3.5
3. Friendship, companionship	3	6.5	6.0	4	4.5	3	1.0	1.0
4. Development of skills	4	3.0	3.0	3	3.0	2	5.5	6.5
5. Measuring self against own ideals	6	4.0	5.0	6	6.5	6	5.5	6.5
6. Emotional release	5	5.0	4.0	7	6.5	8	2.0	2.0
7. Competition, measuring self against others	7	8.0	8.0	5	4.5	1	7.0	8.0
8. Prestige, regard, glamour	8	6.5	7.0	8	8.0	7	8.0	9.0
9. Medatsu	—	—	—	—	—	—	—	3.5
Total autotelic rank	3	1	2	4	5	7	6	—

[a]This column includes the enjoyment of *medatsu*.

Source: Csikszentmihalyi 1975b, Table 2.

enjoyment of *medatsu-koto*) becomes important. "Friendship and companionship" is most important in jovial mock fights during a run and in the lively sociability during intermissions.

"Emotional release" refers mainly to the cathartic feeling one experiences shortly after each session of a run. *Sukkato suru* ("feel completely satisfied," "feel completely refreshed") is the phrase usually chosen to describe the cathartic experiences. The expression also frequently appears in daily conversations among informants and in journalistic accounts. Indeed, emphasis on the cathartic function has misled journalists and scholars into regarding runs only as means of compensating for inferiority complexes and venting frustrations. But as we have seen in the previous discussions and as we shall see in detail in the next section, the run includes various kinds of enjoyment. The cathartic experience is merely one of them.

Medatsu, communitas, flow

Medatsu. Table 6.1 shows that *medatsu-koto* (being seen) was ranked as important as "the activity itself" among reasons for enjoying runs. *Medatsu*, as noted above, is the category that informants use when they emphasize the importance of feedback from the audience. For example:

> If I drive a motorcycle alone, the sound's like *pahn!* [But during a run] It's like *Guwa! Guwa!* Everybody directs attention to us. We carry out a run absolutely because we want to be seen (*medachitai kara*).

The word *medatsu* is frequently found in interviews reported in academic and journalistic publications. It is also used when youths explain why they use "bizarre" and "grotesque" costumes and make extreme modifications to their vehicles.

Scholars as well as journalists usually account for the youths' desires to make themselves conspicuous (*medatsu*), or to show off their belongings, in terms of *jiko kenji yoku* (desire for showing off, desire for self-assertion). The phrase is fine if used as a simple descriptive term, but it becomes circular if used as explanation. Little evidence is given on the relative intensity of this desire. Nor are there detailed descriptions of the ways in which youths try to make themselves and their belongings seen. The results of my field research suggest that *medatsu* is not a straightforward expression of individual desires, but something more complex.

One of the keys to understanding *medatsu* is the nature of the audience's feedback. Note the different ratings of the two very similar activities included in the *medatsu* dimension in Table 6.2. Whereas "playing a theatrical role before a large audience" was ranked 4th, "appearing in a TV program" was ranked 12th among 20 activities in how similar they were to a run. Informants almost uniformly mention the difference in the intensity and directness of the audience's response in accounting for the differences in these two rankings. Many also argue that a run is far more thrilling and full of unexpected events. One informant said:

> Vividness [is different]. . . . We can repeat it again on a TV program, if the director says, "This is no good." But, this [run] is totally different. . . . When I zigzag and crash, who would say, "Cut!"? It's a miserable accident.

Another key is the difference between *medatsu* and "prestige, regard, glamor." Table 6.1 shows that whereas *medatsu-koto* was ranked third, "prestige, regard, glamor" was given the lowest rank. *Medatsu* is akin to "prestige, regard, glamor" in that it requires an audience and that one's performance or appearance attracts the attention of the audience. The most important difference between the two is that "prestige, regard, glamor" presupposes shared value judgments, whereas *medatsu* does not. This difference is clarified further if we examine the informants' distinction between *medatsu* (being seen) and *misebirakasu* (showing off). Informants rarely use the latter in talking about the importance of public display. Most of them agree that *misebirakasu* is somehow different from *medatsu*. Some informants are more explicit on this point:

> *Misebirakasu* is, well, to show off something valuable to others by saying, "It's so good. Don't you think so?" *Medatsu* in run means to attract attention . . . or to get them to see us by doing something wrong and making lots of noise.

> *Medatsu* means to hope that people will pay attention to us when we are doing something. . . . [When we show off (*misebirakasu*) something] we say, "Look at this." We're trying to show off when we ride on gorgeous bikes and show them to someone and say, "It's really a good bike. Don't you think so?" [On the other hand,] we can be noticed by people (*medatsu*) even if we don't say anything.

In Japanese *misebirakasu* is a transitive verb, whereas *medatsu* is intransitive and refers to a state or condition rather than to action. *Misebirakasu* can be characterized as actively insisting on one's own superiority or the superiority of one's own belongings. The superiority must be defined in terms of shared standards. In contrast, one can be in the state of *medatsu* only by commanding the attention of others, whether or not they share the same standards. *Bosozoku* enjoy being watched by people, even if the spectators express shock and dislike. What really matters is the attention of others, irrespective of any moral implications of that behavior. It is obvious that "prestige, regard, glamor" is seen as a more conventional or consensual accomplishment.

Csikszentmihalyi (personal correspondence, 2 September 1983) comments on this point so as to clarify the issue and make explicit the relationship between the enjoyment of *medatsu* and genuine flow experience. After pointing out that both *medatsu* and *misebirakasu* can be regarded as the "basic, primitive *ur*-forms of the motivation out of which more abstract social forms of 'prestige, regard, and glamor' evolve," he mentions two ways to maintain the self strong and ordered. One is to invest one's attention in goals and getting feedback that confirms one's intentions. The other is to get the attention of *others* to recognize one's existence and one's intentions. Csikszentmihalyi suggests that *medatsu* and *misebirakasu* are ways of getting this second type of feedback. He then points out that pure flow activities mainly provide feedback based on personal achievement of goals and thus also strengthen the sense of self, but this is an unintended consequence and not the the main goal of the activity.

As the phenomenon of "stage fright" suggests, feedback from an audience may interfere with the concentration on a flow activity. For instance, heightened self-consciousness due to the presence of bystanders may disrupt the flow experience of rock dancing (Csikszentmihalyi 1975b, pp. l07–8). In contrast, both types of information – feedback from the use of one's skills, and feedback from the audience – are combined in the "ideal" run. This is probably not unlike the experience of actors at the peak of their theatrical performance. In both cases, the audience response does not evoke a monitoring ego but becomes a mirror that transmits immediate and unambiguous feedback. The run is essentially a theatrical stage on which the themes and plots implied in the character images of the *bosozoku* are activated and organized into a "performance," not just a scheme of action written on a script. The character image of *bosozoku* includes many contradictions and inconsistencies, as it includes the traits of both hero and rogue. But the performance is staged as though it were based on a consistent script with coherent themes and plots of a hero narrative (see Chomsky 1965, Chap.1; Levi-Strauss 1966,

Table 6.2. *Ranking of similarity of experience items within each autotelic activity*

Factors	Rock climbers (N = 26)	Composers (N = 22)	Dancers (N = 27)	Male chess (N = 28)	Female chess (N = 20)	Basketball (N = 35)	Bosozoku (N = 45)
1. Friendship and relaxation							
Making love	6.0	6.5	4.5	16.5	17.5	14.0	18.0[a]
Being with good friend	3.0	9.0	4.5	9.0	14.5	8.0	3.0
Watching movie	15.5	5.0	9.0	12.0	17.5	6.0	14.0
Listening to music	6.0	3.0	2.0	10.0	12.5	3.0	5.0
Reading a book	8.0	8.0	6.5	5.0	12.5	15.5	15.5
2. Risk and chance							
Swimming out on a dare	13.0	13.5	15.0	14.0	7.0	17.5	12.0
Exposure to radiation	17.0	10.0	12.0	12.0	10.0	9.5	6.5
Driving fast	10.0	16.5	12.0	12.0	10.0	6.0	1.0
Taking drugs	10.0	13.5	15.0	15.0	14.5	9.5	10.0
Playing slot machine	18.0	18.0	15.0	18.0	16.0	17.5	12.0
Entering burning house	13.0	11.0	12.0	16.5	10.0	4.0	15.5
3. Problem solving							
Math problem	4.0	2.0	9.0	1.5	2.0	12.0	19.5
Assembling furniture	13.0	6.5	17.0	7.5	7.0	15.5	19.5
Exploring strange place	15.5	13.5	18.0	6.0	5.0	12.0	17.0
Playing poker	15.5	13.5	18.0	6.0	5.0	12.0	17.0

4. Competition								
Running a race	6.0	16.5	9.0	7.5	7.0	2.0	2.0	2.0
Competitive sport	10.0	13.5	6.5	1.5	3.0	1.0	5.5	6.5
5. Creative								
Designing, discovering	2.0	1.0	1.0	3.0	1.0	6.0	7.5	8.5
6. Medatsu								
Appearing in a TV program	—	—	—	—	—	—	—	12.0
Playing a theatrical role	—	—	—	—	—	—	—	4.0

"This column includes the *medatsu* dimension.
Source: Csikszentmihalyi 1975b, Table 3.

pp. 66, 232, 237). The aspect of the social drama as a hero narrative is clarified by the emergent quality of the "performance" (Bauman 1975). The immediate demands of the ongoing action pare away the aspect of "rogue" or "fool" potentially implicit in the character image. The script of this hero narrative becomes a set of game rules that make it possible for *bosozoku* to construct their dramatized self-image in an orderly manner. However temporary it may be, they can act as heroes of an ongoing drama (see Leary 1977, p. 63).

Communitas. "Friendship, companionship" was rated highest among the rewards that provide the most enjoyment in the run (Table 6.1). "Being with a good friend" also ranks third among the 20 activities with regard to its similarity to a run (Table 6.2). Many informants emphasized the enjoyment of vivid and unmediated sociability. Two informants described the interaction and mock fighting during a run as follows:

M.:   . . . Yeah. All of us are so happy. Everybody looks so cheerful. Really.
E.:   When passing each other, we wave hands and exclaim, "Wow!"
M.:   When driving side by side, we exclaim, "Peace!" and make the V sign. We get really high.
E.:   If we drive side by side with some guy we know, we may zigzag playfully.
M.:   I may zigzag and kick his bike.

In considering the significance of "friendship and companionship" in the context of the run, we have to take into account the contrast between the pattern of interaction in the hangouts and in the run. Informants spend most of their leisure time talking and gossiping in their hangouts. Roles are undifferentiated in these interactions, and there is ambiguity about who should take the initiative. An intransitive verb, *tamaru*, is used to describe such a pattern of unstructured interaction. The typical answer given to my question, *"Nani shiten nova?"* (What are you guys doing here?) was *"Nani mo shitehen – tamatteru dakeya "* (Nothing – we're just gathering). *Tamaru* is usually used to refer to stagnant water or puddles that have formed on the road. And a Japanese word used for "hangout" is *tamariba*, namely, a place where a group of people gather, like water in a puddle.

In clear contrast to *tamaru*-type interaction, interaction in a run is ordered, exciting, and organized. During a run, roles are differentiated, the flow of time is synchronized, and resources are structured for the sake of a single, simple, and clear-cut purpose. Youth join in voluntarily. They share playlike definitions of the situation about the character image of *bosozoku* and the themes and plots of the run. Synchronized movements of people and vehicles present the "beauty of massed gymanstics." Youths experience a sense of self-transcendence and feel that they belong to a more powerful system (Csikszentmihalyi & Larson 1984, pp. 246–9).

The enjoyment of "friendship, companionship" or that of "collective effervescence" (Durkheim [1912] 1967) derives from a sense of unity in the ordered collective undertaking in which one participates voluntarily. In the carnival atmosphere of a run, the rules governing interpersonal interaction in everyday life are temporarily suspended; and vivid and unmediated sociability becomes possible. A female informant described her experience of euphoria as follows:

> I . . . I understand something, when all of our feelings get tuned up. . . . When running, we are not in complete harmony at the start. But if the run begins going well, all of us, all of us feel for others. How can I say this? When, when we wag the tail of the band. . . . When our minds become, become one. At such a time, it's a real pleasure. . . . When all of us become one, I understand something. . . . All of a sudden, I realize, "Oh! we're one" and think, "If we speed as fast as we can, it will become a real RUN." . . . When we realize that we become one flesh, it's supreme. When we get high on speed. At such a moment, it's really super.

The enjoyment of "friendship, companionship" derives from what Turner called "communitas," namely, "a total, unmediated relationship between person and person" (Turner 1974b, p. 274), which can be found in the liminal phases of society such as rituals, festivals, and initiation rites. The roles differentiated in the performance of a run are not those that segment or separate people. On the contrary, they can be compared to roles in a pretend play (Sutton-Smith & Kelly-Byrne 1984), which make it possible for its participants to liberate themselves from the social roles of everyday life and present an alternative model of human association (Turner 1974a; Garvey 1977; Schwartzman 1978). As Turner says about the hierarchical organizations of the Conservative Vice Lords (a gang of adolescent black youths in Chicago) and Hell's Angels, *bosozoku* youth are "playing the game structure rather than engaging in the socioeconomic structure in real earnest" (Turner 1969, p. 194). Similarly, resources are not divided up against the participants' wills. Nor is time synchronized coercively. Instead time and resources help to create and maintain the playlike definition of the run, to which the participants willingly subscribe.

Flow – the skills and challenges of the run. Whereas *medatsu* and communitas include forms of enjoyment which presuppose feedback from others to one's own actions, the enjoyment of high-speed driving does not necessarily presuppose such a response. Thus, the enjoyment of speed and thrills affords the opportunity for genuine flow experience, in which the actors get feedback that confirms their intentions by engrossing their attention in goals. The results of the questionnaire, the interviews, and the field observations all indicate that the range of this genuine flow in a run is quite limited and that the limitation is due to the peculiar nature of the skills and challenges involved in the run.

Csikszentmihalyi regards the matching of skills and challenges as the essential feature of flow. He argues,

> Activities that reliably produce flow experiences are similar in that they provide opportunities for action which a person can act upon without being bored or worried. . . . When a person is bombarded with demands which he or she feels unable to meet, a state of anxiety ensues. When the demands for action are fewer, but still more than what the person feels capable of handling, the state of experience is one of worry. (Csikszentmihalyi 1975b, pp. 49–50)

This idea of matching skills to challenges is implicit in other psychological approaches to intrinsic motivation, especially the cognitive ones (e.g., White 1959; deCharms 1968; Ellis 1973; Deci 1975). For example, the following statement by Deci is quite similar to that of Csikszentmihalyi:

> One's need to feel competent and self-determining will motivate two general classes of behavior: The first includes behaviors which seek out situations which provide a reasonable challenge to the person. If he is bored, he will seek an opportunity to use his creativity and resourcefulness. If he is overchallenged, and therefore frightened, he will seek a different situation which will provide a challenge which he can handle. In short, this motivational mechanism leads people to situations which provide challenges which make optimum use of their abilities. . . .
>
> The second class of behaviors motivated by the need for competence and self-determination includes behaviors which are intended to conquer challenging situations. In other words, people are motivated to "reduce uncertainty" or "reduce dissonance" or "reduce incongruity" when they encounter it or create it. (Deci 1975, p. 57)

Deci (1975, p. 554) touches on the issue of how people *create* uncertainty or challenge by saying "organisms sometimes seek uncertainty." Csikszentmihalyi's model illustrates how uncertainty or challenge is created and overcome. In his discussion on the theoretical model of flow, Csikszentmihalyi shows two ways in which people in a state of worry return to flow. One way is to decrease challenge. Another way is to increase skills (Csikszentmihalyi 1975b, pp. 52–3). The latter, left unexplored in Deci's argument, is closely related to an integral aspect of flow activity. As the high rankings given to the Creative and Problem-Solving factors in Table 6.2 suggest, flow activities provide a certain degree of uncertainty and novelty. The uncertainty and novelty can be overcome by the actor, if he expands his self toward new dimensions of skill and competence. In this way, flow activities provide people with an opportunity to surpass their own limitations (Csikszentmihalyi 1975b, pp. 29–33). Flow activities not only provide opportunities for matching skills to challenges, but also present the possibilities of elevating a given skill–challenge balance to a higher level. The higher the level of the skill–challenge balance, the deeper the flow experience will be. Flow activities like rock climbing are characterized by potentially boundless levels of skills and challenges, and thus by an almost infinitely expanding "flow channel," or band of skill–challenge balances (Csikszentmihalyi 1975b, p. 52).

The run is a limited flow activity in this sense. This can be seen in the participants' evaluation of its components. Table 6.2 shows that *bosozoku* youths gave lower scores on the factors Creative and Problem-Solving with regard to their similarity to the run, compared to any of the six other activities studied earlier. In addition, they describe the run as involving more risk than any of the other six groups: They gave the highest total scores among the seven groups of respondents to the items in Risk and Chance factor. The peculiar skills and challenges of the run underlie this atypical rating pattern.

The first reason is that the challenges in a run are to a considerable degree unpredictable and uncontrollable. Physical danger is a prerequisite to flow experiences both in rock climbing and in runs. But compared to the danger in rock climbing, physical danger in the run is more contingent upon situational factors that are unpredictable and difficult to control, and thus may intrude upon full psychological involvement. One is frequently drawn "back to reality." Excessive physical danger easily disrupts the skill–challenge balance, and may cause injury or even death. This makes it quite difficult to increase the skill–challenge balance beyond a certain point.

The nature of skills as well as that of challenges sets a limit to the quality of flow. Skills refer mainly to a narrow range of physical skills.

In this respect, the *bosozoku* run stands in contrast to rock climbing, which requires a high level of both intellectual and physical skills. The combination of the two makes it possible to maintain intense concentration in rock climbing, which in turn leads to complex and deep flow (Csikszentmihalyi 1975b, pp. 81–2). This is probably why the Problem-Solving and Creativity factors were rated high and the Risk and Chance factor was rated low by rock climbers. As the rating pattern of *bosozoku* youths in Table 6.2 shows, a run is not thought to resemble other activities that require intellectual skills, and it tends to be characterized by a narrow flow channel. Although some may exhibit a variety of motor skills in acrobatic driving, the participants' choice is severely restricted. It is mainly the leaders who decide the details of a run, and only they use any intellectual skills.

Conclusions

The seemingly irrational behavior of motorcycle gangs has been traditionally explained as being either a way of evading frustrations, or a way of expressing frustrations inherent in the role of dispossessed youths. But as this study has shown, the activities involved in motorcycle runs provide strong positive reasons for participation. The run turns out to be a creative dramaturgical form cleverly crafted to provide a temporarily heightened sense of self to the participants through the enactment of a heroic role in front of a public, and through the use of skills and discipline. In addition, the run provides a sense of belonging to a community and a shared experience of collective effervescence. Finally, participation in a run provides autotelic experiences by structuring the activity in a play form that allows the meshing of personal skills with relevant challenges, and that produces clear goals and unambiguous feedback in a setting that cuts out ordinary stimulation while forcing concentration on a narrow range of stimuli.

Despite these positive characteristics, *bosozoku* activity, like all play forms, has its limitations. It involves many risks without allowing for the development of a great number of skills. Intellectual challenges are almost nonexistent. It is probably for these reasons that few youths remain in motorcycle gangs past the age of 20. With time they realize the limitations of the heroic image they have tried to enact. It is no longer enough to capture the attention of the audience; now they would also like to be accepted and perhaps admired. The run stops providing desirable feedback: The collective effervescence of the gang gradually becomes meaningless. When this point is reached, the activity no longer provides enjoyment, and the youth are ready to move on. But for a few years in late adolescence, the *bosozoku* help bridge the developmental transition into adulthood for many young people in search of a way to express their being with purpose and style.

7. Women, work, and flow

MARIA T. ALLISON AND

MARGARET CARLISLE DUNCAN

Paid work outside the home is becoming the norm for the majority of women in America. Men have traditionally devoted most of their energies to work and have derived from it the main support for their personal identities. How do women experience work? Are they also able to find productive activities in the workplace meaningful and rewarding, or does socialization into the feminine homemaker role prevent women from deriving the same kind of satisfaction from work that men occasionally get from their jobs?

Despite the extensive research on the relationship between work and general quality of life (Spreitzer & Snyder 1974; Pryor & Reeves 1982), on job satisfaction (Wilensky 1960; Dubin, Champoux, & Porter 1975), and on leisure satisfaction (Kando & Summers 1971; Noe 1971; Neulinger & Raps 1972; Bacon 1975; Kabanoff 1980), few studies have incorporated working women in their sample. (For recent notable exceptions see Berk & Berk 1979; and Walshok 1979.) This neglect is particularly unfortunate in that 52.2% of all women and 54% of married women with young children now work outside the home. Participation in the labor force is increasingly required for economic survival (Hesse 1979; Walshok 1979; Mansfield 1982). Of all working women, 77% are now single, divorced, or are married to men with incomes under $15,000 (Mansfield 1982). As these findings suggest, then, women now represent a major sector of the labor force. And since work is such a central aspect of the female worker's life, it becomes imperative to understand more systematically how it influences her perceptions, experiences, and quality of life.

Perhaps the major shortcoming of past research has been the context bias of its design. Some studies have focused on quality-of-life variables in the workplace (such as satisfaction, control, enjoyment), while others

An earlier version of this chapter has been published in *Leisure Sciences*, 9, 3 (1987), pp. 143–61.

have studied them in recreation and leisure activities. This separation hides the interdependence between these spheres of activity within the totality of human experience. The separation of work from the rest of life might in fact be a peculiar gender-linked trait. Female workers do not seem to segmentalize work, leisure, and home life to the same degree as men do (Wilensky 1960; Harrison & Minor 1978, 1982; Iso-Ahola 1979; Pryor & Reeves 1982). There is a tendency to dismiss these findings as spurious by suggesting that working women have not yet fully integrated the worker role into their identity (Oakley 1980; Simpson & Mutran 1981). Yet working women, particularly those who are married and have children, may have a well-developed, yet different, perspective toward the work and home spheres since they have had to maintain responsiblity not only for the worker role, but also for home maintenance and child care (Berk & Berk 1979; Berk 1980; Oakley 1980; Simpson & Mutran 1981). Thus, it is possible that studying work and leisure separately has inadvertently resulted in a male model of the work–leisure relationship, instead of providing a theoretical interpretation that reflects the reality of men and women alike.

A second major shortcoming of past research stems from what Kabanoff (1980) and Kando and Summers (1971) suggest is too great an emphasis on *forms* of activity rather than on the *meanings*. For example, we know a great deal about what types of leisure activities men and women pursue, and for how long a time; but little about how these are perceived, and what importance they have. Researchers have assumed that they know, through their own definitions and context biases, the meaning of such activities for the participants. Dichotomous terms such as extrinsic–intrinsic, instrumental-expressive, obligation–freedom, and seriousness–enjoyment are utilized to characterize the work and leisure experiences, respectively. Clearly, however, two persons engaged in similar work or leisure activities may – and probably do – define the meaning of the experiences in very different ways. Both form and meaning must be considered together in order to develop a comprehensive understanding of the impact of work and leisure on people's lives.

Perhaps one of the most fruitful approaches that helps to overcome these methodological shortcomings is suggested by the work of Csikszentmihalyi (1975b). He tried to understand the essential nature of enjoyment, or "flow," by identifying (1) the experiential components or phenomenological features that characterize the flow state, (2) the nature of the activity engaged in during the experience, and (3) the degree of flow experienced by individuals. By focusing on the subjective condition *first,* rather than on the context, he identified similarities in both work and play environments that did elicit the flow state. This strategy avoids the context-biased compartmentalization of work and leisure; it demonstrates that the entire range of emotions, from joy to absolute boredom and frustration, can be experienced either in work or in leisure. Although this premise seems somewhat obvious now, past research in the area did not really allow for the possibility.

Following the work of Csikszentmihalyi (1975b), the purpose of this chapter is to identify the contexts (i.e., work, home, leisure) in which working women experience their greatest sense of enjoyment or flow, and to examine the nature and meaning of that experience. Flow, according to Csikszentmihalyi (1975b, p. 36) is "the holistic sensation that people feel when they act with total involvement." Similar in nature to Maslow's (1968) concept of peak experience, flow is characterized as an "autotelic experience . . . a merging of action and awareness." The individual feels a strong sense of challenge and control yet there is a "loss of ego" coupled with intensity of focus. Thus, the central question we pose is, To what extent do working women experience these feelings in work, leisure, and home activities? In addition, we attempt to identify the contexts in which working women experience the greatest sense of boredom, frustration, or what is here termed "antiflow." Seen as the antithesis of flow, antiflow is meaningless, tedious activity that offers little challenge; is not intrinsically motivating; and creates a sense of lack of control. Insofar as flow represents absolute enjoyment, antiflow represents extreme disdain or dislike for an activity. In this chapter we hope to identify the nature and extent to which working women experience these feelings in work, home, and leisure spheres.

This approach assumes, first of all, that one's experiences in work and in leisure are not necessarily antithetical; second, that there are dimensions of both work and leisure that maximize flow, and others that are responsible for antiflow. And because the literature suggests that one's relationship to work and to leisure will differ depending on the type of job and on characteristics of the working environment (Noe 1971; Neulinger & Raps 1972), it will be necessary to compare the experiences of women from distinct occupational sectors.

Methods

The purpose of this chapter is twofold. First, through the use of exploratory data, we describe variations in the experiences of work and nonwork in the daily lives of working women. Specifically, we identify the nature and extent to which flow and antiflow are experienced in the work, home, and leisure spheres of professional and blue-collar working women. In addition, the data are used to suggest ways in which past conceptualizations of the work-leisure relationship need to be expanded.

Extensive semistructured interviews were conducted with two groups of working women: professionals (N = 8) from a university setting that included faculty and research associates from a range of specializations (e.g., theater arts, English, biology); and blue-collar women (N = 12) employed as factory workers and service workers. The median income for the professional women was twice as high as for the blue-collar women. Eleven were married, six were divorced heads of household, and three were not married.

Either face-to-face or telephone interviews were used, depending on the respondent's preference. Interviews lasted from 20 to 120 minutes, depending on the depth of information volunteered; most lasted approximately one hour.

Since the goal was to identify the degree to which working women experienced flow and antiflow, the nature of these experiences, and the contexts in which these feelings were experienced, a semistructured interview was developed that allowed for maximum input. Applying the components of flow described by Csikszentmihalyi (1975b) (i.e., challenge, enjoyment, control, and autotelic motivation), and the antithesis of each (i.e., here termed antiflow), core descriptions representing these conditions were read to the subjects. Specific probes about each condition then followed. The statements read to each person follow:

> I am going to read you a description of a state of mind. After I read it I would like to ask you to what degree you experience it and some other questions about it.

(*Flow*):

> When I stop to think about it I realize that an important part of this state of mind is enjoyment. I get so involved in what I'm doing, I almost forget about time. When I experience this state of mind, I feel really free from boredom and worry. I feel like I am being challenged or that I am very much in control of my action and my world. I feel like I am growing and using my best talents and skills; I am master of my situation.

(*Antiflow*):

> When I stop to think about it, I know I experience this state of mind when I'm doing something I have to do. I usually feel bored

or nervous, and I am very conscious of the time. This state of mind exists when I am doing something I don't enjoy and find tedious or beneath my abilities. Or it may occur when I don't have much independence in what I'm doing and I'm not really in control of my situation.

This qualitative inductive strategy (Glaser & Strauss 1967; Barton & Lazarfeld 1969; Denzin 1978) is directed at theoretical sampling of constructs. The goal of such an investigation, and the foundation of the methodology, is to formulate theoretical and conceptual relationships (Glaser & Strauss 1967; Barton & Lazarfeld 1969) rather than to test specific hypotheses.

Findings. The findings that follow are organized into two major sections. The first section describes the experiences of flow and antiflow in the work setting. The second does the same for the nonwork environment.

Flow and antiflow in the work setting

Csikszentmihalyi suggests that one of the major criteria characteristic of the flow state is the "merging of action and awareness . . . a centering of attention on a limited stimulus field" (Csikszentmihalyi 1975b, p. 40). The centering of attention, or intensity, creates a sense of timeless focus on the subject at hand. The quotations in Table 7.1 indicate that the professional women interviewed experienced such focus in their work; blue-collar women, however, instead experienced the strong antithesis that resulted in boredom, followed by frustration.

Bound up in the intensity-of-focus dimension is the experience of time. As the statements in Table 7.2 indicate, the time experience during the flow state is elusive, whereas during antiflow, minutes turn into hours.

Clearly, the blue-collar women found that boredom, due to the lack of things to do, made time move quite slowly. In fact, one person offered that it was not the nature of the work itself, but the unoccupied time that led to the greatest frustration. The professional women, on the other hand, were so involved and focused that they had little awareness of the passage of time.

Another criterion identified by Csikszentmihalyi (1975b) as essential to producing the flow state is the sense of challenge and control that the individual must feel with regard to the situation at hand. The responses in Table 7.3 reflect the differences in the degrees of challenge and control experienced by women in the two work contexts.

Table 7.1. *Intensity of focus experienced in the work setting*

Professional women: flow	Blue-collar women: antiflow
Very many aspects of the career – freedom and liberation from boredom – that is the most prevalent characteristic of having my career... you cannot be bored because in this subject there are continually new discoveries, just reading about it is fascinating to me. My enthusiasm for reading about these things is greater than ever.	When I was on the other end of the line, I'd get so tired, bored, disgusted. We had to hand-pack and wrap, same thing day after day – you have to force yourself to do it.
It's just at some point you've thought about a problem for so long it's almost that you're obsessed with it, not in a negative sense – it's a thing you think about all the time.	When somebody's really made a bad mess – I hate to clean it up..., but the thing that would make it better would be if, in my particular job, I could be busier, and more physical; I get caught with a lot of free time and I don't like that.
If I'm writing a lecture which particularly interests me, or writing a paper, and I'm very interested in what I'm doing, and I'm thinking. Sort of anything that involves sitting and thinking and writing, I guess I'll have that experience. Sometimes reading, I know oftentimes when I'm reading the kind of things that are very difficult and it takes a lot of concentration to follow what the author is saying, and I have to actually solve the problems along with the author.	I've never experienced anything quite like this before. I don't know if other factories are like this but it's always a turmoil – lots of bickering, arguing – I sorta go into myself – it's like a shell.

It is no news that challenge and control on the job are important. Noe (1971) and others have shown that there is a link between the level of satisfaction and enjoyment experienced, and the degree of autonomy and responsibility allowed in the work setting. The professionals in this study were relatively free to determine not only the type, but also the level of difficulty of the tasks to be undertaken on any given day, whereas the blue-collar workers had a relatively fixed and repetitive series of tasks over which they had little control. Although initiative and even

Table 7.2. *The time experience in the work setting*

Professional women: flow	Blue-collar women: antiflow
Most of what I do is economic theory, a lot of problem solving, and I would say that when I'm just sitting at my desk, trying to solve a problem, sometimes I forget about the time, sometimes I have to set an alarm if I'm going to class because I'll forget what time it is.	The thing I hate most about work is the boredom. There are times when I get really busy, but there are often times, a lot of times, when there's nothing to do. You stand around and watch the clock – I hate it.
To be totally absorbed in what you are doing and to enjoy it so much that you don't want to be doing anything else, I don't see how people survive if they don't experience something like that . . . if I went to work every day and just had to sort of wait 'til Miller Time, just do my work and have no feeling of getting anything out of it, I'd look for something else to do.	When there's nothing to do, there's nothing to do. When you've washed all the walls, swept and mopped the floor, and only five minutes have gone by on the clock, there's not much you can do.

creativity are expected in the professional role, they are not encouraged in the blue-collar women. In fact several indicated that they had tried to find more things to do but were chastised by supervisors for stepping outside of their assigned responsibilities.

Professional and blue-collar women have very different experiences on the job. During the interviews, one could not help but sense the frustration that the blue-collar women felt with their work. And several made it clear that it was not the nature of the work itself but the numbing boredom of the unchallenging environment that made each day so frustrating. Thus, their work experience became a source of antiflow, which, as we shall see, had an impact on other aspects of their personal lives.

The professional women, on the other hand, found the work experience very challenging and stimulating. This is not to say, however, that this setting itself was free from frustration. The statements below illustrate some of the activities and experiences that led to antiflow for the professional women:

Sometimes the feelings of boredom have come from the feeling that I'm working on a project that is not of fundamental interest,

Table 7.3. *Degrees of challenge/control experienced in work settings*

Professional women: flow	Blue-collar women: antiflow
[In my career] people are judged very much on their intellectual abilities, so therefore one worries constantly if one can meet the standards, higher and higher standards that are being created in the field . . . my work gives me an opportunity to use whatever intellectual abilities I have to extend and that's the advantage of my career, that the challenges are greater than one's own gifts.	[I find the job] frustrating, there's not enough to do, it's very repetitious. . . . it's not challenging.
The teaching, the contact with students, not as much transmitting information but encouraging them in a particular area – to arouse their interest in a particular area – I think that's one of the most important things I can do. I enjoy the fact that in the position I'm in, I'm continuously learning new things, I have to keep up with current developments which is very exciting, so that is very challenging. It's continuous stimulation. I have to keep on my toes all the time because the way things are developing and changing you can't relax with your current knowledge, you have to keep up, and I think it is very stimulating and I enjoy it.	When I started work here I worked on the line – I didn't like that at all. I had to hand-pack and wrap all day long. Now I've moved up – there's a panel I have to watch – it keeps control of time and temperature – I have to keep the line moving.
Developing curriculum and seeing it successful. Motivating faculty. Having the budget come out right, which I work on all the time . . . recruiting people who work out well. Seeing success in the department that I'm very closely responsible for. Initiating and carrying through is very satisfying.	In my job now I'm supposed to make initial decisions within the scope of what I'm responsible for, but my personnel manager has the prerogative to overrule me and he makes arbitrary decisions and that angers me. The inequity [of the job] really gets in the way of that [i.e., flow] occurring. I have a standard of performance that I don't believe he shares; his ignorance is demonstrated constantly.

Table 7.3. (*cont.*)

Professional women: flow	Blue-collar women: antiflow
Yes [I experience this], even in my everyday activities. When we're working on a show. And it would be working with a student who is excited about what he's doing. And also working on my own, a project of my own within the shop. Sometimes I take some of my more difficult costumes and work on them myself, anything that involves tailoring, which is one of my main loves. I can get very involved in that and I find it interesting.	No stimulation, little new to do. Supervisory staff not willing to deal with people at the bottom – they don't work with us but against us. There's a lot of conflict. Supervisors will come and question everything – they'll tell me I'm doing something wrong when I know it's right.
	The thing that bothers me is that it really doesn't matter how you do on your job, you can do anything you want, it's frustrating – you care about how you do your job but your supervisors don't really reward you. There are those that work and those that never do anything – they treat us all the same.
	When you feel like you're always being watched.

will not open up frontiers of science and will not be of interest to my colleagues . . . and I feel, "Oh, I've started it," but now I find I'm not interested in it and yet I must continue.

I usually feel these kinds of feelings when a lecture's coming up that I need to prepare for that I've given many times before, but I feel obligated to sit down and go over my lecture notes. It's very difficult to look at them. Except the control is not necessarily from outside, but right there. It's just boring.

Well, usually I'm just rewriting something I've already written. . . . I mean I feel like I'm putting a tremendous amount of energy into something that may or may not net me anything at all. I just spent the entire month of September working on a grant proposal. It had already been rejected but it was recommended for revision. . . . Once I get into the actual writing up of the description, I enjoy it. I get into the process of it. But the details, the nitty-gritty details, making sure the budget is right, I find those terrible, I have to push myself to do them. Another thing, looking up references . . . wandering around the library, xeroxing things, collecting articles, following up references, I have to force myself to do that.

In general, these statements indicate that there are moments when the sense of antiflow is strong; during these moments professional women feel tedium and a lack of control. However, most respondents claim that these experiences are the exception and are far outweighed by intense enjoyment and satisfaction. Boredom caused by a lack of things to do never occurred. Rather, what boredom did exist was instead a function of the nature of the task itself. One university woman summarized the feelings experienced by many of the professional women when she stated, "[in this career] one is freed from boredom, but one is rarely freed from worry."

Strategies for dealing with antiflow

Perhaps one of the most unexpected findings of this study was the ways in which both professional and blue-collar women developed strategies to deal with antiflow. With regard to their frustration, the blue-collar women commented:

I talk to myself a lot, I try to use the power of positive thinking. I will talk to myself and feel lucky to have a daughter, a house.

Sometimes I get depressed, there are lots of financial worries, and work and I'm by myself [i.e., divorced with a daughter] and there are only so many hours in a day – you have to cultivate a sense of humor and be flexible – I won't stay up 'til midnight to vacuum.

[on the job] I sorta go into myself, it's like a shell. . . . I gotta do it to keep my sanity, I have to force myself to think about something else, anything I have to sort of turn into myself, and I can pretty much do that by talking to myself – I have to really watch my nerves so I tell myself to cool it and forget about 'em – I get so upset and mad – I stop and get myself not to worry.

Some women can keep control in all different divisions at work – with those above her and people she works with. There's one woman at work that does this all the time. She's like a friendly tyrant – she does her work and nobody hassles her. The supervisors leave her alone – she maintains a gentle control over everything – she has her own territory.

In a similar fashion, the professional women indicated that they developed techniques and strategies to help minimize antiflow experiences at work:

Well, in the course of scientific work, many of the technical aspects are very boring, and it is hard to do them because of the boredom, but the way one gets through it is by thinking of the problem that one is seeking to solve, so that all the time you're doing this tedious work, you think of possible answers that your work may yield.

I used to experience it [i.e., antiflow] more than I do now. I've decided I don't like it, and I'm not going to do it. There are times when somebody higher on the ladder will have me doing things that I really would rather spend my time doing something else. . . . I did it once because I had foolishly committed myself, and now will just not let it happen again.

Every job has some tedium, but it depends on what percent it is, if it's bigger than you can handle or rationalize out of or whatever, then I think it's a shame that a person can't move on. And I have moved on. It's your own life – you should do something about it. I guess I'm a realist, a pragmatist – do something about it. I guess that's unfair to say, because some people can't do anything about it.

It appears, then, that both groups of women develop strategies to deal with the frustrations of the work experience. These strategies are similar to what Csikszentmihalyi (1975b) terms cognitive restructuring, and serve to at least minimize the degree of antiflow experienced.

Flow and antiflow in nonwork settings

Whereas the work setting elicited very different reactions from professional and blue-collar women, the nonwork setting (home, family, leisure) elicited many similar emotions and experiences for both groups. In general, flow was experienced in two situations: (1) interpersonal relationships, and (2) sports and creative activities. The major source of antiflow derived from household chores.

Flow in the nonwork setting. Tables 7.4 and 7.5 indicate that the flow experiences of both groups of women revolve around leisure activities.

Table 7.4. *Sources of flow: interpersonal domain*

Professional women	Blue-collar women
Oh yes, when I'm working with my daughter; when she's discovering something new. A new cookie recipe that she has accomplished, that she has made herself, and artistic work that she has done that she's proud of. Her reading is one thing that she's really into, and we read together. She reads to me, and I read to her, and that's a time when I sort of lose touch with the rest of the world, I'm totally absorbed in what I'm doing.	With my daughter, seeing her happiness, seeing her fascination with a toy, putting a puzzle piece in upside down and watching her work with it. Playing with my children.
I try to involve my children in my work, especially my older daughter who's been coming down here and working with me. There are frequently times when we're home or driving around and talk about my work or something like that ... sort of a sense of joy and accomplishment in what I'm doing and able to bring them into it also.	Go shopping with neighbors ... also visiting my friends and family.
Friendships, very close friendships, very very important to share things with. To me, life wouldn't work well without that.	We're church members and we're pretty much involved ... we get home, dash around and do household chores, then go out and get other things done.

The most frequently elicited responses dealt with the interpersonal domain, where family, particularly children, were the focus of attention (Table 7.4).

Both professional and blue-collar women placed tremendous importance on relationships with their children. And although both groups were very protective of their family time, there was some frustration that more time for the children was not available. As one person indicated:

> It's a physical challenge to maintain a home, and I want to spend as much time as I can [with my daughter] but there are other demands. . . . Every working mother probably has some guilty feelings because they have to spend time away from the kids.

Table 7.5. *Sources of flow: sport/creative activities*

Professional women	Blue-collar women
I generally feel the feeling [flow] when I'm trying to do something I haven't done before, which would for me for the most part be in sports. I'm trying something new – just learning – more or less the "ah ha" experience, that same type of feeling when you first realize you can score a point against someone else in racquetball . . . but it's usually attached to my work or some type of goal-oriented activity such as sports where you can see something happen.	Traveling . . . we love to travel . . . we can go when we want, where we want, and do what we want.
	I feel like that when I'm crocheting or doing ceramics. At home it's relaxing even though I have kids. Like when you have kids you have to learn to sort of turn your mind off every now and then. I go into my own little world – sometimes they have to say something to me three or four times before I come out of it.
[When] I play golf, going to a good concert, I like feeling uplifted. . . . Reading an exciting novel. . . . I have a dog I just love. I play with him a lot, they don't demand anything, they give it all, and you've got it all right there.	Doing something physical around the house, like putting up curtain rods, and knowing I had to fix it – I had to completely reset the whole rod, and it really felt good when I did it!
Reading a book. My mother used to get very angry with me because I'd be away, I'd go outside myself, as it were, when I'd read a book. It would happen a lot because I love to read so much.	Sewing, making afghans and quilts. . . . I do this for about four hours a day.
	My biggest treat is to sit and drink a glass of sherry . . . and watch old movies . . . and work on my needlework.

This frustration appeared particularly marked among respondents who had divorced and were single heads of the household.

The second major area in which these working women experienced the most intense flow was in sport and other creative activities (Table 7.5). In general, then, both groups of women participated in a range of leisure activities, which included sports and creative experiences.

Despite these similarities, several distinctions emerged between the two groups. Perhaps the largest difference was the degree of control perceived to be important within the home environment. Blue-collar women expressed great satisfaction with the sense of control they felt in the home. The following quotations are indicative:

When dinner is ready on time, and the house is clean – the routine is nice to have in family life, to have play time in the tub, play time at the table – it gives you a rootedness, a routine.

[I enjoy it] when everything goes smooth, and when I get home it's pretty well set up, things click, they work.

I like to organize things and set a schedule, just get things done.

[At home] I know what I'm doing, same thing I've done for years. . . . I've got a routine. When I had little kids it was different, I had to feed 'em, dress 'em, stuff like that . . . now it's a little easier.

Such a pattern might reflect these women's needs to compensate (Wilensky 1960) for lack of control on the job. This type of response was not evident among the professional women. Household routines served to minimize antiflow rather than to establish mastery and control. One professional woman offered:

I don't do that much housework and I don't consider it beneath my abilities, some things just need to be done. . . . I feel it's tedious and boring but it has to be done. I do it if I have more time, and if I don't have enough time, my husband will do it. And if we plan efficiently, we get somebody else to do it, so it's not much of an issue.

A second distinction was that the professional women frequently would begin talking of their home life and continually revert to discussions about their jobs, or would link their work with their home life. The blue-collar women, on the other hand, made a clear distinction between the two environments and only referred to work in regard to ways it would inhibit their enjoyment at home (e.g., time, fatigue, aggravation, lack of money).

I don't let my work interfere with my home . . . they're separate, and I keep 'em that way.

I'm on my feet from 6 [A.M.] to 3 [P.M.] every day and when I get home I'm too tired to do anything.

In general, then, blue-collar women segment the work and nonwork spheres more than professional women. This pattern is not only understandable given the blue-collar women's reaction to work, but is also consistent with past research on work–leisure patterns among men (Kabanoff 1980; Kabanoff & Obrien 1982).

A final point that applies to both groups is that home does not elicit the intensity of feelings, either positive or negative, elicited by the work environment. In fact, most of the flow experiences at home reflect more what Csikszentmihalyi (1975b, p. 141) terms *microflow*, or those "trivial" everyday experiences that give structure and meaning to daily life.

> We all engage in small, almost automatic behavior patterns which are not extrinsically rewarded yet appear to have a necessary function. These patterns include idiosyncratic movements, daydreaming, smoking, talking to people without an expressed purpose, or more clearly defined activities like listening to music, watching television, or reading a book. (Csikszentmihalyi 1975b)

Antiflow in nonwork settings. One final similarity between professional and blue-collar women was that household chores were the most consistent source of antiflow in the home. The examples offered were specific and concrete, and although there was a sense of satisfaction when the chores were done, the activities themselves were very much disliked (Table 7.6).

Both groups attempted to minimize the dissatisfaction with the activities by creating a sense of routine. And like the intricate strategies developed by the blue-collar women to decrease antiflow at work, here we find the professional women developing strategies to deal with the antiflow at home. The ultimate strategy, mentioned by several of the professional women, was to hire a housekeeper to help with the household chores, an avenue not financially feasible for the blue-collar women.

Sources of flow

Professional women claim to experience their greatest sense of flow at work, whereas blue-collar women experience flow predominantly at home and in leisure. Several characteristics present in both settings seemed to elicit the flow experience.

First, both groups felt a sense of mastery and control whenever they experienced flow, regardless of the environment. The professionals constantly commented on the degree of mental challenge, creativity, and discipline their jobs required. They utilized *process* descriptors such as "thinking, reading, solving, writing," and focused not so much on the activity itself as on the creative mental processes that must be utilized during the activity.

In a similar fashion, blue-collar women experienced their greatest sense of mastery and control at home and in leisure. They talked about the home as "their castle," an environment wherein they established

Table 7.6. *Antiflow in the nonwork setting*

Professional women	Blue-collar women
Doing dishes, I feel compelled to do them . . . or other household chores like raking leaves.	Washing, housekeeping. Cleaning the house.
I go out of my way to avoid situations like this [antiflow]. Certain kinds of routine things . . . like shopping . . . so I try to make it interesting by only going to stores that have the best vegetables and thinking about what I'm going to eat and picking the vegetables out very carefully. But I still get bored, very bored, because I know I have to do it every week . . . or I'll end up with nothing to eat on Monday and Tuesday. I have a routine every Saturday morning when I get up, I go to the store first thing and get it over with.	Every time I stand at the ironing board and I think of the things I'd rather be doing. Housework.
Yard work . . . I try to make it interesting. I try to decide okay, this is Sunday and I'm going to work in the yard. So I get up early and go out there and I try to figure out what would make it look better. It's generally several months since I did anything . . . my husband cuts the lawn once a week and I sort of every once in a while go out and trim the roses and stuff like that. Housework I hate to the point where I just have someone else do it for me.	Sometimes, when Andy [son] is being a monster. Keeping up with housework. When all I ever do is wash dishes.

control, routine, and a sense of "rootedness." Although discrete household maintenance chores were not particularly enjoyed, there was great satisfaction in knowing that once those tasks were completed, all was in order.

And not unlike the professionals, the blue-collar women experienced a strong sense of flow in some leisure activities. These ranged from quietly "sipping a glass of sherry" at the end of the day, to more active leisure like gardening and traveling. As one blue-collar woman indicated, "We decide when and where we're going to do things." Thus, consistent with the work of Csikszentmihalyi (1975b), the sense of control of one's activities emerges as an important criterion for the flow experience.

A second characteristic, closely related to the previous one, is that a sense of autonomy and freedom was important in eliciting the flow state. Essentially, women enjoyed activities in which they were able to match the opportunities for action in the environment – or challenges – with their personal skills. Both professional and blue-collar women experienced flow in settings in which they were relatively free to determine daily priorities, the type and nature of tasks or activities to be accomplished, and the degree of effort to be put into the task at any given time. For example, the university structure provided the professional women with a relatively open system (a high degree of autonomy and much freedom to structure one's day as one chooses). Although the factory provided a rigid and closed occupational structure, the blue-collar women were able to experience this sense of autonomy in their home and leisure environments. Consistent with past research, this latter finding suggests that blue-collar women may establish a home–work distinction similar to that found for male workers (Kabanoff 1980; Kabanoff & Obrien 1982).

A third shared characteristic of flow for both groups of women was that although it was often experienced alone, it could also be experienced in interaction with others. Several of the university women, for example, commented on the tremendous sense of enjoyment they experienced through work with their students. In a similar fashion, both groups discussed their enjoyment as they watched their children play, or as they read and played with their children. Thus, flow did not need to be a completely individual activity but could be elicited in interaction with others.

The experience of flow, then, seems to involve similar conditions, but very different contexts, for the professional and blue-collar women. This is not to say that the professional women only experienced flow at work and not at home, or that the blue-collar women never experienced flow at work. But both the frequency and the intensity of feelings were triggered in very different domains for the two groups. In contrast to the greatly different settings that produced flow for the two groups, an analysis of those settings revealed many shared characteristics, including the importance of mastery and control, autonomy, and the potential role of other people in eliciting the flow state.

Sources of antiflow

The settings that elicited a sense of antiflow among both professional and blue-collar women were tasks that were tedious, simplistic, and repetitive. These types of tasks led to both frustration and boredom. The professional women, for example, cited cases in the work setting that were boring (e.g., rewriting papers, preparing grant budgets). In the home setting, household chores such as washing dishes, shopping for groceries, were not at all liked. In fact, several of the professional women hired help to keep the maintenance chores going.

Perhaps the most poignant aspect of this study was the tremendous boredom experienced by the blue-collar women at work. The factory workers bemoaned how difficult it was to stand at the assembly line day after day "packing and wrapping, packing and wrapping." Service workers discussed their frustration because their simplistic tasks left them with nothing to do once they were completed. Several said they would be much happier if they were given more work to do with greater responsibility. Boredom was their greatest enemy.

A second source of antiflow for the blue-collar workers was the type of interaction they had with supervisors. Not only were supervisors seen as overbearing and lacking in job competence, but also as erratic and unfair in their decision making. These perceptions heightened the feeling of lack of control and thus increased the sense of antiflow experienced by these women.

What is clear from both characteristics described above is that antiflow appears in situations in which challenge and control are lacking. On the job, workers felt that they were challenged very little and that their skills were used ineffectively by the organization. In the relationship between workers and supervisors the former felt little control over their evaluations and recognition. Thus, each situation brought forth very intense feelings of antiflow.

One might ask why these blue-collar women did not change jobs or move to another community. Although the answer to such a question is quite complex, their interviews suggested some reasons. First, several were divorced single heads of households with young children. Many felt fortunate to have a job at all. Quitting a job and moving a family could create more problems than it would solve from their perspective. A second reason might be that many had family (e.g., parents, siblings) within the community. Family served not only as a recreational outlet (e.g., visiting), but also as an important source of both moral and perhaps financial support. And finally, as several of these women indicated, they really did not have training to move into other jobs. Thus, they felt a sense of frustration and lack of freedom within the work opportunity structure in general.

Coping strategies

One of the most surprising outcomes of this study was the identification of the elaborate strategies developed to decrease or at least inhibit the antiflow experience. Many instances of cognitive restructuring were found among both blue-collar and professional women. Respondents described mental games they played with themselves in order to decrease feelings of antiflow: "turning inside myself," "thinking about how lucky I am to have a job," "making a game out of it (e.g., shopping)." This type of cognitive restructuring appears to be an effective short-term response to antiflow situations. In the case of blue-collar women, however, it appears that a complete restructuring of the job would be essential to decrease the sense of alienation they feel in the work environment.

Conclusions

Working women basically derive the same psychological rewards from interacting with their environment that working men do. They feel a strong sense of enjoyment when they can match their skills with opportunities for action, when they can control their decisions, when they can focus their attention on clear goals that produce consistent feedback. For women who are fortunate to have professional jobs, the work setting provides ample opportunities for such psychic rewards. But jobs that reduce human performance to simple mechanical routines produce the opposite state of mind: a sense of numbing boredom, of a senseless waste of one's life.

All women reported intense flow experiences when interacting with other people, and especially with their own children. The developing skills of children present a constantly increasing, yet manageable, set of challenges to these women; whenever a child does something new, it is interpreted in part as positive feedback to the mother. Similarly, creative, active leisure provided enjoyment to both groups of women. Blue-collar women compensated for the lack of control on their jobs by structuring household routines in orderly, predictable ways. For all women, the more repetitive household tasks were occasions for antiflow, and stimulated ingenious attempts at cognitive restructuring.

These results support Kabanoff (1980) and Kabanoff and Obrien (1982), who suggest occupational differences in the degree of compartmentalization between work and leisure. Kabanoff and Obrien (1982) found that occupational groups differed in what task attributes (i.e., influence, variety, pressure, skill utilization, interaction) they satisfied through work and leisure. It would be particularly interesting to understand the motivations behind the processes of compensation and generalization that past researchers have identified. It might be, for example, that blue-collar men and women separate their work and home lives because their jobs allow so little enjoyment. The relationship between work and non-work for professional men and women, however, might be quite different. Whereas professional men may focus more narrowly on work commitments, their female counterparts (especially those with children) must maintain the multiple role responsibilities encompassed in career, home maintenance, and child care (Oakley 1980; Simpson & Mutran 1981). If this is true, one would expect women who find a strong sense of enjoyment and commitment to their careers, and yet maintain multiple and integrated roles in home and leisure environments, to compartmentalize less.

The rich information shared by the respondents in this study reveals the complexity of human experience and the challenge they pose for understanding enjoyment and its antithesis. There is a need to move beyond the strictly quantitative assessment of constructs such as leisure satisfaction, leisure attitudes, and leisure motivation and to begin to unravel what they mean to various categories of people through more careful qualitative analyses. These constructs and their measurement have served the leisure field well and have been extremely valuable in providing parameters and subscales for a multitude of dimensions. However, future studies, both qualitative and quantitative, must bring us to a better understanding of the meanings that work and leisure have in the daily lives of all individuals.

8. The relationship between life satisfaction and flow in elderly Korean immigrants

SEONGYEUL HAN

What makes for successful aging has been one of the main concerns of psychological and social gerontology since Havighurst's pioneering work over 30 years ago (Havighurst & Albrecht 1953). Since then, many studies have tried to assess qualitative differences in patterns of aging and to find variables related to successful aging (Larson 1978).

Such concepts as life satisfaction, morale, and adjustment have been widely used to measure success in the later years of life. Even though these concepts are different from each other in content and major focus, it is assumed that they refer to the same underlying construct. Lohman (1977), for instance, found that there is a high level of correlation among widely used measures of life satisfaction, morale, and adjustment.

As Neugarten, Havighurst, and Tobin (1961) suggested, life satisfaction is not a unidimensional concept. In their original formulation of the Life Satisfaction Index, five distinct components of life satisfaction were identified: zest vs. apathy; resolution and fortitude; congruence between desired and achieved goals; positive self-concepts; and positive mood tone. This multidimensionality has been confirmed by Adams (1969), who factor-analyzed responses to the Life Satisfaction Index A (LSIA). Knapp (1976) obtained the same results, concluding that the Life Satisfaction Index should be treated as a multidimensional measure. Using this multidimensional framework, Hoyt, Karser, Perters, and Babchuck (1980) found that some dimensions show a better fit than others between life satisfaction and social activity.

The primary purpose of this study was to investigate the relationship between life satisfaction in old age and the flow experience. There is increasing evidence that flow is generally experienced as an optimal

The author wishes to acknowledge the financial help of the Robert Kahn Memorial Fund with this research.

state of consciousness. But less is known about whether the positive relationship lasts over time. Hence the question: Do older people who report more frequent flow experiences also report greater life satisfaction?

The subjects were newly immigrated Korean elderly people residing in Chicago. As Koh, Sakauye, Koh, and Murata (1981) have pointed out, these people are characterized by their intragroup similarities in language, historical and cultural experiences, and especially, by their infrequent exposure to Americans and American culture before immigration. Because life satisfaction is influenced by such variables as subjectively perceived health status, education, and socioeconomic status (Edwards & Klemmack 1973), the influence of these factors was also taken into account in this study.

Method

The respondents were 16 male and 20 female newly immigrated Koreans over 60 years of age residing in the Chicago area. These respondents were selected randomly from the large sample of a study that had investigated the acculturation process of the newly immigrated Asian elderly.

The mean age of the sample was 66.7 years, with a range of 60 to 79 years. On the average, each respondent went through 8½ years of formal schooling. The mean years of residence in the United States was 4.3 years. Fifteen out of 16 men and 10 out of 20 women were married.

The social background of the respondents was basically middle class. In Korea, most of the men had owned small businesses ($N = 6$), or worked as white-collar employees ($N = 6$). Most of the women ($N = 13$) had been housewives, the rest had been employed in business. The respondents were interviewed either at the investigator's office or in their home.

Measuring the frequency of the flow experience. To measure the frequency of flow, respondents were read three quotations describing the flow experience. Afterward, they were asked if they had ever had a similar experience, and if yes, what activities were they engaged in when they had such an experience. The three quotations were originally devised by Csikszentmihalyi (1975b, 1982a, 1985a), and they were translated into Korean for this study by the author. These quotations are as follows:

    1. My mind isn't wandering. I am not thinking of something else.

I am totally involved in what I am doing. My body feels good. I don't seem to hear anything. The world seems to be cut off from me. I am less aware of myself and my problems.

2. My concentration is like breathing. I never think of it. I am really quite oblivious to my surroundings after I really get going. I think that the phone could ring, and the doorbell could ring, or the house burn down or something like that. When I start, I really do shut out the whole world. Once I stop, I can let it back in again.

3. I am so involved in what I am doing. I don't see myself as separate from what I am doing.

Respondents who said they never experienced any of the examples received a score of 0. A maximum score of 3 was given to respondents who identified their experiences with all three quotations.

Measurement of life satisfaction. Life satisfaction was measured by the Life Satisfaction Index B (LSIB, Neugarten et al. 1961).

Measurement of subjectively perceived health status. Perceived health status was measured by adopting one item from the Duke Older American Resources and Services (OARS) Multidimensional Functional Assessment Questionnaire (Pfeiffer 1976), which was originally devised to assess the elderly's function at the social, economic, and mental and physical health level; and other demographic background information. The item used is "How would you rate your overall health at the present time, excellent, good, fair, or poor?". Answers were coded on the 0- to 3-point scale (0 = poor, 1 = fair, 2 = good, 3 = excellent).

Measurement of economic status. Economic status could not be measured directly by actual amount of income, because all but one subject had no other source of income except family or government support. Most subjects are financially supported by their grown-up children, and the difference in actual income is relatively slight. Therefore in this study subjectively perceived economic status was measured. The item used for this purpose was "How well does the amount of money you have take care of your needs: very well, fairly well, or poorly?". Answers were coded on the 0- to 2-point scale (0 = poorly, 1 = fairly well, 2 = very well).

Results

Types of flow activities. Although all respondents agreed that there could be such an experience as flow, only 12 (33%, six men and six women) recognized at least one quotation as being similar to an experience they had had.

Csikszentmihalyi's previous research with adult American workers (Csikszentmihalyi 1985a) yields a much higher figure (86.7%). The more than double frequency of reports by the U. S. sample suggests either age or cross-cultural differences. The Korean elderly had a tendency to interpret these quotations in their literal sense. For example, some said that they sometimes had a flowlike experience but not so deep as to ignore the house burning or a ringing telephone.

Table 8.1 shows the activities in which flow experiences were reported to occur, and the number of persons experiencing flow in each activity. Fifteen different activities were reported. They fall into three large categories: productive activities such as work and housework; leisure; and religious-educational activities. The main difference between the sexes appears to be that men find flow relatively more often in leisure pursuits such as playing *go*, playing a musical instrument, or photography; while women experience it more often in the context of what might be thought of as household obligations such as cooking, sewing, or taking care of grandchildren. Men and women associated flow with religious activities equally often. Only two activities, working and meditation, were common to both males and females, indicating a strong gender differentiation in the types of activities that produce flow.

Of the 31 total reports, 61% were in response to quotation 1, 10% to quotation 2, and 29% to quotation 3. One reason for this difference might be the subjects' tendency to interpret quotations in their literal sense. Because quotation 2 contains the more extreme analogy of the house burning, it was rarely endorsed.

Another way to classify the activities mentioned as producing flow is to recode them in terms of five categories used in previous studies (Csikszentmihalyi & Graef 1979). If this is done, 59% of the total activities are classified in the hobbies and home activities category, 13% in outside work activities, and 13% in the passive attending activities category. No sports and outdoor activities were reported by the Korean sample. It is quite interesting to compare these results (Figure 8.1) with previous

Table 8.1. *Activities mentioned by Korean elderly as being most similar to flow*

			Type of activity			
	Productive	Number	Leisure	Number	Religious/educational	Number
Men (N = 16)	Working	2	Playing *go*	3	Meditation	2
	Planning	1	Playing music	3	Studying	1
			Photography	3		
Women (N = 20)	Cooking	3	Painting	2	Meditation	2
	Sewing	2	Calligraphy	2	Bible	1
	Working	1			Sermons	1
	Handicrafts	1				
	Grandchildren	1				

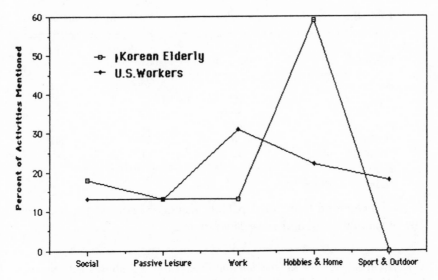

Figure 8.1. Types of flow activities mentioned by Korean elderly and by
U. S. adults.

research with American workers (Csikszentmihalyi & Graef 1979; Csikszentmihalyi 1985a).

As shown in Figure 8.1, work is the most important source of flow
experience for U.S. workers, followed by hobbies and home activities,
and sports and outdoor activities. For the elderly Koreans in this study,
the importance of work and hobbies is reversed. This difference is easy
to understand. All the respondents in this study are retired; in addition,
they may be too weak physically to enjoy sports and outdoor activities.
Accordingly, hobbies and home activities become relatively important
sources of the flow experience for them. Generalizing from this result,
we can suggest that having hobbies and home activities with which they
can be deeply involved is very important for older people.

Of the total 15 flow-producing activities, only 2 – work and meditation
– are shared by both male and female subjects. These results show that
men and women get flow experiences from different activities. This
might be due to the strict division of gender roles in traditional Korean
culture.

Of the 12 subjects who reported flow experiences, 3 (2 males and 1
female) said that their ability to have flow has increased with age: They
can now concentrate more deeply on what they are doing because they
are doing fewer of the things that broke up their concentration before,
and because of more free time. On the contrary, 2 subjects (1 male and

Table 8.2. *Correlations of six demographic variables to life satisfaction*

Variables	Male (N = 16)	Female (N = 20)	Total (N = 36)
Flow	.22	.59**	.44**
Age	−.02	−.13	−.07
Education	.39	.45*	.39*
Residence	−.01	.41	.21
Health	.28	.49*	.41*
Economic status	.18	.21	.29

Note: * = $p < .05$; ** = $p < .01$.

1 female) reported that this capability has been reduced because they feel physically weak and are easily fatigued.

Correlation between life satisfaction and flow. Table 8.2 shows that there is a significant relationship between life satisfaction and frequency of the flow experience ($r = .44$, $p<.01$). However, this finding is mostly due to the female respondents. Although the relationship is positive for males, it does not reach significance. We can see also that there are significant positive relationships between life satisfaction and education ($r = .39$, $p<.05$), and subjectively perceived health status ($r = .41$, $p<.05$). Again, these relationships are stronger for females than for males. There are no significant relationships between life satisfaction and age, years of residence in the United States, or economic status.

To see the relationship between life satisfaction and marital status, a *t* test was performed for the women only, because only one man was not married. The results show no significant difference on life satisfaction between the two groups.

Because males and females clearly differed in the strengths of the relationships between the variables, *t* tests were performed on each variable to see the sex difference more clearly. Even though there are positive relationships between life satisfaction and flow experience, education, and subjectively perceived health status for women but not for men, there are no significant differences in these variables between the two sexes.

Since frequency of flow, education, and health status are all significantly related to life satisfaction, first- and second-order partial correlations were computed to see the relationships between life satisfaction and flow experience more clearly. In the first-order partial correlation,

Table 8.3. *First- and second-order partial correlations between life satisfaction and flow experience*

	First order (education)	First order (health)	Second order (education, health)
Total	.33*	.37*	.30
Female	.55*	.47*	.45*

Note: Variables in parentheses were controlled. * = $p < .05$.

education and health status were controlled for separately, and in the second-order partial correlation, these two variables were controlled for simultaneously. Partial correlations were carried out for the total group and for women only, because there was no significant relationship between life satisfaction and flow for men. Table 8.3 shows the results.

As shown in Table 8.3, for women there is a significant positive relationship between life satisfaction and flow even when either education or health status is controlled for ($r = .55$, $p<.05$; $r = .47$, $p<.05$, respectively). This relationship is still significant when education and health status are controlled for simultaneously ($r = .45$, $p<.05$). For respondents as a whole, the relationship between life satisfaction and flow frequency is significant when either education or health status is controlled for ($r = .33$, $p<.05$; $r = .37$, $p<.05$, respectively), but the relationship disappears when both variables are simultaneously controlled for.

To analyze more specifically which dimensions of life satisfaction are related to flow, differences in each item of LSIB were examined by *t* test, between those respondents who reported flow and those who did not.

For the group as a whole, 11 of the 12 items differed in the expected direction. There were significant differences on items 1, 4, and 10. These items are: "What are the best things about being the age you are now?" "How happy would you say you are right now, compared with the earlier periods in your life?" and "How much unhappiness would you say you find in your life today?" respectively. Those who experience flow answered more positively than those who do not on items 1 and 4, and more negatively on item 10. For women, all of the items differed in the expected direction. There were significant differences on items 4, 7, and 10. Item 7 is, "How often do you find yourself feeling lonely?" Women who had flow experiences answered that they felt lonely less frequently than those who had none. For men, none of the life satis-

Table 8.4. *Correlations between five demographic variables and frequency of the flow experience*

Variable	Male	Female	Total
Age	−.01	.32	.18
Education	.51*	.26	.41*
Residence	−.02	.53*	.23
Health	.09	.45*	.29
Economic status	−.06	.46	.05

Note: * = $p < .05$.

faction items differentiated between those who do and those who do not report flow.

Table 8.2 indicated that at least for females, life satisfaction relates significantly to some of the demographic variables. Correlation analysis was used to see whether these demographic variables also relate significantly to the frequency of reported flow experience.

Table 8.4 shows that education is significantly related to reported frequency of flow ($r = .41$, $p < .05$). But this significance applies to male subjects only ($r = .51$, $p < .05$); for women, there is no significant relationship between flow experience and education. For females it is length of residence in the United States and health status that are significantly related to frequency of flow ($r = .53$, $p < .05$; $r = .45$, $p < .05$, respectively).

Discussion

The primary aim of this study was to investigate the relationship between life satisfaction and the flow experience. Neugarten and her colleagues (1961) identified five distinct dimensions of life satisfaction: zest vs. apathy, resolution and fortitude, congruence between desired and achieved goals, positive self-concept, and positive mood tone.

Csikszentmihalyi (1975b) argued that the affective outcome of the flow experience is enjoyment. Those who have it should feel better about themselves, feel more in control of their worlds, and be less dependent on extrinsic supports.

After considering each dimension of life satisfaction and the affective results of flow, we can suggest that there should be a significant relationship between life satisfaction and frequency of the flow experience. This expectation is confirmed by this study. The two variables are significantly related. Even when either of two moderating variables – education and health status – is partialled out, there is still a significant relationship between life satisfaction and flow. When education and health status, which are significantly related to life satisfaction, were controlled for simultaneously, however, this relationship between life satisfaction and the flow experience was no longer statistically significant. But the still high level of correlation between life satisfaction and flow experiences when education and health status were controlled for ($r = .30$, $p < .08$) suggests that the relationship would be significant with a larger sample. For women, the flow experience had a significant correlation with life satisfaction even when education and health status were controlled for simultaneously.

The study also indicates that there is a strong sex difference in the relationships between life satisfaction and other variables, including frequency of the flow experience. For men, none of the variables related significantly to life satisfaction. For women, three variables (flow, education, and health status) were significantly related to life satisfaction. Women appear to be more sensitive to the affective outcome of flow than men. For men, none of the items in the life satisfaction scale is significantly different between those who experience flow and those who do not. For women, three items are significantly different between those who experience flow and those who do not. Women who experience flow have a more positive attitude toward being their age, feel more happy about their present life, and feel less lonely.

According to Neugarten et al. (1961), the mood tone dimension of life satisfaction differentiates people who express happy, optimistic attitudes and moods; who use spontaneous, positively toned affective terms; who take pleasure in life – from people who express depression and lonelines; who express feelings of bitterness, irritability, and anger.

All items that are significantly different between those who have flow experiences and those who do not in this study are part of this mood tone dimension of life satisfaction. Therefore we can infer that flow is more closely related to the mood tone dimension of life satisfaction than to its other dimensions.

Education was found to have a significant relationship to the frequency of flow. Other variables (age, years of residence in this country, health status, and economic status) did not. One reason for this significant relationship between the flow experience and education may be that some of the flow activities engaged in by the men – like photography, playing musical instruments, painting, calligraphy, listening to a lecture – are associated with a certain level of formal education in Korean culture.

For women, flow and education are not significantly related; instead, years of residence in the United States and health status are. The reason there is no significant relationship between flow and education for females may be that such activities as cooking, taking care of grandchildren, sewing, listening to a sermon, and reading the Bible do not necessarily need a high level of formal education.

The close relationship between length of residence in the United States and flow experiences for women may be due to specific family relationships. Seventy percent of the women lived with their grown-up children. During the day, when the grown-up children and their spouses go out to work, the older women usually take care of their small grandchildren. Accordingly, they have less free time to engage in their favorite activities than the men. The longer their residence becomes, the less their grandchildren need help. At that point they have more free time to engage in their favored activities. This argument becomes more plausible when it is seen that for women, age had a closer relationship to flow experiences ($r = .32$) than for men ($r = .01$) even though the difference is not statistically significant.

The reason that health status is significantly related to flow for women but not for men is not quite clear. It may be due to the women's different family situation, or to their different flow activities.

Finally, this study provides suggestions for further flow research. First, a life-span developmental perspective can be used to see the effect of age differences and age changes. For example, some subjects reported that their ability to have flow experiences was reduced because of physical weakness and rapid fatigue. Others, however, said that their ability and chances to experience flow have increased owing to more free time and a lessening of distracting obligations. Some reported no change. Therefore, it may be important to see what kinds of activities provide flow to different age groups, and to see the changes in the frequency of flow experienced from the same source as a function of aging.

Second, the three quotations used for measuring flow may need to be elaborated before they are applied to older people and to people with different cultural backgrounds. The contents of these quotations are so strong that if taken literally some subjects have difficulty admitting that they have experienced something similar. For example, some said that they sometimes feel deep involvement in what they are doing, but not so deep as to ignore a ringing doorbell or the house burning. It might be difficult for older people to be so totally involved in what they are doing. In this sense, it may be interesting to measure microflow activities and experiences (Csikszentmihalyi 1975b) and investigate their relationship to life satisfaction.

9. Flow and writing

REED LARSON

Activities that produce flow experiences are autotelic and intrinsically motivated; that is, people do them simply because they are enjoyable, even if no rewards follow. Thus flow activities are "useful" in that they provide a state of being that is an end in itself. But it seems that flow is useful in another sense. The negentropic state of consciousness that comes into being when the person is in tune with the environment is the most efficient condition of the organism. A person in flow should be able to function at his or her best. A worker should be at the peak of his or her productivity when the work is enjoyable. This is presumably even more true when that work involves creativity, because the spontaneous investment of psychic energy necessary for an original accomplishment is most likely to occur when the person enjoys what he or she is doing (Amabile 1983).

The task of this chapter is to examine how the writing of an original composition is affected by conditions of psychic order and disorder. The process of writing an English theme was investigated because it represents a creative challenge that everybody who has gone through high school is familiar with. The question is, to what extent do negative emotions such as anxiety or boredom interfere with the completion of such a task? To what extent is the experience of flow in writing related to its successful completion?

Emotions, according to Immanuel Kant, are "illnesses of the mind" ([1798] 1978, p. 155). They blind and derail rational thought and action. Indeed, the Latin and Greek origins of "emotion" and "passion" denote a condition of being moved by forces outside one's control (Averill 1980). Anger, fear, depression, even love are states in which a person's

An earlier version of this chapter was published in the volume *When a Writer Can't Write* (1985), edited by Mike Rose (New York: Guilford).

thoughts may be distorted and command over mental processes may be impaired.

What is the role of emotions in writing? The writer's task is to assimilate facts and ideas into some form of lucid and compelling order, to shape an intelligent organization of thought on the page. In analyzing a poem, discussing a field of knowledge, or developing a theory, it would seem that writers need to be in full command of their faculties. Processes of prewriting, problem solving, attending to audience, and editing presuppose an ability to exercise controlled and rational thought. Emotions, therefore, would seem inimical to successful writing.

Passion, however, is often valued in writing. Nietzsche counters Kant's statement: "Of all writings, I love only that which is written with blood" ([1885] 1964, p. 67). Emotions can bring a person to life. Rage, excitement, desire are motivating and can transform a mechanical text into engaging prose. Emotions, therefore, have an uncertain status in the writer's experiential world. They may disrupt as well as facilitate the creation of a valuable composition. In what follows we shall see how the thinking and writing of high school students is affected by various emotional conditions, as viewed in terms of the flow model of consciousness.

A research approach

Investigations of this topic began with two tactical decisions. First, I decided to work with people involved in major writing projects, projects that stretched over weeks, because emotional disruptions of intellectual work are magnified in major assignments (as often witnessed in the writing of master's theses and doctoral dissertations). Second, I decided to study adolescents, who according to previous research are more vulnerable to emotional fluctuations than other older age groups. Adolescents report experiencing higher highs and lower lows during their daily lives, and their emotions appear to shift more quickly than those of adults (Larson, Csikszentmihalyi, & Graef 1980; Csikszentmihalyi & Larson 1984). Indeed, emotional reactions to writing are extremely common in this age group (Daly & Miller 1975; Hogan 1980).

The high school students were working on a research paper for English classes, known in their school as the "junior theme." This paper is expected to incorporate library research and to be 6 to 10 pages long. Students are given 6 to 9 weeks to carry it out, and they receive feedback from teachers at several stages along the way. The subject matter is unspecified in most classes; hence students often choose topics that are personally engaging and less likely to be aversive.

Writing samples from students who experienced different emotional states while working on this assignment are presented, and how these states affected their final papers are discussed. These examples have been selected to demonstrate certain theoretical points; thus it should be understood that I am developing a hypothesis rather than attempting to prove one.

The cases to be discussed come from two studies. In one, students were interviewed at about the time that they were completing their papers (Larson & Csikszentmihalyi 1982). In the other, they filled out questionnaires on repeated occasions before, during, and after starting the assignment. For both studies, a colleague in the English Department of the University of Chicago evaluated the final papers, employing the same criteria he normally uses to evaluate student writing. Although he was aware of the general purpose of the study, he was unaware of the emotional experiences reported by the particular students. Thus the students' reports of how they felt while writing their papers could be compared with professional evaluations of the quality of their products.

For some students emotions were clearly disruptive, whereas for others emotions helped in the writing task. Before presenting these cases, I should mention that the two groups were approximately matched on several measures of cognitive performance. They were similar in verbal achievement tests scores, in grade-point averages, and in the amount of experience with large writing assignments. Hence the likelihood is reduced that differences between the two groups of students are due to cognitive variables. Rather, the differences are more related to the ways that these two groups experienced and responded to the emotional dimensions of the task.

First to be considered are the students who had disruptive emotional experiences. These experiences are divisible into those involving overarousal, with anxiety being the prototype, and those involving underarousal, with boredom being the prototype.

Overarousal: the anxiety scenario

Clinical picture. Overarousal takes many forms, from slight agitation to existential dread, from impatience with the assignment to contempt for what one has done. A person might be afraid of getting a bad grade or of not being able to transfer what was in his soul to the written page. Students in this condition become angry at the teacher, at the school, and at parents or friends who have nothing to do with the assignment. They describe being "flustered," "overwhelmed," "pissed off," and "scared." They report being plagued by inner voices that are critical of everything they write.

At the core of these different experiences is the state of anxiety. Nearly everyone in a sample of 90 students we studied described encountering some version of anxiety at least once while writing the junior theme (Larson, Hecker, & Norem 1985). It was generally episodic; however, for some it became endemic to the task. They could not sit down to work without experiencing apprehension, worry, and distress.

The first example is a girl, E. S., who did her paper on "how advertising influences the women's fashion industry." This girl was interested in becoming a fashion designer someday, so it was a pertinent topic. She had done a number of similar projects in the past and received As and Bs; hence, there was no particular reason for her to expect trouble. The information on her experience comes from questionnaires she filled out on eight different days before, during, and after her work.

Before beginning, she reported feeling slightly positive toward the assignment. She was somewhat enthusiastic and anticipated that her paper would be well organized and would say something meaningful. However, she was having a hard time making choices and narrowing her focus. She felt unsure of the topic and could not figure out how to combine the materials – she wanted to get all the information in. As a result, she began doubting her abilities, and a variety of other negative feelings cropped up in her experience: She felt confused, overwhelmed, and unable to find time to work on the paper.

As the deadline approached, E. S. began feeling so anxious that she was unable to concentrate. At the outlining stage there was a period of excitement; but when she started writing, she was overtaken by anxiety and was unable to focus her thoughts. She reported that she could not find the right words and was confused and extremely unhappy. Only at the last minute, under pressure of the deadline, was she able to pull something together; and when she turned it in, she had no idea whether her paper would deserve a B or C or A. The experience culminated in a state of emotional and cognitive disorder.

The second case, G. J., is an intelligent and articulate boy who did a paper on the architect Mies van der Rohe. At first he had been unenthused by his topic. But then an evening at the library raised his excitement. He said, "It was like a hot flash. I went through the card catalogue and got as many books as I could. They were all in front of me; I was going through them and was just eating them up." The problem was that this experience set up very high expectations for the paper. Thus, in subsequent work sessions, he was repeatedly dissatisfied with what he was accomplishing. Stubbornly determined to write a good paper, he would work until he "dropped," even though the sessions were becoming less and less productive. He appeared to have been unable to distance himself from the project and, as he reported, couldn't quite trust it to leave it alone: "I was really intense with it: I'd eat it, sleep it, and drink it." As a result, he went into a state of clinical depression – he described it as a "sickness" – which cast a pall over everything else he did during this period.

Both of these individuals wrestled with expectations for their papers that were greater than they could meet. The girl kept trying to push herself to "try harder," but this just didn't help; and the boy worked himself into a debilitating frenzy. These students lacked the skills to accomplish the grandiose papers they kept imagining, and they were unable to establish expectations for themselves that were consistent with what they could realistically do. Hence they became overwhelmed and lost control of their work; and the writing project turned into a nightmare of worry, frustration, and internal anger. How these internal states were manifested in the papers they ended up writing is examined next.

Effects of anxiety. Physiologically, anxiety is a state of extreme arousal, including increased adrenaline levels, rapid neural firing, increased heart rate, and greater muscle tension (Izard 1977). In small amounts these changes can aid a person's functioning, but beyond a certain point they become disruptive (Hunt 1965).

Cognitively, anxiety is associated with diffused and "disintegrated" attention. Research shows that anxiety reduces one's capacity to hold things in short-term memory, thus effectively reducing the amount of information one can juggle and think about simultaneously (Easterbrook 1959; Izard 1977). Fear, a state akin to anxiety, is often associated with blindness to anything other than the source of threat. States of anxiety, fear, and anger are also associated with impulsive behavior: People act without thinking; they are less able to discipline their actions and to contain sudden dispositions.

The students reported all of these symptoms when writing. Emotions

E.S.'s paper:
Why do people by certain styles of clothing? Why do you choose the style you do? Do you choose the style because you like it? Or is it because everyone else has it?

What affects your choice of style? Do you want to be different and stand out in the crowd? Or do you want the least amount attention as possible and just blend in? Most people purchase the certain style of clothes, because they want to conform with their favorite group or organization and also because an admired person wears that style, that makes a way of becoming more like him.

But what exactly influences the consumers to purchase the latest fashion styles and product?

G.J.'s paper:
Architectural styles in the past fifty years have changed greatly. They have gone from beauty and ornateness to stark and coldness, one of the reasons is an architect named Ludwig Mies van der Rohe. Mies came to America with a new architectural style and since then architecture hasn't been the same.

Between the years of 1893 and 1920, the architectural style in America was that like the architectural style that was in old Europe, it had some of Europes styles and ideas, but it was not exactly like it. To be specific before Ludwig Mies van der Rohe came to America, there seemed to be a great originality in the design of staircases, loggias, which are the arches that run along ceilings, and roofs.

The main reason that these styles differ from the styles of modern architecture, is ornateness. During this period right before modern architecture, the ornamentation was dictated by the style of the building because " . . . appropriate prototypes did not always exist . . . " A good example is for fireplaces, ceilings, and walls there were inventive adaptations of Greek, Egyptian, or Gothic motifs. While all of this was going on, American architecute was going thru a period of revival. This period of revival was happening in two ways, the first way was related to Gothic architecture, what is meant by that is that the structure built in this time resembled some of the Gothic structures in Europe. The second type of revival, which was more acedimac, was inspired by Italian Renaissance, French Renaissance, and Roman Style architecture. The first trend setters included works by Louis Sullivan and Frank Lloyd Wright.

Figure 9.1. Opening paragraphs of anxious students' papers.

interfered with concentration and weakened their control over thought processes. Anxious students reported wanting nothing more than for the whole thing to be over. The effects can be seen in the opening paragraphs of the two papers presented in Figure 9.1. (Although space

allows only the first paragraphs from each student's work to be presented, the patterns identified in these paragraphs are repeated throughout their papers.)

In our first case, E. S., the influence of anxiety is more than evident
in the opening of the paper. The English professor who served as our
expert critic had this to say about the girl's first three paragraphs:

> E. S. seems to understand perfectly well how her introduction
> should affect the reader: It should first establish a problem or ques-
> tion; it should then give the reader some sense of the specific
> concerns that the paper will address; and, at the end, it should
> establish the main topic that will control the organization of the
> essay. This introduction does all of these things, but in the crudest
> way imaginable. E. S. tries to create a question in the reader's mind
> by asking it directly. She announces subtopics by asking still more
> questions. And she establishes the controlling topic by giving away
> the whole point of the paper. The immaturity of this writing is
> evident in its impatient directness and in its aggressive approach
> to the reader's responses and to the material itself. This kind of
> aggressiveness toward the material is evident throughout.

She knew what she should do, and she had demonstrated an ability to
do it successfully in past papers (she had received As on two such
assignments), but in this case she lacked the internal calm to carry it out
with any subtlety. Lacking the concentration and patience to develop
an argument, she obsessively repeats the same point over and over again
as though she mistrusts her ability to reach the reader. About the paper
as a whole, the expert writes:

> The essay is completely out of control. E. S. has no command over
> her material and consistently shows signs that she is overwhelmed
> by the task at hand and that she cannot separate in her mind the
> material and her reactions to it. There is little indication in the body
> of the essay that E. S. has made reader-oriented decisions; and
> when she does consider the reader in the introduction, she man-
> ages only to grab him by the scruff of the neck and barrage him
> with questions.
>
> It's not that E. S. has nothing to say – she has done her homework
> and has all the pieces for an intelligent essay. It's more that she
> has too much to say. She has no sense of what the material in her
> essay comes to, no sense of the essay as a whole. She has not
> created the distance between herself and her research, between
> her role as writer and herself, or between the reader and herself.

Her fragmented internal state resulted in a fragmented attempt at communication. High expectations prevented her from getting a handle on the ideas and controlling the writing. The result is a diffused jumble of thoughts.

The boy writing on Mies van der Rohe, G. J., manifests his agitation in a similar way. His paper attempts to cover a broad span of material and relies on grand leaps in an attempt to pull things together. There is no clear focus. Furthermore, the paper is full of misspellings, poor grammar, and idiosyncratic metaphors. It is apparent that he became attached to certain wordings and images and was unaware that they had limited meaning to anyone else. This is what his high school teacher wrote about the paper:

> Your paper tackles far too much! Your topic is way too broad, and, as a result, you skip around your topic with no throughness focused on any major part of Mies's life. Much more care was needed, also, with sentences; run-ons are abundant. The whole theme ends with a fragment. Few words of any length are spelled correctly. Much greater care was needed here in the proofreading than you were willing to give.

What this teacher did not realize was just how much this student actually tried to make this a good paper. He put in much time and effort, but excitement and anxiety kept him from getting an objective view on the writing. His psychic energy was wasted in trying to order his feelings rather than his thoughts. He could not use attention effectively, and hence there were major lacunae in what he produced.

Anxiety is a state of overarousal that interferes with concentration and control of attention. Episodes of anxiety may be unavoidable, especially for young writers: It is inevitable for students to be overwhelmed sometimes, to set expectations too high or find themselves facing too many choices. Problems come when these situations – and the accompanying emotions – become inseparable from the assignment, when a student continually feels at odds with the work. Anxiety at best leads to impulsive and poorly controlled writing. At worst, it creates emotional and cognitive havoc that makes writing impossible. Now let us look at a very different emotional situation.

Underarousal: the boredom scenario

Clinical picture. Underarousal includes states of apathy, disinterest, depression, and particularly boredom. Its prime characteristic is lack of motivation. Students describe their work as "drudgery" or "a real drag." One boy related the feeling as follows: "You're always looking up at the clock, and it's only two minutes. Sometimes you picked a certain time when you want to go to bed; you wait and you look up and see time is sure going slowly, and you want to be done with it as soon as you can."

Boredom seemed to occur most often during the actual writing of the paper. Students felt that once they had finished their reading they were done with the exciting part and there was nothing new to be discovered. One student explained it this way:

> Writing it, that's a bore; because when I have all these notecards it's all there, but it's a job to put it down on paper. I know what I want to say, but having to put it into words was boring. I'm just kind of a robot repeating what other people say.

It is apparent that this student had little idea of opportunities for excitement in the writing process. Boredom occurs when there is no challenge in the task, when a student can see nothing in the work that is personally interesting or engaging.

Two cases of students who had persistent problems with boredom follow. The first, M. D., had plans to pursue an MBA and go into business. At first he was going to write his paper on baseball; but everyone did that, so he talked with his teacher and decided to do it on immigrant housing, a topic he had already studied in history class.

Asked whether he had any problems four days before the assignment was due, he said no. "It wasn't a really hard topic where you had to probe into anything, really." He had to do it, so he did it. It was all straightforward. He worked at the same time every day after school: first systematically accumulating notecards, then sorting them, then writing it all up. He reported no feelings, no excitement, and no personally meaningful challenge. He said, "I just rolled it." One had the impression of a steamroller that flattened everything in its way.

The second example, D. V., is a fellow who did his paper on the draft. Conscription was something that would affect him when he reached 18 years of age, so he thought it an important and personal issue. The information about him comes from questionnaires filled out at eight points before, during, and after the start of the assignment.

At first D. V. reported being interested in the paper. He found materials easily and indicated being deeply absorbed. But with each successive report he became less and less enthusiastic. By the time he began writing, he reported feeling detached and bored. The cause of this problem seems to have been that the topic had become frozen: It was not changing or becoming refined. He was unable or unwilling to play with ideas. From the very beginning he said that he was doing lots of "polishing" but little or no "inventing." In sum, there was none of what Getzels and Csikszentmihalyi (1976) have called "problem finding." He knew what he wanted to say about the draft. The process of writing it down on paper was therefore a routine exercise.

For both students the process of writing became a mechanical task. They appeared unaware of possibilities for excitement and challenge in writing. Psychoanalysts sometimes portray boredom as a defense against intolerable internal feelings (Fenichel 1951). It could be that these two students adopted a mechanical and conventional approach in order to defend themselves against pain, threat, and novelty in their materials; but their reports indicated only that they found the process unchallenging. They had never learned to find excitement in writing.

Effects of boredom. Laboratory studies indicate that boredom is usually associated with low physical activation. Adrenalin levels are low; heart rate is slowed; there is a decrease in oxygen consumption. Cognitively, boredom is associated with decreased attentiveness and slower thought processes. People are less able to control their attention; vigilance and performance decline (Smith 1981; Thackray 1981).

The relation of boredom to students' work can be seen by looking at the opening paragraphs written by these two students, which are presented in Figure 9.2. The expert critic made the following comments about the beginning of the paper on immigrant housing.

> The introductory segment of the paper is purely factual and exceptionally uninteresting. There is no hint whatsoever of the topic of the main segment (the horrible living conditions of immigrant housing) and no hint of the point to come. M. D. is working hard here to keep himself and his reader from *any* emotional involvement in the material. Thus he can allow himself to write a sentence as callous as the last one in the second paragraph; or he can write the second sentence of the third paragraph (explaining why they were called "dumbell" tenements), a sentence that makes no sense until the reader realizes that the point of view M. D. has adopted is not the point of view of a person looking at the building from the street but of someone looking from above at a plan of the building drawn on a sheet of paper – only then do "top" and "bottom" make any sense. The development of the paper is about

M.D.'s paper:
The great influx of immigrants to the United States in the 1920's and 1930's created unique housing problems. Since most of the immigration was into industrial urban areas, single or two-story housing became impractical.

In order to accommodate the greatest number of people into the available space, housing had to be built up, rather than out. Another requirement of this housing was low and quick construction. The combination of these conditions required a common form for the tenement house. The houses that were already there wasted space with such things as alleys, halls and stair wells.

The new tenement housing began ot resemble rectangular blocks. These were called dumbell tenements because they were wide on the top and bottom and narrow in the middle. These buildings were erected on uniform city plots, twenty or twenty-five feet wide and 100 feet deep. The structure took up almost the entire area of the lot. It was attached to its neighbor on either side, leaving only a strip about ten feel deep in the rear.

D.V.'s paper:
For millions of young men, the age of 18 is very critical. These young men can choose either to go to college or to start a career, but if the draft were reinstated their plans could be drastically changed. The government could disrupt their lives by putting them in the armed services. Our country is facing a decision now – draft or volunteer army. The United States needs greater manpower than it presently has with the all-volunteer army. Our nation could gain the manpower it needs without the draft and should for the sake of individual rights.

Draft is the random picking of men for the armed services. It originated in France in 1793 and has been used in the United States since the Civil War. It has been used during all major U.S. wars since that time, but has generally been opposed during peacetime. This opposition has become much greater after the unpopular war of Viet Nam. The government is now considering the draft in peacetime because of the decreasing number of recruits for the armed services. There is considerable debate concerning the return to the system.

Figure 9.2. Opening paragraphs of bored students' papers.

the most impersonal treatment of this subject that I can imagine from someone his age.

It is a plodding paper with appalling oversights. M. D.'s rigid approach to the assignment is clearly manifest in his writing. Our critic has similar comments about the remainder of the text.

In the body of the paper M. D. cannot help but become somewhat more personal – at least he has persons doing things. But there are still abundant verbal strategies to shift the point of view as far away from the reader and the writer as possible. Thus, the first mention of filth comes as a complete surprise in the third sentence of the fifth paragraph. In this and the next paragraph M. D. is blaming the filthy living conditions on the architecture of the buildings, especially on the airshafts, but fails either to prepare us for or to explain the "stench-filled hallways." Similarly, he blames the airshafts for lack of privacy just before he explains that many families lived in the same apartment. M. D. consistently seeks the most simplified and objectified explanation that he can find. Thus, when he finally comes around to the main point of the paper, the social problems and the immigrants' surprising ability to overcome them, the reader is totally unprepared. Not only do the social problems come out of the blue – M. D. must think that the reader, too, can see their inevitability – but M. D.'s admiration for the success of the immigrants is greatly blunted by his dogged refusal throughout the rest of the essay to bring the writer close to them.

In concluding, the critic describes it as a "very boring paper" and speculates that this quality reflects the author's "determined effort not to let the distastefulness of the topic affect him." One can take the psychoanalytic position that the boy adopted this rigid approach to protect himself from the materials; his description of this experience, however, provides no evidence for this interpretation. It indicates only that he was unmotivated. He had simply not learned that writing holds challenges; hence he missed the option of becoming more personally involved.

In the second case, that of D. V., there is a clear thesis that has engaged the author's interest; the injustice of conscription. As one reads through the paper, however, it is apparent that there is no real development of the initial idea: He simply lists pros and cons, with no effort to weigh them. The expert summarizes his reactions to the paper as follows:

The paper is unremarkable in most respects. It begins well enough, announcing its topics and setting up its point, but it does so too quickly and gives away too much of the point. The development is logical and the flow of topics relatively consistent, but the transitions tend to be abrupt and sometimes crude. D. V. has enough control and distance from his material to manage the shift to his personal point of view in the last paragraph pretty well and to prepare it successfully in his first sentence. But otherwise this is a pedestrian work; one topic at a time, little attention to the reader's possible reactions, little effort to make the paper interesting.

The text mirrors D. V.'s personal state. Just as he couldn't find any excitement while writing on the topic, he was unable to provide the reader with any challenge to make the work interesting.

While the anxious students suffered from overambitious expectations, these students were stymied because they had too few expectations. They did not envision the papers as anything more than a compilation of notes. They seemed unaware of possibilities for finding challenges in writing.

Order and disorder in emotional states

Diseases of the mind. An extreme example of emotional disturbance is provided by a student who was writing a paper on William James's *The Varieties of Religious Experience.* He was a religious person and was very excited and challenged by this opportunity to refute James's attempt to reduce religion to psychology. The paper was a "platform" for him to say things he had been wanting to say for a long time, and he envisioned himself as a "bellwether," a "spokesman for the future." But these grandiose expectations created a state of anxiety that had his mind reeling. When first interviewed, he had torn up numerous drafts and felt that everything he had written was "bullshit." Several months later he was still in a state of prostration. He had succeeded in getting an extension from his teacher but was still ripping up new drafts and tearing out his hair. The essay had lost all sense of ordered sequence or systematic method; he was going in circles and had lost all conviction of making intelligent headway.

Anxiety, boredom, and their related states do resemble diseases: They are associated with afflictions of thought and action. Students' involvement with materials becomes chaotic or rigid; ideas get put down on the page impulsively or mechanically, without proper development or sensitivity to audience.

Among high school students, this condition of internal disruption is extremely common. Nearly everyone in a sample of 90 students doing the junior theme reported emotional problems: bouts of boredom, worry, and loss of motivation (Larson, Hecker, & Norem 1985). Young writers, it seems, wasted many hours floundering in unproductive, distressed states.

At the heart of the issue is the problem of attention: How can writers maintain concentration on their work? In addition to the internal fragmentation generated by the writing process itself, there were other sources of distraction. These youths were at a stage of life when they were falling in love, falling out of love, having fights with their parents, or enduring herpes scares. They were getting carried away by excitements, panics, and other overpowering emotions. The question is, Where within this avalanche of emotions could they find the peace of mind to organize their thoughts?

Integrative emotions. To understand fully the role of emotions in writing, it is important to examine conditions when things go right, to study people who achieve control over their attention and who experience a more constructive state. To do this it will be useful to step away from writing for a few moments.

Mihaly Csikszentmihalyi has attempted to understand optimal states by researching their occurrence in creative and challenging activities. He studied rock climbers, dancers, composers, surgeons, chess players, and others to understand the dynamics of inner experience when things go well (Csikszentmihalyi 1975b, 1978a,b, 1979). In these activities people describe the optimal state as one of enjoyment or "flow," a state in which they are absorbed in their activities and when actions follow smoothly from their thoughts. The emotional state is positive, yet inconspicuous; it requires no psychic energy to be turned inward. Attention is available to negotiate outside tasks and people feel in command of the situation: Dancers describe experiencing heightened control of their bodies; composers describe feeling in command of the musical notes; students feel that they can cope with the assignment they are working on. People feel motivated to be doing what they are doing, and their attention is effective.

What produces and sustains this state? The answer to this question partly involves cognition. Csikszentmihalyi discovered that people describe a common set of predisposing conditions in how they each perceive and interact with the particular activity. The state of flow seems to occur when people have clear goals and a good sense of how they will reach those goals. They know what they want to accomplish and understand the rules governing how one gets there. In addition, feedback, either explicit or self-generated, appears to be important: One has to know when one is doing something right and something wrong. The most central element, however, seems to be the balance between the perceived challenges of the activity and a person's skills. One must experience the activity as presenting opportunities for action that are well meshed with one's talents. The chess player must have an opponent of matched ability; the rock climber must find a climb that is appropriate to his or her skills.

Only when this balance occurs does the opportunity exist for enjoyment and deep involvement. If the challenges of the activity are too great for a person's skills (if the rock face is too steep, or one's chess opponent far superior), anxiety takes over. And anxiety can occur even if the challenges are only *perceived* to be too great for a person's abilities. This is the scenario encountered by the first two students we considered. On the other hand, if the challenges of an activity are too few for a person's skills (if a climb is too easy, or an opponent too weak) – or if one sees no way to make an activity challenging – boredom takes over. This is what seems to have happened to the second two students. In both circumstances, attention was impaired.

Too often we think of cognition as separate from emotion, as if cognitive processes could be understood independently of affect, and vice versa. But this is clearly not the case. What people think is affected by what they feel, and what they feel is affected by what they think. The perception of goals, constraints, feedback, challenges, and skills shapes a person's engagement. The systemic relationship a person has with the ongoing activity determines his or her level of involvement.

The question is, Do young people have the ability to control their involvement in the activity of writing? Can they engineer the kind of internal balance required to become deeply involved in their work? This issue is considered next.

Optimal arousal: the experience of enjoyment

Creating flow in the process of writing. Debilitating emotions are not the only experiences students feel when they work on their papers. Many report flowlike involvement in their writing. They mention the elements of enjoyment, from deep absorption ("All of my brain was there") to intrinsic motivation ("I just loved it"). They report losing track of time, a common element of flow ("I'd get there at 6 o'clock and, before I knew it, it's 10 o'clock and time to go home"); and control over the materials ("I felt really powerful, like I had the information in the palm of my hand and could mold it any way I wanted"). Several students even used the word "flow" to describe the rapt involvement with their work.

What is most interesting is that these students apeared to be using deliberate strategies to make their work enjoyable. The first example is that of a boy, S. N., who did a paper on the development of the DC-3 prior to World War II. This aircraft had interested him because of his aspirations to be an aeronautical engineer. His ability level was no different from that of the other four high school students already considered, and he had no more prior experience with writing, but he seemed in better control of his emotions.

Like the bored students, S. N. was fairly methodical. He worked at the same time every day and set up goals for each session. The difference was in his willingness to adjust schedules and redirect attention according to where the writing led. He began with a curiosity about the DC-3's use during the war but gradually focused in on its development before the war, because he found this period – before the plane was even flown – to be the most interesting and important. Unlike the others, his interest did not stop with the reading. He recognized the challenge of trying to explain to his reader why this period was interesting and important.

Like the anxious students, S. N. experienced times when he was overwhelmed by the quantity of his materials and the difficult task of bringing them all together. But usually he could anticipate when his work was going to be overwhelming and would plan a shorter session to avoid being consumed: "If I knew it was going to be rough, I wouldn't spend as much time on it, but I wouldn't avoid it either." There was grandiosity in his ambitions for the paper, but he was aware of the need to control this internal impulse: "I had to keep stopping myself and saying, 'Okay, I'm doing a project here.'"

This sensitivity to the project and to his internal states protected him from the kind of overexcitement and anxiety that paralyzed the students writing on Mies van der Rohe and on William James. He put in a lot of effort and closely monitored his energy level: "It's like you're putting everything you've got right into it. It would be like not turning the car on but turning on everything electrical in the car at the same time. Sure they'll work for awhile, but all of a sudden – it'll be time for a recharge."

What is striking in this strategy is how closely it follows prescriptions for creating flow. He seems to have been deliberately adjusting the challenges to his abilities. By moving cautiously through hard parts, by stopping when overexcited, and by monitoring his energy, he regulated the balance of challenges and skills, creating conditions for enjoyable involvement.

He related one occasion of particularly intense involvement, which he described as a "big personal high." His concentration was very deep: "I was really shut off from everything that was happening. My phone rang, and it took me three rings to realize it; I mean I was really engrossed." This was not a session of library work or notecard shuffling; it was a session of writing. He had succeeded in finding challenges and enjoyment in the process of putting thoughts down on the page. For him writing was not just a mechanical process; it was an opportunity for discovery and further exploration of ideas. The challenge was to communicate his excitement about this airplane to readers; in fact, he said that he couldn't wait to read the paper himself.

The second example is that of a girl, A. R., who did a paper on the American composer Charles Ives. Her career goal was to become a graphic designer; however, she was also involved in music and had developed a special interest in this composer.

At the beginning of the assignment she was considering several topics, and she reported confusion and irresolution. However, once she settled on Charles Ives, she reported becoming absorbed in reading and taking notes. Like S. N., she worked methodically, setting up a plan for what she would do and deliberately arranging situations where she would be free from distraction. At this point she indicated that there were numerous parts she could work on and enjoy; the project was challenging, and she found herself wanting to work on it.

While she was gathering notes, she began to get anxious about how to order the wide range of materials collected: "I'm having trouble putting things together in logical order." Rather than give way to panic, however, she found a simple solution: Experimenting with different outlines to see how each worked. She was also prepared to leave things out if need be, even though she had now become tremendously fond of everything about Charles Ives. Indeed, things came into place. Later she stated, "As I was writing the rough draft and converting it to final copy, I sensed a real flow in the materials and I felt as if everything was finally falling together." It is noteworthy that she used an image of "falling" to describe writing, as if she were not in command. The experience of enjoyment is one of personal control, but it is also one in which actions seem to be effortless. If a person is working at a level of challenge matched to his or her skills, the sensation of effort and strain will not be there.

A. R. said she experienced the assignment as if it were a musical piece. Her work was a sequence of discovery, joy, and experimentation, occurring within disciplined emotional guidelines.

Effects of enjoyment. Enjoyment is associated with optimal physiological arousal. Heart rate and oxygen consumption increase; at the same time, muscle tonus is heightened, and visual gaze is steadied. Cognitively, enjoyment is associated with clear attention and command over one's thoughts (Csikszentmihalyi 1975b). A person is more likely to feel strong and competent and perceive fullness and beauty in the world (Izard 1977).

The relationship of this state to students' writing is apparent in the final papers produced by the two students just described. Figure 9.3 shows how invitingly S. N. sets up his topic in the opening paragraphs, establishing the interactions between the idea of this new plane, the changing historic conditions of the prewar period, and the ambitions of the plane's creator, Donald Douglas. S. N. had enough command of his thoughts and feelings to bring these different elements together.

The English professor who acted as our expert critic expressed admiration for S. N.'s skillful topic development in the rest of the paper, particularly for his capacity to hold back with his points while systematically building up to them.

> His point is the success of the DC-3. But he manages to delay that part of the paper until page 5, at which time we get two and a half pages describing its accomplishments. These pages are the heart of the paper, the reason it was written; but by saving that material for the end, S. N. is able to include the other information he has collected without making it seem mere filler. This is a very mature structure – a staple of high-toned, general-circulation journals like *New Yorker* and *Atlantic Monthly*. It requires that the writer have a good command of all his material (so that he can see it whole), that he be self-conscious (so that he can make product-, reader-oriented decisions rather than process-, writer-oriented decisions), and that he have the discipline to be patient.

This boy had no more experience than the other four students had; his basic abilities were no greater; furthermore, he reported putting in no more time than the others. Yet somehow his paper comes out much stronger and more ordered. I would like to suggest that his internal self-regulation and his ability to create enjoyment allowed him the patience and command of thought to lay out his materials in such a deliberate and compelling fashion.

The girl writing about Charles Ives was only slightly above the other students in basic ability level. Her paper, however, is a qualitative step

S.N.'s paper:
On December 17, 1939 at little Clover Field in Santa Monica, California, an aircraft was born. The first Douglas DC-3 took off with Carl Clover, the company's vice president, as chief pilot and flew for over 30 minutes. Something magical had happened. Along with an aircraft an era was born. An era of speed and efficiency that would turn a nation's sagging air industry into an ever expanding business and technological enterprise. Quite soon, and without warning, this young upstart would face an even greater responsibility. It would be pushed into the skies of World War II and be expected to perform many new functions. It proved to be up to the challenge. The Dc-3 withstood virtually every form of punishment imaginable and gained the respect of every airman ever associated with it.

The Model T of the air, as she was soon aptly named, quickly grew to accommodate 90% of all commercial air transport in the United States alone. The DC-3 simply formed the backbone of vicil aviation both in the United States and abroad; in war and in peace. The entire venture stemmed from Donald W. Douglas' ambition to fill the order for an aircraft that would "provide for a crew of two, pilot and copilot, with a cabin capable of carrying at least 12 passengers in comfortable seats with ample room and fully equipped with the many fixtures and conveniences generally expected in a commercial passenger aircraft." The success of this modern concept of the all metal airplane rested solely on the shoulders of Mr. Douglas. His ambition was to change the course of modern air travel and he accomplished this with the DC-3.

A.R.'s paper:
Charles Ives was the first American composer to create symphonic music in the image of his country's ideas rather than in the codes of European tradition. Before Ives, most symphonic music followed a somewhat restrictive harmonic law and just had a pretty sound. Ives, however, "plunged into the abyss of tonal freedom" which enabled him to create music that wouldn't have been possible under conventional standards. By using innovative techniques and American ideas, Ives achieved a more maningful and more American type of music.

Ives was born on October 20, 1874 in Danbury, a small town in Connecticutt. This town was, before Ives' time, hidden away from the European beliefs, conventions, and traditions that were arriving at the east cost in the nineteenth century. But, as Ives was growing up, this town started rapid industrial and population growth. New ideas came pouring through Danbury. Even the traditional folk songs, hymns, and band marches were being performed and experimented with in new and different ways. Certainly a growing of new original ideas. These ideas were being created in the home of Charles Ives.

Figure 9.3. Opening paragraphs of papers by students who experience enjoyment and deep involvement.

above those of the first four we have considered. About this paper, the expert writes:

> The global organization of this essay is as complex and sophisticated as S. N.'s, and most of what I said there applies here as well. A. R. is a little more programmatic (and far less subtle) than S. N. in executing her structure, but she does a good job of setting up the topic and the point. The shift to the background material is also well managed through manipulation of topics. The major difference between A. R. and S. N. is that A. R. is less adept at managing the development of the main section of the essay. I won't speculate about causes, but it is clear that S. N. had much easier material to work with at this level. S. N.'s subtopic falls into a story (a structure that is relatively easy to handle), while A. R.'s subtopic requires her to develop a more analytical organization.

She demonstrates remarkable discipline and control in the manipulation of a difficult topic. Rather than acting as impediments, her feelings about Charles Ives are used to help organize her ideas. The paper becomes an opportunity to explore systematically her admiration for the composer and justify this admiration to her audience. In turn, internal discipline and enjoyment seemed to afford her access to her inner feelings and the ability to adapt them to the rhetorical opportunities.

Both of these papers reflect a higher level or organization than the four earlier ones. Whereas the others were composed of fragmented facts and ideas, these two contain a progressively developed train of thought. The first four students had lost control over their psychic energy, which resulted in the production of impulsive or unreflective prose. These latter two students, in contrast, were able to command their attention and build coherent and sophisticated papers.

In the larger study with 90 students, we found enjoyment to be a strong, independent predictor of the grades students received (Larson, Hecker, & Norem 1985). Irrespective of ability levels, the experience of enjoyment appeared to make a substantial difference in the quality of each student's final paper. Curiously, we also found that students who had experienced enjoyment reported putting no more time into their work: They appeared to get more out of each hour they worked. In sum, the ability to create enjoyment was related to more creative and efficient writing.

It would be presumptuous to conclude from these findings that enjoyment per se *causes* good writing, but it would be equally erroneous to dismiss enjoyment as merely a *result* of good writing. Rather, it is likely that enjoyment as both cause and effect contributes to creating and sustaining flow in writing, that the conditions that create enjoyment and that create good writing are closely related.

Of course six students, or even the 90 in the larger study, cannot provide conclusive proof of a thesis. The information discussed here is only suggestive. Nonetheless, the cases discussed indicate that emotional aspects of writing should not be ignored. There appears to be more to success in writing than cognitive ability or writing skills, since ability and writing experience accounted for only part of the differences among these students. Furthermore, merely having interest does not ensure that a student will avoid the pitfalls of anxiety or boredom – several of the students got into trouble because they were *too* interested, becoming emotionally overexcited and losing control of their work.

Successful writing depends in part on the relationship a writer has with the ongoing work. There must be a system of interaction between the person and the evolving manuscript that engenders and sustains attention, that keeps a person motivated and involved in the task. The two students just discussed provide examples of writers able to maintain a positive relationship with their writing. They deliberately monitored their internal states and regulated the challenges appropriately; they actively cultivated their relationship with the topics and skillfully avoided situations that might create debilitating emotions. Hence they enjoyed their work, and this enjoyment helped keep them engaged and ultimately helped them to produce better papers.

Conclusion

Having quoted Kant in the beginning, it may be indecorous to conclude by quoting Tom Wolfe from *The Right Stuff* (1979). However, in his popular book on the astronauts, Wolfe describes the experience of test pilots in a way that is applicable to the topic at hand. Each new flying machine, we are told, has glorious new performance capabilities. It can roll and twist and climb in ways that previous planes could not. But each new plane also has specific limits: It can turn just so sharply and climb just so steeply without tumbling out of control. The range within which a plane maintains aerodynamic stability is called its performance envelope, and this envelope defines the potential and magnificence of each machine. If the pilot exceeds this range, if he pushes it too far, the plane shatters or careens to the earth.

Young writers, unfortunately, spend a lot of time outside of their performance envelopes. They put themselves in situations they cannot handle. Debilitating emotions result; their thinking becomes fragmented and directionless; and their work tumbles out of control. Often these situations result from challenges they have set that are beyond their abilities, tasks that are too large or undefined for them to deal with. In these cases experience takes the form of anxiety. Other times it is absence of genuine challenge that creates the problem. They are unable or unwilling to find anything engaging within their writing, and boredom ensues.

Optimal conditions occur when a person feels challenged at a level appropriately matched to his or her talents. As Csikszentmihalyi has found in certain occupations and in the performance of music, sports, and art, there are conditions that facilitate the experience of enjoyment, a state that combines positive motivation with command of attention. Maintaining these conditions, sustaining this internal balance is by no means simple. Ultimately it is as complex as the person involved and the topic with which he or she struggles.

Presumably these relationships hold not only for the writing of high school English assignments, but for all tasks that involve the concentration of psychic energy on problems that require original solutions. When creative thinking is necessary, and perhaps whenever sustained thinking in general is required, the role of emotions is likely to be the same. The quality of performance will depend, to a large extent, on how well the thinker is able to arrange his or her thought processes so as to make them enjoyable. If too much anxiety or too much boredom enter the picture, the results will show their presence: The product will bear the mark of the thinker's psychic entropy. These are the conclusions suggested by our studies. How far these generalizations can be trusted only further research will show.

10. Flow in solitary ordeals

RICHARD D. LOGAN

It has been argued that extreme physical ordeals, like the ones polar explorers or concentration camp inmates often encounter, are metaphors for life (Frankl 1963). The difference is that in such situations life's fundamental issues stand out more clearly and in higher relief. Others have maintained that play is also a metaphor for life (Huizinga [1939] 1970). Although it may not follow logically from the above that "extreme ordeals are a lot like play," that statement is in a sense what I propose to address, in the particular form of detailing some striking similarities between the qualities of successful coping with adversity and the qualities of experiences that people find enjoyable.

Csikszentmihalyi's flow concept is the vehicle for linking the psychology of successful coping with the psychology of enjoyment. In his book, *Beyond Boredom and Anxiety* (1975b), he describes the features of experiences that make them enjoyable. These include being able to (1) merge action and awarenes, (2) center attention on a limited stimulus field, (3) lose oneself in one's activities, (4) control actions and the environment, (5) receive coherent demands for action, and (6) see the activity as self-rewarding. These traits might be reduced to three: getting caught up in what one is doing, controlling what is happening, and creating variety and stimulation so as to make activities novel and challenging enough to stay caught up in them. Many play and recreational activities have these qualities; if the work experience has these qualities, then work too can be experienced as enjoyable (Csikszentmihalyi 1975b). Paradoxically, in situations seemingly farthest removed from the enjoyable – namely, solitary prolonged survival ordeals – people also describe having

Originally published as "The Flow Experience in Solitary Ordeals" in the *Journal of Humanistic Psychology* 25, 4 (1985), pp. 79–89.

flow experiences. One characteristic of individuals who manage to survive situations of prolonged hardship (captivity, isolation, trek) is that they arrange their environment and their actions so as to create the elements of flow. Sir Geoffrey Jackson, writing about his many months as a captive of South American guerillas, hints at this:

> Whether it is an original discovery I cannot say; but I have con-cluded that the captive requires two classes of routine, correspond-ing to two distinct human needs – the need to break up his day, and the need to fill up his day. I had already developed many such routines. (Jackson 1973, p. 110)

"Breaking up" one's day refers to the need for variety and stimulation; "filling up" one's day day refers to occupying oneself – both help create conditions for getting caught up in things to do. Establishing routines to achieve these ends provides the element of control over one's surroundings.

Because the quality of being able to get caught up in doing something depends on a balance or match between environmental demands and individual capabilities (Csikszentmihalyi 1975b), a flow experience will not just happen when one is coping with an ordeal, as ordeals by def-inition involve overwhelming environmental demands. Individuals may have to go to extraordinary lengths to create or find activities in which they can get caught up, that will provide control over their situation, and that will provide variety and stimulation. It is also true that some individuals who cope successfully are unusually capable of setting up flow experiences. A key reason for their capability, to be addressed later in this chapter, is what might be termed a non–self-conscious individ-ualism, which enables some people to be highly capable observers of their surroundings and controllers of their actions. They are able to get caught up in mental or physical activities precisely because they do not dwell on themselves.

Creating flow in solitary ordeals

Christopher Burney (1952) spent many months in solitary confinement as a prisoner of the Nazis during World War II. Forced to exist in highly limited circumstances, he created flow by making the most of what was available:

> If the reach of experience is suddenly confined, and we are left with only a little food for thought and feeling, we are apt to take the few objects that offer themselves and ask a whole catalogue of

often absurd questions about them. Does it work? How? Who made it and of what? And, in parallel, when and where did I last see something like it and what else does it remind me of? And if we are dissatisfied at the time, we repeat the series in the optative mood, making each imperfection in what we have at hand evoke a wish or an ideal. So we set in train a wonderful flow of combinations and associations in our minds, the length and complexity of which soon obscure its humble starting-point. . . . My bed, for example, could be measured and roughly classified with school beds or army beds, according to appearance and excepting the peculiarity of its being hinged to the wall. . . . Yet this bed retained a quality of bed-ness which summoned all my associations with all the beds I had ever known. . . . When I had done with the bed, which was too simple to intrigue me long, I felt the blankets, estimated their warmth, examined the precise mechanics of the window, the discomfort of the toilet (perversely, for its very presence was an unexpected luxury), computed the length and breadth, the orientation and elevation of the cell. (Burney 1952, pp. 16–18)

Solzhenitsyn (1976) relates the following ingenious example of mental self-stimulation in a fellow prisoner:

He resisted by striving to use his mind to calculate distances. In Lefortovo [prison] he counted steps, converted them into kilometers, remembered from a map how many kilometers it was from Moscow to the border, and then how many across all Europe, and how many across the Atlantic Ocean. He was sustained in this by the hope of returning to America. And in one year in Lefortovo solitary he got, so to speak, halfway across the Atlantic. Thereupon they took him to Sukhanovka. Here, realizing how few would survive to tell of it – and all our information about it comes from him – he invented a method of measuring the cell. The numbers 10/22 were stamped on the bottom of his prison bowl, and he guessed that "10" was the diameter of the bottom and "22" the diameter of the outside edge. Then he pulled a thread from a towel, made himself a tape measure, and measured everything with it. (Solzhenitsyn 1976, p. 182)

Papillon (Charriere 1970), in solitary confinement in the penal colony in French Guiana, created out of a devastating prospect a mental activity in which he became caught up:

One year equals three hundred and sixty-five days, two years, seven hundred and thirty days, unless one's a leap year. I smiled at the thought. One day more wouldn't matter much. The hell it would not. One day more is twenty-four hours more. And twenty-four hours is a long time. And seven hundred and thirty days each made up into twenty-four hours is one hell of a lot more. How many hours does that make? Can I figure it in my head? No, I can't; it's impossible. Why, of course, it's possible. Let's see. A hundred days, that's twenty four hundred hours. Multiplied by seven – it's easy – it makes sixteen thousand eight hundred hours, plus the thirty remaining days times twenty-four which makes seven hundred and twenty hours. Total sixteen thousand eight hundred, plus seven hundred and twenty which makes, if I haven't made a mistake, seventeen thousand five hundred and twenty hours. My dear Mr. Papillon, you have seventeen thousand five hundred and twenty hours to kill in this [solitary confinement] cage with its smooth walls especially designed for wild animals. And how many minutes? Who gives a shit! Hours is one thing, but minutes? To hell with minutes. Why not seconds? What does it matter? What matters is that I have to furnish these days, hours, and minutes with something, all by myself, alone! (Charriere 1970, p. 219)

At the end of this particular mental exercise, Papillon recognizes that he must continue to create additional ones.

Solitary confinement deprives a person of one of the most precious features of a fulfilling life: freedom. Yet, paradoxically, a key feature of the flow experience, in which people feel so free, is "centering attention on a limited stimulus field," a major feature of confinement. Not only does a confined setting make it possible to center one's attention on a limited physical field, it also can clear the decks mentally and give one the opportunity to focus on a particular topic, such as Burney's bed or Papillon's mathematical calculations.

If flow represents the kind of state that many who seek "freedom" desire to experience, then perhaps Frankl's (1963) contention that he found freedom in the concentration camp is not so incredible, because he was able to create and experience flow despite all of his hardship and suffering.

Furthermore, some persons who seem to be good at creating flow in their lives seek out spartan situations rather than "enriched" ones on purpose. Charles Lindbergh (1953), for example, gave this enlightened account of his view of the cockpit of *The Spirit of St. Louis:*

My cockpit is small, and its walls are thin: but inside this cocoon

I feel secure, depite the speculations of my mind. It makes an efficient, tidy home, one so easy to keep in order that *its very simplicity creates a sense of satisfaction and relief.* It's a personal home, too – nobody has ever piloted the *Spirit of St. Louis* but me. Flying in it is like living in a hermit's mountain cabin after being surrounded by the luxury and countless responsibilities of a city residence. Here, I'm conscious of all elements of weather, immersed in them, dependent on them. Here, the earth spreads out beyond my window, its expanse and beauty offered at the cost of a glance. Here, are *no unnecessary extras, only the barest essentials* of life and flight. There are no letters to get off in the next mail, no telephone bells to ring, no loose odds and ends to attend to in some adjoining room. The few furnishings are within arm's length, and all in order.

A cabin that flies through the air, that's what I live in; a cabin higher than the mountains, a cabin in the clouds and sky. After much travail, I've climbed up to it. Through months of planning, I've equipped it with utmost care. Now, I can relax in its solitary vantage point, and let the sun shine, and the west wind blow, and the blizzard come with the night. (Lindbergh 1953, pp. 227–8; emphasis added)

A confined environment can be conducive to flow because the flow state may be easier to create if, as Lindbergh indicates, one is not freighted with too many things to distract and diffuse one's attention. The artificially limited stimulus field, like the bare cell of the monk or of the Hindu yogi, makes concentration easier. This environment one can control.

Lindbergh (like Burney and Papillon) makes the most of his confined surroundings, and soon is caught up in what there is to attend to. He gets so caught up he almost seems to insinuate himself into the very molecules of the plane:

I become minutely conscious of details in my cockpit – of the instruments, the levers, the angles of construction. Each item takes on new values. I study weld marks on the tubing (frozen ripples of steel through which pass invisible hundredweights of strain), a dot of radiolite paint on the altimeter's face (whose only mission is to show where the needle should ride when *The Spirit of St. Louis* is 2000 feet above the sea), the battery of fuel valves (my plane and my life depend on the slender stream of liquid flowing through them, like blood in human veins) – all such things, which I never considered much before, are now obvious and important. And there's plenty of time to notice them. I may be flying a complicated airplane, rushing through space, but in this cabin I'm surrounded by simplicity and thoughts set free of time. (Lindbergh 1953, p. 228)

After many hours of involvement in flying his plane and pursuing various lines of thought, Lindbergh, toward the end of his flight, relates the following, which seems almost a definition of another feature of flow, the loss of ego:

It's been like a theater where the play carries you along in time and place until you forget you're only a spectator. You grow unaware of the walls around you, of the program clasped in your hand, even of your body, its breath, pulse, and being. You live with the actors and the setting, in a different age and place. It's not until the curtain drops that consciousness and body reunite. (Lindbergh 1953, p. 466)

Others who have managed to survive some of the most horrible ordeals imaginable also talk of a flowlike loss of ego. Admiral Richard Byrd (1938), for example, who once spent four months during the season of 24-hour night utterly alone in a tiny hut in the Antarctic, describes an ordeal of isolation, cold, starvation, and living in a black void that is almost beyond comprehension. Yet he created for himself rituals, schedules, and activities in which to get caught up, and he was able one day to experience the following:

The day was dying, the night being born – but with great peace. Here were the imponderable processes and forces of the cosmos, harmonious and soundless. Harmony, that was it! That was what came out of the silence – a gentle rhythm, the strain of a perfect chord, the music of the spheres perhaps.

It was enough to catch that rhythm, momentarily to be myself a part of it. In that instant I could feel no doubt of man's oneness with the universe. (Byrd 1938, p. 85)

So succesful was Byrd, in fact, at getting caught up that he once wrote, after performing his daily regimen of activities and rituals in this vast solitude, "Then I had an hour to myself."

The preceding excerpts seem to illustrate and to be well summarized by the following quotation from Csikszentmihalyi (1975b):

The ability to control the environment by limiting the stimulus field, finding clear goals and norms, and developing appropriate skills – is one side of the flow experience. The other side, paradoxically, is a feeling which seems to make the sense of control irrelevant. Many of the people we interviewed, especially those who most enjoy whatever they are doing, mentioned that at the height of their involvement with the activity they lose a sense of themselves as separate entities, and feel harmony and even a merging of identity with the environment. (Csikszentmihalyi 1975b, p. 194)

The final question concerns the kind of person who manages to create flow experiences under adversity and to use them as coping devices. Given that the flow experience typically involves the absence of self-awareness (loss of ego), might it be inferred that those who are not absorbed in self-contemplation would be in a better position to get caught up in flow? It would seem that a person too much caught up in concerns with himself would have difficulty in getting caught up in what he was doing. The dynamics of the experience imply that during flow the self manifests itself nondualistically as "I" – acting, controlling, attending, observing, but *not reflecting* dialectically. The "me" is absent when one is fully involved. Even activities in which one is rewarded by feedback are experienced nondialectically rather than reflexively: In the moment of the act, the doing is the sheer pleasure, not the self-conscious awareness of "what it does for me."

This point is essentially that made by Frankl (1978) in his concept of *dereflection*. Although he addresses the concept primarily as a means to improve sexual encounters, he clearly implies application beyond when he says, "Instead of observing and watching [one]self, [one] should forget himself" (Frankl 1978, p. 152). It is also noteworthy that such insights of Frankl's originated in the confinement of a concentration camp.

Other traits that follow from non–self-conscious individualism include being a seeker. That which is subject must ultimately have its object. Thus, many non–self-conscious individualists still are looking for something and have goals toward which they strive. To take one example, Lindbergh all his life was fascinated by "realms beyond," which led him to become a trail-blazing aviator.

The ultimate goal that many an adventurer sought was, in the old cliche, to know him*self*. If that was the ultimate goal, why then have I maintained that concern with self as object is maladaptive in coping? The answer is found, among other places, in hundreds of ancient myths that convey the deep human significance of the Quest. "Finding" the self requires a long period of seeking by the self-as-subject. Jung's theory, for example, hinges precisely on that point: The Self is never truly known until (if at all) late in life. Such could also be said of Maslow's theory. Perhaps, then, the problem so many people who are caught up in themselves have in coping with adversity is that in our inward-looking, narcissistic age *we have fostered a far too premature concern with the self as object* that has led to the need to use artificial means such as drugs to create flowlike nonreflexive "highs." Do the same challenging experiences that individualists convert into flow represent merely obstacles to the narcissists? Maybe a far longer apprenticeship in questing, building, and being caught up in the world needs to precede getting caught up in oneself.

Although it may be that individualists who are not self-conscious can enter into flow experiences more readily, it might also be true that those who are too caught up in themselves may be most in need of flow experiences to compensate for that overinvolvement in self.

Ordeals, then, are more than metaphors for life. They are lessons about life. Jackson's observation about the need to break up and fill one's day applies to more than the captive, just as Frankl's work does. Lindbergh's and many other ordeal seekers' enthusiasm for the sparest of surroundings, and the extent to which this spareness enables them to be caught up in flow, speaks volumes about the dependency of those who need consumer items to occupy, distract, and stimulate them. The "I," on the other hand, can fill up whatever blank slate is set before it, and, in fact, yearns to do so. James Lester (1983), speculating about what drives people into arduous and risky adventures, observes, "Whenever I think about reasons for such activities [specifically, mountain climbing] I always return to the notion of a desire to *pare life down to something essential*, and thereby to a focusing of attention, and a wholeheartedness of purpose" (Lester 1983, p. 40; emphasis added).

The "solitary *ordeal*" of this article also tells us about the "*solitary ordeal*" of everyday life: The simple fact of being alone is a great source of stress to many people today (Peplau & Perlman 1982). Perhaps it is a hardship because we dwell on ourselves so much that we can't get into a flow experience. In fact, we even say it: "I just don't know [what] to do *with myself.*" The challenge to create flow in spare and limited conditions is not just the condition of the captive, but of the ordinary lonely individual; indeed, such has been said by existentialists to be the modern human condition. The experiences of those who have undergone solitary ordeals remind us that this challenge can lead to fulfilling experiences, if we sense that we are subjects and agents in the world.

Another aspect of coping and the self-as-subject deserves attention.

Those who see the self primarily as an object (i.e., "me"; consumer) regard themselves as victims, or at least potential victims, even prior to an ordeal. A "psychology of the victim" is in fact profoundly widespread in our present uncertain age. Many who are hardly oppressed objectively nonetheless feel hassled by life. Many privileged others choose to identify with groups that symbolize victimization: minorities, handicapped, the disadvantaged, the poor. Others go to great lengths to transform themselves symbolically into victims (e.g., the "punk" movement and various cults). In real adversity would these people ever be able to free themselves from the orientation that "this is all happening to *me*," and survive, let alone go on actively to create flow?

The self-as-subject, however, cannot be victimized because it offers no target-object. Only an object in the world can be a victim of it. Here is one way of grasping the "secret" of Bruno Bettelheim, Viktor Frankl, Charles Lindbergh, and thousands of other survivors of ordeals: Those who sense themselves primarily as subjects always have a built-in detachment from victimization in their self-as-subject stance. Bettelheim (1943), in fact, says that it was primarily through observing and analyzing his surroundings that he was able to cope. As subject he saw things in which he could get caught up intellectually. Frankl wrote, paradoxically, of the *freedom* he discovered in the concentration camp. Perhaps it was the irreducible freedom of the self as subject. Those whose essence is that they are nonvictims are the ones most capable of coping with ordeals by entering into the non–self-conscious state of the flow experience.

Part III. Flow as a way of life

11. Introduction to Part III

ISABELLA AND MIHALY CSIKSZENTMIHALYI

Why are flow experiences so few and far between in everyday life? The question is partly rhetorical, since it admits no scientific answer. Yet by thinking about its implications, we may not only clarify what flow is about, but may also shed some new light on important historical and institutional patterns of development, and hence on the evolution of culture.

The relative rarity of flow experiences is due, by definition, to the fact that in everyday life the opportunities for action are seldom evenly matched with our abilities to act. Consequently occasions of intense concentration in which we are not distracted from purposeful involvement, in which we get responsive feedback to our actions, are not easy to come by. Everyday experience is characterized more by listless, low-level involvement interrupted by constant distractions, by boredom, and by periods of worry.

One might blame the social system for such a state of affairs, or the culture, or the individual's lack of enterprise and self-discipline. Any or all of these causes may be responsible for not optimizing experience to its fullest. But in the last analysis the culprit is that quasi-metaphysical entity known as "the human condition."

The fact is that the universe does not run in order to make life easier for man. Thus whatever advantage we can manage to snatch from the environment we do in spite of impersonal forces and in the face of random chance. And as soon as we get comfortable in one niche, boredom begins to nudge us on toward new goals.

There are obvious reasons why effortless living keeps getting interrupted. Because the environment is not built to our specifications, external contingencies constantly break into our concentration. It is either too hot or too cold, too wet or too dry. Then our body requires attention: It is either tired or hungry, sleepy or thirsty. Physical pain forces us to turn attention away from what we are doing, and center it inward. Psychological pain – unfulfilled desires, wishes, disappointments, fears – do the same. Awareness of eventual death, and the consequent shortness of time, force us to choose alternatives that are not the ones we would prefer.

To these universal features of the human condition must then be added the social and cultural factors that might hinder flow. A social institution such as slavery may restrict the opportunities for action of a segment of the population. A given religious system may either reduce or increase the frequency of flow in the culture.

It is reasonable to suppose that in a primitive culture that happened to be well adapted to its environment, people would be in flow most of the time, provided that they were unaware of alternative lifestyles and possibilities. In such ideal-typical communities, according to Redfield (1953), life choices are self-evident, doubts and unfulfilled desires are few and transitory.

An excellent example of how a particular culture was able to build flow into their lifestyle was brought to our attention by Richard Kool of the British Columbia Museum. To quote from a recent letter:

> The Shushwap region was and is considered by the Indian people to be a rich place: rich in salmon and game, rich in below-ground food resources such as tubers and roots – a plentiful land. In this region, the people would live in permanent village sites and exploit the environs for needed resources. They had elaborate technologies for very effectively using the resources in the environment, and perceived their lives as being good and rich. Yet, the elders said, at times the world became too predictable and the challenge began to go out of life. Without challenge, life had no meaning.
>
> So the elders, in their wisdom, would decide that the entire village should move, those moves occurring every 25 to 30 years. The entire population would move to a different part of the Shushwap land and there, they found challenge. There were new streams to figure out, new game trails to learn, new areas where the balsamroot would be plentiful. Now life would regain its meaning and be worth living. Everyone would feel rejuvenated and healthy. Incidentally, it also allowed exploited resources in one area to recover after years of harvesting.

What the Shushwap had discovered is an arrangement that many statesmen have only dreamed about: Both Thomas Jefferson and Chairman Mao thought that each generation needed its own revolution for the people to have an active stake in the political system ruling their lives. But presumably few cultures have ever attained such a perfect fit. Most human efforts at adaptation fall short in some respect or other, either by making survival too strenuous a task to accomplish, or by closing themselves off in a rigid cultural pattern that stifles the possibilities for action of each new generation. Some anthropologists, such as Marshall Sahlins (1972), contend that, even in the harshest environments of the Kalahari or the Australian desert, preliterate men have found ways to lead lives that are more leisurely, free, and enjoyable than anything contemporary urban settings offer.

On our side, we tend to agree more with the views of the historian Arnold Toynbee, who held that most cultures have suffered either from a lack of survival challenges, as in the case of the Pacific Islanders, or from too frequent and intense challenges, as in the case of Eskimo cultures. In Toynbee's view a civilization emerges only when environmental challenges are strong enough to prompt a consistent adaptive response, but not so strong as to absorb all the people's energies just in survival tasks.

Toynbee's thesis might be overly simple, yet it undoubtedly contains more than a grain of truth. But the "challenge-and-response" model should not be taken to apply to objective conditions. What differentiates cultures from each other is in part their differential responses to the same objective factors. Often what prompts the development of a civilization is not a change in objective conditions, but a conceptual reorganization that allows a group of people to recognize challenges where they did not see any before. For instance, the great awakening of Islam in the seventh century or the transformation of Japan in the last two centuries are more easily explained in terms of a reconceptualization of what was possible, rather than in terms of changes in the external possibilities. Such reconceptualizations, according to Toynbee, were the task of "creative minorities" within each culture.

All cultures are defensive constructions against chaos, attempts to reduce the impact of randomness on the course of human life. They are adaptive responses to the environment just as feathers are for birds or fur for mammals. Cultures prescribe norms, evolve goals, discover beliefs that help to make human action more fit to tackle the challenges of existence. In so doing they must rule out many alternatives, and so limit possibilities; but this channeling of attention to a limited set of goals and means is what allows effortless action within the self-created boundaries of the culture.

This is why the analogy between games and cultures is so compelling. Both consist of an arbitrary set of goals and of rules that allow action to proceed in a concentrated fashion. The difference is mainly one of scale. Cultures are all-embracing, they specify how a person should be born, how he or she should grow up, marry, have children, and die. Games fill out the interludes of the cultural script. They enhance action and concentration during "leisure time," when the cultural instructions are otherwise silent, and the person's attention threatens to wander into the uncharted realms of chaos.

Occasionally a culture succeeds in evolving a set of goals and rules so compelling and so well matched to the skills of the population that its members are able to experience flow with unusual frquency and intensity. In such cases the analogy between games and cultures is even closer. We can say that the culture as a whole becomes a "great game." Some of the classical civilizations may have succeeded in doing this. Athenian citizens, Romans who shaped their actions by *virtus*, Chinese intellectuals, or Indian brahmins moved through life with the intricate grace of ballet dancers, and derived perhaps the same enjoyment from the challenging harmony of their actions as they would have from an extended dance. The Athenian *polis*, Roman law, the divinely grounded bureaucracy of China, and the all-encompassing spiritual order of India were successful and lasting examples of how culture can enhance flow – at least for those who were lucky enough to be among the principal players.

A culture that enhances flow is not necessarily "good" in any moral sense. The rules of Sparta seem needlessly cruel to us, even though they were by all accounts successful in motivating those who abided by them. The joy of battle and the butchery that exhilarated the Tartar hordes, or the Turkish Janissaries, were legendary. It is certainly true that for great segments of the European polulation, confused by the dislocating cultural shocks of the 1920s, the Nazi fascist regime and ideology provided a simplified game plan. It set simple goals, clarified feedback, and allowed a renewed involvement with life that many found to be a relief from prior anxieties and frustrations.

Flow is a powerful motivator, but it does not guarantee virtue. Other things being equal, a culture that provides flow might be seen as "better" than one that does not. But when a group of people embraces goals and norms that will enhance its enjoyment of life, there is always the possibility that this will happen at the expense of some other group. The flow of the Athenian citizen was made possible by the slaves who ran his property, just as the elegant lifestyle of the Southern plantations in America rested on the work of imported slaves.

The same argument that holds for cultures as a whole holds for subcultures, or groups of people who attempt to differentiate themselves from others in the same society by adopting distinctive goals, norms, and eventually separate lifestyles. In a society as complex as ours, we have subcultures of Amish and Mennonite farmers in black garb riding their horse-drawn buggies, and surfing subcultures that represent an opposite set of norms and values; in between these two one finds almost every other possible combination.

In evolutionary terms, a subculture is a mutation of the cultural form that tries to establish itself in competition with others. Generally most will disappear, because they do not give any advantage over existing lifestyles. A few, however, will survive in a symbiotic or parasitic relation to the main culture; and occasionally one of them might even supplant mainline goals and norms, and become the dominant cultural form.

Subcultures constitute a network running through society, overlapping and enfolding its spaces. Each person might belong to more than one, in differing combinations. There are subcultures of Masons and of gourmet cooks, academics, and science fiction fans. In each case, the subculture specifies goals and rules for its participants, and thus provides an organized set of challenges, a specialized arena in which to experience flow.

In Chapter 12, Delle Fave and Massimini describe two isolated mountain communities in the Italian Alps. Once part of the mainline farming culture of Europe, the Occitan villagers, cut off from the rest of the world by winter snows, have been left behind as a quaint reminder of a way of life that has long since disappeared elsewhere.

Yet, as the interviews with the older generation of the village show, the way of life that developed in this particular niche of the environment is still unusually conducive to flow. When asked if they ever felt the intense concentration, clarity of goals, effortless action characteristic of the flow experience, all the older villagers recognized in it the feeling typical of their everyday working lives. That is how they felt, they reported, when they took the cows to the high pastures, when they pruned their orchard, when they sat down to carve a piece of furniture out of wood. To the question, "If you had the time and money, what would you rather be doing?" the older villagers answered that they would keep on doing the same things – take the animals to the high meadows, prune the orchard, carve wood.

The Occitan culture is thus an example of that rare adaptation, a way of life that absorbs all the energies of its members in an enjoyable, fulfilling interaction. Work is just as enjoyable as leisure, and leisure is as meaningfully related to the rest of life as work is. Great regrets, unfulfilled desires, or chronic discontent might be present in each person's individual life, but they are not built into the fabric of goals and means that the community provides.

Yet this fine-tuned adaptation to a harsh environment is about to disappear. The fragility of the Occitan culture is shown by the answers of the younger generation of villagers. They no longer enjoy the traditional forms of life. Their concentration is disrupted by goals and desires that come from the culture of the plains. When they herd cattle on the mountains their minds dwell on opportunities suggested by television commercials. For them work is drudgery to be endured only for the money it brings, which then can be spent to experience flow in expensive leisure settings; and since work brings more money in factories, most younger Occitans are settling down to industrial jobs far away from their native valley.

That this may not necessarily be the end of the story is suggested by the second sample described in Chapter 12, which consists of 49 people belonging to the same three-generation alpine family. The oldest generation still lives year-round in a mountain village, while many members of the middle and of the youngest generation work part of the year outside the country or in industrial centers. For the oldest generation, as for the elderly Occitans, work was the most frequently mentioned flow activity. For the next generation work still accounted for 41% of the flow activities, but it accounted for only half as many flow activities in the youngest generation. The fact that optimal experience is less tied to jobs means that people experience flow much less frequently on a day-to-day basis: In the younger generations only half of the flow-producing activities mentioned are reported as taking place every day, whereas the oldest generation reports doing practically all the things that produce flow daily. Needless to say, positive descriptions of work decrease by each generation, with the youngest members finding their work boring, full of effort, distracting, anxiety producing, and uninvolving.

Nevertheless, there is a source for optimism in the above data in that work is still the primary source of flow for some of the younger people. This means that modernized workers are capable of finding optimal experience within the requirements of everyday work. The fact that those who find flow in their work stress personal involvement as a key element suggests this may help them to structure autotelic experiences within their jobs. Since work takes up such a major part of a person's psychic energy, this necessarily affects the rest of daily life. As one young member of the third generation expresses it, when the job goes well, the good feeling stays even after work.

A less optimistic trend emerges in the third study, which deals with white-collar workers from Turin, a large industrial city in northern Italy. The two groups within the sample, the first consisting of clerical workers and the second of executives, found little optimal experience in their jobs. Because everyday productive activities are not a source of optimal experience, these people experience flow rarely. Those few who do associate optimal experience with their jobs tended to rate their work as significantly more challenging and requiring higher skills; not surprisingly, managers, whose job structure tends to be more complex and varied, always rated their jobs as resembling the flow experience more than the clerical workers. Because workers who report flow more frequently tend to actually spend more time working while on the job (Csikszentmihalyi 1982), the dichotomy between work and leisure as sources of flow is not a healthy one for the future of society. The fact that the American workers described in Chapter 18 are able to experience more flow in similar and even lower level jobs may mean that the Turin sample, which is made up of only first- or second-generation urban dwellers (nearly half of the grandparents of the sample are farmers), may be suffering the alienation common to those who have left one type of culture and do not yet feel assimilated into their present one.

The drama sketched out in Chapter 12 is one that is taking place every instant at every point on the globe. It is an example of the uncontrolled process of urbanization eroding traditions that took thousands of years to evolve, and that are now being forgotten in the course of a few generations. Another name for it is "progress."

Unfortunately progress is only a hypothesis. Whether it is true or not only time will tell, for if the technological, value-free lifestyle we call progress turns out to be an evolutionary mistake, it might be too late to retrace our steps. Nevertheless, such cultures suggest the type of psychic integration and identification with productive activities that should be the ideal for structuring the jobs of the future.

Chapter 13 describes a very specialized and unique subculture of the modern, technological world. It is composed of people who, unwilling to follow lifestyles available in the mainline culture, have "dropped out" into a more attractive alternative. The "people of flow" Jim Macbeth interviewed got themselves sailing boats, and disappeared from civilization somewhere between Hawaii and Sri Lanka. They are ocean cruisers who sail their tiny crafts from island to island, following a set of goals and rules that simplify their existence to a manageable, enjoyable routine. Their world is reduced to a few square yards of deck suspended between the seemingly infinite expanse of sky and water. Within these limits, they face the ever-present challenges that the elements throw their way.

Macbeth's interviews clearly show that the motivation to join the cruisers' subculture was to avoid the boredom and the anxiety of contemporary urban life, and enhance the frequency of flow in a setting ideally suited to provide it. Like other subcultures, cruising develops to improve the quality of experience. Macbeth's study describes in great detail how the challenges of cruising, when met by skillful responses, bring about the various conditions of flow.

The cruising subculture is, however, unique in some respects. Its existence at the margins of the social system gives it a somewhat parasitic cast. Cruisers do not produce anything, nor do they try to solve any of those problems that they found so intolerable in the communities they left. Is their escape from the constraints of the human condition nothing but a barren retreat?

Macbeth suggests the the cruisers' lifestyle does make a positive contribution to the rest of humankind: By their radical break with society, they bear witness to alternative values worth preserving. Their way of life becomes a "metacultural commentary," a symbol and an example of what life should be. In some ways, this argument echoes the justification that medieval monks gave for their apparently carefree and comfortable life. The monks escaped the hustle and bustle of everyday life, retreated into monasteries governed by strict rules, so that they could worship God and serve as an example to the rest of society.

Cruisers also worship within strict rules. Their God is not the traditional Christian one, but rather a wholistic concept integrating natural forces and human potentialities. In their neopagan quest they provide a model for a kind of commitment that could help bring order into the lives of many who never dreamed of sailing the South Seas. Whether their example will be seen as a spur to a better life or as an invitation to escape rests ultimately with those who interpret their actions.

In Chapter 14, Isabella Csikszentmihalyi describes another subculture, this time using historical sources as data instead of interviews or questionnaires. She describes the beginnings of the Jesuit order, an institution that swept like wildfire through 16th- and 17th-century Europe, and then through the furthest outposts of Western culture.

The success of the Jesuits was due to the fact that they provided an *order* peculiarly suited to the confusion introduced into the Catholic world by the Renaissance and the Reformation. The order attracted intelligent and ambitious young men because it presented them with cognitive and behavioral challenges graded into finer and finer levels of complexity, and it offered a painstaking discipline to train their native skills.

St. Ignatius of Loyola devised a set of goals embedded in an ideological framework that was responsive to the doubts and anxieties of the period. What is more, he formulated a set of rules that gave purpose and direction to even the smallest details of the Jesuits' lives. It prescribed daily schedules almost minute by minute, and it explained how they should speak, hold their heads, and what they should do with their hands. Yet despite these rigid limitations, the Jesuits were encouraged to tackle some of the most challenging opportunities of the age. They were sent alone to foreign lands to make converts of Indian Moghuls and Chinese emperors; they were encouraged to start utopian communities in the New World; they were trained to take leadership in science and in education.

This combination of clearly structured rules within which a great freedom of initiative was possible made the Jesuit "game" one of the most successful subcultures ever invented. Talented young men vied with each other to join its ranks. And the single-minded enthusiasm of the "professed" Jesuit became a self-fulfilling prophecy in that it provoked respect and fear in those outside the order.

The Jesuits provide an example of the role flow plays in history. It suggests how intrinsic motivation shapes the choices people make over time. Cultural evolution is always happening in the minute actions we take to endorse this belief over that one, to act this way rather than that way. This ever-changing pattern of decisions is guided by the quality of the experience we anticipate as the result of the choices we make. A practice that produces flow is more likely to be adopted. A belief or a technology that helps concentration, that creates order among goals, and that produces clear feedback will be preferred.

Obviously, flow is not the only force that directs historical events. But the course of biocultural evolution cannot be understood without it. Even the Marxist doctrine of social change in the last analysis rests on the assumption that people will try to optimize their experiences. Despite the spurious disguise as an "objective" science, the dynamics of historical materialism rest on the subjective desire to avoid aversive states of consciousness. The class struggle is waged by people who discover that their chances to experience flow are blocked by institutional constraints. In the theory of optimal experience, history gains a powerful tool for understanding.

12. Modernization and the changing contexts of flow in work and leisure

ANTONELLA DELLE FAVE AND FAUSTO MASSIMINI

Cultures differ enormously in terms of the range of opportunities they make available to the people who live in them, and in terms of the skills that the average inhabitant feels he or she possesses. The same culture may vary dramatically along these dimensions at two different points in time. Therefore the quality of subjective experience of a typical member of society will also vary. These days, when anthropologists are more than ever hesitant to breach the neutrality of cultural relativism, and when imposing Western standards of interpretation and description on foreign cultures has become a heresy to be avoided at all costs, it might be that focusing on the self-reported experiences of native respondents will provide a viable comparative method.

Accordingly, this chapter reports on extensive interviews with four European groups that, although living in close geographical proximity, are part of very different ecologies and cultural environments. They differ especially in the degree to which they still follow a traditional agricultural lifestyle, as opposed to being integrated with the technological life of the cities. The purpose is to compare how optimal experience is described in such contexts, to see what different activities it is experienced in, and to infer the effects that modernization is having on the quality of subjective experience.

Traditional rural societies have occasionally succeeded in developing lifestyles that are well suited to the requirements of their particular ecological niche, and at the same time have been able to arrange the tasks necessary for survival in such a manner that the people living in the culture find performing them enjoyable and rewarding. This particular synergy of inner and outer needs is generally lost during the process of modernization, when new techniques of production and new social arrangements temporarily destroy the equilibrium achieved by the older traditional forms.

193

In any given historical period, the quality of life in a given culture will depend in great measure on whether the activities necessary for survival – including work and basic maintenance activities – are able to provide optimal experiences. The progressive development of individual skills takes place mainly in response to the challenges of daily existence, and therefore the structure of everydayness is crucial for the development of human potentialities. In this chapter, we see how the relationship between flow and work is negotiated along a continuum of cultural settings ranging from traditional rural to industrial urban contexts.

In traditional cultures, there are no clear distinctions between what is work and what is leisure, at least as far as subjective experience is concerned. In modern societies, however, new criteria for the organization of work and for technological progress have altered people's perception of everyday tasks. Work often fails to provide varied opportunities for action and the clarity of goals and feedback that facilitate optimal experience; many are thus forced to search for it in the leisure activities that have greatly proliferated in modern cultures.

Data collected by our research group in different cultural contexts suggest that modernization works extremely quickly in separating one generation from the next in terms of which activities produce optimal experiences. The studies described here illustrate that the transformation in the kind of activities that produce flow often has profound effects on the style and quality of life as a whole.

Method

The studies reported in this chapter are based on data collected with the Flow Questionnaire, an instrument that had been used previously for studying optimal experience. It is a paper-and-pencil questionnaire consisting of two sections. In the first section respondents are presented with three quotations that describe the flow experience, taken from interviews with a rock climber, a composer of music, and a dancer who were describing their experiences at times of deep concentration and involvement in the activity (Csikszentmihalyi 1975b, 1982a; Han, Chapter 8). Respondents are asked whether they have ever had similar experiences, and if yes, in what contexts. They are then asked to indicate how frequently they are involved with the activities that they associate with the experience of flow.

The second step consists of rating the flow activity identified in the first section along 12 dimensions related to the flow experience (Mayers 1978). The ratings are made on an 8-point semantic differential scale. The rating dimensions are as follows:

I get involved.
I get anxious.
I clearly know what I am supposed to do.
I get direct clues as to how well I am doing.
I feel I can handle the demands of the situation.
I feel self-conscious.
I get bored.
I have to make an effort to keep my mind on what is happening.
I would do it even if I didn't have to.
I get distracted.
Time passes (slowly . . . fast).
I enjoy the experience, and/or the use of my skills.

According to the theory, a person in flow will describe his experience in terms of being very involved, having clear feedback, wanting to do the activity, not being bored, not making an effort to concentrate, and so on.

After respondents completed these 12 scales in reference to their flow activity, they were asked to repeat the rating in reference to other target activities such as family life, schoolwork, or television viewing. In the studies that follow, all the respondents rated both their first-choice flow activities on the 12 scales, as well as their jobs if these had not been mentioned as the flow activity.

After completing the questionnaire, respondents were asked to describe how the experience that they associated with flow begins, how it continues, and what makes it stop. The same series of questions were repeated with reference to jobs. The interview continued with more specific questions about attentional processes in everyday life connected with flow. For example, respondents were asked what thoughts typically occur when they have nothing urgent to do, how often these thoughts occur, and what distracts them from these thoughts; what they would like to do if money and time were of no concern, and what prevents them from doing such things; and what things they most like to do in life and how frequently they do it.

This group of questions provides concrete information about the place of optimal experience in the life of the individual. It gives a detailed view of how important it is in the total psychic economy of the person, and it shows the types of activities in which it occurs, as well as the alternatives that respondents see for experiencing flow in their lives.

Flow experience in traditional cultures

The first set of studies presented illustrates the deep integration between flow and everyday productive activities achieved in traditional cultures. The research was conducted in two mountain regions of northern Italy: The first sample was the Occitan community in the village of Sampeyre (Val Varaita) and the second a three-generational family group that has lived for centuries in a small community of the Gressoney branch of the Val D'Aosta.

Flow and everyday life among the Occitans. The Occitan sample consists of 20 respondents, aged 16 to 78 years, seven of whom are males and 13 females. The respondents reside in the small Alpine village of Sampeyre, which is situated at an elevation of 5,100 feet in the Varaita Valley. The Occitan culture was the cradle of the Langue d'Oc, and played an important role in the history of the Middle Ages. It survives now as a scattered linguistic and cultural entity, mostly in French territory, but with small extensions into Italy, Spain, and the Principality of Monaco. The ancestors of the Occitan community of this study have lived for centuries in the Val Varaita. The smallness of the current sample is due to the steady attrition through migration out of the mountains, an exodus that has dramatically accelerated since World War II. There are few people left to continue in the traditional peasant lifestyle, which involves farming, orchard keeping, cattle raising, sewing, needlework, and the cultivation of flowers. The Occitans live in traditional stone and wood houses containing only the essential artifacts needed for everyday use. The village is often totally isolated in the winter by frequent and heavy snowfalls.

This type of inhospitable environment requires strong adaptive capacities on the part of the inhabitants. In order to survive, a great number of specific skills must be developed to deal with the high environmental challenges. In such conditions, as in most preindustrial societies, everyday activities are closely connected to clear goals and essential functions: Farming and animal husbandry are necessary for biological survival, social interactions are essential to keep the fabric of mutual support and sociability in working order, and the local crafts are necessary for the maintenance of the Occitan culture through the production of functional artifacts. They are all basic activities for the replication and the transmission of biological and cultural inheritance (Massimini 1982; Csikszentmihalyi & Massimini 1985).

At first glance, this culture appears to be similar to the tribal cultures described by Turner (1982): "What we see here is a universe of work in which the community takes part in its totality out of obligation and not by choice." But if we look at how the Occitans describe the subjective experience of their everyday life, through the answers provided to the Flow Questionnaire, it appears that the life they lead is actually perceived to be the result of a free decision to abide by the traditional forms of their culture. Most respondents had spent time in urban centers, and several had the opportunity of moving in with their children or relatives who were living a much easier existence in such centers. Yet, as we shall see, at least half of the sample in question had chosen not to leave the village.

We compare two groups in this sample, which are distinguished by their attitude toward the traditional lifestyle. The first group consists of respondents who claim to have voluntarily chosen to maintain the Occitan lifestyle. The second group includes those who would leave the village and move to urban or modernized environments if they had the chance. This division also reflects a difference in age: The first group only includes people over 30 years of age, the second only those between 16 and 30 years. The 20 respondents in the two groups were given the three quotations referring to optimal experience; everyone, regardless of age or level of education, recognized the kind of experience described in the quotations.

The most interesting contrast between the two groups is the kind of activity respondents associated with the quotations. As shown in Figure 12.1, the first group, consisting of "traditional" respondents, reported work as the context for optimal experience in 77% of the associations they made to the three quotations. In every case respondents mentioned traditional work activities such as farming or crafts. In terms of frequency, 56% of these flowlike activities were reported to occur every day and an additional 41% once a week or more often. Here are two examples from the interviews:

> I still take care of the cows and tend the orchard. I find special satisfaction in caring for the plants: I like to see them grow day by day. It is very beautiful. (62-year-old female)

> By work I mean tilling the soil, bringing in the hay. It is hard work but I like it. I tried for a little while to work elsewhere, but I didn't like it. I quit and I came back to farming because I like it more. (42-year-old male)

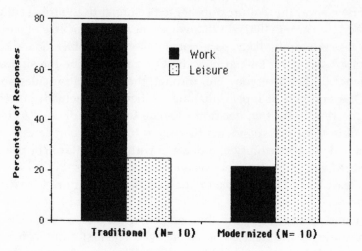

Figure 12.1. Activity context for the flow experience: Occitan farmers.

Few responses in this group paired the flow quotation with leisure activities. Only 24% of all the activities mentioned referred to leisure, and those were almost exclusively of a traditional type, such as playing cards or *bocce* (a form of bowling). Not only was flow more rarely experienced in leisure activities than in work, but the frequency of leisure activities was also reported to occur less often, on an average of once a week.

It seems clear that traditional Occitans have smoothly integrated optimal experience into the fabric of everyday life. The activities that produce flow are those that they perform from morning to night in basic tasks dictated by the implicit behavioral instructions of their biological and cultural inheritance. In addition, however, they have found ways to make such tasks the context of optimal experiences. There is no room in their lives for "meaningless work and useless leisure" (Csikszentmihalyi 1981a), typical of modernized societies. All the psychic energy is focused on essential goals. Challenges are high, allowing the person to test and to develop his or her skills. Work becomes an autotelic activity. The traditional Occitans believe that what they have to do is both inevitable and freely chosen; and because they enjoy their daily tasks, these tasks, and the culture in which they are embedded, are more likely to survive over time. One of our respondents describes knitting, her major flow activity:

> This sensation [referring to the flow experience] begins when I make a difficult stitch – if it is difficult I get great satisfaction when

I see that it came out well. I can spend hours knitting. This way of feeling only happens if I get involved. Once it starts, what keeps it going is the activity itself. (62-year-old female)

This woman also remembers with pleasure how she used to spin wool as a young girl, competing with the other girls of the village in a test as to who could make the thinnest and most uniform thread. Such type of work explains the nostalgia of the elderly respondents for the hard life of the past: "Even the most rigidly determined life makes one feel free as long as one chooses it freely" (Csikszentmihalyi 1985a). This freedom of choice was stressed by several of the interviewees. Some had worked for many years abroad or in cities because of economic necessity, but eventually returned.

For me to work means taking care of the fields and the animals. Especially the animals. For a while I had other jobs in France, but I preferred to come back. I love to work in the open. I could never work indoors in a factory, for example. I like to be close to the animals, it gives me a lot of satisfaction. (50-year-old male)

To the question, "If you could do anything you wanted, regardless of time and money, what would you do?" 21% of the Occitans in the first group answered that they would spend more time with the family, but 50% answered that they would do exactly what they are doing right now. For example,

I really don't know because I'm happy as I am right now, with my family and my beautiful house. I don't wish for anything else. (71-year-old female)

In contrast, the younger respondents of the second group, who would like to abandon the traditional mode of life, do not experience flow in work settings, but rather in "leisure" contexts like skiing, spending time with friends, or playing soccer (Figure 12.1). Such activities account for 68% of their responses.

For these respondents, optimal experiences are rarely reported in productive activities, and consequently only 22% report experiencing them every day. Technology has introduced some new activities to Sampeyre that help structure attention and produce optimal experiences. A good example is a 22-year-old male, who claims to get flow from "practicing motor-cross on the mountain trails." Both of his parents were part of the sample that reported farming as their first flow activity; the son, however, has focused his attention on a modern cultural artifact, the motorbike, which for him has become the vehicle for optimal experience. But the bike intervenes between nature and the individual; the mountains and the natural environment are no longer in his focus of attention. Riding the motorbike isolates him from the web of daily responsibilities; the activity is not as integrated with the pattern of everyday productive and social tasks as those his parents enjoy.

Exclusive focus on leisure as a source of flow is well illustrated by another respondent's description of what he does for a living:

I work as a bricklayer, and occasionally I farm. I have no prefer- ences, I don't like either one.

The enjoyment found in traditional ways of working has not been replicated in modern jobs. Instead we see that split between work and leisure typical of industrial and postindustrial societies (Dumazedier 1985). A woman of 20 who works as a sales clerk and lives in Sampeyre with her parents, who are farmers, describes her work:

I am not particularly interested in my present job. I do it because I can't find anything better. . . . If I could do anything I wanted . . . I would travel. . . . I'd get a job I liked better. I would go live some- where else, not because I don't like this place, but because there are so few opportunities here to work and to have a good time.

The interviews with the Occitans confirm the integration between work and leisure, between obligatory and voluntary activities, among the more traditional respondents. For them work and the entire style of life is free because it appears to be freely chosen each day, and expe- rienced as deeply enjoyable. The younger respondents, on the other hand, are no longer satisfied with the opportunities of their elders. They cannot find joy in productive activities and wish to move elsewhere. Although these conclusions are based on a very small sample, they are confirmed by the results of the next study.

Lifestyle and flow experiences in an extended family of the Gressoney Valley. Forty-nine respondents, all belonging to three generations of the same family from the village of Pont Trentaz, were given the Flow Question- naire and then interviewed. This small village is situated at an elevation of about 3,500 feet in the Gressoney Valley, a defile that branches off at right angles from the much larger Val d'Aosta.

The 10 respondents from the first and oldest generation live in Pont Trentaz year-round. Of the 28 respondents from the second, or middle generation, several spend at least part of the year working abroad or in large urban centers. Several members of the youngest generation only return to the village for the holidays.

The changes in work activities and in life environments brought about

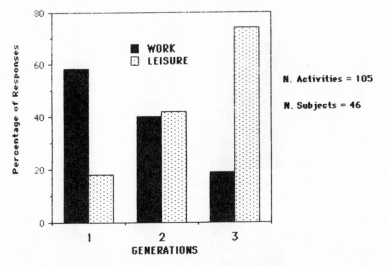

Figure 12.2. Distribution of flow activities in a three-generational family from Pont Trentaz, Gressoney Valley.

by modernization are well reflected in the distribution of responses to the Flow Questionnaire reported in Figure 12.2. For the elders of the first generation (between 66 and 82 years of age), as for the traditional Occitans, work is the most frequently mentioned flow activity. Of the flow activities they mentioned, 58% were related to work. For the second generation (ranging from 24 to 61 years of age), only 41% of the activities mentioned as similar to flow refer to work. The declining enjoyment of work is much stronger in the third generation (ages 20 to 33); only 19% of the flow activities reported by the 11 respondents in this group involved work. In contrast, leisure activities were mentioned as a source of flow in only 16% of the cases by the first generation, in 44% of the cases by the second generation, and in 70% of the cases by the third, and youngest, generation.

The integration of optimal experience with the activities of everyday life is indicated by the fact that the older respondents report doing practically all the things that produce flow daily, whereas in the second and third generations only half of the flow-producing activities are reported as taking place every day.

The generational differences are further highlighted by the results reported in Figure 12.3, which is based on the ratings of work on the various dimensions of flow. As the figure shows, the oldest generation rated their work at the highest level on five dimensions: involvement,

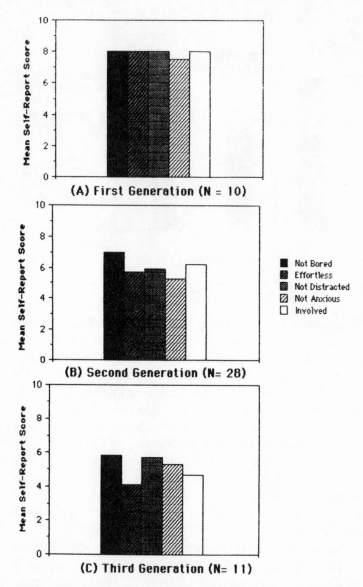

Figure 12.3. Rating of subjective experience while working: extended family from Pont Trentaz, Gressoney Valley.

effortless concentration, few distractions, infrequent anxiety, lack of boredom. The ratings of the second generation were substantially less positive on these dimensions. Finally, the youngest generation rated their work as much more boring, full of effort, distracting, anxiety producing, and as less involving. Analyses of variance showed significant differences between the generations at the .01 level of significance or less on each of these five dimensions.

The way respondents described their work in the interview reinforces the results just reported. For example, here is a woman of the first generation describing the work that is her favorite flow activity:

It gives me great satisfaction. To be outdoors, to talk with people, to be with my animals. . . . I talk to everybody, plants, birds, flowers, and animals. Everything in nature keeps you company, you see nature progress every day. You feel clean and happy: too bad that you get tired and have to go home. . . . Even when you have to work a lot it is very beautiful. (76-year-old female)

Here is another woman from the same generation who finds her optimal experience in her work as a seamstress:

It is rewarding. Even when it did not pay I would do it for the reward of being able to change a length of fabric into a dress. (74-year-old female)

The elderly farmers of the first generation repeatedly stressed the free choice underlying their behavior and claimed they had no unfulfilled desires. The following answer is very typical:

I am free, free in my work, because I do whatever I want. If I don't do something today I will do it tomorrow, I don't have a boss, I am the boss of my own life. I have kept my freedom and I have fought for my freedom. Now I'm getting Social Security and if I want to buy something I can do it without asking my husband and without having to thank anybody. (74-year-old female)

In answer to the question of what she would do if money and time were no object, the same woman states:

If I could do whatever I wanted, I would get some suntan on the balcony, which I never do. I would take some walks across the mountains with the family. And I would do a lot of needlepoint . . . I would help others more than I do now. I would visit some of the holy shrines. . . . What keeps me from doing these things is the lack of time, and then I have to take care of my husband . . . and you do get tired when you work all day.

For these people, the entire pattern of life is autotelic. It is enjoyable, serene, and free, despite the fact that – or rather, because – it is a continuous source of highly complex challenges that call for equally developed skills. This kind of life not only provides a steady sequence of optimal experiences but it does so within activities that are complex and meaningful for the individual as well as for the community. An elderly carpenter describes the flow experience in his work as follows:

This feeling usually comes toward the end when I begin to see how the piece is coming out. It is a very rewarding and happy feeling. To get to this feeling one must become involved in the work. One must be persevering in life. Willpower and perseverence are necessary for every task and for every thing. (66-year-old male)

The man in question is a disabled veteran who had been severely wounded in World War II and had been given an easy clerical job by the government; nevertheless, he also kept working as a carpenter full-time.

Csikszentmihalyi (1982b) claims that "the self grows as the result of continuous learning stimulated by freely chosen goals. This is the same process that optimizes the frequency of flow experiences; therefore one might say that lifelong learning is the best recipe for happiness." The oldest generation of this family seems to have been able to follow that recipe rather closely.

The sons and daughters, however – the family members of the second generation, most of whom live in towns and work at clerical occupations – are split in their attitudes toward work. About half of them look at work exclusively as a source of income that provides little opportunity for creativity or freedom. For instance,

For me, my current job is just a way of making a good living. It is a job that makes it difficult for me to express my personality because the tendency nowadays is to stifle the individual so as to make him more interchangeable and productive. (26-year-old male)

Another white-collar member of this group describes her work:

It takes up a great part of my time and my energies and I think it is important to keep me in balance even though I would prefer to be less involved in it so that I could do things which I believe are more important. (26-year-old female)

The other half of the members of this generation do, however, list work as their primary source of flow. Clearly, modernized workers are also able to find optimal experience in the requirements of everyday work. For instance, a 28-year-old technical draftsman reports the characteristics of flow in "assignments that are especially challenging." A 41-year-old contractor reports optimal experience in the planning of his building jobs, which to him present an opportunity to "express to the utmost my professional skills as well as giving freedom to my imagination."

Both of these respondents stress personal involvement as a key element in their jobs. Such involvement leads to a search for new challenges. Persons who experience flow in activities that are rich in challenge tend to develop increasingly complex personalities; optimal experience is linked to a constant increase in challenges, which in turn leads to gradual increments in skill and a resultant balance in the upper reaches of the flow channel.

These trends hold true also for the third generation. In this group the tendency to find optimal experience in the typically modern jobs of a technological society is even more pronounced. The young members of the family describe their jobs very differently from their older relations. A young tool-and-die maker reports:

> My job is a close relationship between man and machine and it must take into account the requirements of the shop and of the finished product. It requires great concentration from the initial drafting stage to the setting up of the machine all the way until the piece is finished. . . . When the job goes well the good feeling stays with me even after work. If the work is rewarding it will carry over to outside the job. (29-year-old male)

Here the respondent is stressing the impact of flow on the whole life of the person: Its effects color his general attitude toward the entirety of his everyday experience. It should be added that the youngest respondents report optimal experiences in a great variety of activities that were formerly unavailable to their grandparents: listening to recorded music, for instance, and especially the practice of a number of sports, ranging from track to basketball to mountain climbing.

The fact that all three groups recognize the characteristics of flow but differ in the activities in which they experience it confirms the existence of a practically unlimited number of potential flow activities in both traditional and modern contexts. In the modern urban settings, however, the environmental constraints are less severe. Work often loses the complexity and relevance it still has in the farming milieu. The great number of artifacts simplifies everyday life, lowers the average level of challenges, and creates long stretches of free time in which it is not clear what one is supposed to do. Thus many people must search for optimal experiences in specialized environments: The separation between work and free time begins.

In part, this phenomenon is certainly the result of social conditions; however, the way each individual perceives the opportunities for action in the social environment is also important. Half of the people in both the second and third generation found flow in their work environment whereas the other half did not; that there is such a difference suggests the possibility of individual differences in the ability to structure autotelic experiences. When confronted with similar jobs, two persons may see completely different challenges, different skills, and therefore different possibilities for enjoyment. Since work takes up the largest part of the psychic energies of the individual, unless one sees it as a source of optimal experience, it is very difficult to enjoy the rest of daily life.

Flow and work in urban contexts

White-collar workers. Industrial society is organized in terms of strict criteria of work organization, and – to use Max Weber's (1922) term – a general "rationalization" of life. The attention of the workers is structured by technologically defined goals, and it is this predictable exploitation of the psychic energies of the people that supports the myth of efficiency and of the endless increase in productivity ascribed to industrialized societies. As Mitchell (1983; and Chapter 3) has pointed out, this is what leads to the large industrial corporations of our era, to the so-called division of labor, and on a larger scale, to the fragmentation of everyday life. Under such conditions work tends to require the performance of limited and partial tasks. In the absence of personally meaningful goals and of flexible challenges, industrial jobs often turn into externally imposed obligations. Yet as Csikszentmihalyi and Massimini (1985) have pointed out, people will seek out activities that produce optimal experiences and will replicate them selectively. If work makes it impossible to experience flow, people will search for it in the context of free leisure time. However, this leads to the split between useful but coercive instrumental activities on the one hand, and voluntarily chosen expressive activities providing little more than fleeting pleasures on the other.

These trends were illustrated in a study of 64 white-collar workers in Turin, a large industrial city in northern Italy. The sample consisted of 32 males and 32 females between 20 and 61 years of age. In terms of occupational status the sample was further subdivided into Group 1, consisting of 32 clerical workers (telephone operators, file clerks, typists, cashiers, and so on), and Group 2, which included supervisory employees with greater responsibility over budgets and personnel, as well as managers and executives. Although thoroughly urbanized, a sub-

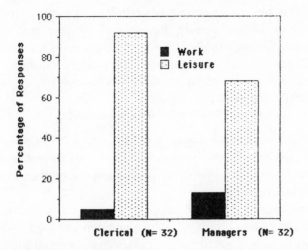

Figure 12.4. Activity context for the flow experience: Turin workers.

stantial number of the respondents were first- or second-generation urban dwellers; 38% of the paternal and 39% of the maternal grandparents of the sample were farmers. Thus these respondents, like so many other recent immigrants from the countryside, could not relie implicitly on family traditions for finding optimal experiences in the environment of the city.

After being read the three quotations of the Flow Questionnaire, 91% of the respondents claimed to have had similar experiences. Figure 12.4 shows the distribution of the two groups' responses with regard to work and to leisure. It is striking that in the first group only 5% of the activities linked to flow had to do with work, and this proportion was not that much higher for the second group – 14%. In contrast, 92% of the first group and 70% of the second associated optimal experience with leisure activities, primarily "listening to music" and "sports." The ratings that respondents gave to these activities matched theoretical expectations (see Figure 12.4). The average score on the 12 variables measuring the various dimensions of the flow experience (e.g., involvement, not being bored, not being anxious) was between 7 and 7.8 on an 8-point scale.

Members of the first group had jobs involving essentially repetitive tasks with little room for personal initiative or responsibility. Such work environments often lead to alienation, as Marx noted long ago, and as the chapters by Mitchell, Macbeth, and Allison and Duncan show in this volume. Not surprisingly, only 10% of the workers in this group mentioned their jobs as a source of flow, and work constituted only 5%

of the activities mentioned. In describing what their work meant to them, most of the people in this group used phrases such as: "For me, work is simply a necessity for survival," "It's a job that provides money for my family," "It keeps me going," "Work is an obligation – a duty."

The three respondents in this group who did mention work as a source of flow gave opposite answers. For instance,

> For me, work means involvement. (37-year-old male)

> By work I mean something that reflects my personality, a productive activity that mirrors our needs, that allows us to realize our skills and our knowledge. Work occupies an important place in my life. (21-year-old female)

It is possible that these three people have jobs that are more autotelic than those of the rest of this group; that they have more responsibility, more initiative and challenge at their workplace than is usual for employees of their type. But this does not seem to be the case. From their interviews it appears more likely that they find flow in work not because the job is structured differently, but because their personalities are more autotelic: They have developed an ability to perceive opportunities in an otherwise rather barren environment.

For the majority of people in this group optimal experience does not happen in everyday productive activities. Thus, on the whole, they experience flow relatively rarely in comparison with the more traditional workers described earlier, or with their three colleagues who associate optimal experience with their jobs. Less than half the people in this group report flow daily, while 28% say they experience it "once a week," and 22% "once a month or less often."

The supervisors and managers of the second group rated their jobs as being much more similar to the flow experience than the clerical workers did. As Table 12.1 indicates, on 6 of the 12 variables there were large differences, with the managers always rating their jobs as resembling the flow experience more than the clerical workers. In addition, they also saw their jobs as significantly more challenging and requiring higher skills. Because their jobs are in fact more autotelic, these respondents are more likely to give autotelic definitions of what work means to them:

> For me working means to build something that is very rewarding. (28-year-old male)

> To be mentally and physically involved, so I can contribute to society. (49-year-old male)

Table 12.1. *Comparison of clerical workers' and managers' mean ratings of their jobs on the flow scales*

Dimensions of the experience	Group 1, white-collar (N = 32)	Group 2, managers (N = 32)	t value	Probability
Involvement	5.18	6.46	−3.14	.003
Feedback	6.56	7.40	−2.47	.02
Intrinsic motivation	3.93	6.56	−4.25	.000
Not distracted	4.93	6.71	−4.00	.000
Clear goals	6.65	7.56	−2.35	.02
Time goes fast	5.21	6.84	−3.14	.003

It is a way of fullfilling myself, to accomplish something, to do something. (26-year-old female)

It means to carry out my principles in practice, because my work is based on an ideal way of being. (44-year-old male)

But even in this privileged group there are sharp individual differences, reminding us again that persons as well as social contexts vary along an autotelic continuum. For the eight persons in this group who mention work as a flow activity, "the traditional distinction between work and leisure is not terribly useful; the essential component of flow can be found in any activity" (Csikszentmihalyi & Graef 1979). For them, 47% percent of the activities they mention as being flowlike involve work, and the other half leisure. Consequently they report flow activities much more often; 56% daily, and an additional 38% at least once a week.

Earlier studies have suggested that those workers who report more frequent flow experiences spend more time actually working when they are on their jobs, and that they enjoy more almost every other aspect of their lives (Csikszentmihalyi 1978b). Hence the ability to tie optimal experience with productive activities benefits both the person (by improving the quality of his or her life) and the community (by increasing the level of psychic energy available to pursue productive goals). It is clear that new forms of social intervention will be needed to alleviate the schism between work and free time. One obvious target is the educational system, which currently keeps emphasizing extrinsic values tied to future income, prestige, and other material goals and pays almost no attention to the quality of experience. To counter these trends, it is necessary to educate young people to recognize the limitless opportunities for action in everyday life. This task becomes particularly urgent if we consider that "if adolescents are ever to grow up willingly they must be convinced that it is possible to enjoy instrumental roles" (Csikszentmihalyi 1981a).

Flow and work rejoined: a sample of dancers. This chapter began with a description of traditional lifestyles wherein everyday life activities are inseparable. It continued by showing that with increasing modernization people are less and less able to experience enjoyment in their work and are forced to seek optimal experiences in often trivial leisure pursuits. Yet even in highly industrialized urban contexts it is possible to find opportunities for an almost complete merger between vocation and flow experience. This possibility is illustrated with a sample of 60 modern dancers who were tested with the Flow Questionnaire.

With the exception of two men, the respondents were all women. Their ages ranged from 18 to 44 years. They fell into five natural groupings: Groups 1 to 4 included students enrolled in the second to fifth year of modern dance training; Group 5 included 16 teachers of dance. For the women in the first three groups dance was still a leisure activity. Each spent only 1–4 hours per week dancing. But the students of the fifth year were already in transition toward a professional dance career and took lessons every day. For the teachers, the transition had already happened: They spent the major part of each day teaching dance and most of them took part in performances and otherwise practiced their professional skills.

It is the teachers that are particularly interesting, because they seem to have been able to achieve the conjunction between work and optimal experience that was possible in more traditional cultures, but that has become so elusive in modernized settings.

When the flow quotations were read to the respondents, all of them recognized dance as a flow activity, but in different proportions, depending on their level of training. Figure 12.5 shows that whereas only 50% of the first group mentioned dance as a flow activity, that proportion increased with each year of study and reached 100% among the students of the last year and among the teachers.

The dance instructors are able to derive optimal experiences from everyday life within an extremely complex activity that requires constant commitment at a very high level of professional performance. Here is how one respondent describes the way in which the flow experience begins for her:

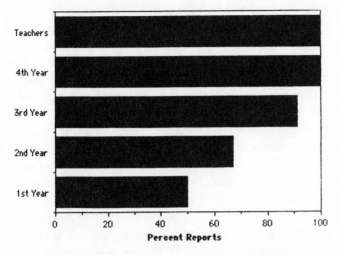

Figure 12.5. Dance mentioned as flow activity: sample of 60 dancers.

This type of feeling begins roughly after one hour of warmups and stretching when one has achieved a fine-tuning of muscle strength and psychological security. I feel happy, satisfied, light. Training helps to make it come about, but I must be very serene and mentally relaxed to get into it. What makes it go on is fitness, willpower, and enthusiasm. (25-year-old female)

In describing the origins of her career choice, and the difficult steps of her professional development, another woman says:

My professional choice was only realized because of my love of dancing. I have met many obstacles on the way and I expect I will meet still many more. But these are part of the fascination dance has for me. . . . Naturally one has to come to terms with one's body. It is very hard work and your body is under constant stress. The only reason I go on is because I love this work. (31-year-old female)

The effort and hardship that one must put up with to learn this art can only be overcome if one finds passion and pleasure in the dance. (25-year-old female)

Almost half the teachers (44%) claim to have started on the way to becoming dancers for purely intrinsic motives with no other incentive than the desire of doing the activity, and often in conflict with their parents' alternative plans for their future. Another third of the sample started dancing in the context of courses they took early in life with parental urging. For both of these groups dance has become part of a life theme (Csikszentmihalyi & Beattie 1979). For example, one of the teachers who started dancing at 14 years of age describes her career:

> From the very first I wanted to become a professional ballerina. It has been hard: little money, lots of traveling, and my mother always complaining about my work. But the love of dancing has always sustained me. It is now part of my life, a goal, a part of me that I could not live without. (23-year-old female)

As already noted elsewhere (Massimini, Csikszentmihalyi, & Delle Fave 1986), this group of 16 teachers is made up of women between 18 and 35 years of age: Yet only three of them are married and only one has a child. For them, the optimal experience obtained through dancing has become – at least temporarily – a priority over the biological reproduction that would force them into a long period of inactivity, with negative consequences for their physical fitness and the decay of skills needed to practice dancing. Instead of biological motherhood, the transmission of optimal experience to students becomes one of the main concerns of these teachers:

> I get an immense amount of pleasure from dancing and I'm quite sure that I communicate it to my students. In fact I think it is very important to pass this on because one can only dance if one enjoys it. It should not be a hassle but true joy. (31-year-old female)

> I think I'm able to communicate my personal joy but this is not enough. The students must find a way to feel the same thing. . . . This appreciation on the part of the students gives value to my work: the fact that I help them reach a vital dimension of mental and physical activity. (31-year-old female)

These dancers recognize that to make the subject one teaches enjoyable is the best way to ensure learning. Educators can help young people learn successfully only if they show that they are enjoying what they teach and if they can communicate that enjoyment to the students (Csikszentmihalyi 1982c, 1986). Similarly, it it important for young people to learn to derive optimal experiences from their everyday activities, learning to find in them ever new opportunities and challenges. As Csikszentmihalyi (1975b) writes, "One of the basic things to be taught to children is to recognize opportunities for action in their environment. This is the skill on which all other skills are based."

The possibility of educating people to build flow into their lives opens up a very broad range of social implications. It is the key for improving the quality of everyday experience. The example of the dancers returns us back full circle to the lifestyle of the Occitans and the old farmers of the Gressoney Valley: Optimal experience permeates their whole life, freeing the individual from unreachable desires and frustrations. When asked "If you could do anything you wanted, what would you do?" most of the dance teachers answered "I would dance more," "I would go to more dance workshops," "I would learn new techniques." In other words they wished to cultivate the activity that already takes up most of their energy, a cultivation that they described in terms of seeking new challenges and ways to improve their skills.

This integrated lifestyle well known to at least some traditional societies can also be actualized in modern urban contexts. Such conjunction can be accomplished when the necessary goals that organize the activities of each day are experienced as freely chosen, and when the challenges encountered are met with confidence.

In the tenth volume of his *Works*, Descartes noted: "Wisdom remains always the same even when applied to the most disparate objects. It is unchanged by their diversity, just as sunlight remains unchanged by the variety of objects it shines upon." As we have seen, flow is experienced in the same way by people who belong to very different cultures and styles of life. Learning how to maximize its occurrence in the context of the productive activities of everyday life is one of the greatest accomplishments of human wisdom.

13. Ocean cruising

JIM MACBETH

Ocean cruising is an example of one of the more exotic and esoteric ways of living when viewed from the perspective of Western industrialized society. Cruisers are people who sail the oceans for years at a time, and do so for pleasure rather than profit. They forsake the security and safety of land-based life for the formidable challenges of ocean and weather. Many of them give up "successful" careers, and all must overcome the work ethic as they move their productive activities from the center of their lives to its periphery. In making this choice they deviate from the usual goals that society suggests people seek, and so imply that they are dissatisfied with mainstream society. Cruisers challenge societal values by altering their whole way of life, abandoning their careers, income, social mobility, the community, and the security of a fixed family life.

The flow model can be used to explain why cruisers are motivated to pursue the lifestyle of this subculture. Clearly, this way of life must be intrinsically motivating, since it requires much effort, involves considerable danger, and provides no extrinsic rewards such as fame or money. Previous studies of intrinsic motivation have focused on autotelic *activities* like chess or mountain climbing (Csikszentmihalyi 1975b). The present study extends the concept to an autotelic *lifestyle*, one that represents an attempt to restructure everyday life activities into a continuous flow experience.

The purpose of the study was to discover the motivations, attitudes, and way of life of this particular splinter from Western society. The usable sample consisted of 59 cruisers who were interviewed by the author during two field trips in the Pacific Ocean, one in 1978 and the other in 1981. The first trip involved 6 months of interviewing while living in the cruiser community and sailing some 5,000 nautical miles. The 1981 field trip involved 2 months of interviewing cruisers in Fiji.

Many people sail on weekends and during vacations, and may even take occasional extended journeys. Cruisers differ from these other sailors in that sailing is central to their daily lives – it is much more than an activity or hobby in a life dominated by an occupation. Cruisers interviewed in the present study were defined as (1) persons without any conscious or imminent deadline (such as a job) for returning to their home port and (2) those who have been cruising for at least 15 months.

During these interviews I questioned cruisers about their motivation, background, and sailing experience and administered personality scales. The latter included Csikszentmihalyi's Eight Reasons for Enjoying an Activity and the Cantril Self-Anchoring Striving Scale (Cantril 1965), which tests for meanings and values across cultures. In addition, cruisers were asked to list the personal characteristics they thought were required to survive as a cruiser. Their responses provided insight into the types of goals and challenges that form the attraction and motivation for adopting the cruising life.

Rejection of the mainstream lifestyle

One way of explaining why some people opt for the difficult life of ocean cruising is to consider what alternatives they are rejecting. The reasons that the respondents in this study and other sailors give for becoming cruisers point to familiar sources of discontent with modern life: the 9-to-5 "rat race" with its stresses and deadlines; the same schedule every day; working in a windowless building (S. 021); the "hundreds of business conferences where everyone said the same thing over and over again, and hundreds of martini lunches where everyone said the same thing over and over again" (Mann 1978, p. 9). Others place their decision within a larger context: "I was able to throw off responsibility, cast off a hum-drum life, be a bit adventurous. I had to do something with life besides vegetate" (S. 062); "It was a chance to do one really big thing in my life; big and memorable" (S. 052).

The reasons given by the cruisers suggest that our system of urban living – with its material consumption, business organization, and social control – fosters meaningless goals and is basically antagonistic to the autonomy of the individual. Cruisers blame modern society for alienating the person from the rhythms of nature, and substituting instead the pace and process of artificial creations – work schedules, payment schedules, business hours, lunch hours, rush hours, and so on. The adjectives the interviewees chose to describe cruisers suggest the qualities these individual are searching for when they abandon conventional lives: adaptable, flexible; self-reliant, self-sufficient; resourceful; careful; optimist; curious; independent; adventurous; nature lover; organized; self-confident.

The cruisers' criticisms are similar to those reflected in other counter-culture lifestyles, like those of surfers and commune members. Although all these groups are critical of the corporate state and the human alien-ation they associate with that state, the alternative community adherents appear to be concerned primarily about the loss of community, which they translate into a loss of individual power and meaning, whereas cruisers appear to focus directly on the powerlessness of the individual in modern society. Thus cruisers put more stress on the individual than on community. Their solution, like that of the surfers, is to take the individuated aspect of capitalism – for example, the notion of self-interest – to its logical extension by opting out of active participation in society and taking care only of themselves. The alternative communities differ in that they seek shared ownership and a stronger sense of mutual commitment or community. None of these groups is actively involved in a wider effort at social change, but all three can be seen as agents of social change – they all question the status quo and by example suggest alternatives to the taken-for-granted. They try to alleviate alienation by getting closer to nature in their place and pace of living. It appears that being "in" and "with" nature in such an intimate fashion can help to overcome the sense of "homelessness" (Berger, Berger, & Kellner 1973) associated with large urban agglomerations and the lifestyle and occu-pational demands associated with city life.

Although cruisers are reacting against their social milieu, their reaction is more than simple escapism. Their reaction is also creative. At this point in their lives their concerns are oriented almost exclusively to quality-of-life issues. They are concerned with "being needs," not merely "deficiency needs"; they are searching for individual autonomy, fulfill-ment, satisfaction, and personal growth instead of being preoccupied with illness, "maturity," and neurosis (Maslow 1968). Humanistic psy-chology embodies a model of human nature that encompasses these empirical and normative concepts, including the central notion of in-trinsic rewards. A humanistic orientation to psychology is distinguished by its concern for personal psychological health and the full development of human potential. The common theme is that of autonomy and choice. In line with such orientation, cruisers act on their own perception of personal freedom. They seek to change their life space and lifestyle in ways that will enhance their identity and sense of competence. The risks they take in this process of reaching out often involve physical danger and an interaction with the unknown, both human and non-human. However, when integrated, these processes are potentially part of a cruiser's identity and sense of fulfillment, part of the enjoyment of life.

Lifestyle as a flow experience

It is not enough to know what cruisers are escaping *from*. By considering the positive attraction of cruising in terms of the flow model, it is possible to understand what they are moving *toward*. Although the flow model was developed in conjunction with the study of activities that appeared to be self-rewarding, here it is extrapolated to the study of a *lifestyle* with a fundamental orientation to the enjoyment people find in cruising.

Csikszentmihalyi (1975b, p. 38) sees flow as a state of experience that is engrossing, intrinsically rewarding, and "outside the parameters of worry and boredom." He cites rock climbing, dancing, music composition, and surgery as examples of activities that provide a combination of elements that allow the flow experience to develop, and assumes that such activities are autotelic, that is, contain rewards in the experience itself. These intrinsic rewards result when a pursuit is freely engaged in, when there is a sense of control, and when "a person's physical, sensory, or intellectual skills" are involved (Csikszentmihalyi 1975b, p. 25). There is also "the underlying assumption that all such activities are ways for people to test the limits of their being, to transcend their former conception of self by extending skills and undergoing new experiences" (Csikszentmihalyi 1975b, p. 26). Csikszentmihalyi points out that the meanings attached to such activities cannot be fully understood simply by identifying, categorizing, and analyzing their objective characteristics; it is also necessary to know the person's own evaluation of the experience in order to understand why the activity was enjoyable.

An autotelic activity carries few extrinsic rewards and usually no material rewards, while still attracting participants who devote time, energy, and money to that pursuit. According to these criteria, the lifestyle of cruising is definitely autotelic. Extrinsic rewards such as income and public acclaim are largely absent. No income is derived from cruising, but income may be necessary to pay for it. Some cruisers who write about their sailing experience do earn enough from royalties to support themselves, but there are few, if any, who actually cruise in order to make money. None of those interviewed cruised for this reason.

Table 13.1. *Rankings given to the eight reasons for enjoying an activity*

| | Csikszentmihalyi[a] | | | |
	Cruisers	Climbers	Composers	Basketball Players
1. The activity itself; the pattern, the world it provides	7.1 (1)[b]	5.9 (2)	6.9 (1)	5.2 (4)
2. Enjoyment of the experience and use of skills	6.6 (2)	6.3 (1)	6.9 (1)	5.0 (5)
3. Development of personal skills	5.4 (3)	4.9 (4)	5.6 (3)	5.4 (2)
4. Friendship and companionship	5.1 (4)	5.2 (3)	2.6 (6)	5.3 (3)
5. Measuring self against own ideals	4.4 (5)	4.3 (6)	4.9 (4)	3.7 (6)
6. Emotional release	3.4 (6)	4.6 (5)	4.6 (5)	2.8 (8)
7. Competition, measuring self against others	2.0 (7)	3.1 (7)	2.2 (8)	6.1 (1)
8. Prestige, reward, glamour	2.0 (8)	1.5 (8)	2.6 (6)	3.3 (7)
Autotelic score	9.7	7.9	9.1	0.7
N =	59	25	21	35

[a]1974, p. 323.
[b]The numbers in parentheses are the rank order for that column.

For an activity to be autotelic, "the most basic requirement is to provide a clear set of challenges" (Csikszentmihalyi 1975b, p. 30). And the most general challenge is that of "the unknown, which leads to discovery, exploration, problem solution" (Csikszentmihalyi 1975b, p. 30). To take a small boat to sea and to foreign lands for extended periods of time is intellectually, emotionally, and physically challenging; it requires constant problem solving; it is freely engaged in; there is a sense of personal control; and there are no extrinsic rewards of consequence. It follows, then, that as the lifestyle provides intrinsically rewarding experiences, and as there are no obvious extrinsic rewards, people must engage in the lifestyle because the lifestyle itself is the intrinsic reward.

Quantitative support for this conclusion is found in the results from the 8 Reasons ranking questionnaire. The data in Table 13.1 show that cruisers see their lifestyle as autotelic. Their score was higher than the score for any of the groups in Csikszentmihalyi's study. Cruisers find their rewards in the lifestyle itself: the pattern, the world it provides, the use of skills, and the development of skills.

These results suggest that the concept of intrinsic motivation central to the flow model applies to a lifestyle as well as to episodes within that lifestyle. This means, first, that discrete activities contribute to the autotelic nature of the lifestyle and, second, that while on one level a lifestyle is simply made up of the sum of its parts, on another, it also transcends that sum.

To take the second point first, cruisers have a meta-episodic view of their life. They talk in terms of cruising as a whole way of life that one "grows into." Also, it is obvious that since all the various activities of cruising can be engaged in by noncruisers, there must be something beyond the separate episodes that makes cruising a lifestyle.

One further point helps confirm that a lifestyle is not conceptually different in this context from an activity. The studies of flow involving activities do not suggest that the person is in flow throughout the duration of the activity. Rather, over the period of hours (or days) encompassing an activity such as rock climbing or composing a piece of music, the person will fluctuate through a variety of levels of flow and nonflow experience. That this fluctuation occurs in an activity lends support to the assertion that an activity-based model can be applied at a lifestyle level of analysis.

The flow model applied

Most people see sailing as a leisure activity – a peripheral part of life, something to be squeezed into the spaces of so-called free-time between work and sleep. For a few people, however, sailing and the activities surrounding it constitute their whole life, a life of hardship and insecurity counterbalanced by powerful intrinsic rewards.

To the dreamers and outsiders, cruising is a romantic life of ease and beauty on tropical islands, with luscious jungle fruits waiting to be picked by the vagabond sailor. To others, it is a boring life lacking in stimulation, with few conveniences, little security, and too much time spent wet and cold on the open sea. The research, however, suggests a more complex picture. Cruising is all of the above, and more. At its best, it is a life of freedom and constant challenge, a life in which results follow efforts and one is confirmed existentially simply by surviving. Life is dominated by the ultimate logic of nature, wherein each element of existence flows and merges with each other element. There is a holistic and total involvement with the processes of living and being, especially on extended passages.

Csikszentmihalyi's flow model contains six elements: (1) the merging of action and awareness, (2) a centering of attention on a limited stimulus field, (3) a loss of ego, (4) control of actions and environment, (5) coherent demands for action and clear feedback, and (6) an autotelic nature. According to Csikszentmihalyi, it is these six elements that distinguish such experiences or activities from other aspects of life. Therefore, I have applied these six elements to the lifestyle of cruising, at both the activity and meta-episodic level. Much of the evidence used is related to specific experiences central to the total lifestyle of the subjects. The evidence is drawn from three sources: books and articles about cruising and blue water sailing; experience and observation as a participant observer; interviews with the 59 cruisers, who have a total of some 295 years of cruising experience among them.

The merging of action and awareness. Ocean passages fit the elements of flow in many ways. Of course, since they are so encompassing and so variable, they do not always involve the merging of action and awareness. However, although there are times when self-consciousness is made more acute, there are also times when one is lost within the experiences: "So one forgets oneself, one forgets everything, seeing only the play of the boat with the sea, the play of the sea around the boat, leaving aside everything not essential to that game in the immediate present" (Moitessier 1971, p. 52). Action and awareness most often merge during bad conditions at night when the person must sit at the helm for hours at a time and maintain the boat safely on course in the midst of high winds and rough seas. One may lose complete consciousness of the self just in keeping the boat safely on course. In fact, one can become so engrossed that hours later, when relieved by another person, one emerges from a cocoon of consciousness wondering where the night went. The self has been absorbed by the sea and the night, and the action of controlling the boat has merged with awareness to the point where there is nothing but the compass light and the hand on the tiller. The activity is all demanding.

The merging of action and awareness is a difficult concept to transfer from an episodic level to a lifestyle level. The loss of the duality of action and awareness that brings about a kind of "thoughtless concentration" applies to a much longer time span. It would seem that at a lifestyle level this element of flow may be found in the integration of activities. Cruising is not segmented in the way the work–leisure dichotomy segments life in modern society. There is a unity between the various aspects of cruising that appears to be lacking in modern society, where the work–leisure split is so evident. This is facilitated by the fact that the income-earning activities we call work are not dominant in most cruisers' lives. Earning income is usually restricted to a period of a few months each year. The concept of a career or occupation is irrelevant in relation to work in the cruising context. These two facts mean that life does not focus on income-earning activities, which therefore do not contribute to the work–leisure dichotomy or to a sense of multiple and possibly incompatible roles. Thus, there is a merging of activities so that they need not be, or are not, consciously split from the totality of the lifestyle.

A centering of attention on a limited stimulus field. The compass and tiller provide a focus, a centering of attention that facilitates the merging of awareness and action. Intense concentration is needed to keep the boat safe in difficult and dangerous conditions. This centering of attention can only be momentarily relaxed in order to take in the powerful beauty of the surroundings.

But there is another level of the centering of attention:

> My uncluttered life was indeed sweet, and it seemed – as it always does – that the simplest pleasures were best. Not only is the sea unspoiled and without artificiality, there is a primeval quality, a *purity* surrounding its environment. Maybe you appreciate the sea because when you are lost upon its vastness your life is not jammed up with trivia, the meaningless detail, and the foolish stuff of civilization. (Roth 1972, p. 100)

This is a level of centering that is exemplified by long passages, but that occurs throughout the whole life space. It is the process whereby the issues and concerns of land-based urban living lose their significance: They are dropped from conscious consideration; they no longer matter.

> But no matter how many little discomforts there may be at sea, one's real cares and worries seem to drop out of sight as the land slips behind the horizon. Once we were at sea there was no point in worrying, there was nothing we could do about our problems till we reached the next port, and there anything might happen – and usually did. Life was, for a while, stripped of its artificialities; rationing and devaluation and nationalisation seemed quite un-

important compared with the state of the wind and the sea and
the length of the day's run. (Crealock 1951, pp. 99–100)

Of course, there is more to the limiting of the stimulus field per se
than simply being out of a city or on an ocean. It takes time and a state
of mind for one to get close enough to the sea. One member of the study
(S. 020), who sails alone on a 22-ft yacht, said that he finds a 4-week
passage the ideal length for him. He recounted that it takes a week for
the previous port to clear from his consciousness; then he has about 2
weeks of nothing to consider but the sea. Four weeks is the necessary
length from landfall to landfall because about a week before his next
landfall he finds his mind beginning to dwell on the land-to-be, considering the problems of navigation, officials, provisioning, and so on.

> I do not like short passages as I don't get into the rhythm or used
> to the confinement quickly. (S. 020)

There were other expressions in the interviews that pointed to the limited
stimulus field as a positive benefit of cruising in general and passages
specifically.

> It is also true that the Spartan existence gives you contrasts so that
> showers, fresh food, walking a path, riding in a car become exciting
> events. Being in this life sharpens the experience of these things.
> You appreciate a minor miracle. (S. 032)

Pirsig identified similar factors. When he moved from motorcycles to
an ocean sailing yacht, he moved into a new space:

> Modern civilisation has found radio, TV, movies, nightclubs and
> a huge variety of mechanized entertainment to titillate our senses
> and help us escape from the apparent boredom of the earth and
> the sun and wind and stars. Sailing returns to these ancient real-
> ities. (Pirsig 1977, p. 67)

His implication is clear: By cutting down external stimuli, especially
artificial ones, we return to the more limited but less limiting stimuli of
nature.

Although the interviewees do not always isolate the concept of a
limited stimulus field, they clearly identify the factors of nature that lead
to such an effect:

> We enjoy the life in places like Suvarov as we like the wildlife and
> the ability to catch food, to subsist in isolation. We fish each day,
> dig a well, collect coconuts, go reef walking to see shells and birds,
> photograph birds – just live. Our life is to appreciate the world of
> nature around us and to keep the home/boat together. (S. 016/017)

What we see, then, is a limiting of the stimulus field at two levels in cruising. Passage making, as one part of the lifestyle, is much more than a mere activity, in part because it is so multifaceted and in part because it usually involves longer periods of time (e.g., 2–3 weeks) than are normally associated with flow activities. Passages clearly foster and contribute to a focused consciousness; that is, there is a centering of attention on and in a limited stimulus area. Concomitantly, the total lifestyle is seen as less complex than modern society because of a variety of factors. An important one is that living on a small yacht generally means a simpler life in terms of possessions – especially clothes and consumer durables. Although an ocean sailing yacht is a major and complex item, its possession and use are so integral a part of the sailing experience that it becomes not an external irritant but a major part of the effort-and-reward system. If the boat becomes a major problem or irritant as an "external" item, the cruiser is likely to leave cruising. One interviewee (S. 013) expressed a feeling of being trapped by the boat and being overpowered by the realization that everything he owned was tied up in something that could be lost at any time. After 3 ½ years he was heading back to his home port in order to set up a land base.

Cruising can be seen as limiting the stimulus field at both a micro and a macro level. At the micro level, specific activities require and develop a focus, whereas at a macro level the lifestyle is more unified, less cluttered, and less fragmented.

A loss of ego. An activity that fosters a merging of action and awareness with a centering of attention on a limited stimulus field will lead inevitably to a loss of the ego construct, a loss of awareness of the "I" as actor. This is clearly the case in some of the situations mentioned above, as the sailor merges with the sea and its life. However, here this loss of ego will be applied more broadly (because of the lifestyle orientation of cruising) to three levels of the sailor's experience: (a) the union of the sailor with the yacht; (b) the merging of the sailor with the forces of the sea; and (c) the loss of status ranking of profession, wealth, and social class.

Literary references to the union of the sailor with the yacht go back to the earliest of modern-day cruisers. Joshua Slocum personifies his yacht, the *Spray* , and often talks to it in the first person: "Almost aboard the last breaker! But you'll go by, *Spray* , old girl! 'Tis abeam now! One surge more! And oh, one more like that will clear your ribs and keel!" (Slocum 1900, p. 499).

Michael Mermod, who sailed his yacht most of the way around the

world, only to have it put in a museum in Switzerland, clearly lost part
of himself when the voyage came to an end:

> Before going back, I take a last look at *Geneve*. From now on we
> shall never be alone together, she and I, in the marvellous shared
> intimacy of joys and sorrows, memories and hopes . . . no one can
> take these memories from us. (Mermod 1973, p. 293)

Jean Gau, in his 70s and with 2 circumnavigations and 11 Atlantic
crossings behind him, reflects on the complex relationship between skip-
per and craft and on the craft as a person:

> Frankly, I consider *Atom* as a living being, intelligent, sensitive.
> When the wind blows, this assembly of wood, metal, and canvas
> becomes a living thing to me. With all her whims, defects, and
> qualities, *Atom* does her job and I do mine. I love her as a . . . a
> good servant, as a man loves an animal, or a car. Let's just say
> that we're friends. (Quoted in Tazelaar & Bussiere 1977, p. 59)

The experience has been so great, so profound, that boat and human
merge, often to the point where the boat is in control, is dominant:
"People who do not know that a sailboat is a living creature will never
understand anything about boats and the sea" (Moitessier 1971, p. 4).

The merging of the sailor with the ocean environment that happens
in extreme conditions also occurs in benign situations. Moitessier, for
example, talks to seabirds and often has a daily routine with a few who
follow him for weeks at a time. In another case, he writes that the
dolphins "talked" to him and through their actions showed him that he
was on a dangerous course; they communicated that he must turn, and
when he did follow their instructions, they played around the boat for
hours – as if to show their joy that he had missed the rocks he was
unwittingly sailing toward. Two stayed with him, one on either bow,
until he was clear of the danger (see Moitessier 1971, pp. 101–5).

David Lewis also recognized this merging of self with the sea when
on a circumnavigation in a catamaran: "You cannot live on the face of
the ocean, in intimate association as you must in a small vessel, without
it becoming a part of you" (Lewis 1967, p. 81). But it is not just the sense
of being part of the sea and its life that is important in relation to this
loss of ego. There is, under many conditions, simply a transcendence
of the I – you are simply not conscious of the self, even the physical self
in some cases. The task requires such concentration, focus, and action
that the sense of being an actor, the sense of self, is irrelevant and
ignored.

To the extent that a reduction in consciousness of social status is a loss of ego, cruising is a lifestyle in which the ego plays a lesser role than in modern society. Whereas people in society continually monitor their status positions, this happens much less often while cruising. Social status and the ego derived from it have no use in a lifestyle in which respect comes from getting oneself across the ocean.

> Cruisers are down-to-earth; not usually country clubbish, usually not society conscious; even wealthy ones get this way. (S. 007)

> Class and economic distinctions are dissolved by the closeness to the ocean and adventure. Yachts really open up all these contacts with all types of backgrounds and lifestyles, contacts that are prevented from occurring in normal life by social graces. (S. 006)

> Another thing about this life is that you can really make your own choice of friends whereas back in regular life a lot of friends are dictated by your occupational, political, or class situation. (S. 037)

> In every country I have seen, a caste system of some sort exists, however much it is denied. Even amongst the most civilized and democratic countries, true equality of opportunity is something that has still to be attained.
>
> The sea and ships are great levellers. There is certainly no room on a small boat for a person who is incompetent or won't pull his weight, whatever his "caste." All share the same risks in a storm and no earthly influence will select you above the rest to be saved if the ship founders. (Knox-Johnston 1969, p. 172)

Similarly, the kind of social interaction and simplicity of life in the cruising context remove many of the social forces to which a Western city dweller becomes accustomed: "Free from the pressures of others around us, with no compulsion to wear any sort of social mask, we found that we could think more clearly and find peace in doing so" (Saunders 1975, p. 238). An aspect of the flow experience, then, is that self-awareness, consciousness of self, is reduced. In the cruising lifestyle, this loss of ego can be seen on a number of levels ranging from the personal to the social.

Control of action and environment. This element of the flow experience is at the heart of the lifestyle of cruising and of the activity of passage making. The interviewees stressed again and again that this lifestyle provided them with a degree of control over their own actions that was impossible to achieve while living in an urban, industrialized society.

Cruisers are fleeing from a whole range of restrictions, from the least obvious and insidious social controls to the most obvious legal and occupational controls, including the highly bureaucratized operation of industrial societies. Unable to "do anything without the approval of society" (S. 046), they try to regain some of that lost control over their personal life through cruising.

> You are trying to get away from normal routine and get personal power from the freedom you build yourself. (S. 006)

> Passages are marvelous – detached from the land – totally under your own jurisdiction – you make your own laws. (S. 030)

> I was a fighter pilot in WWII and find that sailing and cruising is like that, as you are your own determiner, are independent – looking for Germans to shoot down is like looking for dragons, for adventure. In the 9-to-5 rat race you lose choices and identity as you are just a cog in a big wheel of the system; now out here again we have to make our own decisions. (S. 037)

The feelings of control and of successful negotiation of the ocean provide direct satisfaction and confidence. Dr. David Lewis, writing of his lone sailing voyage to the Antarctic, comments that we cannot know our own powers unless we can somehow remove ourselves from a society that does everything for us (Lewis 1977, p. 19).

Lewis makes another pertinent point when discussing the response of his 11-year-old daughter, veteran of their circumnavigation in a cat-amaran, to a TV interviewer's question about whether she was not worried about her father's safety: "Vicky and I have spent half of our lives at sea in yachts. A storm at sea is safer than crossing roads on land, and Daddy knows what to do" (Lewis 1977, p. 37). Although her assertion may not have applied to her father's imminent voyage to the Antarctic – a fearsome cruising place – cruisers clearly believe the sentiments expressed by Lewis's daughter. In the more frequented parts of the world's oceans, with proper preparation of the person and the yacht and careful reading of the pilot charts, there is comparatively little risk in taking a small yacht to sea.

> One of the best things about ocean voyaging and cruising, as a sport, is its safety record. . . . Once you sail out the breakwaters, a good watch will eliminate almost all danger of injury or loss due to other people's negligences. Your own preparations, skill, and care will make you safe. (Pardey & Pardey 1982, p.149)

The risk, then, is seen more as a challenge to one's own skill and competence, and within the realm of personal control. This is in contrast to the random risks that individuals face from crime and from cars within the everyday life of modern cities. The essence in cruising is a feeling of control over the self and the interaction with the environment:

> Our lives lay in our hands alone – no one knew where we were – and the independence was a good feeling. I felt exuberant and reassured somehow. I knew that I was in charge of the ship and what we did, but I also had the notion that I was in control of the sea that I could see around me – a foolish idea, I suppose, for it is manifest that the sea knows no master. Yet as long as we paid proper respect to the might of the ocean I felt sure that our tiny ship would be safe. (Roth 1972, p. 8)

As Laurence Le Guay says in his *Sailing Free*, "Any well found yacht of sound construction with an able crew can usually cope with anything the sea can deliver, barring unusual conjunctions like fibreglass and coral, or wood and killer whales" (Le Guay 1975, p. 65).

This sense of control is an important aspect of the experience of ocean passages specifically and the cruising lifestyle in general. Cruising is a choice individuals make to remove themselves from an environment where they have little control but face a multitude of external and random risks. The choice places them in an environment where they have, or believe they have, more control and fewer externally generated, random risks. Concomitantly, the external risks associated with modern society are only occasionally encountered and so do not dominate the cruising lifestyle.

Coherent demands for action and clear feedback. Cruising is inextricably entwined with the forces of nature, as cruisers are never divorced from the forces that surround their floating homes. They are always alert to the ebb and flow of the tides, to the changes in the weather, to the ever-changing tapestry of color that is the progression of the days and nights. Cruising means constant contact and interaction with nature. Because it is a lifestyle that is close to nature, cruising makes clear demands for action and lets you know, in no uncertain terms, whether the demands were met.

> At sea you are all the skills, plumber, electrician, light company; you've got to do it yourself. These tasks are physical and mental and emotional challenges that don't let you atrophy. The challenges on land are governed not by you but by rules and regulations so

in cruising you can escape from that and get down to basic life.
(S. 032)

Navigation is a good example of where a totally noncontradictory
demand is made for action and where feedback is both immediate and
definite. It is immediate in that a path is marked on a chart; as feedback,
it is marred only by the doubts of the navigator as to its accuracy. The
feedback becomes definite as land is sighted when and where expected:

> Just as on other occasions I, as navigator, experienced a sense of
> satisfaction coupled with some astonishment that my observations
> of the very distant sun from an unsteady platform and the use of
> some simple tables . . . enable a small island to be found with cer-
> tainty after an ocean crossing. (Hiscock 1968, p. 45)

Others also note the thrill of navigating to a perfect landfall: "Each time,
I feel the same mixture of astonishment, love and pride as this new land
is born which seems to have been created for me and by me" (Moitessier
1971, p. 159). He knew what he had to do and he found out in no
uncertain terms that he had done it right. The feedback was satisfying.

A demand for action in the cruising life entailed by the self-imposed
self-sufficiency is to be able to fix things, usually by improvisation. A
couple of incidents reported by Knox-Johnston in his single-handed
circumnavigation illustrate the kind of situations that develop at sea. In
the first case, he had broken a self-steering rudder and, lacking spares,
had to repair it:

> The repairs took me three days. The old rudder blade was hope-
> lessly split, so I made a new one out of one of the teak bunkboards.
> The bar had broken by the middle of the blade, and to rejoin it I
> cut the handle of [sic] a pipe wrench and then filed it down until
> it fitted inside the bar, like an internal splint. (Knox-Johnston 1969,
> p. 71)

Later he describes how he made a new reefing handle by modifying a
bottlescrew (a turnbuckle used in tensioning the wires that support the
mast):

> I cut the bottle part of the screw in half and then heated it on the
> primus [stove] until it was red hot. Then I hammered it until it
> cooled and repeated the process until I had the right shape. I had
> to file out the corners a bit which took time but I ended up with
> a snug fit. (Knox-Johnston 1969, p. 79)

My interviewees also referred to the same concept of self-reliance:

> You must be adaptable and practical – the average cruiser is like

the remote farmer, he has what he needs and when something breaks he goes to work to make something to fix it. (S. 037)

This is as true in most anchorages as it is at sea. Lack of tradespeople in many areas and lack of funds means cruisers must improvise and do the jobs themselves. The result is rewarding:

The pride you'll feel as your skills develop can't be easily described. The first time you sail your 6-tonner up to the dock so she stops within a foot of the cleats, the first hatch you build that doesn't leak a drop, the first repair job you successfully complete – each is a triumph that will bring a glow to your life. Eventually this self-sufficiency will grow to be a sport. You'll set new goals and reach them. Then some day there will be an ultimate test. I am convinced that to every person who goes to sea for long periods of time there comes at least one time self-sufficiency will save his life or his boat. (Pardey & Pardey 1982, pp. 303–4)

Success is immediate and tangible: A sail that has been stitched up by hand at sea, a delicious fish dinner, a good day's run and, eventually, arrival at his destination on the other side of an ocean. Failure also is immediate and tangible: a jibsheet that chafes on the shrouds and parts in a squall, a knot that unties in use, a wet bunk under a leaking hatch, a poor day's run on a good wind because the helmsman steered all over the ocean. (Griffith 1979, p. 259)

Cruising is governed by rules that are noncontradictory and clear. Wind, sea surface, and sea bottom impose logical demands on the cruisers. Navigation and boat maintenance have specific needs, and noncompliance (through ignorance or sloth) will give clear results. On a social level, rules are not so immediately obvious and are often contradictory, for example, when dealing with customs, immigration rules, and various bureaucratic situations. Subculture rules also must be learned, but these are small aspects of the cruising life compared to the interaction with nature.

Autotelic nature. Cruising is a set of activities for which no external rewards are offered. No one, with the exception of a few publishers and admiring would-be cruisers, offers monetary rewards for cruising. In fact, the reverse is more likely the case, as employers and governments will often put up disincentives. Social pressures from family and friends often militate against departing. David Lewis (1969, p. 280) sums up the fundamental reward of an extended cruise: "At the end we had the satisfaction of having accomplished what we had set out to do."

But it is Moitessier who best describes the deeper autotelic nature of sailing and the commitment to this particular way of life that some cruisers are able to achieve: "All our earth's beauty . . . all the havoc we wreak on it. God, how good it is to be here, in no rush to get home" (Moitessier 1971, p. 73). In fact, Moitessier never went home to France. He was the leading contender in a lucrative "race" to be the first to sail single-handedly nonstop around the world when he crossed his outward path in the Atlantic Ocean. He had completed about two-thirds of the course but instead of continuing north in the Atlantic, Moitessier turned his helm for the Cape of Good Hope – a second time – because "I really felt sick at the thought of getting back to Europe, back to the snakepit. . . . Sure, there were good, sensible reasons [for going back]. But does it make sense to head for a place knowing you will have to leave your peace behind?" (Moitessier 1971, p. 164). The "sensible" reason was an extrinsic reward offered by the English *Sunday Times*. Extrinsic and intrinsic rewards need not be in conflict. But Moitessier saw the extrinsic rewards as a risk, especially in conjunction with his perception of other aspects of European society.

The foregoing examples point to a lifestyle that requires no extrinsic rewards, a lifestyle rewarding in and of itself. Its essence is a closeness to nature, and the very essence of nature is intrinsic value.

Conclusion

This chapter uses the flow model as a lens through which to view cruising. The main features of the model, originally developed to explain the motivational value of activities, have been applied to the understanding of a lifestyle. Cruising is dominated by intrinsic rewards and is of itself autotelic. It provides clear demands for action and constant feedback, and participants experience a sense of control over their lives that they missed in other contexts; they perceive their lives as simple, self-contained, and manageable. Being cut off from "normal" society centers their attention and narrows the stimulus field. Actions are at one with the setting, that is, at one with the environment itself and its relation to other flow elements. Not only does the oneness with the natural environment allow for a loss of ego boundaries, but the roles and facades that are part of urban living are of no use or value in the cruising context.

Occasionally, especially in storm conditions, a total loss of ego occurs while action for survival takes over completely.

The flow model has helped to show the shared features in the ideology of the subculture and to explain the depth of individual involvement in cruising. It reveals why the experience has a great impact on the view of self and the world. This is part of what distinguishes cruising from other sailing "subcultures," and also from the predominant lifestyle of modern society.

Deviating from the norm is not uncommon in modern Western society. Cruisers are archetypal models of escape from the frustrations of technological living. But the escape they enact is not a regression to the protective womb, to a safe and comfortable lifestyle. Rather, it is a creative escape into growth. Because cruising requires existential choices and personal reflection, it fosters psychological development. And because it provides experiences of competence, independence, and enjoyment, it highlights those ingredients necessary for the fulfillment of individuality that are so often lacking in our current social environment.

14. Flow in a historical context: the case of the Jesuits

ISABELLA CSIKSZENTMIHALYI

For about two centuries after its founding in 1540, the Jesuit order of the Roman Catholic Church played a leading role in the religious and political history of Europe, and through its far-flung and energetic missions it was instrumental in the development of European influence in the rest of the world, particularly the Americas and the Far East. During its heyday, the order spread very quickly through Italy, Portugal, France, and Spain and into Central and Eastern Europe, attracting some of the most brilliant and ambitious young men of that day to its ranks. By 1556, when St. Ignatius of Loyola died, some 1,000 Jesuits were already working throughout Europe as well as in Asia, Africa, and the New World. Their number increased to 15,544 in 1626 and to 22,589 by 1749.

The question addressed in this chapter is, Why was this particular monastic order so successful during the 1500s and 1600s? Obviously one could cite many causes suggested by a materialist approach to history and list various economic, social, and political reasons for the Jesuits' influence. Important as such "extrinsic" causes may have been, a historical event also requires a psychological explanation. Impersonal historical forces must be translated into ideas and emotions before they can systematically affect human action. A psychological explanation should account for the role of intrinsic motivation, because given the opportunity, people tend to select differentially those courses of action that provide the most positive experiences. A primary rule governing choices is to maximize flow, or the matching of personal skills with the opportunities of the environment that produces enjoyment.

In this particular case, the question is, What made the system of life represented by the Jesuit order so attractive to men living in the second half of the 16th century? The thesis to be developed is that the Jesuit rules provided an optimal set of conditions by which young men could live the entirety of their lives as a single flow experience. Whereas cultural forms such as games of chess or tennis provide rules that allow people to lose themselves in an involving flow activity for short periods of time, the Society of Jesus provided a system of all-embracing rules by which a young man could organize his total experience. Its success depended on its ability to integrate the lives of its members into a challenging yet unified game plan.

The Society of Jesus was founded at a time when Roman Catholic dogma and authority had been seriously challenged by the events associated with the Reformation. Christianity had been and continued to be one of the major factors in the historical and cultural development of Western Europe as well as in the extension of European culture to other continents that began in the 15th century. However, until the Reformation, Roman Catholicism could claim to be the only true church of Jesus Christ on earth. By the mid–16th century, with the presence of Lutheranism in Northern Europe and Anglicanism in England, the hegemony of Catholicism had become severely threatened. One Catholic defeat, ecclesiastical and political, had followed another, and Catholic failures were to blame for many of them. The goodwill that the church had gathered as a bulwark against the Muslims and as a keeper of peace among the European princelings through the 13th century was squandered away in the next two (Hollis 1968, pp. 5–6).

A major psychological effect of this fragmentation was that the faithful began to question what they had been taught about proper sequences of thought and behavior. Doubt about the right course of action to take is a prime source of anxiety; but the Society offered a lifestyle that created a coherent system and worldview for thinking and acting and thus helped remove the incapacitating doubts ushered in by the Reformation (Nussbaum 1953, p. 179).

The order that Ignatius founded reflected to a large extent the personality and experiences of its founder: It incorporated the knowledge of a former soldier and a courtier into the deep religious faith that he acquired during a long recuperation from a serious injury sustained in battle. Not surprisingly, he saw the service of God as a holy chivalry and envisioned the order as a spiritual army whose members would find their battleground in the struggle for men's souls (Barthel 1984, p. 26).

The social structure of the order

The idea of the *Compania Jesu Christi* being led by a "general" was nothing new – the Dominicans and Franciscans each had a general of their own

– but these figures did not have the almost unlimited power of the Jesuit leader. Here we find the first hint of the psychological attraction of the company: As we know from current studies of human development, adolescent males and young men are particularly responsive to the "bonding" camaraderie of peers, as well as to the appeal of strong "dominance" hierarchies that in humans are often expressed through the symbolism of military ranks and discipline. The Ignatian doctrine of obedience and the emphasis on hierachy are no different from what was stressed by many military institutions of the past and is still considered important in military training academies. By combining these with spiritual goals, however, Ignatius achieved a unique and powerfully attractive amalgam of instinctual and cultural motivations (Brodrick 1971, pp. 101–2).

This rigidity of internal structure was tempered by the physical freedom that the members of the Society of Jesus enjoyed, in contrast to other monastic orders. From the beginning, Ignatius saw the order as an *active* rather than a contemplative organization. Like other monastic orders, it was concerned with converting souls and interceding on behalf of sinners, but the diplomatic background of its founder added another dimension, which became evident in the order's use of flexible and creative means to achieve these goals.

Briefly, the main differences betweeen the Jesuits and previous orders were these: (1) The Jesuits wore no distinctive habit; (2) they were un-cloistered – they were to remain in the world; (3) they were not to be a contemplative order, so that chanting of liturgy or communal prayer was not required and these became strictly an individual matter; (4) fasting or other types of self-deprivation were given little or no emphasis; (5) in addition to pledging the usual monastic vows of poverty, chastity, and obedience, the "professed" Jesuits who completed the very long probationary period pledged particular obedience regarding apostolic missions and special obedience to the pope (this is the famous Jesuit fourth vow); (6) a Jesuit was expected to remain a Jesuit and not accept any other ecclesiastical office or higher rank not bestowed by the order; and (7) Jesuit spiritual activity was not sharply defined, nor restricted to the parish and the pulpit (Ganss 1970, pp. 64–72; Barthel 1984, pp. 47–8).

How these particular attributes of the order helped it to become so influential and wide-ranging is best understood in light of the steps that were preliminary to becoming a full-fledged Jesuit. To want to lead a life of poverty, chastity, and obedience means that a strong preselection process is already operating. Serious religious commitment and feeling are necessary to consider such a course of action. Certainly a sense of idealism had to be present in those Jesuits who joined the order in its infancy, since it had not had time to develop the power and other extrinsic rewards of older orders. Emphasis on a life of action, the freedom of dress, and freedom of movement would necessarily attract those who felt at ease and thrived in such circumstances. These would be action-oriented men with enough faith and initiative to maintain their purpose without the support provided by group rituals and familiar settings; this is perhaps best illustrated by the preference shown by many Jesuits for solitary overseas missionary careers. In addition, the fact that spiritual activity was not strictly defined or restricted to the parish and the pulpit opened many new opportunities that the Jesuits were quick to utilize. Moreover, the prohibition against accepting ecclesiastical offices outside of their own order probably freed the Jesuits from outside influences and competition and made them concentrate on successful activity for the benefit of their own order.

The structuring of psychic energy

One of the chief appeals of the Company of Jesus has been its ability to develop a set of rules that, when applied to the thoughts and actions of its members, produces a harmoniously ordered set of experiences. The progression from novitiate to that of a "professor" (vows are called "professions") able to take the fourth and highest vow takes place in the context of a highly structured, hierarchical society. The novitiate lasts for 2 years, twice as long as in most other orders, and continues the blueprint of discipline and religious training developed by Ignatius.

Following a pattern that was to remain unaltered right up to the 1960s, a novice's day was structured from approximately 5:00 A.M. to 9:15 P.M. It included common housekeeping chores and studying (e.g., Latin and Greek) as well as devotions, meditation, and the crucial twice-daily examination of one's conscience. Very little of the social interaction was extraneous to the scheduled activities. The strictness of the schedule taught the discipline and obedience expected of a Jesuit and weeded out those unsuited to that type of life: Over half of every seminary's entering class did not complete the 2-year novitiate. The *Constitutions* of the order instructed the novice in the code by which as a Jesuit he would be governed for most of his life. He would select the form of prayer that he found most congenial to his temperament, and think out his role and rank within the society for the future (Ganss 1970, pp. 67, 349–51; Barthel 1984, p. 51). Perhaps most important, the trainee would participate in a 4-week course of instruction based on the *Spiritual Exercises*.

The *Spiritual Exercises* were originally written by Ignatius for his first disciples in 1522, but he kept revising them until he produced the final version of 1541 (Hollis 1968, p. 10). Their purpose was to teach not only how to meditate, but also how to have reaffirming and even ecstatic religious experiences. They were addressed to the individual devotee rather than to a community of believers as a whole. Whereas other orders relied primarily on lengthy prayers, fasting, and other austerities for this type of experience, the Jesuits were trained to reach it *consciously*, and these other means were to be used only rarely as an auxiliary or backup system.

The desire on Ignatius' part to do away with external rituals and mortifications, except insofar as they might be useful for the training of character and mind, was mainly due to the deep impression made on him by Thomas à Kempis's widely read book, *Imitation of Christ*. The book's emphasis on the state of the *inner* life as opposed to outward devotions, its call to shape one's life through a personal imitation of the life of Christ, represented a desire on the part of many Catholics for a deeper spiritual life within the church structure. It reflected the wish for worldly and ecclesiastical renewal that the hierarchy of the church was failing to provide (Foss 1969, p. 97). Many educated and thoughtful men were influenced by these ideas, and in adapting them through the *Spiritual Exercises* Ignatius allied himself with the more advanced religious thinkers of his time.

Although the *Spiritual Exercises* have been criticized for lacking originality, that attribute was never claimed by Ignatius. His genius lay in developing a detailed set of instructions for attempting to reach, maintain, and reaffirm the values of early Christianity and its emphasis on service to mankind. Their endurance through the centuries is due to the "logical coherence into which the teaching was all bound together . . . apart from telling the retreatant what are the ends at which he ought to aim it gives him practical advice on how he is to achieve them" (Hollis 1968, p. 12). In other words, the exercises are structured in such a way that the participant knows what goals he is to achieve, how to go about achieving them, and whether he is on the path toward his goal – in short, the steps are there for the process of achieving a religious flow experience.

In line with Ignatius's methods, the instructions are both flexible and very detailed and precise: Ignatius suggests the type of environment in which they ought to be performed, including the optimal lighting in a room; desirable postures, and ways of breathing. Yet they are not the same for everyone. They are varied according to the age, attainment, and spiritual predisposition of the participant: "In this way nothing will be imposed on them that they cannot easily bear and from which they cannot get some profit" (Barthel 1984, p. 72). The exercise master (a Jesuit father) must treat each individual as unique and select a program "to suit the individual capacities and character of his charge" (Foss 1969, pp. 96–7).

The function of the instructions is to successfully instill in the participant a pattern for examining his conscience and to develop a technique of meditation that will enable him to have a "direct experience . . . of the Passion and Resurrection of Christ, all through the medium of the kind of visual and mental image projection that Ignatius [had] developed" (Barthel 1984, p. 73; see also Boehmer 1975, pp. 48–49). After first visualizing the torments of hell that follow sin, the participant is led by his spiritual guide to experience, "down to the last detail, the suffering and ultimate sacrifice of Jesus Christ"; after this, he is guided in vicariously experiencing "Christ's resurrection and is given a foretaste of the Christian's eternal reward" (Foss 1969, pp. 95–98; see also Spence 1984, pp. 14–16; Barthel 1984, p. 73). Urged to use all his senses, the novice's belief in the basic tenets of Christianity that made it such a powerful and appealing force is thus graphically reinforced.

The importance of the *Spiritual Exercises* in the life of a Jesuit, once the institutional, training years are over and he is on assignment, whether as teacher or missionary, is not to be underestimated as a source of spiritual and moral reinforcement (Spence 1984, pp. 54–6, 230–1). No matter how busy he is, a Jesuit is expected to examine his conscience twice a day. By directing attention systematically to his past actions, with Christ's life as the model, he can evaluate his activities in terms of the spiritual ideals and goals he has set for himself. This restructuring of consciousness provides a constant infusion of psychic energy for renewing one's purpose and is one of the reasons that others were always ready to step forward when called, whether it meant going to North America where Jesuits had just been massacred by Indians or smuggling themselves into Japan knowing that their predecessors had suffered fates of unspeakable horror (Hollis 1968, pp. 50–1). One writer suggests that "the essential motivation of the Order itself . . . that one should present oneself to the world not as oneself, but in imitation of

Jesus Christ by means of one's service to mankind . . . [that it is this spiritual and psychological transformation which] . . . later gave the Order such a profoundly individual character" (Barthel 1984, p. 26). This is not to say that other orders did not have in mind the same lofty goals, but the method Ignatius systematized proved to be psychologically sound, and more adapted than earlier monastic systems to the specific conditions of the Counter-Reformation.

The all-inclusiveness of Jesuit training and the personality of its founder are further illustrated by the *Rules of Modesty*, which formed a crucial part of the *Epitomes*, a manual of behavior that shaped many generations of Jesuits. The *Rules* prescribe everything from the proper demeanor for a Jesuit (an expression of humility and modesty) to the desirable way of holding the head or gazing at other people. For example, the lips should not be compressed too severely, nor should the mouth be kept open too wide; and the hands should be kept decorously still. In short, all of one's gestures and bodily motions should be examplary and unobtrusive (Barthel 1984, pp. 69–70). The thoroughness of the instructions may seem excessive, but here Ignatius is trying to shape the whole man – to impart knowledge that will ease the burden of social situations so that energy can be spent on the task at hand instead of worrying about one's self-image. Just as the rules of a game provide the structure necessary to keep the attention on the activity itself, so Ignatius strove to keep his followers' attention on the goals they were taking on.

The *Rules* are believed to be an adaptation of the type of discipline of body, tongue, and action (*sosiego*) that a Spanish gentleman sought to achieve in all moments of life, large and small, and which Ignatius had striven for as a soldier and diplomat. With this outward discipline went such *ideal* mental attributes as being able to judge quickly every situation and recognize departures from the usual, the ability to distinguish the right command and the right obedience, the "capacity to grasp all necessary decisions instantly and comprehensively," and the "accurate knowledge of the speech, customs, and manners of the great world" (Boehmer 1975, pp. 18–19). Even a modicum of such an ability to discriminate would be helpful in deciding what type of sermon to deliver to a given audience, or how to treat most effectively the penitent in the confessional. Thus Ignatius employed the attributes used to achieve worldly success to achieve his spiritual goals.

Once out in the field, another freedom that the Jesuits had was that they were not a mendicant order. Although Ignatius had gone through a long period in life when he supported himself through begging, he later decided that it was a time-consuming and distracting activity. Because it was believed that freedom from financial worries would facilitate the attainment of their goals, the Jesuits were not forbidden to accept gifts for the Society from the faithful, and with time they accumulated large amounts of property and instituted a banking system of their own. An example of their practical approach to finances is the fact that the first five generals only allowed the order to open new schools "when it was clear that they could be financially self-sustaining and could attract a qualified staff" (Ganss 1970, pp. 70, 180; see also Barthel 1984, p. 115). Their expanding holdings and financial practices eventually led to much criticism (Ridley 1938, pp. 259–62), but one must remember that *individual* Jesuits, especially in the early days of the order, were willing to undergo personal hardships and privations that would be difficult to even imagine today (Brodrick 1947, 1971).

This methodical attention to the structuring of everyday life allowed the Jesuits to concentrate on their tasks with an intensity unparalled in the Catholic church – with the exception, perhaps, of the conventual orders, whose concentration, however, was usually paid for by withdrawal from the stimuli, demands, and activities of the world outside the walls of their spiritual refuge.

Feedback and a complex environment of challenges and skill

An important factor once a Jesuit was out on assignment was the feedback he received both from superiors at hand, or if these were not available, from the general himself. By the time of his death, Ignatius had written over 5,000 letters, many of them to the Jesuits in the field: The *Monumenta Historica* contain more than 9,000 printed pages of Ignatius's letters and instructions (Brodrick 1971, p. 97). So careful was Ignatius of giving the right response and encouragement that he usually read each letter over twice before affixing his signature. Yet, in spite of his stress on obedience, Ignatius was not dogmatic about the instructions and suggestions he penned – he preferred to "keep the spirit at the expense of the letter" (Brodrick 1971, p. 101). For example, before Peter Faber left on a mission to Germany, Ignatius provided him with detailed instructions on how to conduct it. When Faber later wrote back that "I have done just the opposite of what you commanded me to do, since I found the situation to be quite different," Ignatius praised him highly for his flexibility and initiative, and called his actions "true obedience" (Barthel 1984, pp. 68–9).

Correspondence was particularly important to some of the missionary Jesuits, who often were confronted with alien cultures and surroundings and had few colleagues available for guidance and the sharing of problems. The Jesuit general Claudio Aquaviva, aware of the spiritual attrition such assignments usually entail, sought, in the letters he wrote to Matteo Ricci and other missionary Jesuits, not only to provide moral support, but also to foster a "sense of excitement compounded of service to God and a sense of participation in history" (Spence 1984, p. 124). Moreover, when Ricci was in China hoping to convert that nation to Catholicism, Aquaviva accepted as valid and helped implement many of Ricci's requests for such Western items as prisms, clocks, books, and paintings. These were to be given to influential Chinese, not only in keeping with Chinese custom, but also as a way of arousing the interest of the ethnocentric Chinese in European culture (Spence 1984, pp. 140, 180, 258).

The Jesuit generals and others in command seemed to be aware that if the Jesuits were to keep to the primary objective, that of converting souls to the Christian doctrine, they had to develop various strategies to maximize their opportunities for action. Thus as early as 1550, Francis Xavier, who in India had gone around in rags of poverty, decided that in Japan one could get a hearing only if dressed like a man who possessed some influence. He also encouraged the other Jesuits who would be tackling that country's prominent citizens and the bonzes (the Shinto leaders who controlled religious life in Japan) to display their scholarship: "It was only because they believed we were scholars that they were disposed to listen to us on the subject of religion" (Hollis 1968, p. 38). Matteo Ricci followed the same pattern in China when he dressed in upper-class Chinese fashion and dazzled the Chinese mandarins with his discourses on the maps, globes, and astronomical instruments he had brought with him – he was able to interest them in his religion only after commanding their attention and convincing them that, at least in some ways, the Europeans were superior to the Chinese (Hollis 1968, p. 62; Spence 1984, pp. 258–9).

The Jesuits seem to have acknowledged very early the necessity of respecting the local customs whenever possible: They discovered that direct efforts to discredit such customs were counterproductive. In countries like India, China, and Japan, they did not treat the local religious beliefs as total errors, as the first missionaries had done. By making a point of learning the local languages and customs as well as possible, they were usually able to find some similarities on which to base a starting point and would treat these beliefs as first, although imperfect, hints at the truth. They attempted to express their teachings as far as possible "in the terminology to which their listeners were accustomed" (Hollis 1968, p. 56). Thus the converts of India were allowed to incorporate some of their original rituals and use their own liturgical language (the problems leading to this decision were known as the Malabar Rites controversy), and no attempt was made by the Jesuits to discourage their Chinese Catholics from continuing the practice of Confucianism. When Ricci died in 1610, he had begun petitioning for permission to use Chinese during mass – he foresaw the day when all foreigners would be expelled and hoped to build up a reserve of native clergy.

South America provides another example of the Jesuits' initiative in their attempts to achieve their goals. Although Ignatius had made a point of working with the local authorities whenever possible, the Jesuits of South America became convinced that the native Indians would not be treated decently by the white Portuguese colonists who wanted to enslave them, and founded eleven self-sufficient Indian communities (Reductions) in Paraguay and Brazil. Only missionaries and government officials were allowed to enter these Christian communities, and no white traders were allowed to establish their business there: Eventually an army was even created to prevent incursions from local settlers (Bangert 1972, pp. 257–61).

The generals of the order supported such measures whenever their necessity was convincingly explained to them; later problems on these issues came from those with opposing financial interests and from their rivals, among them the Dominicans and Franciscans, who "had come to look on the Church as a predominantly European institution . . . [and were intolerant of] Christianity that was not dressed in European clothes" (Hollis 1968, p. 58).

Thus the initial success of the Jesuits was in part due to the fact that the independent initiative of its members was recognized and acted upon by the central authorities.

The special skill of the Jesuits: the perfection of reason

The ascendancy of the Jesuits took place in the period of European history generally known as The Age of Reason. After the humanistic revival of the Renaissance, and the discipline of critical thought introduced by the Reformation, reliance on faith as a basic epistemology was becoming increasingly difficult. Intelligent young men needed the challenge of an intellectually demanding training. The attraction of the Jesuit order lay in great part in its attempt to develop a rational approach to the study and practice of religion. The temper of the times, Ignatius foresaw, was such that examples of piety and good works could no longer counter the intellectual attacks on the church (Foss 1969, pp. 77–80).

Although the first draft of the statutes of the order indicates that Ignatius intended to break away from the old monastic tradition of scholarship, he quickly realized the possibilities of a thoroughly educated cadre in furthering his goals and made the pursuit and transmission of knowledge one of the order's main concerns. One obvious result of this decision was the extensive involvement of the Jesuits in all levels of education. The spread of Jesuit academies and colleges even in Protestant countries was due in a large part to the abilities of their teachers: As one Lutheran pastor wrote despairingly at the end of the 16th century, "Yet, how many of our own are so learned and well-instructed as the Jesuits? How many as diligent and as skilled in imparting that knowledge to the young as these emissaries of the Romish Antichrist?" (Barthel 1984, p. 118.) No wonder that at certain times the demands by heads of states and by cities for their services outstripped the order's ability to produce the requisite number of trained Jesuits (Brodrick 1971, pp. 207–18).

Certainly, the decision by Ignatius and his successors to try to train young Jesuits "to be in the intellectual forefront of the cultural life of their time added immeasurably to the work that each student [novice] had to undertake and to the amount of literary work that he had to try to absorb" (Spence 1984, p. 140). It is probable that Ignatius' military career had taught him the value of careful preparation. The future Jesuit who during the novitiate acquired discipline and religious training next spent years acquiring a thorough knowledge of theology, the classics, mathematics, and science. In addition, in order to prepare Jesuits to battle heathens and heretics, the curriculum came to include the methodological training of "disputations," during which a student had to defend a given point of theology against a wide range of counterarguments by his fellows. When such sessions were rigorously conducted, "they gave extraordinary training to the young in structuring argument, analyzing their own faith, and sharpening their techniques of memory" (Spence 1984, p. 100). All such training was useful in any of the myriad activities undertaken by the Jesuits, whether debating theological points with Protestants, Japanese priests, Chinese learned men, or in carrying on their pedagogical activities.

As a result of their training, the Jesuits' number came to include not only many notable teachers but also exceptional historians, astronomers, mathematicians, and scientists. As the first systematic anthropologists, they brought back to Europe the knowledge of new languages and people, and different ways of life. They introduced new methods of agriculture to these new areas, and took with them and brought back medicinal herbs and knowledge of new plants and animals. Because nearly all their works were permeated with one purpose – to serve the "Greater Glory of God" – they produced very little in the areas that require more imagination, such as poetry, literature, painting, or music. But they were eminently successful in those areas useful in furthering their endeavors, such as education.

The first Jesuit college opened in Messina, Sicily, in 1548; by 1615 the Jesuits were operating 372 colleges, and by 1755 nearly double that number – 728. In Germany, the heart of Protestantism, progress came through upgrading the level of the Catholic clergy, education, and public lectures and debates explicating theological points (Thompson 1913, pp. 208, 214, 225; Ogg 1960, pp. 103–4). Inspired by the advice of Peter Canisius, Ignatius founded the Collegium Germanicum in Rome (1552) to train young Germans to meet the challenges of Protestantism in the future. Canisius was also instrumental in founding Jesuit colleges at such places as Vienna, Prague, Ingolstadt, Innsbruck, and Freiburg; in the last city he founded a printing press, on which he and others produced tracts that challenged Protestant claims through a comprehensive literary defense of the church (Hollis 1968, pp. 23–7). In a country like Poland, where the Protestant influence was much more negligible, the growth of Jesuit presence was very dramatic: from the 11 Jesuits who were first admitted into Poland in 1565 their number increased to 466 by 1590 and to 2,097 by 1773 as the order became internally self-perpetuating. By 1590 the Jesuits had opened 11 colleges and one university, and the number of colleges increased to 50 by 1648 (I. Csikszentmihalyi 1968, 1986). Such wide-ranging growth was due to the multifaceted and energetic activities of the Jesuits in the pulpit, in the press, the confessional, and the classrooms.

Involvement in social problems

Education was only one of the important skills the Jesuits came to be known for. On a more practical level, they were able to fill in voids that the Church hierarchy had not taken care of: Realizing that alms and occasional acts of charity were not enough, the Jesuits energetically undertook to aid the sick, the poor, and the unfortunate. They ministered to the sick in hospitals, to the wounded on battlefields, and to the prisoners in their cells. They spoke out for their beliefs to people in the streets and marketplaces, piazzas, and public gardens; to the laborers in the countryside (accompanied by choral groups to "sweeten" their labor); among the prostitutes in the brothel areas; and in the front of houses of notorious usurers. They founded orphanages for the the many street children and homes of refuge for prostitutes. They formed congregations among lay persons both to reinforce their commitment to the Catholic faith and to enlist their aid in various useful and charitable activities (Spence 1984, pp. 98, 240–42).

The role of the Jesuits as confessors has been much written about, epecially the amount of "casuistry" involved in their dealings with sinners (Ogg 1960, pp. 331–8). But one must remember that the order began at a time when even the slightest transgression could be considered a mortal sin, and fear of a hard penance dampened participation. An additional problem was that the religious questioning and turbulence of the times had caused many people to forego the habit of the confessional. The feeling of the "naturalness" of religion was being lost, and even devout persons began to think that God could be worshipped and served on an individual basis, without the mediation of the clergy (Foss 1969, pp. 52–4). To Ignatius the important thing was to somehow get them back into churches. To this end much stress was put on preaching to the masses, and the Jesuits introduced some reforms into the confession process – in effect, they "humanized" the all-important doctrine of Grace. The believer was no longer simply to admit his sins, but to open up his heart and tell his troubles to his confessor, who thus became a "spiritual adviser" rather than a "sentencing magistrate." One could now expect to deal with a congenial confessor; and a distinction began to be made between mortal sin and venial sin.

A more controversial aspect of Jesuit confessional activity was that when imposing a penance or suggesting any kind of behavioral instruction, the confessor was allowed to "temper his remarks to suit the social circumstances and the spiritual attainments of the individual" (Barthel 1984, p. 86). For this and the previous reasons, the Jesuits became greatly in demand as confessors, especially among the princes and rulers of Europe; at the same time, they did succeed in involving many others in the church and the confessional process (Ogg 1960, pp. 337–8; Boehmer 1975, p. 69). Jesuit literature assures us that their members did not think that only the souls of the powerful were of value – or that their tolerance of much less than perfect behavior in influential persons was hypocritical. Rather, "It was simply a recognition of the fact that in the world as it was in the 16th century, whether in Europe or in Asia, it was not possible to carry out missionary work except with the goodwill of the secular authorities" (Hollis 1968, p. 38). As a recent historian has expressed it, people like Pascal were "wrong in always attributing a wicked motive to the Jesuits. Most of them were men who, if they made Heaven easy for others, made it difficult for themselves; they had not interest in promoting vice or immorality . . . [they tried] to retain their hold on that large class which many churches have had to give up in despair – the indifferent, the worldly and the frivolous. That end was admittedly a good one, though the means might be . . . hard to understand" (Ogg 1960, pp. 337–8).

That the Jesuits proved to be extremely enterprising in their roles as confessors is illustrated by this final example: For the pilgrims visiting the Holy City of Rome, they set up a system of bilingual confessors, each fluent in Italian and one other language – the name of the second language would be displayed above the confessional. "By the 1590s the Jesuits could produce priests to speak in any of the twenty-seven different languages" (Spence 1984, p. 98).

Later developments

Basically, the Jesuits used whatever means they thought would be beneficial to "the defense and propagation of the faith and for the progress of souls in Christian [Catholic] life and doctrine" (Ganss 1970, p. 66), ranging from basic proselytizing to such sophisticated endeavors as putting on spectacular theatrical dramas and oratorios (Nussbaum 1953, p. 42; Spence 1984, p. 99). Their enthusiasm was reinforced by the order's members who were distinguishing themselves in scientific research as well as in their voyages to the new worlds. For a long time, they were both part and leaders of the intellectual and political currents and interests that activated the life and policy of Europe. Their importance did not necessarily increase with their numbers; rather, it decreased as the beliefs of the order became less relevant to the evolving itellectual ideas and spiritual needs of their milieus. The religious wars culminating in the Treaty of Westphalia ushered in an era of skepticism and a general decline in religious ardor and belief, and the growing nationalism necessarily clashed with the goals of a "universal" church. The Jesuits were also hampered in their intellectual exploration by the limits imposed on them by a church dogma that feared being obsoleted by new ideas. Another factor was the tendency for institutions to lose the zeal and dynamism of the originating founders and ideas as they expand in number and power. Who, after all, could duplicate Ignatius's genius for "attracting, inspiring, leading and ordering men exactly as was needed" (Hollis 1968, p. 129)? When one considers that even the charismatic founder had problems with maintaining some of his original companions on the right spiritual track (Brodrick 1971, pp. 237–51), how much more difficult it must have been to channel effectively the energy of this organization as the numbers increased tremendously.

For the Society, which started with 10 members and no residences in 1540, by 1640 counted some 280 residences and missions and more than 16,000 members. Much of the energy given previously to maintaining and monitoring the spiritual goals of the organization would need to be spent in just keeping track of the deployment and needs of the growing number of members scattered over various countries and continents. For much the same reason, codification and an increase in rules and regulations was seen as necessary to assure some uniformity of behavior. Thus the *Ratio Studiorum* crystallized Jesuit education from the theology in colleges to the grammar of the lowest classes, while the *Directorium* was produced as a guide to the *Spiritual Exercises*. Although probably necessary, such steps were the beginning of an increasing tendency "to see truth as something already completely known, . . . [where] towards any new speculation authority has no duty but to look up the book and see if it is right or wrong" (Hollis 1968, p. 126).

Later developments should not obscure the fact that the Jesuits achieved many remarkable things in a relatively short period of time; and such a high level of energy and performance could not be realistically maintained. Whatever one's prejudices, it is generally acknowledged that many of their activities were admirable, and have been justly recognized as such. For instance, a Protestant historian describes their work in Mexico, where one of the chief obstacles to the conversion of the Indians was the the appallingly non-Christian conduct of the supposedly Christian colonists: "They spread education among all classes, their libraries were open to all and they incessantly taught the natives religion in its true spirit . . . their efforts in the conversion of the natives were marked by perseverance and disinterestedneess, united with love for humanity and prayer" (Hollis 1968, pp. 77–8). The Reductions that the Jesuits founded in Paraguay and Brazil aroused the admiration and imagination of many intellectuals and thinkers in Europe, including Montesquieu (Hollis 1968, p. 80). Only 50 years ago, a historian could still credit them with an additional remarkable accomplishment, one of many secular by-products accompanying the Jesuits' spiritual efforts:

> The geographical labours performed in China by the Jesuits and other missionaries of the Roman Catholic faith will always command the gratitude and excite the wonders of all geographers. . . . one hundred and fifty years ago a few wandering European priests traversed the enormous state of China proper and laid down on their maps the positions of cities, the direction of rivers and the height of mountains with a correctness of detail and a general accuracy of outline that are absolutely marvellous. To this day all our maps are based on their observations. (Thornton, *History of China* [1921], quoted in Hollis 1968, p. 64)

Conclusions

The reason Ignatius of Loyola and his followers were able to develop such a successful institution is that they created a set of rules and practices that attracted the voluntary attention of a substantial number of able young men. These rules attracted attention because they provided a unified structure of consciousness whereby psychic energy could be invested in an ordered way. They offered a graduated set of challenges commensurate to the skills of the novice, and later to those of the full-fledged Jesuit. These challenges included ways of thinking, praying, behaving – in short, they encompassed almost the entire range of consciousness.

Most important, the unified rules that structured the psychic energy of the Jesuits were well integrated both with the cultural realities of the period, and to an extent perhaps unparalleled by previous religious systems, they were congruent with biologically programmed goals. The reliance on reason, the emphasis on individual autonomy and education, the concern with social and political realities fit the Company within the worldview of the Counter-Reformation. Although the vows of celibacy ran counter to biological selection, the military discipline and the wide scope for the development of physical, intellectual, and organizational skills provided young men who joined the Jesuits with a great number of challenges.

These factors brought the Jesuits intrinsic rewards that sustained their behavior and thought, whether they were facing the tribulations of classroom teaching or the often difficult and sometimes deadly privations of life on the frontiers of Canada, Brazil, Russia, India, and China. As with all cultural forms that command the allegiance of its members, the selection and continued survival of the Society of Jesus cannot be completely understood without accounting for the enjoyable experience it provided to those who followed its norms.

IV. The measurement of flow in everyday life

15. Introduction to Part IV

MIHALY AND ISABELLA CSIKSZENTMIHALYI

Flow is a useful concept not so much because it accounts for rare and exotic activities like rock climbing or ocean sailing, but because it helps explain the texture of everyday life, the rise and fall of motivations that follow one another as normal people respond to the human and inanimate contours of their changing environment. It is the sum of these momentary motivational states that shapes the life of the individual over time, and it is the sum of these individual lifetimes that shapes the evolution of social and cultural forms. As Massimini has observed, flow experiences in everyday life are reminiscent of Darwin's image of the tiny, soft-bodied organisms whose calcareous skeletons slowly build rock-hard reefs on the ocean floor. Flow experiences, too, seem ephemeral, but they form habits and institutions that stand the wear of centuries.

The study of fairly exceptional cases, such as individuals undergoing solitary ordeals or joining motorcycle gangs, is an important first step that helps reveal the parameters of autotelic experience. That was the initial goal of the work reported in *Beyond Boredom and Anxiety*. But the ultimate goal was "to find out piecemeal and experimentally what combination of challenges and skills can be accommodated in a schoolroom, a neighborhood, or a home . . . [in order to] maximize flow involvement in as many people as possible" (Csikszentmihalyi 1975b, p. 203). In the last chapter of that book, work and schools were targeted as the two institutions in which research on flow was most needed, because people spend most of their lives first in school and then on the job, and therefore the quality of their overall life experience is most deeply affected, at least in quantitative terms, by what happens to them in those contexts.

The following chapters show some of the consequences of following this advice. They report studies of flow in everyday life, especially in schools and at work, as well as in the third major context of life – the home. These studies are distinguished by a common conceptual framework and by a common methodology. The theoretical model is based on the ratio of the quantity of subjectively experienced challenges to the quantity of subjectively felt skills. The shared methodology is what we decided to call the Experience Sampling Method, or ESM for short. The steps leading to its development follow.

The Experience Sampling Method. At the conclusion of the research that went into *Beyond Boredom and Anxiety*, all of which was based on interviews and questionnaires, the limitations those methods imposed had become somewhat frustrating. Interviews are indispensable at the initial stages of any research into the subjective dimensions of experience. They provide integrated self-reports, personal reminiscences that alone could yield the broad outlines of a sequence of phenomenological events. But the limitations of the interview as a way of reconstructing the stream of consciousness are also obvious. Being retrospective, the interview cannot easily separate the actual event from the cultural forms and the personal wishes that may influence its retelling. More than anything else, interviews are limited by the vagaries of memory and by the difficulty that persons unused to reflection have in reporting events, especially internal events that only take place in consciousness. Interviews are tools with a very rough resolution; they yield only the most general, the most obvious features of the landscape they are designed to reveal. Therefore by the mid 1970s we were looking for a new tool, for an instrument that could magnify and bring into sharper relief events in the everyday stream of consciousness.

The first experiments were with diaries and other forms of systematic reporting. These methods were able to give a finer resolution of everyday experience, but they also were open to the slight rearrangements that a person brings to his or her experience when engaged in formal reporting. A more immediate, a more spontaneous measure of inner life was needed.

The tool we were looking for was developed at the University of Chicago in 1975 and 1976. The first prototype of the ESM came about when Suzanne Prescott, then a student in the Committee on Human Development, suggested to M. Csikszentmihalyi the idea of using electronic pagers as the stimulus for respondents to report on their thoughts and feelings *on the spot* (Csikszentmihalyi, Larson, & Prescott 1977). If a transmitter was programmed to send signals to the pagers at random times of the day, and the respondent was asked to fill out a series of questions and rate a number of items whenever the pager signaled, it would be possible to get instantaneous accounts of inner lives at random, unexpected moments. Combined with a booklet of self-report forms, the pager – or "beeper" as it is less formally known – makes it possible for the investigator to prompt respondents to give a high-resolution description of their mental states right as these are happening.

Various versions of self-report forms were developed and pre-tested; these eventually yielded a self-report booklet that measured a set of items that capture the main dimensions of consciousness (affect or emotion, activation or potency, cognitive efficiency, and intrinsic motivation) as well as the main contextual dimensions that influence the state of consciousness (e.g., where a person is, with whom, doing what).

The ESM was developed as a tool to study flow in everyday life. Our first systematic study, conducted in the spring of 1976, described the daily fluctuations in experience for 107 workers in the Chicago area. But in using this new instrument, we found ourselves in the situation of the fabled sorcerer's apprentice: The tool took on a life of its own independent of the user's intentions. What happened was that the ESM gave such detailed insight into changes in consciousness in everyday life, that we felt compelled to use it first for a comprehensive description of what people do day in, day out, from morning to night. The logical next step was to prepare a systematic record of the changes in consciousness in everyday life, which in turn meant fine-tuning the recording instrument to make sure that the method measured the most salient dimensions of consciousness.

But soon it became clear that any description had to classify respondents by major categories such as sex, age, or social class, since variations in consciousness were presumably dependent on such demographic characteristics. Then we became curious as to whether the responses we were getting were culturally specific to the United States, or whether they had a wider validity. These and many other urgent questions were brought up by the new instrument. The richness of the data produced was such that during this decade, ESM research was primarily data-driven or method-driven rather than concept-driven. Almost 10 years of very active investigations went by before we felt ready to return to the original question, namely, Can flow be measured in everyday life?

How the ESM and similar in situ self-reporting techniques developed around the same time is a story of its own, documented by Hormuth (1986), Massimini and Inghilleri (1986), and Csikszentmihalyi and Larson (1987). The chapters in Part IV of this volume illustrate the application of the ESM to the purpose for which it was primarily developed: the study of flow.

How the ESM measures flow. Every time the pager signals, which usually means 8 times a day for a total of 56 times a week, the respondent fills out one Experience Sampling Form (see Figures 15.1 and 15.2 for an early and a later ESF). Each form contains open-ended items (e.g., "As you were beeped, what were you thinking about?"), as well as numerical scales that indicate the intensity of various emotions (e.g., "Describe your mood as you were beeped: alert . . . drowsy; happy . . . sad, etc." on a scale from 1 to 7). Each ESF yields over 30 measurement points on which to base an estimate of the respondents' subjective state. The question then becomes, Which of these items should be used as a measure of flow?

It could be argued that the intensity of response on the happy–sad scale would make a good index of the intensity of flow. Or the amount of concentration reported. Or the lack of self-consciousness. Or the degree of control experienced. Or one might make a case that the degree to which a person disagrees with the statement "I wished to be doing something else" when beeped would be the best index of flow. All of these dimensions were represented by quantified scales on the ESF. Or perhaps one could have used a combination of all of the above items as a global measure of flow. Instead, we decided to take an alternative route.

To take items measuring positive states of consciousness, like happiness or concentration, as representing the flow state would have been probably accurate, but on the other hand it would also have prejudged the issue. To do so would have amounted to defining flow as happiness, or high concentration, and so on; but our task was to ascertain whether this was indeed the case, not to make it so by definition. We felt that the relationship between flow and a positive state of consciousness was a *synthetic* relation, not an *analytic* one (Popper 1965). Therefore it was necessary to find a measure of flow that was independent of the more direct measures of positive states of consciousness.

The obvious choice was to define flow in terms of the balance between challenges and skills. This ratio has been one of the fundamental features of the flow model, and it was logically (i.e., analytically) independent of how happy, concentrated, motivated, or strong a person felt. We expected an empirical correlation between the balance of challenges and skills on the one hand and positive experience on the other; but because

Date: __8/4/76__   Time Beeped: __5:30__ am/(pm)   Time Filled Out: __5:40__

AS YOU WERE BEEPED

Where were you? _in living room at home_

What was the MAIN thing you were doing? _watching T.V. news -_
Jimmy Carter interviews

Why were you doing this? (circle answers)   I had to do it...............yes
                                              I wanted to do it..........(yes)
                                              I had nothing else to do.....yes

What other things were you doing? _eating pie & milk_

What were you thinking about when you were beeped? _Jimmy Carter's_
campaign

	no	some	quite	very
How well were you concentrating?				(9)
Was it hard to concentrate?	(1)			
How self-conscious were you?	(0)			
Were you in control of your actions?				(8)

0 1 2 3 4 5 6 7 8 9

Describe your mood and physical states as you were beeped:

	very much	quite much	some what	do not feel either	some what	quite much	very much	
hostile	0	o	.	-	.	(o)	0	friendly
alert	0	o	(○)	-	.	o	0	drowsy
happy	0	o	(○)	-	.	o	0	sad
tense	0	o	.	-	.	(o)	0	relaxed
suspicious	0	o	.	-	.	(o)	0	trusting
irritable	0	o	.	-	(·)	o	0	cheerful
strong	0	o	(○)	-	.	o	0	weak
active	0	(o)	.	-	.	o	0	passive
lonely	0	o	.	(·)	.	o	0	sociable
creative	0	o	(○)	-	.	o	0	dull
resentful	0	o	.	-	.	(○)	0	satisfied
free	0	o	.	(·)	.	o	0	constrained
excited	0	(o)	.	-	.	o	0	bored

	none	slight	bothersome	severe
headache	(0)			
body aches	(0)			
other physical symptoms _____	(0)			

0 1 2 3 4 5 6 7 8 9

S. 183

Figure 15.1. Sample of an early version of the Experience Sampling Form (ESF).

Were you: ( ) alone ( ) with friends ( ) with co-workers ( ) with supervisor

(✓) with family ( ) with strangers ( ) other _____

CIRCLE THE NUMBERS BELOW THAT BEST DESCRIBE HOW YOU FELT ABOUT WHAT YOU WERE DOING WHEN YOU WERE BEEPED. For example, if you felt that the activity was very challenging for you, you might circle a number toward the right hand side of the scale.

```
                                   0  1  2  3  4  5  6  7  8  9
Challenges of the activity        +--+--+--+--+--+--+--(7)--+--+
                                   low                        high

Your skills in the activity       +--+--+--+--+--+--+--+--(8)-+
                                   low                        high

Do you wish you had been doing    (1)--+--+--+--+--+--+--+--+--+
  something else?                  not at all              very much

Was anything at stake for you in  +--+--+--+--+--+--+--+-(7)-+--+
  the activity?                    nothing                 very much
```

List all the things you remember doing since you were last beeped (or in the last hour or so). CHECK YOUR ANSWERS--WRITE DOWN HOW OFTEN IF MORE THAN ONCE.

✓ _____ day dreaming
_____ talking or whistling or singing to yourself
✓ _____ watching people or things or just staring into space
_____ watching TV or going to a movie
_____ listening to the radio or a record
_____ listening to a presentation or lecture
_____ reading a book or magazine or newspaper
✓ _____ reading something related to work or school
_____ snacking, smoking, or chewing on things
_____ chewing on objects (pencil, paperclip, finger . . .)
✓ _____ walking, pacing, or running
✓ _____ small muscle movements (tapping your finger, swinging your leg)
_____ rubbing, grooming, or scratching yourself
_____ typing or working some other office machine
_____ doing something different on your job
       (specify _____)
✓ _____ driving a car or motorcycle
_____ riding a bicycle
_____ playing a game or sport alone
_____ shopping or browsing
_____ doing art work, playing a musical instrument or other hobby
       (specify _____)
✓ _____ cleaning, cooking or other work at home
_____ talking or joking with friends or relatives
_____ talking with coworkers or fellow students
✓ _____ talking with supervisor or teacher
✓ _____ talking on the telephone related to job or school
_____ talking on the phone to a friend or relative
_____ parties or games with others
_____ touching or holding a child or adult

FILL OUT ONCE EVERY 24 HOUR PERIOD

Time you went to bed last night: _____

Approximately how long did it take you to fall asleep (in minutes): _____

Time you woke up this morning: _____

How would you describe the quality of your sleep last night?
```
        0    1    2    3    4    5    6    7    8    9
        +----+----+----+----+----+----+----+----+----+
      very poor      moderately      moderately      very good
                       poor            good
```

Figure 15.1 (continued)

Date:_____ Time Beeped: 12:06 am/pm Time Filled Out 12:07 am/pm

As you were beeped...

What were you thinking about? Romeo & Juliet

_____

Where were you? English Class

What was the MAIN thing you were doing? Reading / Reviewing
Romeo & Juliet

What other things were you doing? Chewing on pen

_____

WHY were you doing this particular activity?
　　　(/) I had to　　( ) I wanted to do it　　( ) I had nothing else to do

	not at all		some what		quite			very
How well were you concentrating?	0	1	2	3	4	(5)	6	7	8	9
Was it hard to concentrate?	0	1	2	3	4	5	6	(7)	8	9
How self-conscious were you?	0	1	2	3	4	(5)	6	7	8	9
Did you feel good about yourself?	0	1	(2)	3	4	5	6	7	8	9
Were you in control of the situation?	0	1	2	(3)	4	5	6	7	8	9
Were you living up to your own expectations?	0	1	2	3	4	(5)	6	7	8	9
Were you living up to expectations of others?	0	1	2	(3)	4	5	6	7	8	9

Describe your mood as you were beeped:

	very	quite	some	neither	some	quite	very	
alert	0	o	.	-	(o)	o	0	drowsy
happy	0	o	.	-	(o)	o	0	sad
irritable	0	o	(o)	-	.	o	0	cheerful
strong	0	o	(o)	-	.	o	0	weak
active	0	o	.	(o)	.	o	0	passive
lonely	0	o	(o)	-	.	o	0	sociable
ashamed	0	o	.	(o)	.	o	0	proud
involved	0	o	.	-	(o)	o	0	detached
excited	0	o	.	-	(o)	o	0	bored
closed	0	o	.	(o)	.	o	0	open
clear	0	o	.	(o)	.	o	0	confused
tense	0	o	.	(o)	.	o	0	relaxed
competitive	0	o	.	(o)	.	o	0	cooperative

Figure 15.2. Sample of a recent version of the Experience Sampling
Form (ESF).

Did you feel any physical discomfort as you were beeped:

Overall pain or   none   slight   bothersome   severe
discomfort   0   1   2 ③ 4   5   6   7   8   9

Please specify: _I hate english_

Who were you with?

( ) alone   ( ) friend(s)   How many? _____
( ) mother   female ( )   male ( )
( ) father   ( ) strangers
( ) sister(s) or brother(s)   (✓) other _students_

Indicate how you felt about your activity:

	low									high
Challenges of the activity	0	1	2	3	4	5	6	⑦	8	9
Your skills in the activity	0	1	2	3	4	⑤	6	7	8	9

	not at all								very much	
Was this activity important to you?	0	1	2	3	4	5	6	7	⑧	9
Was this activity important to others?	0	1	2	3	4	5	6	7	⑧	9
Were you succeeding at what you were doing?	0	1	2	3	④	5	6	7	8	9
Do you wish you had been doing something else?	0	1	2	3	4	5	6	7	8	⑨
Were you satisfied with how you were doing?	0	1	2	3	4	5	⑥	7	8	9
How important was this activity in relation to your overall goals	0	1	2	3	4	⑤	6	7	8	9

If you had a choice. . .

Who would you be with? _Anybody_

What would you be doing? _Anything_

Since you were last beeped has anything happened or have you done anything which could have affected the way you feel?

Lunch

Nasty cracks, comments, etc: ***

English sucks

Figure 15.2 *(continued)*

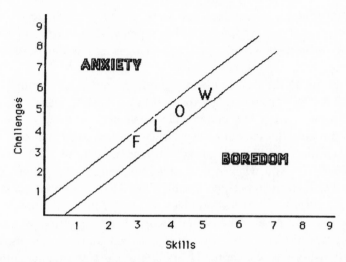

Figure 15.3. The original flow model. Optimal experience is predicted in the diagonal area where the ratio of challenges to skills equals one. (Adapted from Csikszentmihalyi, 1975b.)

the two sets of variables were conceptually distinct, this expectation could be falsified by the data. In other words, results might show that in fact people were not better off when challenges and skills were in balance than when one of the variables was larger than the other. This logical independence recommended the challenge-skill ratio as the most economical and persuasive measure of flow.

Accordingly, on each ESF there were two items: "What were the challenges in this activity?" and: "What were your skills in this activity?" scaled from zero ("none") to 9 ("very high"). The theoretical model based on our extensive interviews predicted that the optimal flow experience would occur whenever both these items were given the same numerical value; for example, when challenges were scored zero and so were skills, or when challenges and skills were both scored 9, and so forth. This relationship is illustrated visually in Figure 15.3.

The diagonal line in the figure represents the optimal ratio of challenges to skills. It is then that consciousness performs most effortlessly, that attention, awareness, and memory work with the fewest impediments. Accordingly, this negentropic state should be experienced as a very positive condition; people should feel happy, strong, concentrated, and motivated whenever the ratio of challenges and skills approaches unity.

However, when the thousands of self-reports generated through the ESM were initially analyzed, the theoretical predictions were not confirmed. People did not feel better when challenges and skills were in balance. The only dimension of experience that followed the expected pattern was the item that measured intrinsic motivation: "When you were beeped, did you wish to be doing something else?" When challenges and skills were in balance, people tended to answer that question "Not at all." When one of the variables was larger than the other, they tended to say that they wished to be doing something else to a degree that was proportionate to the imbalance between challenges and skills. This relationship was conceptually gratifying, since the main claim of the model is that flow is intrinsically motivating. Yet it didn't quite seem enough: We had expected people in flow also to feel more alert, more concentrated, more strong, more in control, less self-conscious. Why weren't the predicted relationships appearing?

For years this remained a frustrating puzzle in an otherwise fruitful research program. Was the conceptual model wrong? Did the ratio of challenges and skills have very little to do with the quality of experience? Or was our method at fault, unable to capture the shifting patterns in consciousness? The wording of the ESFs was changed, and new samples were recruited and tested in the hope of clarifying the problem. But nothing helped bring about the expected results.

A conceptual and methodological breakthrough in the measurement of flow occurred in 1985. At the University of Milan, where Professor Massimini and his team had been replicating some of our ESM work with samples of Milanese teenagers, a simple but ingenious idea was proposed: the flow experience begins only when challenges and skills *are above a certain level*, and are in balance. In operationalizing this concept, the personal mean for challenges and skills (which is represented by the zero-point when the raw scores are transformed into z scores) was used as the starting point above which the experience should turn positive. When both challenges and skills are below what is customary for a person, it does not make sense to expect that person to be in flow, even if the two variables are perfectly balanced. In such a condition, when opportunities for action are less than normal, and when personal

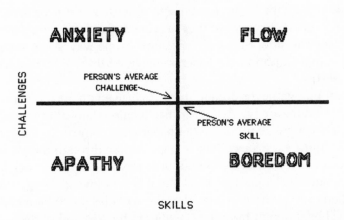

Figure 15.4. The flow model applied to the ESM. The origin for the optimal experience is the personal average of challenges and skills – only above that starting point does flow begin. (Adapted from Massimini and Carli, 1986.)

abilities are underutilized, a person might feel apathetic or in a state of vegetation. The new flow model, as revised by Massimini and Carli, looks like the illustration in Figure 15.4.

The model in Figure 15.4 does not contradict the one in Figure 15.3; it simply adapts it to the specific research design of the ESM. Figure 15.3 is a composite diachronic model illustrating how the flow experience proceeds through time, *in a single activity*, from enjoyment of small challenges when a person's skills are limited, to an ever-complexifying enjoyment of higher challenges requiring increasingly rare skills. For instance, a beginning piano player will see learning the keys corresponding to the various notes as challenging, and might feel in flow simply by running the scales on the keyboard. As soon as the player feels confident with the scales, however, new challenges need to be found or he or she will get bored.

In the model represented by Figure 15.3, it would be very difficult for a person to return to a lower level on the diagonal. A piano player who has reached a certain skill level can get bored or anxious, but it is almost impossible for him to lose both his piano playing challenges and skills at the same time. This is the reason why flow is a force for growth: Unless people get better at what they are doing, they can't enjoy doing it any longer. The flow diagonal represents a one-way street toward increasing complexification (Csikszentmihalyi 1982b; Csikszentmihalyi & Larson 1984).

But in real life we never do one thing exclusively: Nobody can play the piano 24 hours a day. Activities that require skills alternate with routine, unchallenging episodes: After playing the piano even the greatest musician must eat a snack, take a nap, browse through the papers, and talk to someone. In everyday life, it is possible to move back and forth from high-challenge, high-skill situations to low-challenge, low-skill situations several times a day – but the activities at the high end of the scale will be different from the activities at the low end of the scale. Figure 15.4 takes this reality into account, and predicts that only the high-challenge, high-skill situations produce flow, whereas apathy will be the result when challenges and skills are in balance but below the mean. In other words, when the musician is rehearsing a difficult piece that he can barely master he will be in flow; when he is tired in the evening and watching television he will not be in flow even though he might feel that his depleted skills are in balance with the scarce challenges in the environment.

Chapter 16 shows how the Milanese team operationalized the new conceptual model. When the model was reformulated this way, the ESM data fell beautifully in line with the theoretical expectations. People reported the most positive states when challenges and skills were in balance and when both were above their mean levels for the week of testing. In the sample of Milanese teenagers, for instance, 18 of the 27 dimensions of experience were significantly more positive in this condition than in any other. Teenagers concentrated much more, felt more in control, were more happy, strong, active, involved, creative, free, excited, open, clear, motivated, and satisfied with their performance when both challenges and skills were in balance above the mean (Massimini & Carli 1986; Massimini, Csikszentmihalyi, & Carli 1987).

When skills are above average and challenges below (conceptually this would correspond to the condition of "boredom"), control is above average but concentration falls – the remaining variables show only slight deviations from the mean. When challenges are above average and skills are below (the condition of "anxiety"), concentration is significantly high but control is lower. The quality of experience is lowest when both challenges and skills are below the mean (the low condition of "apathy");

in the Milanese sample, 20 out of the 27 dimensions of experience were significantly lower than average in this condition. These relationships have been now replicated with a variety of samples in the United States and in Italy.

Chapter 17 shows a comparison of the responses of teenagers from Chicago and Milan, using the ESM data analyzed in terms of the eight-channel flow model. The distribution of responses in the various channels was very similar for both groups of students. However, the most positive feelings for the American students occurred when they felt that their skills were somewhat above the level necessary to meet current challenges (channel 3), and their most negative feelings were in the anxiety channel, when they perceived the challenges to be above their skill levels. The Italian adolescents' most positive feelings occurred while in the flow (high-challenge, high-skill) channel, and they exhibited the strongest negative feelings in the region of apathy (low challenge, low skill). In their daily lives, the American adolescents found themselves more frequently in flow while in school, while the Italians felt more often in the region of control. The same findings obtained for studying at home. Nevertheless both groups find school and studying a generally positive experience. For the Italians, the ideal curriculum would provide more opportunities to mach their skills with the appropriate challenges. For the American adolescents, it would encourage them to employ more the growth-producing challenges present in the schools.

Chapter 18 focuses on work, which is the productive activity that takes up the bulk of adults' psychic energy, as studying does among adolescents. Unless adults learn to enjoy productive work, society will be in trouble. The findings reported by Judith LeFevre, gleaned from an early ESM study of over 100 typical workers in the Chicago area, are in some respects reassuring, in that they do not indicate any widespread alienation from work. First of all, the data confirm the flow model. When challenges and skills are both high, the respondents report the highest quality experience, as did the Milanese teenagers. Second, the more time workers spent during the week in the flow condition, the higher the levels of overall experience they reported; that is, the more happy, strong, concentrated, satisfied, and so on, they were. Third, and perhaps most important in its consequences, the occasions of flow were more frequent on the job than anywhere else, including leisure settings. This was most true of managers and professionals, but it was also true of blue-collar assembly line workers. Even though most jobs are not designed to maximize flow, it seems that compared to the opportunities in the rest of life work still offers the most consistent setting for enjoyment and growth.

Chapter 19 reports a comparison between two equally talented groups of teenagers. Both are exceptionally able in mathematics. The students in the first group, however, are developing their talent while the students in the second group are not. Jeanne Nakamura shows that the key difference between the two groups is that the achieving math students are twice as often in flow when studying compared to the students who are not using their talent. The latter, in contrast, are in the condition of "anxiety" much more often when studying. To compensate for negative experiences when studying, the lower achieving students spend much more time socializing with peers and friends, an activity that is accompanied by positive moods. The dynamics of flow and antiflow in these two groups illustrates clearly the process by which young people grow up to either develop or to neglect the intellectual talents with which they are endowed.

In Chapter 20 Anne Wells looks at an increasingly numerous and important segment of the population: working mothers. She is specifically interested in the opportunities for experiencing flow that mothers of small children who also work have, and how these opportunities relate to their sense of self-esteem. By including items from Rosenberg's self-esteem scale on each ESF, Wells has been able to measure fluctuations in self-esteem as well as the other dimensions of consciousness. Her data again replicate the findings concerning flow: Both self-esteem and the other dimensions of experience are most positive when challenges and skills are above the mean, and significantly worse in apathy, boredom, and anxiety situations. Moreoever, flow experiences occurred in all types of activities and with all groups of companions. Mothers who spent more time in flow during the course of the study reported higher levels of parental self-esteem. The amount of time spent in this high-challenge and high-skill channel was related to several other factors, such as the age of the youngest child, the socioeconomic status of the family, and whether or not the person liked her job.

In Chapter 21, Kevin Rathunde takes on an ambitious task: to identify whether there is such a thing as an autotelic family context that can facilitate and encourage a child's capacity to derive optimal experiences. Basing his conclusions on data from an ESM study of some 190 adolescents, Rathunde found that the subjects who perceived their family context as being autotelic did in fact report more optimal experiences than their peers who saw their family context as nonautotelic while at home with their parents, when involved in productive activities in school, and while doing homework and studying at home. Defining the autotelic family context as one that structures a child's subjective experience with a balance of choice, clarity, centering, commitment, and challenge, Rathunde sees these qualities as providing an economy of *attention* by avoiding the wasteful extremes of boredom and anxiety. The structure provided by the autotelic home allows the child to devote his or her resources to the task at hand by not diverting attention to problems with the structure itself. The lower scores on affect, activation and motivation, and the lower self-concept displayed by the teenagers from nonautotelic context homes suggest that these adolescents may be focusing on the rules and restraints represented by the school and its demands, such as homework, rather than on finding intrinsically motivating or flow experiences that may be available within such obligatory situations. Because other studies on flow have suggested that some persons may possess an autotelic personality that is capable of finding flow experiences in the least encouraging or even inimical situations, being able to identify the components of a home that encourages the growth of persons who can find opportunities for meaningful action in many and varied settings has important implications for human well-being.

16. The systematic assessment of flow in daily experience

FAUSTO MASSIMINI AND MASSIMO CARLI

In considering possible future empirical research on flow, a central desideratum was expressed in the last pages of *Beyond Boredom and Anxiety*: "The flow model could be extended to work situations and other 'nonleisure' settings . . . it is important to find out piecemeal and experimentally what combination of challenges and skills can be accommodated in a schoolroom, a neighborhood, or at home, so that . . . [we] can maximize flow involvement in as many people as possible" (Csikszentmihalyi 1975b, p. 203). The present chapter describes such a project.

The transition from theory to empirical validation is never easy, especially when the phenomenon is a complex one. When it belongs to the class of "subjective experiences," the methodological challenge becomes even more baffling. In this context, the problem consists of finding a way to describe variations in the quality of subjective experience as a function of variations in the conditions of flow – that is, as a function of the relationship between the levels of perceived challenges and perceived skills.

Flow is a relatively rare experience, difficult to encounter every day, at least in our culture and for the majority of people. It was first described in groups of people who, because of their specialized activities and because of their strong involvement, were able to come in contact with this experience in its highest forms – chess masters, rock climbers, surgeons, and so on (Csikszentmihalyi 1975b). It was from interviews with such performers that the basic principle of the theory was derived: the importance of reaching a balance between opportunities for action and personal abilities in order to enter the flow state. Applied to a broader theoretical context, the implications of this principle have become central to the paradigm of psychological and cultural selection, which in turn helps explain the evolution of culture and of the individual self (Csikszentmihalyi & Massimini 1985; Massimini 1979a,b; Massimini & Inghilleri 1986).

Instead of studying select groups, we try to verify the validity of the consequences of balancing challenges and skills on the part of ordinary individuals in relatively "normal" situations. The interaction between opportunities for action and individual skills is not a rare occurrence. It is constantly happening in everyday life, and follows a molecular process that repeats itself every moment throughout our life spans, resulting in psychological effects that slowly shape the habits and personalities of individuals – like those tiny shifts and movements of the terrestrial crust that in time bring forth massive mountain ranges. It is from this flux of daily experiences that flow occasionally emerges. The stream of ordinary experiences, ranging from the faintly pleasant to the boring and the anxious, is made up of a random collection of discordant notes. Occasionally the notes fall into a harmonious chord – when that happens, information in consciousness is ordered, and we experience flow.

Applying the principle of a balanced ratio between skills and challenges to ordinary events makes it possible to search for those contexts of everyday life that make the flow experience more likely to occur. The study of everyday life, in turn, presents unique problems of its own. Whereas flow is a well-ordered state of consciousness, everyday life appears confused: "It is more like a turbulent sporting event in which hopes and frustrations, elation and disappointment follow each other in no particular sequence" (Csikszentmihalyi & Larson 1984). It is not easy to identify patterns of coherence in such an unpredictable flux. Even if we consider one person only, the intricacies of the problem become readily apparent. In the experience of a single individual, moments of high and low concentration and involvement will alternate in an apparently random fashion in conjunction with positive and negative emotional states. The same activity, the same thoughts, within the space of a few minutes may produce very different emotions. The problem becomes even more intractable if we are to seek rules to encompass two or more persons.

It is therefore essential to use a variable that will help to identify and reflect the order underlying such apparent anarchy, a variable based on clear theoretical principles providing "some guidance for what kind of models can be constructed and what sort of prediction can or cannot be sought" (Boyd & Richerson 1985). Order in consciousness will be most easily detected in the context of flow; or in the more mundane settings of everyday life, in those situations where experience most closely approximates flow. It is in such contexts that one would expect a "positive convergence" of the dimensions of consciousness, an ordered state of optimal experience. The thread of Ariadne that makes it possible to untangle the convoluted fluctuations characteristic of everyday life is the balancing of challenges and skills. This balance is important not only to the climber moving up a rock face. It is in the ordinary life of every day that we learn, moment by moment, how to evaluate opportunities for action and how to match them with appropriate skills until the matching becomes as automatic as breathing. And the relationship between this parameter and the optimal emotional state is presumably the same in everyday life as it is in the extreme situations encountered by rock climbers or chess masters.

From the viewpoint of empirical research, the problem is to develop a method that will be capable of describing as precisely as possible fluctuations in the perception of challenges and skills, and the related changes in the quality of experience in normal situations.

Method

The method of choice, based on self-reports and developed specifically for this purpose, is the Experience Sampling Method (ESM) (Csikszentmihalyi, Larson, & Prescott 1977; Larson & Csikszentmihalyi 1983; Csikszentmihalyi & Larson 1987). It consists in providing respondents with an electronic pager and a questionnaire booklet. The investigators activate the pagers through a radio transmitter seven or eight times a day according to a random schedule, and each time the pager signals, the respondent fills out one sheet of the booklet. By the end of a week the booklet will contain a systematic description of the external parameters of the person's life (the activities performed, the places visited, the people encountered), and of the personal experiences and dimensions of consciousness of which the person was aware when the signal occurred (the affect, the cognitive efficiency, the motivational states, and so on).

In our case, an average of seven signals were sent between 8 A.M. and 10 P.M. to each respondent for the period of 1 week. Each sheet of the response booklet included 25 self-report scales based on those developed by Csikszentmihalyi and Larson (1984). The sample consisted of 47 respondents between 16 and 19 years of age, students of a classical lyceum in Milan. There were 14 males and 33 females in the sample, which reflects the actual gender distribution in the Italian classical ly-ceums. The study was conducted in May 1983.

Our task was to have the ESM reflect the parameters of experience during various levels of perceived challenges and skills. The ratio be-tween these two variables, rather than the type of activity a person is engaged in at any given moment, should serve as an indication of the presence of flow. One might expect dramatic differences between the flow experiences of a painter and those of a scientist or a housewife. Similarly, what might produce flow in everyday life for one person may not be the same for anyone else. Thus, theoretically, the most meaningful reference point for the presence or absence of flow is the perception of challenges and skills reported on the ESM sheets.

Furthermore, in order to interpret the data meaningfully it is necessary to account for individual differences in response to the scaled items. Some respondents consistently describe their action opportunities as very high, whereas others rate them consistently low. The same differ-ences hold true for the rating of personal skills. In the present sample, the rating of skills was an average of 5.8 on a 9-point scale, with indi-vidual means ranging from 2.4 to 7.8. The sample mean for the level of challenges was 3.8, with individual means ranging from 1.2 to 6.0. For a person whose mean level of challenge is 6.0, the rating of a specific situation as presenting a challege level of 5.0 would be relatively low, but for another person whose mean challenge level was 2.0, the same rating of 5.0 would constitute an exceptionally high level of challenge. What should we consider a high level of skills and challenges when the values on the scale are rated so differently by different respondents? In order to provide a common reference point for comparison among sub-jects, we turn to the traditional statistical procedure of standardizing individual responses around individual mean scores. The raw scores reported in each booklet were changed into numbers representing stan-dardized deviations relative to the average of that respondent. These standard z scores are comparable with each other across individuals and indicate on a unified scale the degree of deviation from the average response.

The various combinations between the level of perceived challenges and skills are reported in terms of eight different ratios between the individuals' standardized challenge and skill scores:

1. High challenges and average skills
2. High challenges and high skills (flow)
3. Average challenges and high skills

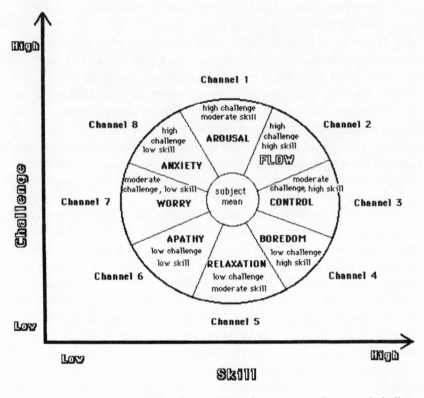

Figure 16.1. A model for the analysis of experience. Perceived challenge is on the ordinate, and perceived skill is on the abscissa.

4. Low challenges and high skills (boredom)
5. Low challenges and average skills
6. Low challenges and low skills (apathy)
7. Average challenges and low skills
8. High challenges and low skills (anxiety).

These eight situations are represented visually by the model in Figure 16.1. The center of the figure represents the average level of the individual's weekly challenges and skills. It corresponds to the point of origin of two Cartesian coordinates, with challenges on the ordinate and skills on the abscissa. The eight "channels" represent various ratios between these two variables.

This model implies that each respondent will describe his or her experience differently, depending on the channel in which the response occurs; depending, in other words, on the ratio between challenges and skills. The theoretical expectation is that the optimal situation as well as the most congruent one will be reported when respondents describe their situation as having both high challenges and high skills (channel 2). The verification of this fact is the first test for the validity of the model. But how should we define optimal experience? What combination of variables would one expect to be present in the flow experience? The respondents, in filling out the ESM sheets, described their states of consciousness along a very broad spectrum of dimensions. Some of these dimensions refer to affective states (e.g., the items happy–sad; cheerful–irritable), others reflect motivational states (how much a person wished to be doing something else); still others reflect cognitive involvement (e.g., level of concentration, ease of concentration). The positive end of each of these dimensions was expected to be more typical of flow, and the coincidence of all the positive dimensions was the expected characteristic of that optimal experience.

In the tables that follow the average self-report scores on these various dimensions will be reported as standardized z scores in order to make it possible to compare deviations from individual means across people who might have been using the response scale in different ways. Table 16.1 reports the mean standard scores of the 47 adolescents on the various dimensions of experience in each of the eight channels defined by the ratio of challenges and skills. Twenty-three dimensions of experience are compared in the table, and the analysis of variance shows significant effects of the channels on each one of these 23 dimensions of experience.

As predicted, channel 2 is the most positive of the eight channels and the one in which the quality of experience clearly approximates the optimal flow experience. When challenges and skills were both high, respondents were concentrating significantly more than usual, they felt in control, happy, strong, active, involved, creative, free, excited, open, clear, satisfied, and wishing to be doing the activity at hand. The opposite state of experience was reported in channel 6, where both challenges and skills were below the person's average, and a similar, although somewhat less negative, state was reported in channels 7 and 8, which theoretically reflect situations of anxiety. Channel 4, which theoretically corresponds to the situation of boredom, reflected an essentially neutral experience: below-average concentration, a feeling that nothing important was at stake, an adequate sense of control, and oth-

Table 16.1. *Average z-scores (N = 47)*

Channels	1	2	3	4	5	6	7	8	ANOVA F	Significance
Number of subjects	45	47	41	45	44	46	45	42		
Concentration	0.60***	0.56***	0.01	−0.36*	−0.44**	−0.46**	−0.02	0.41*	23.32	0.000
Ease of concentration	0.04	0.16	−0.13	0.23	0.15	−0.31*	−0.48**	−0.36*	7.65	0.000
Unself-consciousness	0.01	0.20	0.23	0.25	−0.07	−0.07	−0.35*	−0.65***	9.33	0.000
Control of situation	0.19	0.44**	0.41*	0.30*	−0.05	−0.55***	−0.71***	−0.58***	29.03	0.000
Alert-drowsy	0.15	0.28	0.09	−0.01	−0.26	−0.38*	−0.05	0.07	5.98	0.000
Happy-sad	0.19	0.38*	0.26	0.10	0.00	−0.37*	−0.43**	−0.16	10.37	0.000
Cheerful-irritable	0.08	0.27	0.27	0.18	−0.08	−0.24	−0.28	−0.19	6.42	0.000
Strong-weak	0.15	0.35*	0.17	0.08	−0.25	−0.41**	−0.35*	−0.14	8.43	0.000
Friendly-angry	0.13	0.26	0.36*	0.10	−0.05	−0.23	−0.37*	−0.17	9.71	0.000
Active-passive	0.40**	0.45**	0.17	−0.12	−0.41**	−0.54***	−0.34*	0.21	17.04	0.000
Sociable-lonely	0.10	0.12	0.03	0.16	−0.18	−0.18	−0.26	0.06	2.67	0.010
Involved-detached	0.40**	0.42**	0.00	−0.14	−0.21	−0.42**	−0.23	0.45***	13.29	0.000
Creative-apathetic	0.27	0.52***	0.14	0.00	−0.37*	−0.45**	−0.30*	0.22	18.97	0.000
Free-constrained	0.14	0.45**	0.15	0.12	−0.11	−0.33*	−0.61***	−0.30	16.68	0.000
Excited-bored	0.36*	0.49**	−0.05	−0.09	−0.29	−0.47**	−0.25	0.19	14.68	0.000
Open-closed	0.25	0.32*	0.19	0.06	−0.28	−0.40**	−0.35*	−0.07	10.00	0.000
Clear-confused	0.20	0.53***	0.24	0.13	−0.15	−0.37*	−0.57***	−0.30	17.12	0.000
Relaxed-anxious	0.04	0.25	0.34*	0.28	0.08	−0.23	−0.33*	−0.44**	12.19	0.000
Wish doing the activity	0.36*	0.53***	0.02	0.02	−0.27	−0.47**	−0.42**	−0.10	15.98	0.000
Something at stake in activity	0.79***	0.47**	−0.01	−0.67***	−0.46**	−0.55***	0.29	0.56***	43.45	0.000
Time speed[a]	−0.31*	−0.26	0.08	0.03	0.29	0.28	0.09	−0.43**	9.54	0.000
Satisfaction	0.39*	0.73***	0.30	0.07	−0.31*	−0.63***	−0.50***	−0.25	36.97	0.000
W.B.S.E.[b]	−0.31*	−0.33*	−0.02	0.02	0.22	0.30*	0.23	0.05	7.50	0.000
Number of reports	200	354	112	279	152	330	133	122		

Note: * $= p < 0.05$; ** $= p < 0.01$; *** $= p < 0.001$.

[a] Time speed: negative values mean that time is perceived to go faster.

[b] W.B.S.E.: Wish to Be Somewhere Else, negative values mean the absence of the wish to be somewhere else.

erwise average mood states across the board. Table 16.2 indicates the amount of congruence between positive and negative extremes of experience in the eight channels. The table helps illustrate that each channel has a characteristic experiential profile.

Channel 2 brings together the positive extremes on almost every dimension of experience, whereas channel 6, and to a lesser extent channel 7, bring together all the negative poles. Channel 1 is characterized by cognitive involvement, activity, excitement, and satisfaction; next to channel 2, it is the most positive experiential setting. Channel 3 is characterized by friendliness, relaxation, and control. Moving on to channel 4, control is still present but concentration lapses and the experience seems to become generally more passive. Channel 5 already shows the apathy syndrome that becomes much more pronounced in channel 6. Finally, channel 8 shows characteristics of stress: high concentration, high involvement, high stakes, but difficulty in concentrating, lack of control, and a feeling of anxiety.

The patterns reported in Tables 16.1 and 16.2 closely replicate the theoretical expectations based on the flow theory. It is clear, however, that the model using 8 channels is a relatively arbitrary one. In order to study in greater detail the relationship between the ratio of challenges and skills on the one hand, and the quality of experience on the other, it is possible to double the number of reference points and analyze responses in terms of a 16-channel model. Figure 16.2 shows the means of four variables (concentration, control, creativity, and satisfaction) in each of 16 channels. In this model, it is channels 2 and 3 that correspond to channel 2 in the 8-channel model, and channels 10 and 11 correpond to what was formerly channel 6. Again the convergence of the lines in these two extreme settings shows the homogeneous quality of the optimal experience on the one hand, and the uniformly depressed syndrome of apathy on the other.

It is also possible to move in the opposite direction and reduce the number of channels from eight to only four. This would involve a model that uses the four basic quadrants considered by the theory: (1) a balance between challenges and skills, both variables being above the individual mean; (2) balanced challenges and skills, both variables being below the individual mean; (3) unbalanced situation with high challenges; and (4) unbalanced situation with high skills. Figure 16.3 shows the distribution of means on four experiential variables (concentration, creativity, control, satisfaction) according to this 4-channel model. Again, as expected, the model yields the predicted profile of experience. Whether one needs

Table 16.2. *Congruence of the experience*

Channels	1	2	3	4	5	6	7	8
Concentration	▓	▓				▦		▓
Ease of concentration				▦	▦	▦	▦	▦
Unself-consciousness							▦	▦
Control of situation			▓	▓		▦	▦	▦
Alert-drowsy						▦		
Happy-sad		▓				▦	▦	
Strong-weak		▓				▦	▦	
Friendly-angry			▓				▦	
Active-passive	▓	▓			▦	▦	▦	
Involved-detached	▓	▓				▦	▦	▓
Creative-apathetic		▓			▦	▦	▦	
Free-constrained		▓				▦	▦	
Excited-bored	▓	▓				▦		
Open-closed		▓				▦	▦	

| Clear-confused |
| Relaxed-anxious |
| Wish doing the activity |
| Something at stake in activity |
| Time speed[a] |
| Satisfaction |
| W.B.S.E.[b] |

Positive Negative

Note: The table shows the association of positive and negative levels of the variables describing the experience in the 8 different situations defined in terms of challenges/skills ratio.

[a]Time speed: negative values mean that time is perceived to go faster.
[b]W.B.S.E.: Wish to be somewhere else; negative values mean the absence of the wish to be somewhere else.

QUALITY OF THE EXPERIENCE

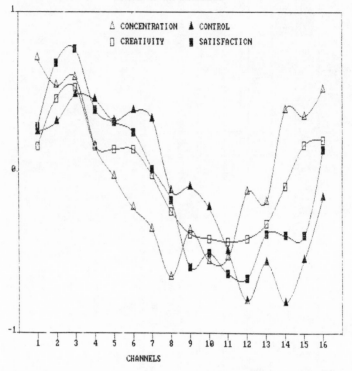

Figure 16.2. Italian high school students' ESM reports of the quality of the experience (N = 47 means based on 1,682 self-reports).

the simplicity of a 4-channel model or the complexity of the 16-channel one depends on the depth of analysis required.

Frequency of flow experience in various activities. One of the first questions in applying this method to the study of flow experience in everyday life is, In what types of activities does optimal experience typically occur? Figure 16.4 shows that for these Italian teenagers the majority of responses in channel 2 were reported while the respondents were either engaged in class work or in studying (for a total of 34% of all responses in channel 2), followed by situations in which they were socializing with peers (28%), thinking (8%), involved in art and hobbies (7%), and reading (5%). In contrast, only 1% of the reports falling into channel 2 were given while watching television. The overall implication of Figure 16.4 is that almost any activity in daily life can produce flowlike experiences.

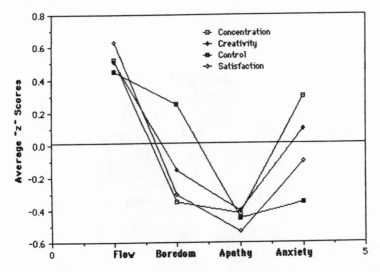

Figure 16.3. Quality of experience reported in different challenge/skill contexts.

Moreover, the encouraging suggestion is that productive activities like studying and schoolwork are potentially as conducive to the flow experience as any of the more typical leisure activities are.

Table 16.3 shows the percentage of time that each of 15 main activities were reported in each channel of a 4-channel model. Again the table shows that each of the 15 activities is represented in every channel, which suggests that, at times, every activity can be boring, anxiety-producing, or apathy-producing, as well as being a context for optimal experience. On the other hand, there are huge differences in the proportion of times in which activities are associated with each of the basic experiential settings. Television watching was reported in the flow channel only 2.8% of the time, whereas arts and hobbies were in the same channel 47.2% of the time; personal care was experienced as boring 69.4% of the time, whereas listening to music was in the boredom region only 17.6% of the time. The activity most often associated with apathy was television watching (39.3% of the time), whereas the least apathetic activities were art and hobbies (3.8%) and sports and games (5.3%). One unexpected result in the anxiety column of Table 16.3 is that the highest proportion of anxiety is reported while listening to music (52.9%). One possible explanation for this high figure is that teenagers turn to music when they perceive their emotional life as being out of control; thus the

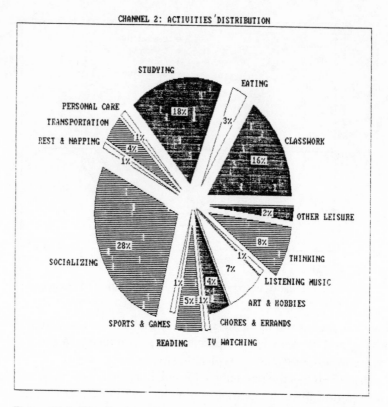

Figure 16.4. Distribution of optimal experiences (reports in Channel 2, N = 354), by types of activities.

causal connection is not that listening to music produces anxiety, rather the opposite may be true. The activities least associated with anxiety are eating and personal care.

Patterns of individual differences

The flow model and the ESM methodology make it possible also to compare adaptive strategies that differentiate one individual from another. We now present a few case studies to illustrate this more clinical approach.

Flow and the restoration of order: Paolo's case. Paolo is a third-year student in the classical lyceum. His average scores on the ESM are generally very close to the sample means. What makes his case interesting is an

Table 16.3. *Activity and quality of the experience (percentages)*

	Flow	Boredom	Anxiety	Apathy
Classwork	23.8	20.1	37.2	18.8
Studying	23.7	22.2	37.4	16.7
Socializing	32.2	24.5	31.5	11.7
Sport and games	26.3	36.8	31.6	5.3
TV watching	2.8	45.8	12.1	39.3
Listening music	11.8	17.6	52.9	17.6
Art and hobbies	47.2	20.8	28.3	3.8
Reading	24.6	34.8	24.6	15.9
Thinking	18.2	21.4	36.5	23.9
Other leisure	10.8	41.5	20.0	27.7
Eating	9.9	56.0	7.7	26.4
Personal care	3.5	69.4	7.1	20.0
Transportation	19.2	41.1	17.8	21.9
Chore and errands	16.1	54.0	10.3	19.5
Rest and napping	10.5	44.7	13.2	31.6

Note: Distribution of the main activities in four situations defined by the challenges/skills ratio. Flow refers to channel 2 (high challenges and high skills); boredom sums up situations referred to in channels 3, 4, 5 (skills prevalence); anxiety situations refer to channels 1, 8, 7 (challenges prevalence); apathy refers to channel 6 (low challenges and low skills).

event that happened halfway through the week of responding: He fell from a bicycle and had to have his foot put in a cast. This traumatic event destructured the normal course of his daily life, forcing Paolo into near immobility for the remainder of the week (and incidentally reducing the number of his responses to a total of 24).

Whereas optimal experiences result in an "ordering" of conscious states, such an accident has the opposite effect: It disorders the contents of awareness. In other words, the accident made it more difficult for Paolo to use customary strategies to achieve the optimization of experience. With the help of our model, we may try to show how Paolo coped with the disorganizing effects of his accident during that week. Taking the whole week into account, Paolo's experience involves situations mainly in channel 2 (29.2%), as well as channels 1 and 4 (16.7% each; see Table 16.4). In what situations did Paolo report optimal experiences? Of the seven times that he reported being in channel 2, five, or 70%, refer to studying either at home or at school. In fact studying is always associated with high, or at least average, challenges for Paolo

Table 16.4. *Distribution of reports for Paolo, Carlo, Carmen, Maria, and Mariarita (percentages)*

	Paolo (N = 24)	Carlo (N = 31)	Carmen (N = 50)	Maria (N = 47)	Mariarita (N = 49)	Whole sample (N = 1,682)
Channel 1	16.7	3.2	6.0	2.1	14.6	11.7
Channel 2	29.2	32.3	28.0	19.1	2.1	20.2
Channel 3	4.2	—	8.0	14.9	—	6.2
Channel 4	16.7	9.7	24.0	10.6	47.9	16.2
Channel 5	4.2	6.5	4.0	2.1	4.2	8.6
Channel 6	12.5	25.8	16.0	23.4	14.6	18.6
Channel 7	12.5	—	—	8.5	8.3	7.6
Channel 8	4.2	6.5	12.0	14.9	6.3	6.9
Central area	—	16.1	2.0	4.3	2.1	3.7

(channels 1, 2, 7, and 8), and of all the responses during which he was studying, 50% of the time he reported being in channel 2. It seems clear that for Paolo schoolwork provides an optimal integration of personal abilities and situational opportunities. This does not mean that Paolo only exists for his books and for his homework. When he is studying, he wishes to be elsewhere as most of his classmates do; he is involved in sports and has an active social life. Nevertheless, schoolwork represents for him an opportunity to apply his personal skills, and Paolo always describes studying as an activity in which there is a lot at stake.

The day of the accident Paolo did not fill out any of the ESM sheets. The next day and the two successive ones none of his answers were in channel 2. Because he was constantly thinking about his cast and trying to negotiate his crutches, all of his answers fall into the low regions of channels 5, 7, 4, and 6. It took 2½ days after the accident for Paolo to restore a sense of balance with the environment and to channel his attention into a concrete task. In a series of three responses between 3:30 and 8:00 P.M. on the third day after his fall, Paolo rediscovered a way of meshing his personal skills with opportunities in the environment. He returned to channel 2 by using the same means for ordering experience that he had perfected in the past: studying. At 3:30 he started on a physics assignment and his concentration was high, but he reported difficulty in concentrating. He was confused; he described high challenges but low skills. The situation is typical of a channel 7 response.

At 6:00 p.m. Paolo was still studying physics. By now he had achieved a moment of extreme experiential congruence: concentration was still high, but it was also easy; instead of being confused, Paolo reported being clear and in control. He was not self-conscious and felt satisfied; and both challenges and skills were equally high. The situation is a clear example of a channel 2 response. By 8:00 p.m. Paolo was still in the same situation, still doing physics and still in channel 2. He reported the same positive dimensions of experience as before, except that he was having a somewhat harder time concentrating and was being distracted by a wish to go with his friends to a country music concert.

It looks as if Paolo, recovering his habitual attentional structures, had succeeded in restoring a relative state of order to his consciousness. He may not have been in a complete flow state because he was still not very highly motivated as he was working, but he was extremely close to that optimal state. Studying is rarely a complete flow experience for an adolescent because the motivation for it usually tends to be extrinsic. However, to the degree that teenagers approach the flow experience while studying, they learn to use a strategy for giving order to the self that provides them not only with intense satisfaction rarely available in the rest of life, but also with the discipline and skills necessary to achieve a productive integration with adult social roles.

The following day Paolo has returned to a state of normalcy, with more of his responses in channel 2 and no great discrepancies between challenges and skills for the rest of the week. But not all students are as proficient in using the opportunities in their environment to achieve order in experience. The next two examples describe students for whom schoolwork appears to offer very little challenge and hence no opportunity for optimal experience.

The case of Mariarita: alternating between boredom and apathy. The attentional strategies developed by Mariarita are in certain respects the mirror image of those developed by Paolo. Only one of her 49 responses fell into channel 2, which shows a pronounced inability to find ways of expressing her skills in the environment she finds herself in. Most of the time Mariarita's experience is in the boredom region of channel 4 (47.9%); the next two most frequent situations are those of apathy in channel 6 and arousal in channel 1, both reflecting 14.6% of her answers (see Table 16.4). Although she is involved in a great variety of activities, not one of them seems to have an ordering effect on her consciousness. Studying is one of her major activities (36% of her week is spent studying), but none of the responses while studying fall in channel 2. Most of them belong either in the boredom or the apathy situations.

The only response in channel 2 occurred when she happened to be fixing the frame of a painting at home, an almost random event that was not integrated into any coherent overall plan. The positive pole of her experience, given the almost total absence of responses in channel 2, is represented in her case by situations of high arousal in channel 1. For Mariarita the way to overcome boredom is to be in situations with high challenges even when not completely matched with adequate personal skills. Among her answers in channel 1 there are several in which she is listening to music, and they represent for her the closest approximations to the optimal experience.

With only one week's worth of responses, it is not possible to diagnose what the problem with Mariarita's strategy may be, and whether it is caused by elements in her environment, or by her way of perceiving her environment. It is important, however, to show that such divergences between processes of individual selection and the culturally structured action opportunities exist (Csikszentmihalyi & Massimini 1985), and it is equally important to begin investigating their causes.

Entropy and the disruption of flow: the case of Maria. Maria's week is characterized by emotional problems concerning a boyfriend. It is a dynamic situation rich in high and low moments. Thirty-five of her 50 responses make reference to the boy with whom she is emotionally involved, either as a focus of Maria's thoughts, of her wishes, or as an actual partner of interactions. Of these 35 instances, only 7 involve actual interaction between Maria and her friend. Not once does the interaction take place in the region of optimal experience (channel 2). In each case the challenges are higher than the skills (three answers fall in channel 7, three in channel 8, and one in channel 1); in fact, the quality of experience with her friend is typified by anxiety, confusion, sadness, and lack of satisfaction – joined, however, with high involvement, high concentration, and high stakes.

Maria's strategies for achieving optimal experience are, however, more efficient than those described previously in the case of Mariarita. She seems to have a capacity to structure experience similar to that shown by Paolo. Despite boyfriend problems, 19% of her total responses fall into channel 2, which is almost exactly average for the sample. These situations involve a variety of activities such as study, sports, and socializing with friends. They are also related to her boyfriend (e.g., when she talks about him with her girlfriends or when she is getting ready to go out with him). But for the time being, quantitatively the most important attentional structure for Maria is this relationship, which she is incapable of integrating into a balanced ratio of challenges and skills. Therefore she is unable to achieve a real congruence between positive experiences whenever she is involved directly in the relationship. This inability affects the rest of Maria's experiences. Her most frequent type of response is that of apathy (23.4% in channel 6), and she has the highest mean score on anxiety as well as one of the three highest ones on boredom in the whole sample. The fact that Maria's responses in channel 2 are decidedly more positive than the average suggests that she can restructure her experience along more positive lines once she is able to resolve the entropic pressures of her current sentimental attachment. We now turn to situations in which emotional relationships add stability to the respondents' inner life, instead of producing entropy.

Negentropy and stabilty: the cases of Carlo and Carmen. Both Carlo and Carmen reported relatively high proportions of responses in channel 2: Carlo 32.3%, and Carmen 28.0%. Their cases contain nothing exceptional; they are examples of normality with respect to the sociocultural context to which they belong. What differentiates these two students from the previous cases is the way in which they describe the quality of their relationship with the environment, including the school, a friend of the opposite sex, and the family. Carlo, for instance, is very involved with a girl in his school. She appears in 14 of his 31 ESM responses, but whereas Maria's relationship was a constant occasion of anxiety and disruption, Carlo's was an opportunity for order and optimal experience. Figure 16.5 compares some of the average moods that Maria and Carlo reported when they were with their respective partners. It is clear that the emotional relationship is in one case a source of uniformly positive experience, whereas in the other it produces the opposite set of moods.

Whenever Carlo is alone with his friend, he reports high challenges and high skills in channel 2, and a completely positive experience. But there are several other situations in which his experience approximates flow: studying, music, and particularly drawing, which for Carlo is the activity that best represents the flow experience.

Very similar is the case of Carmen, whose entire week is filled with positive and serene self-reports. Like Carlo, she also finds a great number of opportunities for the application of her personal skills: She is in flow when with her boyfriend, when she is reading, and very often when

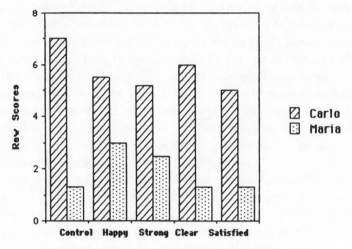

Figure 16.5. Average quality of experience with partner.

she is studying (35% of her responses in channel 2 refer to studying either at home or in school). In contrast to Paolo, her optimal school-related experiences involve the humanities. When she is studying physics and other science subjects, her state of consciousness is usually in apathy. Nevertheless, the fabric of daily life provides Carmen with a variety of meaningful goals into which to channel her psychic energy.

Conclusions: the growth of complexity

The five case studies illustrate some of the possible applications of the theoretical model when tested empirically with the ESM. They are examples of how individuals integrate their experiences in the course of normal life. The self-reports provided by this sample of high school youth confirmed the theoretical expectations concerning the relationship between optimal experience and the balance of challenges and skills. Both at the group level and at the level of individual cases, the flow model makes it possible to provide a meaningful interpretation to these segments of behavior and consciousness.

If it is true that the ability to structure experience so as to provide a balance between challenges and skills at a high level of complexity is the means toward personal growth (Csikszentmihalyi & Larson 1984), then the five cases described earlier could be classified into two broad groups. The first would include Paolo, Carlo, and Carmen, who seem to be mastering the strategies necessary to structure experience; the second group includes Maria and Mariarita, who have not yet learned to do so. As a consequence, the teenagers in these two groups also differ in terms of the quality of their weekly experience: The three in the first group tended to score above the group mean on most of the dimensions of experience (of the 25 ESM variables, Paolo scored higher than the sample as a whole on 13, Carlo on 21, and Carmen on 20 variables; in contrast Maria and Mariarita had average scores higher than the group mean only on 4 and 3 variables, respectively).

There is another way to test out the question of whether persons who spend more time in flow benefit by it in terms of an overall improvement in the quality of their lives. It consists in correlating the proportion of time each individual spent in the various channels throughout the week, with his or her mean scores on the 25 ESM variables. Is more time spent in flow related to more positive experience overall? Is more time spent in the conditions of boredom and anxiety related to a generally more negative state of consciousness? To simplify matters, the 4-channel model was used in this analysis (i.e., flow = channel 2; anxiety = channels 1, 7, and 8; boredom = channels 3, 4, and 5; apathy = channel 6). Table 16.5 shows the results. The first column of Table 16.5 indicates that the amount of time spent in flow is indeed positively related to the quality of experience – not only momentarily, at the time of occurrence, but cumulatively over the week. Teenagers who report a greater frequency of responses in channel 2 also report being more happy, cheerful, friendly, and sociable over the course of the week. These four variables comprise the "positive affect" dimension of experience, and on each the correlation is high and significant. In addition, frequency in channel 2 is related to how excited, relaxed, and satisfied teenagers rate themselves over the course of the week, and how much they see being at stake in their daily life.

The amount of time spent in anxiety yields only one significant correlation: Students who spent more time in that condition report being more sad. The frequency of time spent in boredom is more diagnostic: Teens who spend more time in low-skill channels are more sad, bored, anxious, and less satisfied and feel that there is less at stake for them. And finally the condition of apathy does not correlate very highly with any of the variables, except (negatively) with both challenges and skills, which is of course tautological. Thus although apathy is the most neg-

Table 16.5. *Global experience and challenges/skills strategy (N = 47)*

	Flow	Anxiety	Boredom	Apathy
Concentration	.05	.01	.07	−.11
Ease of concentration	−.20	−.09	.15	.21
Unself-consciousness	−.04	−.04	−.03	.15
Control of situation	.03	.01	.10	−.05
Alert-drowsy	−.06	.10	.14	−.16
Happy-sad	.53**	−.37*	−.38*	.08
Cheerful-irritable	.45**	−.24	−.20	−.06
Strong-weak	.27	−.18	−.20	.06
Friendly-angry	.41*	−.23	−.14	−.06
Active-passive	.17	.04	−.08	−.10
Sociable-lonely	.36*	−.08	−.07	−.05
Involved-detached	.14	.03	.08	−.17
Creative-apathetic	.26	.09	−.15	−.23
Free-constrained	.14	−.08	−.08	.02
Excited-bored	.42**	−.27	−.45**	.13
Open-closed	.32*	−.22	−.16	.03
Clear-confused	.25	−.24	−.17	.08
Relaxed-anxious	.42**	−.12	−.38*	−.05
Challenges	.64**	−.09	−.36*	−.32*
Personal skills	−.00	.26	.37*	−.52**
Wish doing the activity	−.01	−.00	.00	−.02
Something at stake in the activity	.53**	−.10	−.42*	−.14
Time speed	−.14	.08	−.00	.06
Satisfaction	.43**	−.12	−.36*	−.04
W.B.S.E.	.05	−.01	−.01	.02

Note: Correlations between the individual averages of the variables measuring the quality of the experience and the percentage of reports in four main situations defined in terms of challenges/skills ratio. * $=p < 0.01$; ** $= p < 0.001$.

ative experiential state when measured concurrently, the long-term effects of spending time in that condition appear to be less noticeable than the effects of spending time in boredom.

Adolescents who repeatedly succeed in matching demanding opportunities for action with their personal skills are on the way to a complex personal development. The kind of order they are learning to establish in consciousness is not easy to attain. It requires the disciplined investment of psychic energy over time, and the constant honing of skills. But to develop one's potentialities one must take a daily dose of high challenges. The secret is to come as close as possible to the deep enjoyment of the flow experience while doing it. The teenager who learns to enjoy physics homework (as well as enjoying friends, family, music, and the rest of the opportunities in the environment) is well on the way to a rich and rewarding life.

The adolescents we studied are just now in the process of learning to structure their experiences, and of building a self based on the patterns of attention they are investing in various goals. The kind of adults they will turn out to be will depend directly on the experiential strategies they are enacting in this period of their lives. But the theoretical model of the flow experience and the data marshaled for its measurement are more broadly applicable and have more general implications for human psychology.

17. The quality of experience in the flow channels: comparison of Italian and U.S. students

MASSIMO CARLI, ANTONELLA DELLE FAVE, AND
FAUSTO MASSIMINI

This chapter compares responses to the Experience Sampling Method from a sample of American students in the Chicago area studied by Csikszentmihalyi and Larson (1984) and a sample of Italian students from a classical lyceum in Milan (Carli 1986; Gallina 1986; Toscano 1986; Massimini & Carli, Chapter 16). The purpose of the comparison is to ascertain whether and to what extent respondents in these two cultures report similar experiences across their daily life in terms of the flow theory as operationalized by the challenge/skill ratio. Given the importance of the high school in the lives of these two groups of adolescents, the chapter also focuses on studying.

In the case of cross-cultural comparisons, it is important to keep the variables defining the two groups identical as far as possible, except for the one variable that is to be compared, namely, the national or cultural difference. In the present case, the matching is close but not perfect. First of all, the relative standing of the two high schools in their respective communities is similar but not absolutely comparable. The American high school from which the sample of 75 U.S. adolescents was drawn was a diversified community high school with about 4,000 students of quite different academic interests and abilities. The Italian lyceum from which the 47 Italian adolescents were drawn is a much more select and academically oriented institution. Although the socio-economic background of the two samples was quite comparable, the Italian students may thus have been more motivated toward scholastic activities than their American peers.

An additional difference concerns the ages of respondents in the two samples. The U.S. sample consisted of equal numbers of 14-, 15-, 16-, and 17-year-olds. The Italian one was made up of students between 16 and 18 years of age. Usually 2 years would not make a great difference in psychological responses, but in this period of the life cycle it could affect the pattern of reports of subjective experience.

Distribution of responses in the flow channels

The first step in the analysis was to tabulate the reported responses into each of the eight channels defined by the ratio of challenges to skills and described in Chapter 16. A comparison of the two tabulations (see Table 17.1) reveals a very similar distribution.

The only significant difference appeared in channel 8, the theoretical region of anxiety, which encompasses a significantly higher number of the American adolescents' responses ($p < .02$). The Italian sample reported one-fifth of its responses to be in channel 2 (flow), with the second highest proportion in channel 6 (apathy): These proportions were reversed in the U.S. sample. On the whole, however, the patterning of responses never differed by more than 3 percentage points, and therefore was essentially very similar.

The quality of experience in the flow channels

The second question we asked was whether the two groups reported similar experiences within each channel, in other words, whether the different ratios of challenges to skills have similar meanings in the two cultural settings. Table 17.2 shows the average z scores for 20 experiential variables in the 8 channels of the flow model of U.S. adolescents. The analogous table reporting the values for the Italian sample is found in Chapter 16 (Table 16.1).

A comparison of the responses that American adolescents reported (Table 17.2) with those of the Italian teenagers (Table 16.1) shows that whereas the theoretically expected pattern of optimal experience in channel 2 is strikingly confirmed for the Italians, for the American adolescents the most positive responses tend to emerge in channel 3, where the ratio of skills is relatively higher than the challenges. Although 15 out of the 23 variables have their most positive mean in channel 2 for the Italian adolescents, for the Americans only 7 out of 20 have their positive peak in the flow channel, and 10 in channel 3. Another way of reporting the difference is that for the Italian teenagers 15 variables are significantly different from the mean value of the experience in a positive direction while in channel 2, and only 3 variables are significantly more positive

Table 17.1. *Percentage of responses in each flow channel for Italian (N = 47) and U.S. (N = 75) adolescents*

	Channels							
	1 (Arousal)	2 (Flow)	3 (Control)	4 (Boredom)	5 (Relaxation)	6 (Apathy)	7 (Worry)	8 (Anxiety)
Italy	11.7	20.2	6.2	16.2	8.7	18.7	7.6	6.9
United States	10.3	18.1	5.9	17.3	6.5	21.1	7.2	9.8

Table 17.2. Average z-scores, United States

Channels	1	2	3	4	5	6	7	8	ANOVA	
									F	Significance
Number of subjects	76	77	61	73	60	78	63	63		
Concentration	.55***	.43***	.16	-.23*	-.39*	-.45***	-.17	-.22	33.78	0.0000
Ease of concentration	-.30**	-.18	.09	.19	.03	.20	-.17	-.49***	9.85	0.0000
Unself-consciousness	-.20	-.18	.04	.13	.08	.14	.008	-.22	4.13	0.0002
Control of situation	-.08	.14	.24	.08	-.02	-.13	-.20	-.09	3.76	0.0005
Alert-drowsy	.29*	.29*	.18	-.26*	-.18	-.19	-.05	.01	12.07	0.0000
Happy-sad	-.06	.12	.31**	.07	.02	-.03	-.11	-.14	4.01	0.0003
Cheerful-irritable	-.14	.11	.29*	.01	-.01	.02	-.06	-.14	3.67	0.0007
Strong-weak	.15	.17	.14	-.07	-.00	-.08	-.05	-.08	2.51	0.0150
Friendly-angry	-.14	.04	.26*	.11	-.02	.04	-.12	-.09	2.65	0.0106
Active-passive	.28*	.31**	.14	-.11	-.10	-.18	.01	-.03	6.29	0.0000
Sociable-lonely	.02	.03	.13	-.04	.01	-.06	-.009	-.007	.56	0.7807
Involved-detached	.25*	.33	.25*	-.16	-.19	-.26*	-.06	.01	8.62	0.0000
Free-constrained	-.25*	.06	.27*	.25*	-.001	.06	-.04	-.30*	8.20	0.0000
Excited-bored	.01	.20	.13	.03	-.09	-.05	-.26*	-.23	4.22	0.0002
Open-closed	-.08	.15	.15	-.01	-.15	-.04	-.07	-.26*	2.85	0.0063
Clear-confused	-.32**	.16	.39**	.11	.04	.02	-.06	-.50***	9.60	0.0000
Wish doing the activity	-.13	.12	.25	.18	.03	-.01	-.32*	-.40**	9.59	0.0000
Something at stake in the activity	.70***	.53***	-.06	-.36**	-.42**	-.53***	-.03	.52***	55.48	0.0000
Time speed[a]	-.008	-.25*	.01	-.03	-.09	.08	.07	.14	2.54	0.0141
Satisfaction	-.18	.16	.48***	.14	-.09	-.03	-.12	-.37**	9.90	0.0000

Note: * = $p < 0.05$; ** = $p < 0.01$; *** = $p < 0.001$.
[a]Time speed: negative values mean that time is perceived to go faster.

than average in channel 3, whereas for the U.S. adolescents only 6 are significantly more positive in channel 2, and 9 are more positive in channel 3. Thus, although the general pattern of association between challenges and skills on the one hand and the quality of experience on the other seems to hold true in both national samples, the American teenagers report a subjective preference for situations of higher personal control in which their skills are perceived to be more than adequate for coping with the situational opportunities for action.

The variables that both groups report as being highest in channel 2 are alert, strong, active, involved, excited, open. These common variables belong to the activation or potency cluster of experiential dimensions, and these are the highest in the flow channel in both samples. The variables that have their peak in channel 3 for the U.S. adolescents tend to belong to the affect cluster of experiences (happy, cheerful, friendly, sociable), as well as to the motivation cluster (i.e., free, wish to be doing the activity, satisfied). Whereas for the Italian teenagers all dimensions of positive experience peak in channel 2, the American teenagers appear to split their optimal experience between channels 2 and 3, with the experience of activation and potency peaking in the flow channel, and the experience of positive affect and motivation peaking in channel 3, where the ratio is more favorable to personal skills.

When one looks at the situations in which the two samples report the most negative experience, certain differences between the two national groups also emerge. For the Italian sample, channels 6 and 7, which theoretically describe the state of apathy, are clearly the worst: Almost every variable has its highest negative value in one of those channels. For the American adolescents, the most negative channel appears to be channel 8 (anxiety), but compared to the Italian group, even this situation is not uniformly negative.

Therefore both positive and negative experience is more polarized in the Italian sample around the axis of flow and apathy, respectively. The quality of experience, at least when observed in terms of the challenge–skill axis, is much more congruent in the Italian sample, whereas it is more diffused and less polarized among the U.S. adolescents.

In comparing the pattern of responses to single variables across the two samples, it appears that some of them are answered in almost the same way by Italian and U.S. adolescents in each of the eight channels. For instance, the variables at stake, concentration, involvement, alert, and sociable follow almost exactly the same pattern (see Figures 17.1a and 17.1b).

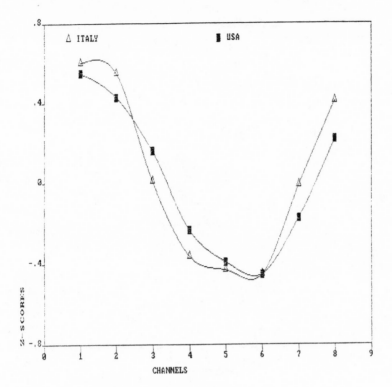

Figure 17.1a. Italy–USA: Concentration.

The remaining variables describing the quality of experience tend to follow the pattern shown in Figures 17.2a and 17.2b. In both of the curves reported in these two figures the following cross-national trends can be discerned: (a) The variation in the level of response across channels is much greater for the Italian sample; (b) the peak of positive experience for the Italian group is in channel 2, and for the U.S. in channel 3; (c) the most negative experience is reported by the Italians in channel 6 (apathy), whereas for the U.S. sample the worst experience tends to be in channel 8 or in the neighboring channels characterized by high challenges.

Another way of illustrating the similarities and differences between the two national samples is to compare the quality of experience in the two channels that are theoretically most significant in terms of the model: channels 2 and 6. Figure 17.3 shows the average z scores for 20 variables, as reported by the two samples, that fall into channel 2. The similarity

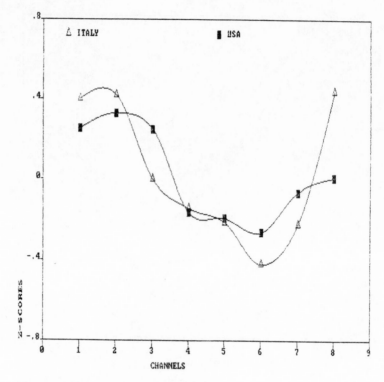

Figure 17.1b. Italy–USA: Involvement.

in the responses is shown by the fact that for both groups the quality of experience is predominantly positive: For the Italians 20 out of the 20 variables, and for the Americans 18 out of the 20 variables, diverge from the individual means in a positive direction. Both samples reported almost identical levels of high concentration, high alertness, much being at stake, and time passing fast in the flow condition.

The difference between the two samples is highlighted by the fact that in the flow channel, the positive quality of the experience for the Italian teenagers is on the average almost half a standard deviation above their mean, but is generally only half as large, on the order of .2 of a standard deviation, for the American teenagers. This pattern again suggests the congruence of positive moods and the accentuation of positive experience in the flow channel as typified in the responses of the Italian adolescents, and the still positive but more muted experience reported by the U.S. teenagers. The largest differences between the two groups are

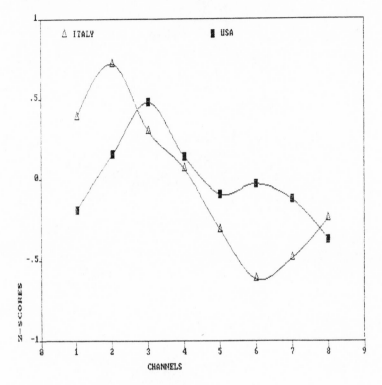

Figure 17.2a. Italy–USA: Satisfaction.

that the Italians' flow-channel responses show relatively much higher levels of satisfaction, wishing to do the activity, clarity of thought, and freedom.

The pattern shown in Figure 17.4 is in many ways the mirror image of the one presented in the previous figure. Both samples show a generally negative experience in the apathy channel. The Italian and U.S. teenagers report almost identically low levels of concentration and a low level of feeling that there is something at stake. However, the differences on the other variables are striking: Whereas for the Italians most variables are about .4 of a standard deviation below average, for the U.S. adolescents the experience in channel 6 is barely negative at all. The largest differences in single variables are in terms of satisfaction, wish to be doing the activity, excited, in control, and ease of concentration; on each of these, the Italian teens report much more negative experiences in channel 6.

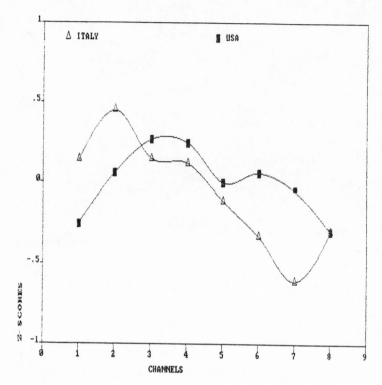

Figure 17.2b. Italy–USA: Free.

In conclusion, the application of the flow model to the analysis of the quality of experience in these two samples shows that in both cultures the flow experience is generally a positive one. However, whereas for Italian teenagers flow is an extremely positive state and apathy an extremely aversive one, the U.S. adolescents' experience is less extremely affected by the ratio of challenges and skills. For them, the flow channel is in general positive but the axis of experience is rotated so that a slight preponderance of skills over challenges is experienced as the most positive situation, and the preponderance of challenges over skills is experienced as the most negative.

The subjective experience of study

The high school, together with the studying associated with it, plays a central role in the life of the contemporary teenager. This is true both

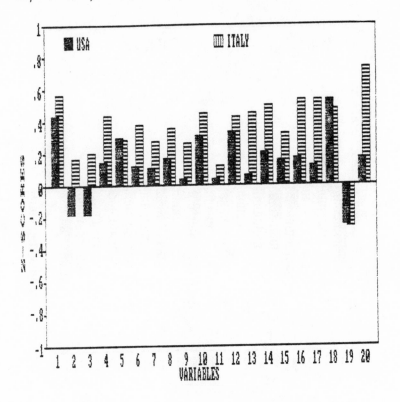

VARIABLES LEGEND

1.CONCENTRATION
2.EASE OF CONCENTRATION
3.UNSELFCONSCIOUSNESS
4.CONTROL OF THE SITUATION
5.ALERT
6.HAPPY
7.CHEERFUL
8.STRONG
9.FRIENDLY
10.ACTIVE

11.SOCIABLE
12.INVOLVED
13.FREE
14.EXCITED
15.OPEN
16.CLEAR IDEAS
17.WISH DOING THE ACTIVITY
18.AT STAKE
19.TIME SPEED *
20.SATISFACTION

* TIME SPEED: negative values mean that time is perceived
to go faster.

Figure 17.3. USA–Italy: Channel 2.

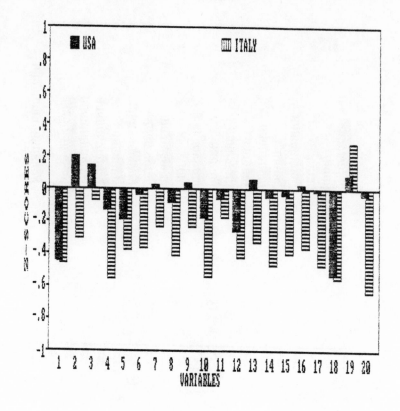

VARIABLES LEGEND

1.CONCENTRATION
2.EASE OF CONCENTRATION
3.UNSELFCONSCIOUSNESS
4.CONTROL OF THE SITUATION
5.ALERT
6.HAPPY
7.CHEERFUL
8.STRONG
9.FRIENDLY
10.ACTIVE

11.SOCIABLE
12.INVOLVED
13.FREE
14.EXCITED
15.OPEN
16.CLEAR IDEAS
17.WISH DOING THE ACTIVITY
18.AT STAKE
19.TIME SPEED *
20.SATISFACTION

* TIME SPEED: negative values mean that time is perceived
   to go faster.

Figure 17.4. USA–Italy: Channel 6.

in terms of the amount of attention invested in its goals and in terms of the importance such activities will have for the future of the student. Therefore it is an important area in which to study in more depth the effects of the relationship between challenges and skills on the subjective experience of adolescents.

Tables 17.3 and 17.4 indicate the distribution of answers in the various channels, as related to studying, for the Italian and U.S. adolescents. Table 17.3 shows the percentage of responses in each channel during the period in which the students reported they were studying outside of school, that is, doing homework.

The comparison clearly shows that, for the American sample, studying is perceived as presenting higher challenges than for the Italian one. The American adolescents' responses while in the channels with high challenges (1, 2, and 8) refer to studying between 24% and 31% of the time, as opposed to a range 16 to 24% for the Italians. In contrast, the Italian adolescents report studying much more often when they are in low-challenge channels such as 4, 5, and 6. The U.S. adolescents report studying significantly more often in the flow channel ($p < .05$), whereas the Italian teenagers report studying significantly more often in apathy ($p < .01$), as well as in channels 3 and 4 ($p < .05$), which indicates a greater frequency of control and boredom responses while studying.

Table 17.4 gives the percentage of time in each channel that students reported while attending classes. The major significant difference is that, in comparison with the U.S. students, when doing classwork the Italian students gave twice as many apathy responses ($p < .01$), and twice as many worry responses ($p < .05$). Adding up the percentages from Tables 17.3 and 17.4 shows that 49.4% of all the responses in the flow channel for the U.S. adolescents involved schoolwork; the corresponding percentage for the Italian adolescents was 32.6%. Conversely, of the responses falling into apathy, only 10.2% have to do with studying for the American sample, whereas 26.9% of the apathy responses involve schoolwork for the Italians.

These numbers relating to the frequency of scholastic activity in the flow channels seem to indicate that, despite the obligatory nature of scholastic activity, a positive psychological selection may be operating in favor of school-related activities. This is especially true for studying as opposed to class work, and particularly for the American students, for whom the free structure of homework appears to produce a much more positive experience than studying in school (cf. channels 1 and 2, Tables 17.3 and 17.4). In any case, it is

Table 17.3. *Studying and homework as a percentage of each flow channel, Italian and U.S. adolescents*

				Channels				
	1 (Arousal)	2 (Flow)	3 (Control)	4 (Boredom)	5 (Relaxation)	6 (Apathy)	7 (Worry)	8 (Anxiety)
Italy (N = 47)	24.0	16.8	22.4	8.5	11.1	12.1	18.2	21.5
United States (N = 75)	31.3	30.0	10.7	2.5	6.7	2.6	13.6	24.5

Table 17.4. *School classwork as a percentage of each flow channel, Italian and U.S. adolescents*

	Channels							
	1 (Arousal)	2 (Flow)	3 (Control)	4 (Boredom)	5 (Relaxation)	6 (Apathy)	7 (Worry)	8 (Anxiety)
Italy (N = 47)	14.6	15.8	18.9	3.8	13.1	14.8	25.7	25.5
United States (N = 75)	20.7	19.4	13.3	5.0	9.0	7.6	13.1	20.5

clear that in both cultures studying is experienced as a high challenge activity that may provide the context for optimal experience a
surprisingly high proportion of time.

The comparison between the two national samples reported in Tables
17.3 and 17.4 suggests an advantage in favor of the American teenagers
with respect to the subjective experience of studying. Almost half of the
U.S. teenagers' experiences in the flow channel have to do with studying
or schoolwork. The corresponding figure for the Italian adolescents is
18% lower. Thus the American high school seems to offer a greater
opportunity for optimal experience than does the Italian one. However,
we must recall that the Italian and the U.S. adolescents respond somewhat differently in the various channels. Whereas channel 2 is clearly
a positive experience for the Italians, it is less so for the Americans.
Thus the greater opportunity for optimal experience may not result in
such a strong advantage for the U.S. teenagers after all. Although they
spend more time in channel 2 while studying, the peak of optimal experience is in channel 3, where skills exceed challenges. Only 11% of
the responses in channel 3 involve studying, and 13% involve
schoolwork.

When the quality of experience involving schoolwork is charted
across the eight channels, the resulting patterns are very similar to
those obtained for experience as a whole and reported in Figures
17.3 and 17.4. Although the quality of experience is generally always
somewhat lower when studying than in the rest of the students' activities, it tends to be the most positive in channel 2 and the most
negative in channel 6. The differences between the two national
groups presented in the context of experience in general also hold
true for schoolwork; that is, the Italian teenagers are much more polarized, with a positive peak in channel 2 and a negative one in
channel 6, whereas the experience of the Americans is less sharply
differentiated among the channels.

Figure 17.5 shows how the variable at stake is perceived by the two
samples when they are doing homework. The two curves are very similar: Both the U.S. and the Italian teenagers report extremely high values
on this variable in every channel. Clearly, they perceive that there is
much at stake for them while studying, even when the challenges and
skills in the situation are low. However, the stakes are especially great
when studying involves high challenges, as in channels 1, 2, and 8.

Figure 17.6 charts the responses to the variable happy as reported by

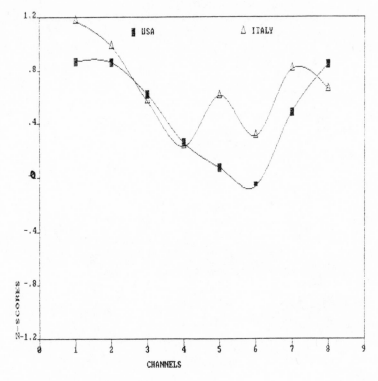

Figure 17.5. USA–Italy studying: At stake.

the two samples when doing homework. Both groups of teenagers tend to be below average in happiness while studying, but here the national differences appear to be greater than the similarities: Whereas the Italian adolescents are happier in the high challenge channels (1, 2, and 8), the U.S. adolescents are happier in the high skill channels (3, 4, and 5). Similar patterns obtain for several of the other variables, especially those relating to motivation.

Given these differences, it is remarkable how similarly the Italian and U.S. adolescents experience studying overall. Of the 20 variables on which the two samples can be compared, the U.S. teens are significantly more positive on 4: They report that concentration is easier, that they feel more sociable, involved, and free while studying. The Italian teens are more positive on three variables: They say that they are less self-conscious and more active, and that time passes faster while studying.

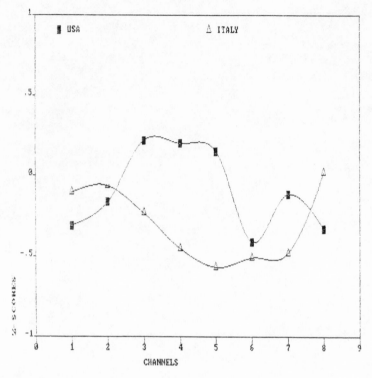

Figure 17.6. USA–Italy studying: Happy.

On the whole, despite differences in the amount of time spent in the flow channels while studying and despite the different quality of experience in the various channels, the two groups of students end up having relatively similar scholastic experiences.

These patterns suggest that Italian students would enjoy their school experience more if they could feel that they had relatively higher challenges when doing homework, and higher skills when they are in the classroom. The American students would enjoy school more if they felt that it held fewer challenges. Although the U.S. adolescents spent more time in the flow context at school than the Italians, this did not appreciably improve the quality of their scholastic experience, because they preferred the situation of control, in which there is a surplus of skills over challenges – and this was a relatively rare experience for them when doing schoolwork.

Discussion

In conclusion, we see that, in terms of the frequency of situations of flow, boredom, anxiety, and apathy, Italian and American adolescents are extremely alike over the course of a typical week. The largest difference is that the American teens spend about 3% more of their time in the situation of anxiety – hardly a noteworthy difference.

Whereas the distribution of responses in the various challenge–skill combinations was similar, the quality of experience in response to these ratios indicates a somewhat different subjective response to flow in the two cultures. In both groups flow was a very positive experience; but for the Italians it was clearly optimal, whereas the American adolescents preferred to be more in control. Conversely, whereas the most aversive experience for the Italians was apathy, for the Americans it tended to be anxiety.

These slight differences might have important implications in the long run. If a person prefers a situation in which the challenges are not as high as his or her skills, over time that person might avoid challenging situations, and consequently will tend to choose contexts that are not optimally conducive to growth. This would be especially true in productive activities, such as those involving study and learning. Ironically, the social structure of the school system seems designed to frustrate students in both cultures. The Italians, who prefer to be in flow, spend more of their time at school in the region of control; the American teens, who prefer to be in control, spend more of their time at school in flow. Yet the data suggest that studying could be a relatively positive experience for both groups. The school seems to present an adequate level of challenges and skills, at least in comparison with alternative opportunities available to teenagers.

Although this chapter compared Italian and American adolescents, the two samples are not representative of the two cultures, nor are they exactly matched on all relevant variables except for culture. Hence the differences reported might not be a reflection of how Italian and American teenagers as a whole differ from each other. It is possible that the two years' seniority of the Italians accounts for why they like challenges more; or it is possible that, as members of an academically competitive classical lyceum, this preference is due to their greater academic skills. Thus age or selectivity might be responsible for the differences, rather than culture. However, the findings are suggestive of the kind of comparison that is likely to reveal divergent patterns for optimizing experience in various cultures or subcultures, patterns that in turn might lead to different rates for the selection and replication of behaviors and artifacts over time. In this sense, day-to-day subjective reactions to situations and events constitute the process of psychological selection that in the long run is responsible for the direction of sociocultural change.

18. Flow and the quality of experience during work and leisure

JUDITH LEFEVRE

In adults, flow has been described in the context of specific activities, such as chess playing, rock climbing, and surgery (Csikszentmihalyi 1975b), but not as it occurs during the course of the ordinary activities of everyday life. However, studies of teenagers during everyday life have shown that flow is characterized by higher levels of motivation, cognitive efficiency, activation, and satisfaction (Csikszentmihalyi & Larson 1984; see also Massimini & Carli, Chapter 16; Carli, Delle Fave, & Massimini, Chapter 17). Furthermore, high as opposed to low achievers report a greater proportion of flow during academic work (Csikszentmihalyi & Nakamura 1986; Nakamura, Chapter 19). These findings with teenagers suggest that flow during everyday life is an optimal experience that facilitates the fulfillment of individual potential.

To confirm that the experience of flow is an optimal experience for adults as well as teenagers during everyday life, this study first describes the amount of time adults spent in flow (identified as a balanced ratio of challenges to skills above average weekly levels) and then compares self-ratings of the quality of experience with ratings given during the rest of daily life. In addition, it examines whether increased time in flow enhances the overall quality of experience.

Most adults spend a large part of their time at work. However, the quality of the working experience varies considerably. It has been proposed that well-being on and off the job relates to the opportunities for self-actualization and growth available at work, which in turn depend on the nature of the job (Herzberg 1966; Davis & Cherns 1975; Karasek 1979). Previous findings on teenagers suggest that occupations involving high levels of challenge and skills would enhance well-being by increasing self-actualization through flow. However, it has also been argued that self-actualization can occur during leisure, where it compensates for lack of opportunity at work (Blackler & Shimmin 1984). An additional

307

purpose of this report is to compare flow in work and in leisure and assess the effects of different occupations on how people are feeling in these two contexts. To this end, the amount of flow in work and leisure is described, and the quality of experience in both contexts is compared. Then the effects of occupation on the experience of flow in both contexts are evaluated to determine if higher level, skilled jobs are associated with more flow and a better quality of experience than less skilled jobs.

Methods

Sample

The respondents were workers recruited from five large companies in the Chicago area that agreed to cooperate in a study of work satisfaction. The study was described at company assemblies to a total of 1,026 workers. Of these workers, 44% volunteered to participate in the study. Proportionately more skilled than unskilled workers volunteered (75% and 12%, respectively). From the volunteers, 139 representative respondents were selected to participate, and 107 completed the study (for a more complete description of the sampling procedure see Graef 1978).

The respondents' occupations included management and engineering (27%), clerical (29%), and assembly line (44%) jobs. About half of the subjects were married (53%), 31% were single, and 16% were separated or divorced. The respondents' ages ranged from 19 to 63 years (mean age = 36.5 years), and 37% were male and 63% were female. Most were white (75%). Therefore, this group represented a diversified sample of workers whose responses are presumably typical of average urban American adults.

Procedure

The Experience Sampling Method (ESM) was used to investigate flow in adults during the course of everyday life (Csikszentmihalyi, Larson, & Prescott 1977; Larson & Csikszentmihalyi 1983; Csikszentmihalyi & Larson 1987). As in other ESM studies, self-reports of experience were obtained from each respondent throughout the day for a week. Respondents carried electronic paging devices, or "beepers" such as doctors carry, which emitted seven daily signals or "beeps." Radio signals were sent randomly within 2-hour periods from 7:30 A.M. to 10:30 P.M. Thus, approximately 56 signals were sent out during the week. An average of 44 responses per person were completed, for a total of over 4,800 responses (85% of all signals sent). Missed signals occurred because of mechanical failure of the pager or because the respondents turned the pagers off in situations in which they did not want to be disturbed. Ninety-nine percent of the responses were given within 20 minutes of the signal.

When a signal occurred, respondents were instructed to immediately fill out one page of a response booklet (ESF, or Experience Sampling Form) that they carried with them. It took 1–2 minutes to fill out a page of the ESF. The ESF included items asking about current challenges and skills (to identify flow), about the quality of experience, and about the kind of activity engaged in at the moment of the signal.

Challenges and skills. On the ESF, respondents were asked to rate the "challenges of the activity" and their "skills in the activity" using 10-point Likert scales. To minimize individual response bias, the responses of each subject were transformed into individual z scores. Then the z scores were used to determine which of four challenge and skill contexts the subjects were in, using a 4-channel model (see Chapter 16). These contexts, which included flow, were defined in terms of the balance of challenges and skills as defined by the flow theory (Csikszentmihalyi 1975b; Csikszentmihalyi & Nakamura 1986; Massimini, Csikszentmihalyi, & Carli 1987):

1. The flow context. Both challenges and skills are greater than the respondent's average.
2. The anxiety context. Challenges are greater than the respondent's average, and skills are less than his or her average.
3. The boredom context. Challenges are less than the respondent's average, whereas skills are greater than his or her average.
4. The apathy context. Both challenges and skills are below the respondent's average.

The quality of experience. Quality of experience was measured by 12 additional items on the ESF, which asked about the respondent's psychological state. As described above, each response was transformed into individual z scores to control for response bias. Then activation and affect scales were created from eight items (7-point Likert scales), based on previous research (Csikszentmihalyi & Larson 1984), and on confirmatory factor analysis of all continuous variables on the ESF. For this analysis, the four items making up each scale were averaged. Affect included the items happy–sad, cheerful–irritable, friendly–hostile, and sociable–lonely. Activation included the items alert–drowsy, strong–weak, active–passive, and excited–bored.

In addition, motivation, concentration, creativity, and satisfaction were also measured, since these dimensions of experience have often been mentioned as being important components of the quality of working life. Motivation was assessed by the item "When you were beeped ... did you wish you had been doing something else?" This item was scored on a 10-point scale from "not at all" to "very much," and scores were reversed so that a higher score indicated higher motivation. Concentration was also scored on a 10-point scale from "very low" to "very high." Creativity was measured by the 7-point Likert scale creative–dull, and satisfaction by the 7-point Likert scale satisfied–resentful.

The current activity. The activity was determined from response to the item "What were you doing?" Each response was coded into one of 154 activity categories such as seeing the doctor, typing, or preparing a meal (intercoder reliability = 86%). These detailed categories were reduced to 16 broader categories (intercoder reliability = 96%). The work category included all instances in which respondents indicated that they were actually working on the job (e.g., writing a report, filing, meeting with coworkers). When respondents indicated that they were *not* working while at the job (e.g., socializing with coworkers, taking a coffee break), the responses were not included. The leisure category included activities such as watching television, daydreaming, socializing, going to a museum, reading, or writing letters, when respondents were not at their jobs.

Analysis

Differences in the amount of time spent in each challenge–skill context and the quality of experience in each of the channels were tested with ANOVAs in which the channels were the repeated measures. Most tests of differences compared all four challenge–skill channels. Associations between the percentage of time spent in flow and the overall quality of experience were tested with the Pearson correlation. To measure the overall quality of experience, the mean level of each psychological state across responses was computed. For this last analysis raw rather than z scores were used, since the mean z score always equals zero.

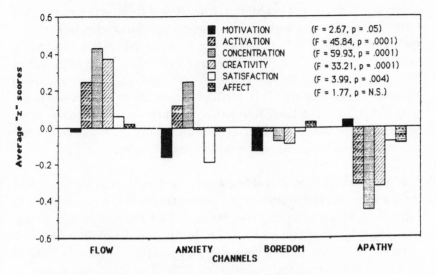

Figure 18.1. The quality of experience in the flow channels.

Results

The challenge–skill contexts

Time in each channel. The adult workers in this study spent a greater percentage of time in the flow (mean ± S.E.M. = 33 ± 1%) and apathy contexts (34 ± 2%) than in either the anxiety (12 ± 1%) or boredom contexts (19 ± 2%) (F = 51.00, $p <$ .0001, ANOVA). Thus, they spent the majority of their time (67%) in a state of balance between the perceived challenges of the environment and their skills.

The quality of experience. The quality of experience varied significantly in the challenge–skill channels, with the exception of affect (see Figure 18.1). In flow, motivation, activation, concentration, creativity, and satisfaction were all relatively high; this result confirms that flow is an optimal experience for adults. However, in the anxiety, boredom, and apathy channels, these psychological states differed. First, motivation was higher in the apathy context as well as in flow, but was lower in the anxiety and boredom contexts. Thus, motivation was higher when challenges and skills were balanced. Second, activation, concentration, and creativity decreased progresssively in the anxiety, boredom, and apathy contexts, compared to flow. The level of these states was higher when challenges were high. Finally, satisfaction was higher in the boredom context as well as in flow, but was lower in the anxiety and apathy contexts. Thus, satisfaction was highest when skills were high. Affect did not differ among the four challenge–skill contexts, possibly because it is a stable personal trait that does not change much in response to the factors that influence flow. Alternatively, it may be influenced by other factors besides the level of challenges and skills, such as the specific activity a person is doing when he or she is signaled.

Time in flow and the overall quality of experience. Increases in the time spent in flow were associated with improved overall quality of experience (see Table 18.1). This relationship was strongest for activation, concentration, and creativity. However, the relationship was also significant for motivation, satisfaction, and affect. The relationship between the overall quality of experience and the time spent in flow is at least partly accounted for by the improved quality of experience that occurs during flow. However, there may be a carryover effect to other times as well. For example, although affect was not significantly better *during* flow, people who spent more time during the week in balanced high-challenge, high-skill situations did feel more happy, cheerful, friendly, and sociable over the entire week than people who spent less time in flow. It is possible that during a flow episode affect is not heightened, but after a flow episode affect improves.

Flow in work and leisure

The amount of time that the workers spent in flow and the quality of their experience during flow differed in work and leisure. First, the amount of time they spent in flow during work (mean ± S.E.M. = 54 ± 4%) was considerably higher than during leisure (17 ± 3%), where they spent more time in the apathy state (52 ± 4%). Second, the quality of experience in flow compared to all the other channels combined differed during work and leisure (see Table 18.2). During work, motivation, activation, concentration, creativity, and satisfaction were all higher when in flow, whereas affect was not. A mild negative affect characterized most responses from work, whether the person was in flow or not.

In contrast, during leisure, affect as well as activation, concentration, and satisfaction were higher during flow, whereas motivation was not.

Table 18.1. *Correlations between
the proportion of time spent in
flow and the quality of experience
(N = 107)*

Quality of experience	
Motivation	.20**
Activation	.43***
Concentration	.38***
Creativity	.41***
Satisfaction	.17*
Affect	.23**

Note: 1-tailed * = $p < .05$;
** = $p < .01$; *** = $p < .0001$.

Thus, affect was higher when respondents chose to do flow activities during leisure (high-flow activities included hobbies, sports, viewing art), yet the motivation to do these activities was no higher when people were in flow than at other times. Instead, strong positive motivation was characteristic of leisure responses whether the person was in flow or not.

Occupational effects on the quality of experience and flow

Overall quality of experience. Occupation affected the overall quality of experience more during work than leisure. The managers and engineers rated themselves significantly higher on motivation, concentration, and creativity when working, compared with the other two groups. During leisure, the occupational groups differed only in creativity, with the managers and engineers rating themselves lowest. In both work and leisure, the assembly line workers were usually at the opposite end of the continuum from the managers and engineers.

Flow. Consistent with the above findings, occupation also affected the workers' experience of flow more during work than in leisure. During work, the manager–engineer group differed from the clerical and assembly line workers in both the amount of time they spent in flow and in the quality of the flow experience. Thus, the managers and engineers spent significantly more time in flow while working than the other workers did (see Table 18.3). They also had higher levels of activation ($F = 3.68$, $p < .03$), concentrated more intensely ($F = 4.74$, $p < .02$),

Table 18.2. *The effect of occupation on the quality of experience during flow and nonflow by context*

Psychological state	All (N = 93)		Managers and engineers (N = 35)		Clerical workers (N = 38)		Assembly line workers (N = 20)		ANOVA channel		ANOVA occupation		ANOVA channel by occupation	
	Flow ($\bar{x}$)	Nonflow ($\bar{x}$)	Flow ($\bar{x}$)	Nonflow ($\bar{x}$)	Flow ($\bar{x}$)	Nonflow ($\bar{x}$)	Flow ($\bar{x}$)	Nonflow ($\bar{x}$)	F	p	F	p	F	p
Work														
Affect	-.04	-.12	-.10	-.12	-.01	-.14	.00	-.10	1.62	ns	.18	ns	0.33	ns
Activation	.22	-.09	.33	-.04	.12	-.17	.20	-.06	45.88	.0001	2.98	ns	0.53	ns
Motivation	-.19	-.52	.00	-.30	-.25	-.65	-.39	-.66	10.39	.0018	5.28	.0068	0.15	ns
Concentration	.55	-.04	.72	.10	.50	-.14	.35	-.10	76.62	.0001	5.13	.0078	0.68	ns
Creativity	.45	-.12	.71	.00	.33	-.36	.24	.08	36.61	.0001	8.96	.0003	3.62	.03
Satisfaction	-.01	-.22	.00	-.20	-.01	-.26	-.04	-.18	6.32	.0137	.08	ns	0.14	ns
Leisure														
Affect	.14	-.09	.12	-.04	.15	-.07	.13	-.20	9.11	.0035	.33	ns	0.39	ns
Activation	.12	-.35	.15	-.36	.12	-.29	.08	-.42	34.94	.0001	.39	ns	0.19	ns
Motivation	.35	.30	.56	.28	.42	.32	-.01	.30	0.06	ns	2.37	ns	2.81	ns
Concentration	.35	-.31	.36	-.35	.31	-.21	.41	-.42	50.31	.0001	.13	ns	0.92	ns
Creativity	.13	-.33	-.10	-.44	.30	-.16	.13	-.47	36.57	.0001	6.17	.003	0.84	ns
Satisfaction	.21	-.07	.22	-.01	.17	-.01	.26	-.22	7.76	.0069	.20	ns	0.73	ns

Note: n.s. Not significant.

Table 18.3. *The effect of occupation on the time spent in each channel by context*

Channel	All (N = 106) ($\bar{x}$)	Managers and engineers (N = 36) ($\bar{x}$)	Clerical workers (N = 43) ($\bar{x}$)	Assembly line workers (N = 27) ($\bar{x}$)	Univariate ANOVA within channel		ANOVA channel		ANOVA occupation		ANOVA channel by occupation	
					F	p	F	p	F	p	F	p
Work												
Flow	.54	.64	.51	.47	3.28	.05	61.46	.0001	.93	ns	2.17	ns
Anxiety	.11	.10	.12	.11	.05	ns						
Boredom	.17	.14	.21	.15	.94	ns						
Apathy	.16	.11	.17	.23	3.00	ns						
Leisure												
Flow	.18	.15	.16	.20	.72	ns	79.08	.0001	2.01	ns	2.41	.04
Anxiety	.14	.09	.15	.18	3.83	.02						
Boredom	.14	.14	.16	.11	1.14	ns						
Apathy	.52	.61	.49	.46	3.49	.03						

Note: n.s. Not significant.

and were more creative ($F = 5.78$, $p < .005$) during flow than the other workers. However, they were not more motivated or satisfied. Again, the assembly line workers were usually at the opposite end of the continuum from the managers and engineers.

In leisure, the workers' experience of flow was less affected by their occupations. When involved in leisure activities, the workers in all three occupations spent similar amounts of time in flow, although the manager–engineer group and the assembly line workers spent more time in the apathy and anxiety states, respectively (see Table 18.3). In addition, only their motivation was affected by occupation. In this case, the assembly line workers were less motivated during flow than the other workers ($F = 3.26$, $p < .04$).

Discussion

The results of this study support the hypothesis that flow is an optimal experience for adults. However, they also demonstrate that the amount of time spent in flow and the quality of experience during it are affected by the person's activity and occupation.

One-third of the adults' daily life was spent in a balanced state of relatively high challenges and high skills. In this context, which theoretically corresponds to flow, the workers' motivation, activation, concentration, creativity, and satisfaction were relatively high, in contrast to their level in the other challenge–skill contexts. This confirms and extends previous findings that the immediate quality of experience during flow improves. Furthermore, the overall quality of experience during daily life improved as the time spent in flow increased; this suggests that there is a carryover effect of the flow experience to the rest of life. This relationship between flow and the overall quality of experience extended to affect, as well as to the other psychological states. Therefore, either increasing the time spent in flow makes people feel happier as well as more satisfied, motivated, creative, and so on, or people who are generally more happy and satisfied are able to find opportunities for flow more often.

One unexpected finding was that the average level of motivation in flow across all situations, although higher than in anxiety and boredom, was surprisingly low (see Figure 18.1). An inspection of the data showed that the low average motivation in flow was actually the result of a bimodal distribution. About 40% of the sample reported high motivation in flow and low motivation in apathy. Another 40% had the opposite pattern: They were motivated in the condition of apathy and not in flow. This difference suggests that the first group consists of individuals who have a more autotelic personality; that is, they are more motivated to seek out flow than the average person.

A second unexpected finding was that the respondents spent proportionately more work than leisure time in flow. Apparently the ordinary leisure activities of everyday life, such as reading, talking, and watching TV, are not very conducive to flow.

When the respondents were working, all the dimensions of experience improved significantly in the flow channel compared with the other channels except for affect, which was essentially the same in all challenge–skill contexts. During leisure, all dimensions of experience were higher in flow except for motivation, which was uniformly high regardless of channel. Thus, during leisure, the adults did not prefer to do the activities in which they were in flow, even though they were happier then. Consequently, when in leisure they were rarely in flow, but rather spent their time in the apathy context. It is possible that the higher levels of concentration and activation in flow cannot be tolerated by most people for extended periods of time. In making the choice to spend their leisure time in the low-challenge, low-skill context rather than flow, the workers may be indicating their preference to rest from the demands of work, even at the cost of an overall reduction in the quality of experience. Contrary to previous suggestions (Blackler & Shimmin 1984), they do not compensate for lack of opportunities for self-actualization at work by increasing flow during leisure.

Occupation affected the experience of flow primarily in work, rather than in leisure. During work, but not leisure, the amount of flow and the level of motivation, concentration, and creativity were higher among the manager–engineer group than among the other workers. The experience of flow during work may differ in the three occupations because of job characteristics. For example, managerial and engineering jobs are more complex and flexible than the clerical and assembly line jobs, and these characteristics may allow workers to control their challenges and skills to maintain flow. In contrast, less skilled jobs involving simple, repetitive tasks with little flexibility provide few opportunities for control. In addition, characteristics of the workers may also lead them to pick jobs with more or less opportunity for flow and to respond differently to the opportunities that exist.

Despite possible individual differences among workers, our findings indicate that restructuring jobs to increase flow in the workplace would benefit all workers, since flow uniformly improved the quality of experience. These benefits should carry over to company productivity as well. Since flow enhances activation, concentration, and creativity, it is likely that performance would improve by increasing the amount of time spent in flow. In addition, increases in flow may improve morale and prevent burnout, since motivation and satisfaction are also enhanced.

19. Optimal experience and the uses of talent

JEANNE NAKAMURA

There is more than enough evidence confirming the fact that flow is a powerful source of positive experience, and thus that it contributes to the quality of life by improving subjective states as they occur in the present. There is less evidence about the long-term effects of flow on the quality of life. It has been argued that enjoyment of high-challenge, high-skill situations makes personal growth and sociocultural evolution possible (Csikszentmihalyi 1985b; Csikszentmihalyi & Massimini 1985), but the kind of longitudinal data neccessary to test such assertions are not yet available. In the meantime, it is possible to use cross-sectional evidence to answer some related questions, namely, Do young people with high cognitive ability who use their talent show the same patterns of flow experience as similarly talented students who fail to use their talent? The answer to this question might reveal why some individuals are able to fulfill the promise of their early talents, whereas others are not.

In the same classroom, some students with the potential for exceptional performance develop their skills whereas others who are equally talented do not. A substantial body of research has explored possible causes, focusing either on traits of the individual (such as positive or negative self-esteem) or factors in the environment (such as parental education or divorce) as contributing to the differential achievement of students with equivalent cognitive endowments (Raph, Goldberg, & Passow 1966; Zilli 1971; Whitmore 1980; Dowdall & Colangelo 1982; Tannenbaum 1983). But no systematic study has been done on the day-to-day relationship *between* talented individuals and their environment, or the ways in which this relationship influences their inner experience. Yet whether a person uses his or her talent is likely to be affected by the motives and emotions he or she experiences when using that talent. It would seem necessary to understand how students perceive and experience their transactions with the environment in order to explain differential achievement. The research reported here explores the relations between subjective experience and the use of talent in a small sample of teenagers with high mathematics ability.

The model of subjective experience adopted here is the flow model (Csikszentmihalyi 1975b, 1982a). In previous research, a picture of an experiential state that motivates sustained involvement in various activities has emerged. It has been described as "flow": a state of enjoyment, control, and focused attention that obtains when the opportunities for action perceived in the environment fully utilize the capacities for action; that is, when challenges and skills, as subjectively perceived, match. Both possible imbalances of challenges and skills are hypothesized to produce negative experiential states; anxiety, when overchallenged, and boredom, when overskilled.

The relation between flow and the realization of potential is this: Flow is achieved when an activity challenges the individual to fully engage his or her capacities; as these capacities grow, staying in flow requires taking on increasingly greater challenges (Csikszentmihalyi & Larson 1984). Drawing on this theoretical model, one factor that might distinguish those students of high potential who develop their intellectual ability from those who do not is the extent to which the students find academic activities to be intrinsically enjoyable – to be like "flow activities."

In order to explore the inner states experienced in actual transactions with the environment, a naturalistic method is necessary. The Experience Sampling Method (ESM) makes it possible to collect descriptions of thoughts and activities, and assessments of inner states, at random moments during the course of a typical week (Csikszentmihalyi, Larson, & Prescott 1977; Larson & Csikszentmihalyi 1983; Csikszentmihalyi & Larson 1987).

Method

Participants in the study were students of superior math ability attending the public high school that runs Chicago's magnet program in math. *Ability* was measured by performance on a nationally normed test of academic potential (Tests of Academic Proficiency, TAP). Students invited to take part in the study had scored in the top decile on the test as a whole and in the top 5% on the math section of the test.

Teacher ratings provided the measure of *achievement*. One or more teachers in the math department evaluated each student on a 9-point scale, ranging from "far below" to "at or above," in response to the item: "Compared to what you see as this student's potential, their actual performance is———." Scores on this item were averaged when provided by more than one teacher. The sample was then divided into three groups of approximately equal size based on students' mean scores. This study compares the top third of the sample, defined as high achievers (N = 14), with the bottom third defined as low achievers (N = 12).

The groups did not differ by gender, age, parents' occupations, or race. Average age was 16 years. Participants were predominantly white and primarily from white-collar or professional families. The high achievers' mean percentile score on the math section of the TAP was 97.4, that of the low achievers was 96.9 (t = 1.02, NS). Thus the two groups did not differ in terms of mathematical ability.

Each student carried an electronic pager and a booklet of self-report forms, completing a form whenever the pager signaled (once, at random, within each 2-hour period between 8 A.M. and 10 P.M., for 7 days). The form included 27 items concerning the students' subjective states: were they alert or drowsy, happy or sad; to what degree were they in control of the situation; and so on. In addition, it asked where they were, whom they were with, and what they were thinking about and doing. Over the week of sampling, the 26 respondents completed a total of 873 self-reports.

Results

Two aspects of these teenagers' day-to-day experience are explored here: first, the kinds of activities in which they invest their psychic energy, and, second, the quality of their transactions with the environment in terms of the flow model.

How high- and low-achieving students use their time. Our first question concerns the differences between high- and low-achieving students with respect to the amount of time they invest in academic activities (see also Robinson 1986). The two groups do not differ in the amount of time they spend in school. Yet the low-achieving students spend a significantly smaller proportion of time doing classwork than do the high achievers (as a percentage of total time in school, low achievers, 32.9%; high achievers, 49.5%, t = 2.70, p < .05). Outside of the classroom as well, the low achievers invest significantly less time in academic activities than their high-achieving counterparts (as a percentage of all time out-side of school, low achievers, 8.0%; high achievers, 18.1%, $t = 2.19$, $p < .05$). Combining classwork and homework, the low achievers spend only 15% of their time engaged in academic activities compared with the high achievers' 27% ($t = 3.03$, $p < .005$). As each percentage point in an activity corresponds to roughly 1 hour a week spent in that activity, another way of stating this difference is to say that low achievers study about 15 hours a week, high achievers almost double that time, or about 27 hours.

What are the low achievers doing with the time not devoted to school-work? They report spending the same proportion of time as high achiev-ers in routine maintenance activities such as personal care, eating, and getting from place to place. More surprisingly, they channel no more time than the high achievers into structured activities other than school-work, such as jobs, hobbies, sports, and the arts, and no more time into passive leisure activities, such as watching television and listening to music. What they *are* doing is spending significantly more time than the high-achieving students simply chatting and "hanging around" with friends, family members, and acquaintances. Socializing on average ab-sorbs 27% of their time, as compared to 14% for the high achievers. This difference of almost twice the number of hours each week spent in unstructured leisure appears to be quite important in relation to the students' degree of academic involvement, and is returned to later.

Flow and achievement. On each self-report form, the students rated the challenges of the activity they were engaged in, and their skills in it. Following Carli (1986), we have standardized ratings on these two scales around each respondent's own mean, in the belief that it is the relative rather than the absolute levels that are experientially significant; that is, how much the challenges and skills in an activity differ from the indi-viduals' average levels. Combining the two dimensions defines four categories of experience. When challenges but not skills are high (de-fining the upper left quadrant), anxiety is predicted; when skills but not challenges are high (defining the lower right quadrant), boredom is expected. This method has revealed a distinct experiential state in which the challenges and skills are both below average (the lower left quad-rant). In the Italian sample, this combination was experienced as highly aversive on all measured dimensions, producing a "low" state that was unpredicted by the original theoretical model. This finding suggests that it is only when challenge and skill ratings are *above average*, in addition to being in balance, that a state of flow is experienced (the upper right quadrant).

When all of the reports over the course of a typical week are considered, high and low achievers spend very similar proportions of time in each quadrant. Two points are especially important. First, the two groups do not differ in the proportion of time they spend in the high-challenge, high-skill "flow" situations. Second, both groups spend a greater proportion of time in the "boredom" quadrant, where skills are higher than challenges, than in any other.

The next step is to determine whether the ratio of challenges and skills in an activity influences the quality of subjective experience. In particular, the question is whether a state of optimal experience characterizes everyday activities in which perceived challenges and skills are simultaneously high.

Previous research using the Experience Sampling Method has identified four clusters of variables that define major dimensions of the quality of subjective experience. These dimensions, indexed by averaging the component variables, are: affect, or mood; activation, or potency; cognitive efficiency; and intrinsic motivation. The revised flow model suggests that when challenges and skills are both above average all of these dimensions of experience will be elevated. Thus one might evaluate the levels of these four dimensions in each quadrant. One other dimension was also added, the degree of satisfaction with self as reported each time a response was made. This item is particularly important in light of the fact that self-esteem, of which this item is considered to be a part, has often been implicated in studies of academic achievement. The latter proved to contrast in an intriguing way with the aspect of positive experience represented by elevated affect.

Repeated measures ANOVAs show significant main effects by quadrant for all of the variables except affect ($p < .01$ in each case). That is, affect levels appear to be independent of the challenge–skill combinations, whereas the other dimensions vary significantly across the four quadrants.

In order to show the relative levels of these subjective states directly, Figure 19.1 presents the mean z scores in each quadrant on the four dimensions that showed significant effects. The top chart shows the pattern of the high achievers and the bottom chart that of the low achievers. When challenges and skills are simultaneously above average, a broadly positive experience emerges. Both high and low achievers feel more satisfied with themselves than usual and experience higher than

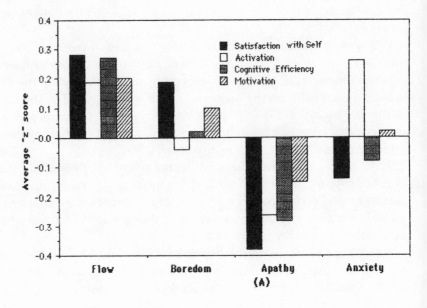

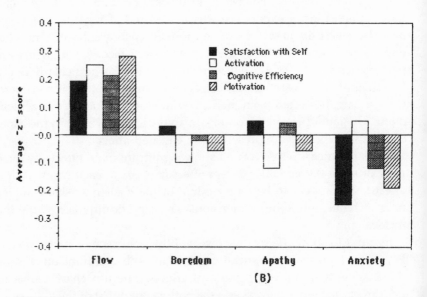

Figure 19.1 (A) High achievers' average quality of experience in flow
quadrants (N = 14 subjects and 472 responses). (B) Low achievers'
average quality of experience in flow quadrants (N = 12 subjects, 401
responses).

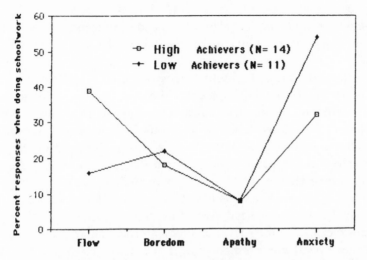

Figure 19.2. Percentage of schoolwork responses that fall in each flow quadrant, for high and low achievers (total N of responses: high achievers, 125; low achievers, 50).

usual activation, cognitive efficiency, and intrinsic motivation when the conditions for flow are present.

The character of subjective experience in the other three quadrants is always less positive than in the flow quadrant. For the high achievers, the most negative state is clearly experienced in low-challenge, low-skill activities, consistent with the findings of Massimini and Carli (Chapter 16). But for the low achievers, the most negative experiential state appears to be associated with the "anxiety" quadrant, in which they confront relatively high demands equipped with relatively low skills. On these occasions they feel markedly less satisfied with themselves and less intrinsically motivated.

Figure 19.2 shows that when involved in academic activities, the high achievers spend a substantially larger proportion of time than the low achievers in the high-challenges, high-skills quadrant associated with flow. For the high achievers, studying is like a flow activity four times out of ten. For the low achievers, studying is like flow less than half as often: only about 16% of the time. The low achievers spend a substantially greater proportion of time than the high achievers in the state of anxiety, those high challenges, *low* skills situations that are experientially very negative for them. Both groups spend about equal amounts of time in the "boredom" and "low" quadrants while involved with academics. On the whole, high and low achievers spend significantly different proportions of time in the four quadrants while studying ($F\ 3,\ 69\ =\ 2.84$, $p < .05$).

These patterns suggest why high achievers invest the time in schoolwork necessary for the development of their intellectual potential – they experience flow. On the other hand, low achievers study less in order to avoid anxiety. Consistent with previous findings about motivations for academic success and failure, high achievers enjoy academic challenges (Lloyd & Barenblatt 1984; Gottfried 1985), whereas low achievers find them overwhelming (Raph, Goldberg, & Passow 1966).

The low achievers spend as little time as possible in productive academic situations, and instead invest their time in socializing. Whenever they are socializing, their level of affect improves significantly over the times they spend doing schoolwork ($t\ =\ 5.31$, $p < .001$). In the short run, they avoid psychic entropy by this transfer of psychic energy from productive to unstructured leisure activities. The problem is that in doing so they will not develop those potential skills that their level of tested ability shows they have, thus forfeiting the enjoyment that the high achievers experience in productive activities. By avoiding academic challenges, they run the risk of limiting themselves for the rest of their lives to enjoying only relaxing, low-intensity social situations.

20. Self-esteem and optimal experience

ANNE J. WELLS

One of the most intriguing aspects of flow theory concerns the effects of the experience on the sense of self. On the one hand, a person in flow is supposed to be unself-conscious. On the other hand, the self is said to emerge strengthened from the experience (Csikszentmihalyi & Graef 1980; Csikszentmihalyi 1982a, 1985b). Presumably, even though the self need not be in the focus of awareness during optimal experience – when rules and goals are clear – the positive feedback obtained from it stays on and contributes to a more sturdy self-concept after the flow episode is over and self-consciousness returns.

The first aspect of this apparently paradoxical relationship has been documented empirically by previous studies. It seems clear that when people report being self-conscious, their subjective states are less positive than when they are unself-conscious (Wicklund 1975; Csikszentmihalyi & Figurski 1982). Thus on a moment-to-moment basis, flow and a sense of self appear to be mutually exclusive. However, the second aspect, namely the relationship between flow and a person's overall sense of self-esteem, has not been approached empirically before. The present study addresses this question: Is there a positive association between flow and self-esteem?

Wells (1985, 1986) used the Experience Sampling Method (ESM) to study variations in the self-esteem of 49 mothers and found several factors that were significantly related to fluctuations in self-esteem as the women went about their daily lives (e.g., presence vs. absence of their children, aspects of the interpersonal situation). Self-evaluation theories have long suggested that one feels best about oneself when one is capable of meeting life's challenges and has the skills necessary to handle the tasks of life. However, some of life's tasks are more challenging than others, and people are more skilled at some tasks than others.

Flow is characterized by involvement, concentration, and feelings of enjoyment. Using the ESM to study the ongoing daily experience of a group of men and women who worked, Csikszentmihalyi and Graef operationalized flow in terms of the relationship between people's perceptions of the challenges of their immediate situation and the number of skills they were using to deal with the situation (Graef 1978; Csikszentmihalyi & Graef 1980). According to the model developed by Csikszentmihalyi (1975b, 1982a), when challenges are greater than the skills being used, a person may experience anxiety; when the challenges are less than the skills being used, a person may experience boredom; but when challenges are roughly equal to skills being used, a person experiences a feeling of enjoyment and involvement called "flow." Csikszentmihalyi and Graef (1980) found that such a state is experienced by people in everyday life and suggested that people with higher frequencies of flowlike experiences will feel better about themselves and feel more in control of their lives.

It is this relationship between perceived challenges and skills, on the one hand, and self-evaluations, on the other, that is explored in the present chapter. At a "within individual" level of analysis, it is expected that when skills used are at a level nearly equal to challenges, self-esteem will be highest. It is also expected that at a "between-individuals" level of analysis respondents who more often report being in flow will also have higher average overall self-esteem. The self-reports will be divided into four Challenge/Skill (C/S) channels, similar to but not identical to the ones reported by Carli (1986) and used elsewhere in this volume (see Chapters 16, 17, 18, and 19).

Method

Sample

Participants were 49 middle-class Caucasian working mothers from intact families with at least two normal children between the ages of 2 and 14. Since self-esteem (SE) has been found to vary with socioeconomic level, intact vs. broken homes, normal vs. disadvantaged children (Wylie 1979), a relatively homogeneous sample was desirable. Women with at least two children between the ages of 2 and 14 were sought to reduce the possibility that mothers would be in a period of significant life cycle or self-concept change. Most of the mothers interviewed expressed a desire to work. Thus, the findings of this study cannot be generalized to mothers who choose not to work or who have to work. Participants were located by several methods (e.g., from school directories; from recommendations of principals, teachers, and others; and from lists of two firms that did market research). Of the mothers contacted who fit the criteria, 71% agreed to participate and 62% finished the study.

Procedures

Before beginning the ESM procedure, respondents completed two over-all SE measures, the Index of Adjustment and Values (IAV) (Bills, Vance, & McLean 1951) and the Self-Esteem Scale (SES) (Rosenberg 1965); and one SE measure in the more specific parental role, the Parenting Sense of Competence Scale (PCS) (Gibaud-Wallston & Wandersman 1978). This was done in order to explore the relationship between SE measured with ESM, and SE measured with earlier self-report methods (i.e., one-time generalized methods).

Rosenberg's SES (1965, 1979) is a 10-item scale that measures overall self-esteem. Rosenberg (personal communication 1980) advised expand-ing the four original responses (from strongly agree to strongly disagree) to six responses, and then scoring each from 1 to 6. Summing these items yielded a score that ranged from 10 to 60. The mean of the present sample (N = 49) was 48.2, the standard deviation 5.6, and the scores were normally distributed.

The IAV (Bills, Vance, & McLean 1951) is a 49-item measure of overall self-esteem, defined as evaluations made on traits considered to be de-sirable. The measure contains 49 descriptive terms (e.g., "considerate") and three response columns. In the first column people indicate how well a particular word describes them, in the second whether they like or dislike the way they are, and in the third how much they would like to be that way. Although the IAV was designed to yield three scores, the self-ideal discrepancy score was not used owing to methodological difficulties (Wylie 1979). The two scores used were (a) a self-concept score (IAV Self) acquired by summing responses in the column describ-ing self; and (b) a self-acceptance score (IAV Accept) acquired by sum-ming the column describing how much a person liked or disliked the way he or she is.

The PCS (Gibaud-Wallston & Wandersman 1978) is a 17-item measure of competence as parents. Since its authors thought self-esteem was the cognitive outcome of a self-evaluative process, they focused upon the perceived ability to meet the demands of parenting. The purpose was to look at competence instead of just self-acceptance, and to focus upon a specific context. There are two subscales: (a) PCS skill/knowledge (PCS Skill) measuring parents' perceptions of the degree to which they have acquired the skills and understanding to be a good parent; and (b) PCS value/comfort (PCS Value) measuring the degree to which parents value parenthood and are comfortable in that role.

The ESM (Csikszentmihalyi, Larson, & Prescott 1977; Larson & Csikszentmihalyi 1983; Hormuth 1986; Csikszentmihalyi & Larson 1987) was used to report on present activity in response to randomly activated paging devices by filling out a one-page Experience Sampling Form (ESF) 4 to 5 times a day for 2 weeks from 8:00 A.M. to 10:00 P.M. Mothers were instructed that this was a study of their everyday life, and all thoughts and feelings were important. Inspection of the data showed that of the possible 3,136 total signals sent, 71% were responded to within 5 minutes and 73% (2,287) were responded to within 30 minutes. Since current experience was being studied, only the questionnaires answered within 30 minutes were included in the analysis. The total number of valid EEFs responded to per mother ranged from 25 to 62, with a mean of 47.

The ESM self-esteem scores. Self-evaluation was considered a process of appraisal; and SE viewed as a perceived evaluation of self that might change over time and context. Each time mothers were signaled, their perceptions of two core aspects of SE were measured (how good they felt about themselves and how satisfied they were with how they were doing), as well as other aspects of their present experience that might be related to SE. These included (a) aspects suggested by SE theory (e.g., control of the situation, anxiety); (b) aspects of the interpersonal context (e.g., whether goals were compatible with others present); (c) the presence vs. absence of children; and (d) how challenging their present activity was and how much skill they were using. Then, the correlations between these various factors were looked at to determine which other aspects of experience correlated highly with the two core aspects measured. In other words, was there a cluster of items that appeared to be measuring self-esteem? In order to answer this question, I computed the average levels of each of the aspects of experience asked about on the ESF over the 2-week period of data collection. Then, these averages were intercorrelated. Analysis showed (Wells 1985, 1986) that three aspects of experience were highly intercorrelated with the two core aspects of experience initially designed to measure SE (average r [49] = .77,

$p < .0001$; in addition, the next highest correlation of any other item with this cluster was .68 or less). Thus, when experience was looked at on a moment-to-moment basis and then averaged over time, mothers' SE appeared to be made up of five interrelated aspects: (a) how good they felt about themselves; (b) how satisfied they were with how they were doing; (c) how much in control of the situation they felt; (d) how much they were living up to their expectations of themselves; and (e) how much they were living up to the expectations of others important to them. The above five items were used to measure SE each time a person responded to the signal (sum/5). Then an overall ESM self-esteem score was calculated (ESM SE [Average], which was the average SE score of all of a particular respondent's items over 2 weeks) as well as ESM SE scores when they were in particular contexts (ESM SE [Context], which was the average of SE scores on a mother's ESF when she was in a specific context, e.g., when with children vs. when with adults). The average intercorrelation between items that made up the overall ESM SE (Average) score was .77, $p < . 0001$, and Cronbach's alpha = .94. To give an estimate of test–retest reliability, average ESM SE scores for the first half of the data collection period were correlated with average scores for the second half (r [49] = .86, $p < .0001$).

Correlational analyses showed that the ESM procedure measured information that overlapped with the generalized SE measures. The overall ESM SE (Average) scores were moderately correlated with scores on the RBS, IAV, and the PCS, ranging from a nonsignificant .13 to a significant .55 ($p < .0001$) with a mean of .36, which was within the range usually found between tests of similar constructs (i.e., $r = .35 - .50$, Fiske 1971).

Categorizing experience by challenge and skill. Mothers' reported experiences were divided into four clusters depending on the relationship between challenges and skills. This was done by coding each response into one of four Challenge/Skill (C/S) channels according to the reported level of challenge of the present activity and the skill being used. The method used was as follows:

1. First, the average levels of challenges and skills were located for each respondent. Then z scores (z challenge and z skill) with a mean of 0 and a standard deviation of 1 were calculated for each ESF response.
2. A distance measure was calculated for each response by subtracting z challenge from z skill.
3. Then, for each response, if the distance between z challenge and z skill was between 0 and .55 or between 0 and −.55 (i.e., within approximately 1/2

332   Anne J. Wells

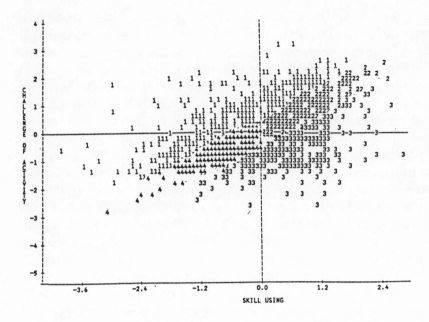

Figure 20.1. Distribution of responses in four challenge/skill channels. A total of 2,287 responses are included. The scattergram does not indicate multiple responses with the same values.

standard deviation of each other), challenges and skills were considered to be roughly equal. In addition, if z challenge and z skill were above the person's mean, then the mother's experience was coded into channel 2, which corresponded to the theoretically proposed flow channel. If z challenge and z skill were below the person's mean, then the response was coded into channel 4, which corresponds to the proposed apathy channel (see Figure 20.1).
4. If the distance between z challenge and z skill was greater than .55, then z challenge was greater than z skill, and the response was coded into channel 1, which is the theoretically proposed anxiety channel.
5. If the distance between z challenge and z skill was less than − .55, then z skill was greater than z challenge, and the response was coded into channel 3, corresponding in theory to the boredom channel.

As noted previously, the C/S channels used here are similar but not identical to those used in Chapter 16 of this volume. If the eight channels are collapsed so that channels 1, 7, 8 are channel 1, channel 2 = 2, channels 3, 4, 5 = 3, and channel 6 = 4, the correlation between mothers' responses coded by the 4-channels method and by the method used in this chapter is r (2,190) = .70, $p < .0001$.

Figure 20.1 shows a plot of mothers' respones (N = 2,135) by C/S channels (two mothers were not included in this analysis because of missing data). Of the total 2,135 responses, 558 (26%) fell into channel 1; 484 (23%) were coded into channel 2; 551 (26%) into channel 3; and 542 (25%) into channel 4. ESM SE (Context) scores were computed for each C/S channel by locating all the times a particular mother's experience was coded in a particular channel (e.g., in channel 1 or anxiety, when z challenge was greater than z skill), and finding the average ESM SE score for that mother in that channel. It was expected that self-esteem would be highest in channel 2 and lowest in channel 4. For this analysis respondents were also sorted into three groups according to the amount of time they spent working, because the percentage of time at work (worktime) had a significant negative correlation with overall ESM SE (Average) scores (r [49] = $-.29$, $p < .04$). These groups were (a) 17 mothers who worked full-time (100%), (b) 20 who worked at least half-time (50–80%), and (c) 12 who worked part-time (25–40%).

Results

The results of a 3×4 (worktime × channel) multivariate analysis of covariance for repeated measures (Finn & Bock 1985) show that self-esteem was significantly higher in flow than in the three other channels (see Figure 20.2). Self-esteem in channel 2 (when challenges and skills were roughly equal and both were above average), was higher than in channel 4 (when challenges were roughly equal to skills but both were below average) (univariate F [1, 44] = 31.09, $p < .0001$), than in channel 1 (when challenges were higher than skills) (univariate F [1, 44] = 23.03, $p < .0001$) or in channel 3 (when skills were higher than challenges) (univariate F [1, 44] = 8.91, $p < .004$).

There was also a significant worktime effect (univariate F [2, 44] = 3.59, $p < .03$). All three worktime groups were significantly different from each other, with mothers who worked the least having the highest self-esteem and those who worked the most having the lowest self-esteem. There was no significant interaction effect between worktime and channel. Thus, as predicted, respondents did feel better about themselves in flow, and significantly worse in apathy, boredom, and anxiety. Levels of current ongoing self-esteem were related to amount of time spent working, with mothers working full-time reporting the lowest average levels of ongoing self-esteem. It was interesting to note that mothers'

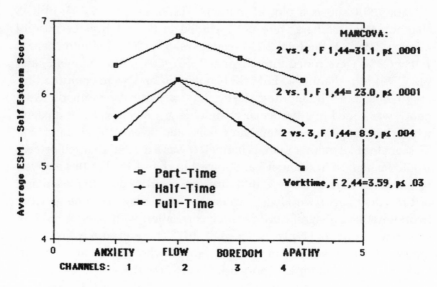

Figure 20.2. Working mothers' self-esteem in flow channels (N = 47).

descriptions of their lives (although not measured systematically) often included discussion of how difficult they found the task of juggling their family and work responsibilities. Such descriptions and the above finding raise questions such as Do mothers who work more have less opportunity to fulfill both work and family responsibilities? and Do mothers' estimates of how well they are balancing these two sets of responsibilities affect their current evaluations of themselves?

The second prediction of this study was that those respondents who spent more time in channel 2 (flow) would have the highest overall self-esteem. Three measures of overall self-esteem were available: two generalized ones, the RBS and IAV, and an overall measure of averaged ongoing self-esteem, the ESM SE (Average) scores. In addition, self-esteem in the more limited context of being a parent was measured by the PCS. The percentage of time spent in each C/S channel was found by locating all the times a mother was in a particular channel and dividing the number of responses in that channel by her total number of responses. Subjects varied a great deal in terms of how much time they spent in each channel. The mean percentage of time spent in each channel was as follows: 25% in channel 1, with a range of 6–43%; 23% in

Table 20.1. *Correlation between self-esteem and percentage of time in C/S categories*

Self-esteem (N = 47)	Percentage of time spent in C/S category			
	1	2	3	4
ESM Self-esteem	−.05	.23	−.10	−.14
Rosenberg's Self-esteem Scale	.00	.20	−.10	−.09
Index of Adjustment and Values Self-esteem	.21	.05	.08	−.26
Index of Adjustment and Values Accept	−.11	.36*	−.14	−.08
Parenting Competence Scale— Total	−.36*	.57***	−.45**	.17
Parenting Competence Scale— Skill	−.31*	.50**	−.43*	.17
Parenting Competence Scale— Value	−.34*	.48**	−.33*	.14

Note: * $= p < .05$; ** $= p < .001$; *** $= p < .0001$

channel 2, with a range of 4–40%; 26% in channel 3, with a range of 4–47%; and 26% in channel 4, with a range of 8–56%. Table 20.1 shows the correlational analysis between percentage of time in particular channels and self-esteem scores.

Only one of the generalized measures of self-esteem, the IAV Accept, was significantly related to percentage of time in channel 2 (the flow channel) (r [47] $= .36, p < .01$). Nor was the overall average ESM measure of ongoing self-esteem significantly related to percentage of time in flow. However, the generalized measure of self-esteem in the more specific context of being a parent, the PCS, was significantly related to three of the four C/S channels. All three PCS scores – PCS total, PCS Skill, and PCS Value – were (a) negatively related to percentage of time spent in anxiety, when challenges were higher than skills (with N $= 47$, $r = -.36, p < .01$; $r = -.31, p < .03$; $r = -.34, p < .01$, respectively); (b) positively related to flow ($r = .57, p < .0001$; $r = .50, p < .0003$; $r = .48, p < .0006$, respectively); and (c) negatively related to boredom, when skills were higher than challenges ($r = -.45, p < .001$; $r = -.43, p < .002$; $r = -.33, p < .02$, respectively).

One of the factors believed to facilitate the flow experience is having clear expectations about one's behavior, and receiving feedback as to how one is doing (Csikszentmihalyi 1982a). It is interesting to note that the percentage of time in channel 2 does predict self-esteem in the more limited context and role of being a parent, but is unrelated to a more generalized self-evaluation (with the exception of the IAV Accept). One could speculate that mothers may have clearer ideas about what they expect of themselves as mothers, and receive clearer feedback about themselves as parents, than they are clear about what to expect of themselves as persons. Certainly this finding raises a number of interesting questions about the interaction between self-esteem and flow.

The question arises, Is the percentage of time spent in each of the C/S channels related to other internal and external factors? External factors such as socioeconomic level, education, occupation, time spent at work, age, and age of youngest child, shape and limit mothers' experiences so that they have somewhat different experiences and external realities to deal with. Since each person has only limited amounts of time, energy, and attention to spend in the various activities (Csikszentmihalyi & Massimini 1985), one can ask: Is the time mothers spend in the various C/S channels significantly related to external factors? For example, is the age of the youngest child related to spending less time in flow, or more time in boredom and apathy? Do women in more professional occupations spend more time in flow, as Allison and Duncan (Chapter 7) suggest? Csikszentmihalyi (1982a) and Csikszentmihalyi and Graef (1980) have found that people report flow not only when composing music or winning a chess game, but also in everyday experience, for example, at work or in class. Thus, one would predict that channel 2 experiences could be found in any occupation.

There were no significant differences in the mean percentage of time mothers spent in each of the four C/S channels by age of mother, her education, occupation, time spent at work, or number of children. (Hollingshead's Index of Social Position [1957] was used to categorize mother's education and occupation and to derive a family socioeconomic rating.) There was one significant difference by family socioeconomic status rating. Mothers with an upper-middle-class family rating spent significantly less time in channel 1 (when challenges were greater than skills) than mothers with a family rating of middle class (F [47] = 4.05, $p < .02$). Also, channel 4 (when challenges and skills were roughly equal, but below average) approached a significant difference ($p < .07$), with mothers from the upper middle class spending more time in channel 4 than mothers from the middle class. However, this "difference" should be viewed with caution until replicated.

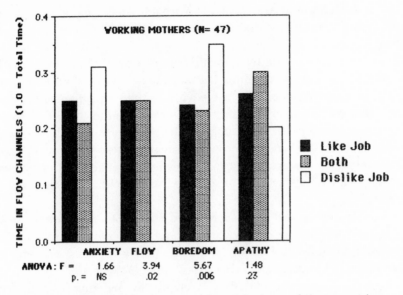

Figure 20.3. Relationship between job satisfaction and time spent in flow channels.

Age of youngest child was also significantly related to mean percentage of time spent in channel 2 (flow). Mothers whose youngest child was between 2 and 4 years old reported significantly lower percentage of time spent in channel 2 than mothers whose youngest child was 5 to 6 years of age (F [47] = 6.06, $p < .01$). It does appear that having a young child in the home is related to mothers spending less time in flow.

How much a woman liked her job was significantly related to mean percentage of time spent in flow and in boredom (see Figure 20.3). Mothers who said they liked their jobs reported a significantly higher percentage of time spent in channel 2 (F [47] = 3.94, $p < .02$), and significantly less time spent in channel 3 (F [47] = 5.67, $p < .006$) than mothers who said they disliked their jobs. Thus, whether or not a mother liked or disliked her job was related to the percentage of time spent in two C/S channels, with more flow experiences being related to liking one's job and more time in boredom being related to disliking one's job. Such findings do not tell us whether flow experiences lead to liking one's job or liking one's job leads to flow experiences. However, follow-ups of such findings are important since job satisfaction may be related to such factors as productivity, less job time lost, and less worker turnover.

Next we explore the relationship between percentage of time in the C/S channels and two contextual factors, mothers' reported activities and companions (whom they were with). Is there a relationship between activities and companions and time spent in each of the C/S channels? In other words, what percentage of the time were mothers in each of the C/S channels when they were primarily involved in work, home maintenance, self-care, child care, or leisure interaction, when they were alone, with adults only, with children only, with both children and adults?

The results of this analysis showed that mothers reported all C/S channels of experience in each activity and companion group. However, when mothers were working on the job, they were twice as likely to be in channels 1 and 2 than in channels 3 and 4 (32% and 36% vs. 16% and 14%). If they reported they were primarily involved in child care, they were more likely to be in channels 3 and 4 than in channels 1 and 2 (30% and 25% vs. 22% and 21%). If mothers reported they were alone or with children only, they were more likely to be in channels 3 or 4 than in channels 1 and 2 (alone 27% and 29% vs. 21% and 21%; with children, 24% and 27% vs. 22% and 20%), whereas if they were with adults they were more likely to be in channels 1 and 2 (28% and 33% vs. 19% and 18%). In addition, when mothers' experiences in channel 2 were examined, mothers were about equally likely to report they were primarily involved in work (29%), home maintenance (26%), or leisure interactions (26%). It would appear that for mothers there is more than one activity in which flow experience is likely. However, in terms of companions, when in channel 2 mothers reported more often being with adults only (31%) rather than being alone (22%), with children only (23%), or with children and adults (22%). Thus flow experiences did occur in the other companion groups, but appeared slightly more likely in the company of other adults.

Finally, we turn to the relationship between percentage of time in C/S channels and the quality of experience. Overall average levels of certain ESM variables were correlated with percentage of time spent in each C/S channel ($N = 47$). Percentage of time in channel 2 (flow), for instance, was significantly related to the reported overall average levels of being interested ($r = .48$, $p < .0001$), energetic ($r = .32$, $p < .05$), organized ($r = .34$, $p < .05$), feeling smart ($r = .37$, $p < .001$), involved in the present activity (r =.31, $p < .05$), and appreciated ($r = .34$, $p < .05$). Percentage of time in channel 3 (boredom) was negatively related to overall average levels of concentration ($r = -.29$, $p < .05$), being interested ($r = -.38$, $p < .001$), and feeling smart ($r = -.31$, $p < .05$); and negatively related to being nervous or tense ($r = -.32$, $p < .05$).

It is interesting to note that the percentage of time spent in C/S channels was not significantly related to overall average levels of moods such as happy–sad, contented–discontented, or to most of the interpersonal variables such as friendly–angry, cooperative–uncooperative, feeling involved with others present, and also not related to overall average levels of motivational variables such as wishing to be doing something else and likely to take the initiative. Although frequency of flow experience has been reported to be related to motivation (Csikszentmihalyi 1982a; see Massimini and Carli, Chapter 16; LeFevre, Chapter 18), mothers' overall average levels of wanting to be involved in their experiences was not related to percentage of time in flow. One might speculate that mothers may have a number of reasons for wanting to be involved in doing something. For example, being good parents and caring for their children may be motive enough for wanting to do their tasks. Mothers may report wanting to do what they are doing, even though they are not being challenged or able to use their skills at the present time, because they may feel that certain routine maintenance tasks need to be done.

Summary and conclusions

In this chapter the relationship between self-esteem and the flow experience has been examined. Respondents did report significantly higher levels of ongoing ESM self-esteem when in channel 2 (flow) than when in channel 1 (anxiety), channel 3 (boredom), or channel 4 (apathy). Self-esteem as a parent was also related to percentage of time spent over the course of the 2-week period in channels 1, 2, and 3, with mothers who spent more time in flow and less in anxiety and boredom reporting higher levels of parental self-esteem. Certainly these findings demonstrate that self-esteem and flow experiences are related and, in addition, point to the possibility that flow experiences may be more important to the evaluation of self in more specific contexts and roles. These findings suggest further questions: Do flow experiences raise self-esteem, or does feeling good about oneself make it more likely that one will experience flow? And how do clearer expectations and positive feedback affect both self-evaluation and flow experience?

Results also show, as expected, that flowlike experiences can and do occur in all types of activities and with all groups of companions. Also, percentage of time in the various channels was essentially the same no matter what the mother's age, occupation, education, amount of time spent at work, or number of children. Such findings are important because they show that it is possible to structure experience optimally despite clear external constraints. Mothers reported that they often felt considerable pressure because their time was tightly scheduled by the responsibilities of their work and families. However, the results show that, even with these very real constraints, mothers somehow managed to structure their experiences so that they did have time when challenges and skills were roughly equal and both were above average. Two external factors did appear to be related to the percentage of time in the C/S channels: The age of youngest child was related to lower percentage of time in the flow channel and higher percentage of time in boredom; a family SES rating of upper middle class was related to lower percentage of time in anxiety. In addition, percentage of time in flow was related to liking one's job, and to quality of experience in terms of overall average levels of concentration, being interested, organized, energetic, involved in one's activities, and feeling smart and appreciated.

The main contribution of these findings to the flow theory is to confirm that momentary variations in self-esteem are linked to changes in the ratio between challenges and skills: When both are high and in balance, self-esteem is highest; but self-esteem is low when both are low, as well as when challenges are greater than skills (anxiety) and when skills are greater than challenges (boredom). Although these relationships do not prove causality, they suggest that changes in the challenge–skill ratio could *precede* the variations in self-esteem. Whether the relationship is in fact sequential will have to be ascertained by future research. An opposite line of causality is suggested by the relationship between parental self-esteem and time spent in flow. It is possible that mothers who feel competent as parents will be able to structure their experiences so as to be in flow more often – thereby increasing momentary levels of self-esteem. A process of circular causality might then be in effect, whereby flow experiences first bolster the self, and then a stronger self increases the probability of experiencing flow.

The findings with working mothers of small children also raise at least one question for the flow theory. Are there groups of people (e.g., mothers of small children, who work) for whom motivation to do tasks is related not only to the relationship between challenges and skills, but also to other important factors such as wanting to be good parents? Such questions remind us of the complex nature of the interaction between the factors that affect and make up our experience.

21. Optimal experience and the family context

KEVIN RATHUNDE

Many studies have attempted to understand the influence of the family by observing its impact on a child's behavior; they have left – hidden from view – the subjective experience of the child. Although valuable insights have been gained through behavioral observations, the present study adopts the Experience Sampling Method (Csikszentmihalyi, Larson, & Prescott 1977) to begin filling in this subjective aspect of our understanding of the family. There has been a convergence of thought in several disciplines around the simple idea that a person's subjective interpretation of a situation will influence subsequent behavior. Paradigm shifts in philosophy (Langer 1957), the social sciences (Taylor 1979), and developmental thought about children and families (Maccoby 1980) have stressed individuals' active role in defining their environment. Thus to understand the influence of the family context, it is important to know how it affects the way children subjectively interpret their current situations.

The flow model (Csikszentmihalyi 1975b) focuses on one kind of interpretation of a situation – the ability to find in it opportunities for meaningful action or challenge – which leads to the optimal experience of flow and appears to have many healthy and beneficial consequences, including a path for differentiation and growth (Csikszentmihalyi 1982a). How might a family foster this form of interpretation – or way of paying attention – in its children? The general questions motivating this study are

1. Can we identify a context that facilitates optimal experience and flow in children?
2. What are the dynamics of that context?
3. Does it produce children who are more able to experience flow in new surroundings?

These questions can be answered only by applying some of the theoretical constructs of the flow model in new directions. The model specifies the dynamics concerning the salient dimensions of challenge and skills in the *foreground* of one's awareness. Flow occurs only when both challenges and skills are high and there is a perceived balance between them. When attempting to understand the context in which flow might occur, attention must shift to the dynamics or optimal balance of information in the *background* of awareness, which is often taken for granted and processed automatically. When one is in the enjoyable state of flow and focused on an interesting task, an implicit and organized context exists that helps to focus attention. This context may be so thoroughly incorporated into one's perspective that it virtually disappears into the background of awareness.

One can picture this process by considering how the rules of baseball continue to direct the players' actions on the field long after the rules "disappear" from awareness. The structural design of a family, a game, or even a theory (see Kuhn's 1970 notion of a paradigm) creates a context or filter through which attention is focused and directed. Although the rule-bound context may often be in the background, its existence and importance become obvious in an in-depth phenomenological analysis (Schutz & Luckmann 1973). Different structural designs or symbol systems will throw the spotlight of attention on different opportunities for action. As a result, they will influence the potential rewards of experience, that is, whether or not it is autotelic (enjoyable for its own sake: *auto* = self, *telos* = goal). For example, the context of an artist's life may contain rules of artistic expression that support and encourage the artist to recognize opportunities for action, new ideas, and works that elaborate important themes in the artist's life, and therefore highlight opportunities for autotelic experience. The artist's "work" thus becomes something that is less motivated by an external reward structure. In contrast, a businessman pursuing goals defined by a company's rules of profit would have a much harder time obtaining optimal experience in the absence of extrinsic rewards. It seems reasonable to assume that contexts will also vary from one family to the next in regard to which goals they bring into the light of attention. Given the enormous influence that the family's symbolic structure exerts on a child's entire world view (Berger & Luckmann 1967), it may be reasonable to assume that the family context will greatly affect whether a child ever develops the kind of interpretation and style of paying attention that facilitates autotelic experience.

From the autotelic experience to the autotelic context

An autotelic family context may be thought of as the organized, rule-bound environment that structures a child's attention in ways that enhance the playlike quality of experience that is enjoyable in itself. Simply put, an autotelic context is a place where autotelic, or self-rewarding behavior is facilitated. Four aspects of the autotelic family context are examined in this study: (1) its component features, (2) the optimal balance of these features, (3) the beneficial function of the autotelic context in regard to the economy of a child's attention, and (4) the effect of an internalized autotelic family context on a child's experience in different contexts.

By first examining the characteristic features of the flow experience, it is possible to restate these features in terms of the context in which flow occurs. In other words, if one were to describe one's experience while playing a particular game, one can analyze how the game's rules help to support and structure this experience. The qualities of flow are a sense of control, the centering of attention on a limited stimulus field, clear goals with unambiguous feedback, its autotelic or intrinsically rewarding nature, the merging of action and awareness, and the lack of ego awareness. To state these qualities in terms of a family rule-context it might be said, first, the context must be such that it provides a perceived *choice*, and thus a feeling of control to the child. Second, the context must have *clarity* so that it highlights a stimulus field for a child that can then be attended to and manipulated with high concentration. Third, the family context must *center* attention on the immediacy of the task rather than exclusively on its consequences, so that the intrinsic rewards of the activity itself are experienced. Fourth, the context must encourage a *commitment* or trust that allows the child to feel comfortable enough to put aside the mediation and defense of the ego. Fifth, a context must support opportunities for meaningful *challenge* to set the whole process of flow in motion.

The five contextual factors identified above must exist in a dialectically balanced state between rigidity and looseness in order to facilitate optimal experience. To operate efficiently within the parameters of our information-processing capabilities (Broadbent 1958), this processing should not be disrupted by the extremes of under- or over-arousal (Berlyne 1971). In a phenomenological perspective, information is most efficient or "flowlike" between the extremes of boredom and anxiety. A family context must exhibit certain parameters to engender optimal experience: (1) it must provide choices in order that the child feels in control, but must not be coercive in determining where the child should focus attention or leave the child completely on his or her own; (2) must provide clarity so that the child may efficiently focus and adjust attention, but not be so rigid or loose that the feedback from the environment is redundant or uninterpretable; (3) must center attention on immediate tasks in order that the child experiences autotelic rewards, but must not disrupt a task with too much attention to rewards exclusively outside the particular activity or exclusively inside the child; (4) must support a commitment or trust in order that the child may emerge from behind a defensive ego, but not call for dogmatic adherence or leave one alone or alienated; and (5) must provide challenge to give the impetus to action, but must not overwhelm the child's affective and cognitive potential for turning information into meaning. A family context that strikes this balance between choice, clarity, centering, commitment, and challenge will be defined here as an *autotelic family context*. A context that typically provides too little or too much of these five factors will be referred to as a nonautotelic context, which is one that facilitates either boredom or anxiety.

When an autotelic family context is in operation, it will ordinarily direct attention without itself being the focus of attention. In this way it will both conserve and liberate the attention of a child within it. This foreground–background dynamic can be illustrated with the analogy of game rules. The rules of a game are not the focal point of the player who is absorbed in performance. They conserve the attentional energy of the player by providing preformulated guidelines that direct attention to certain goals. They simultaneously liberate the attention of the player who submits to the rules by eliminating the distractions that would disrupt performance and the enjoyment of the game itself. When the rules become a point of contention, the enjoyment of the game momentarily ends and attention is turned toward working out the difficulty. If the game truly provides an autotelic context, most problematic contingencies will have been foreseen and the rule structure can quickly and efficiently remedy the problem.

It is assumed here that these foreground–background dynamics are also at work in an autotelic family context. Here one might imagine a simple scenario concerning one of the five theorized factors that create an autotelic context – clarity of rules. A child in an autotelic context might clearly know the rules for painting with watercolor paints at home, such as wearing a painting smock, sitting at the kitchen table, and so on. Once the rules help structure the context for painting, however, there are no rigidly detailed steps that would make painting a boring or redundant activity. Another child may sometimes paint with a smock on and sometimes off, and sometimes paint at the kitchen table and sometimes not. One particular day the parents might demand that the child wear the smock and sit at the table. The child, knowing that these rules have been inconsistent in the past, may get into an argument with the parents that disrupts the activity. The autotelic context would have facilitated a flow experience in the activity of painting. The other child's attention will have been wasted in an unproductive way.

If something like this seemingly trivial negative outcome, which could easily have been modeled on any of the four other factors, happens repeatedly over the years in many different activities, a serious deficit in the quality of experience might occur. If the former positive outcome is repeated often, the rules that structure the activity of painting will probably become second nature and automatic because they have not been *recognized* as standing in the way of an enjoyable experience. To summarize this point, whenever the rule-bound context that normally acts as a focusing lens for attention to experience in *itself* becomes the focus of attention, the possibility for optimal experience or flow is disrupted until the particular contextual factor is optimally balanced and recedes to the background. Since rules in any domain must undergo challenge and modification, and rule negotiation in play may help to develop important social skills in a child (Bettelheim 1987), it can be added that rules that are autotelic to begin with can be modified more productively.

The beneficial impact of an autotelic family context is theorized on the basis of its "fit" to the active and intrinsically motivated child learner (Piaget 1962; Maslow 1968; Deci & Ryan 1985). A good fit occurs because boredom and anxiety are less often taking center stage to the child's natural absorption in growth-orientated behavior. Through socialization the typical patterns of paying attention at home may be internalized and carried over into new contexts. Schutz and Luckmann (1973, pp. 256–61) make the following argument about the transfer effect of previous socialization to new situations: The individual "enters the situation with a socialized store of interpretational and motivational relevances. . . . The subjective system of relevances . . . conditions what is experienced in the current situation as *obvious and routine* or as *problematic* and needing explication and mastering" (emphasis added). If a child is socialized in a context in which the rules are not typically the focus of attention and seen as the cause of one's boredom or anxiety, these same attentional patterns may condition him or her to see the rules in a current situation outside of the home the same way. We can use the school context to illustrate this point.

A child from an autotelic home may tend to move into the school context and operate "as if" its conditions fit with his or her intrinsic motivation, even though they may not. In this case, the situation may be analogous to the healthy benefits that have been observed for individuals who operate under an "illusion of control" (Alloy & Abramson 1979). A second way in which socialization in an autotelic context may affect school experience is through the increased ability to concentrate and not be distracted. A child from an autotelic context may have more attention free to work at restructuring a chaotic situation in order to find the control and meaningful feedback necessary to sustain a flow experience. In contrast, a self growing up in and habituated to the relatively chaotic or rigid patterns of attention of a nonautotelic context will likely "see" the same issues of choice, clarity, centering, commitment, and challenge as problematic and unresolved also in a new context. They will remain in the foreground of awareness and drain attention. Since an autotelic context may help economize the resources of energy and attention, one would expect that differences between children from these two contexts would be apparent when they are involved in productive activities, that is, activities that require a greater amount of effort.

Many of the five contextual factors important for flow have been the subject of empirical investigation in family research. Studies of attachment behavior relevant to the factor of commitment demonstrate that securely attached infants have a greater propensity for exploratory and mastery behavior (Ainsworth, Bell, & Stayton 1971; Main 1973; Matas, Arend, & Sroufe 1978). Investigations of the influence of parental styles on creativity (Getzels & Jackson 1962) suggest the beneficial effects of greater flexibility, perceived choice, and a positive emotional context. Perhaps the most relevant for the ideas being developed here is Baumrind's (1977) influential study of the family. In discussing the importance of family balance through the comparison of permissive, authoritative, and authoritarian parental styles, she found that avoiding the two extremes – permissive and authoritarian – was optimal for developing the active disposition or "agency" of children. The dimensions that were looked at – parental control, maturity demands, parent–child communication, and nurturance – in many ways overlap with the dimensions identified in the present study as important for optimal experience. A clear analogy can be drawn between permissive styles and anxiety-provoking contexts, authoritarian styles and contexts that are experienced as boring, and a balanced style that facilitates agency or intrinsic motivation. Kohut's (1978) psychoanalytic writings on the concept of "optimal frustration" suggest that a balance of freedom and restriction is necessary for children to navigate successfully important developmental challenges. The present study adds to these studies the realization that balanced choice, clarity, centering, commitment, and challenge produce their impact on the child by avoiding the wasteful extremes of information processing, thus allowing the optimal operation of consciousness.

Despite the presence of isolated studies of choice, clarity, centering, commitment, and challenge, and some previous thought about dynamics and balance, there is not an approach to the family that (1) unites this cluster of factors and (2) specifies the dynamics operating. Approaching the study of the family by way of the phenomenology of the child provides an opportunity to accomplish both of these objectives, in that the five factors themselves and the dynamic of optimal balance are meaningfully integrated by the concept of flow.

Method

Subjects

A total of 395 freshman and sophmores from two suburban high schools were nominated by their teachers in the fields of math, science, art, music, and athletics for participation in a 4-year longitudinal study of talented adolescents. Letters were sent to the homes of the students explaining the project, and meetings were scheduled to invite questions; 228 of the talented adolescents agreed to participate. Approximately 193 adolescents who had completed all the instruments make up the present sample.

Procedure

Each student met with a member of the research staff three to four times in an office at the school. Over the course of these meetings the student filled out several questionnaires designed to gather background, personality, and sex-role identity information. In addition, students were assigned electronic pagers and given instructions on how to fill out the Experience Sampling Method booklet (see Csikszentmihalyi & Larson 1984). Students carried their pagers for 1 week while being sent 7–9 random signals daily between the hours of 7:00 A.M. and 10:00 P.M. during the week and 7:00 A.M. and midnight on the weekends.

Hypotheses

Three hypotheses were proposed about the effects of autotelic family context on the adolescents' experience: (1) that those who perceive their family context as autotelic will have more optimal experience at home while with their parents than peers who perceive their family context as nonautotelic; (2) that the group with an autotelic home context will have more optimal experience while at school and involved in productive activities; and (3) that talented adolescents who perceive their family context as autotelic will also have more optimal experience while doing homework and studying at home.

Measures

The items used to measure the autotelic context were a combination of items chosen from two previous family questionnaires used by Devereux, Bronfenbrenner, and Rogers (1969) and Olson, Bell, and Porter (1982). Both of these previous surveys were organized around theoretical notions that recognize the importance of "balance" in family contexts; for this reason they were well-suited to the purposes of the present study.

Of the 27 responses that constituted the final autotelic score, 20 came from the Devereux et al. parent-practices questionnaire. This questionnaire uses variables that are organized under four general dimensions: supporting, demanding, controlling, punishing. Bronfenbrenner (1961) and Devereux (1970) propose a "theory of optimal levels" that states that a balance of support and control (love and discipline) are optimal in the socialization of responsible and mature children. Too much or too little of either of these components would lead to immature development. For example, high control–low warmth would lead to aggressiveness in children, high warmth–low control would lead to impulsivity. Seven of the items that measured the autotelic context came from the Olson, Bell, and Porter FACES II questionnaire, which is organized under two general dimensions: cohesion and adaptability. As does Bronfenbrenner's theory of optimal levels, this approach suggests a curvilinear relationship between important variables and optimal family systems. Extremes on the cohesion dimension produce disengaged or enmeshed families whereas extremes on the adaptability dimension produce rigid or chaotic families; optimal interactions are hypothesized to be in the midrange for each variable.

The contextual factors – choice, clarity, centering, commitment, and challenge – were chosen as relevant based on empirical reports of the "flow" experience (Csikszentmihalyi 1975b); this experience epitomizes the highest concentration of attentional energy. These factors are similar to others identified as important in research on children's intrinsic motivation (see deCharms 1976). They allow the construction of an independent measure phenomenologically relevant to the ESM-dependent measures, which yielded momentary reports of the subjective state of the child. In this way a theoretical continuity is established between the measures.

Some of the questions from the previous family surveys fit these dimensions. For example, choice was measured by responses to the items "S/he lets me make my own plans about things I want to do even though I might make a few mistakes" (Devereux et al. 1969); and "In solving problems, the children's suggestions are allowed" (Olson et al. 1982). However, not all of the questions on the two surveys had a clear link to the proposed phenomenological dynamics. For example, it is not clear what phenomenological effects one might expect from factors that measured "physical punishment" or "protectiveness" (Devereux et al. 1969), or factors that measured a family's "coalitions" or use of home "space" (Olson et al. 1982). For these reasons, such items were not included in the autotelic score.

Before looking at the dependent variables on the ESM measures, preliminary analyses were done on the autotelic context measure. Pearson correlations were computed to assess the intercorrelations between the individual items on the questionnaire. In addition, descriptive statistics were computed to assess the distribution of scores, and t tests were done to look for sex differences.

The pattern of results in the correlation matrix supports the assumption that the items reliably discriminate between autotelic and nonautotelic family contexts (see Rathunde 1987). Composite scores were computed for each family on three dimensions: autotelic, boredom/

rigidity, and anxiety/ambiguity. Correlations between these composites on the entire sample confirmed their distinctiveness. The autotelic score was negatively correlated with the anxiety/ambiguity score $r = -.57$ and negatively correlated with the boredom/rigidity score $r = -.36$. A final autotelic context score was computed by subtracting the anxiety and boredom scores from the first autotelic score. This score was correlated negatively with both anxiety and boredom $r = -.68$ and is the basis for subsequent analyses reported below.

Measures of optimal experience were obtained with six composite variables from items on the ESM self-report form: affect, activation, cognitive efficiency, intrinsic motivation, system negentropy [negative entropy or a state of order], and self-esteem. Five of the six variables, each composed of three to four items, have been used in previous ESM research to define the major components of subjective experience (see Csikszentmihalyi & Larson 1984 for more information about these measures). The self-esteem dimension is the same cluster of intercorrelated items used by Wells in Chapter 20. In the flow experience – operationalized by the balance of challenge and skills when both are above average levels – these dimensions of experience have consistently been shown to be enhanced. While the present study is not indexing the flow experience per se, it is expected that these dimensions of experience will differ for the two groups on the basis of the fact that the contextual conditions are optimally balanced and therefore generally more conducive to autotelic experience.

The results below treat the autotelic context measure as a discrete variable in order to contrast the upper and lower quartiles of the distribution of scores. Although this results in a loss of statistical power, there are two theoretical reasons for doing it. First, the theoretical concept of an autotelic context describes a context in which a cluster of five factors are *all* highly present and operating in an optimal balance. In other words, it makes more sense in terms of the theory to arbitrarily choose two cutoff points, and for heuristic purposes, think of a family context as either autotelic or not. The scores in the midrange would more often be high on some factors and low on others and not either consistently high or consistently low. Second, in a particular situation (for example, in class), there will be many sources of variance operating. If an autotelic family context is going to make a difference in competition with these other sources of variance at school – such as a disliked subject or teacher – then the effect of the home context will have to be relatively strong.

Table 21.1. *Quality of experience at home for adolescents in autotelic vs. nonautotelic contexts*

ESM items	Autotelic context (N = 45)	Nonautotelic context (N = 45)	t	p
Happy	5.29	4.46	3.79	<.001
Cheerful	4.91	3.94	3.98	<.001
Sociable	4.99	4.36	2.63	<.01
Affect	5.07	4.25	4.23	<.0001
Clear	4.86	4.32	2.03	<.05
Open	4.85	4.32	2.30	<.05
Cooperative	4.43	4.10	1.66	<.10
System negentropy	4.71	4.24	2.59	<.01
Alert	4.91	4.42	1.91	<.05
Active	4.30	4.07	.87	ns
Strong	4.61	4.24	1.76	<.05
Excited	4.44	3.73	3.04	<.01
Activation	4.57	4.13	2.27	<.05
Concentration	4.50	4.09	1.15	ns
Ease of concentration	7.01	6.80	.59	ns
Unself-consciousness	6.50	6.37	.29	ns
Clear	4.86	4.32	2.03	<.05
Cognitive efficiency	5.74	5.39	1.73	<.05
Wish doing activity	5.04	3.97	2.26	<.05
Control of actions	6.20	4.80	3.59	<.001
Involved	4.97	4.41	2.35	<.05
Motivation	5.42	4.39	4.25	<.0001
Feel good about self	6.12	4.62	3.97	<.001
Up to own expectations	6.37	5.11	3.58	<.001
Satisfied how doing	6.41	5.28	2.67	<.01
Self-concept	6.30	5.06	3.85	<.001

Note: Figures are means of individual raw score means based on approximately 560 ESM signals. All significance tests are one-tailed.

Results

The quality of experience at home

As expected, adolescents who perceived their family context as autotelic showed a strong pattern of more positive experience when they were with their parents (see Table 21.1). The following results are based on those signals that happened to catch the adolescents in the presence of at least one of their parents while siblings may or may not have been present. Three activities – talking, watching television, and eating – accounted for approximately 50% of the signals with parents.

As Table 21.1 shows, when teenagers who belonged to the autotelic group were randomly signaled in their home environment, they reported experiencing higher affect ($t = 4.23$, $p < .0001$), higher activation ($t = 2.27$, $p < .05$), higher cognitive efficiency ($t = 1.73$, $p < .05$), and higher motivation ($t = 4.25$, $p < .0001$) than their peers from the nonautotelic context. They also experienced the social context of the family as more ordered or negentropic ($t = 2.59$, $p < .01$), a result that holds for direct face-to-face communication with their parents ($t = 2.54$, $p < .01$ – not reported in Table 21.1). Adolescents from the autotelic group also reported a higher self-esteem ($t = 3.85$, $p < .001$) when with their families.

Alternatively, the more optimal experience of the autotelic group can be described in terms of the 19 items that made up the composite scores, 15 of which showed significant differences between the two groups (see Table 21.1). These teenagers were happier, more cheerful, more sociable, cooperative, and open with their families. They thought more clearly and felt more alert, strong, and excited. They wished more to be doing what they were doing, were involved with it, and felt a sense of control over their actions. They felt good about themselves, were living up to their own expectations, and were satisfied with how they were doing at the time. In addition, on 16 of the 19 items the non-autotelic group showed more variance in the distribution of their responses. On four of these items the groups differed significantly (two-tailed test): satisfied how doing ($F = 1.84$, $p < .05$), cheerful ($F = 1.86$, $p < .05$), strong ($F = 2.17$, $p < .05$), and wish doing activity ($F = 1.81$, $p < .05$). One of the composites – cognitive efficiency – also showed more variance in the non-autotelic context ($t = 2.24$, $p < .01$). This pattern of results, although not predicted, is consistent with the above findings. In other words, not only does the high autotelic context facilitate optimal experience at home, but it seems to do so more consistenly.

The quality of productive experience

The second and third hypotheses proposed on the basis of the theorized effects of an autotelic context predicted that the quality of productive experience, both at home and at school, would be more optimal for the group accustomed to an autotelic context at home. Table 21.2 compares the autotelic and nonautotelic groups while they were engaged in studying or doing schoolwork at home. The first set of figures refers to signals

Table 21.2. *Quality of experience at home for adolescents while studying or doing homework*

	Autotelic context (N = 33)	Nonautotelic context (N = 34)	t	p
ESM composites for homework alone or with parents present				
Affect	4.24	3.85	1.80	<.05
Activation	4.20	3.81	1.82	<.05
Cognitive efficiency	5.90	5.41	1.80	<.05
Motivation	4.74	4.22	1.87	<.05
Self-concept	6.00	5.51	1.30	<.10
ESM composites for homework alone				
Affect	4.14	3.80	1.58	<.10
Activation	4.19	3.71	2.29	<.05
Cognitive efficiency	5.93	5.47	1.60	<.10
Motivation	4.90	4.42	1.84	<.05
Self-concept	6.25	5.77	1.39	<.10

Note: All significance tests are one-tailed. The first set of figures above is based on approximately 220 ESM responses; the second set is based on approximately 184 responses, reported as means of individual means.

responded to when the adolescents were working either alone or with their parents present (see Table 21.2).

As expected, students belonging to autotelic family contexts show a pattern of more optimal experience while doing homework and studying. When signaled, they were experiencing higher affect ($t = 1.80$, $p < .05$), higher activation ($t = 1.82$, $p < .05$), higher cognitive efficiency ($t = 1.80$, $p < .05$), and higher motivation ($t = 1.87$, $p < .05$). They also tended to have a higher self-concept ($t = 1.30$, $p < .10$). The second set of figures is a subset of the above information – the 180 ESM signals for when the adolescents were doing homework or studying alone. Two notable changes are that for doing homework at home alone, the effect for both affect ($t = 1.58$, $p < .10$) and cognitive efficiency ($t = 1.60$, $p < .10$) seems somewhat weaker than when the additional signals with the parents were included. The other items remain essentially unchanged. In the case of the affect measure (happy/cheerful/sociable) this change is misleading because it reflects a rise in the nonautotelic group's feeling more *sociable* when they are doing homework alone than when

Table 21.3. *Quality of experience for adolescents while in school*

	Autotelic context (N = 47)	Nonautotelic context (N = 48)	t	p
ESM composites				
Affect	4.82	4.44	2.22	<.05
Activation	4.47	4.28	1.25	ns
Cognitive efficiency	5.40	5.07	1.75	<.05
Motivation	4.52	4.10	2.12	<.05
System negentropy	4.41	4.20	1.58	<.10
Self-concept	5.94	5.23	2.67	<.01
Individual items on which groups differ				
Happy	4.87	4.52	2.00	<.05
Cheerful	4.55	4.13	1.98	<.05
Sociable	4.94	4.67	1.35	<.10
Alert	5.09	4.73	1.70	<.05
Ease of concentration	5.85	5.37	1.56	<.10
Control of actions	5.78	4.93	2.59	<.01
Feel good about self	5.66	4.81	2.72	<.01
Satisfied how doing	6.03	5.42	2.27	<.05
Up to own expectations	6.12	5.47	2.18	<.05

Note: All significance tests are one-tailed. Figures are means of individual raw score means based on approximately 1,120 ESM responses.

they are with their parents. Since this item loses its positive connotation in this context, the rise in the sociable score, which diminishes the difference between the two groups on the affect composite, in fact suggests a conclusion that supports the theoretical predictions. The smaller effect for cognitive efficiency may suggest that it is slightly easier for the nonautotelic group to concentrate when their parents are not around or may simply be due to chance. Overall, the means on the individual items go in the predicted direction on 18 of the 19 items, with the exception of the item "sociable." Individual items on which the groups differ significantly ($p < .05$) suggest that the biggest differences between the two groups while doing homework and studying are that the talented adolescents from autotelic contexts are more happy, cheerful, alert, strong, and feeling better about themselves. They also show a tendency ($p < .10$) to be able to concentrate more easily, be in control of their actions, and wishing to be doing what they are actually doing.

Table 21.3 presents the results for the analysis of the quality of experience for the two groups while doing productive work at school. For this comparison, only signals that caught the two groups either in class, studying, or doing homework were used.

Consistent with the results thus far, the autotelic group showed a clear pattern of more optimal experience at school as well. They experienced higher affect ($t = 2.22$, $p < .05$), higher cognitive efficiency ($t = 1.75$, $p < .05$), and higher motivation ($t = 2.12$, $p < .05$). Although their activation composite was higher, the difference was not large enough to draw a clear conclusion. In addition, the autotelic group maintained a higher self-concept ($t = 2.67$, $p < .01$), and the marginally significant results suggest that they find the social context of the school more negentropic ($t = 1.58$, $p < .10$). Of the 19 individual items, all went in the predicted direction. Individual items on which the groups differed significantly are also summarized in Table 21.3. When comparing them across productive activities at home and at school, it seems that the group with an autotelic home context were consistently more happy, cheerful, and alert when engaged in productive work. They concentrated more easily, felt more in control of their actions, and felt better about themselves than their peers whose home context is less supportive of playful, self-rewarding experience.

The quality of experience with friends

Owing to the highly positive descriptors chosen by the adolescents from the autotelic home context, an objection might be raised that what the above findings reflect are not differences in phenomenological experience but different response biases of the two groups. Perhaps the group from the home contexts we have been calling autotelic endorse any item higher in any situation. The counterargument can be made that even if this were the case, such a response bias still reflects something important about the way these adolescents experience their daily lives. However, in order to address this objection in an empirical way, various activities when the adolescents were with their friends were explored by way of the ESM measure. Of particular interest was the context of passive un-structured leisure with friends, such as socializing, attending a party, playing games, listening to music, watching television or video movies, and the like. In these activities, where high affect, activation, cognitive efficiency, and motivation are more easily achieved than when in school or studying, one might expect more similarity between adolescents regardless of whether their parents provide an autotelic context.

Table 21.4. *Quality of experience for adolescents with friends in passive unstructured leisure*

ESM composites	Autotelic Context (N = 33)	Nonautotelic Context (N = 26)	t	p
Affect	5.68	5.58	.34	ns
Activation	4.94	5.18	−.72	ns
Cognitive efficiency	5.58	5.70	−.44	ns
Motivation	6.01	5.64	.97	ns
System negentropy	5.10	4.66	1.63	ns
Self-concept	6.33	5.54	1.44	ns

Note: All significance tests are two-tailed. These figures are means of individual raw score means based on approximately 150 ESM signals.

Table 21.4 summarizes the findings for the two groups. Results are drawn from 150 ESM signals for these two groups of adolescents.

In this context the two groups show almost no differences. None of the six comparisons are significant, and two of the composites – activation and cognitive efficiency – reverse direction and show that the group from the low autotelic home context is slightly higher. Of the 19 items that make up the composites, 18 show no significant differences between the groups. Teenagers from autotelic home contexts do feel more satisfied with how they are doing ($t = 2.70$, $p <$ .05). Seven of the items – happy, alert, active, strong, concentration, unself-consciousness, and wish to be doing what they are doing – reverse direction and show higher scores for the adolescents from nonautotelic home contexts. In comparison with the other observed contexts – home, homework, and school – being with friends in the relatively passive context of unstructured leisure is for them the most positive time of the week. It is the only context in which they show higher levels of positive experience than the autotelic group. Although friends are also a positive context for the autotelic group, they are able to move in and out of the productive contexts across the week and maintain their positive level of experience.

Discussion

The general questions motivating this study were (1) Could a family context be identified that facilitates optimal experience in children? (2)

Could the dynamics of such a context be understood? and (3) Does its effect carry over into new contexts such as school? The results suggest that an autotelic family context – a context that structures a child's subjective experience with a balance of choice, clarity, centering, commitment, and challenge – consistently facilitates the optimal experience of adolescents. These findings held for experience at home and experience at school.

The assumption underlying this interpretation is that the teenagers' perception of their family context is accurate, and that this context affects the quality of their experience. An alternative explanation would deny this causal assumption and simply hold that some teenagers are more prone to see their families as autotelic, and these same teenagers also report better moods when with the family or when studying. Thus the reasons for the differences observed are to be sought in the adolescents' style of responding to questionnaires, rather than in any effects of family context. This alternative explanation would not explain, however, why the same teenagers did not also report higher moods when they were with their friends. The specific character of their optimal experience suggests not a general positive response bias, but rather a positive adaptation to family and study in addition to peer interactions. This, in turn, suggests a specific link between family context and optimal experience.

The effect of an autotelic context has been theoretically explained by the *economy of attention* resulting for the adolescents who come from families where the rules structure experience in ways that avoid the wasteful extremes of boredom and anxiety. In other words, an autotelic context provides a surplus of attentional resources to be devoted to the task at hand because important contextual conditions for optimal experience and flow have been efficiently balanced and operate in the background of awareness. In the following discussion I explain how the results of the present study support this theorized dynamic and what additional questions are important to ask in future studies. I also point out other relevant studies or views that help to illustrate how this dynamic may be operating.

In their moment-to-moment experience, teenagers from autotelic contexts are more happy, cheerful, sociable, open, cooperative, and clear when with their parents. This observation is consistent with the theorized economy of attention in that an autotelic context seems to be providing a structure for family interaction that is not diverting attention to problems with the structure itself. Just as a game could not be enjoyed unless one accepted and played within the rules, family interaction presumably would not be enjoyable unless the same acceptance of the rules allowed attention to be placed on the actual interaction. The autotelic context seems to be sustaining the structure of the family's life; but, like breathing, doing so in ways that are effortless, automatic, and therefore economical. Current thought in cognitive psychology (Schneider & Shiffrin 1977; Shiffrin & Schneider 1977) has made the distinction between "controlled" and "automatic" information processing, which helps to clarify what might be at work in the autotelic context. With repeated activation and feedback in a particular domain, one develops expertise that allows information processing to become more habitual and automatized. For example, as one becomes an "expert" in taking particular roads home from work, less attention needs to be paid to street signs and landmarks to stay on course. More of the processing resources are available for the intricacies of the situation at hand (see also Sternberg 1984).

Although the present study investigates a general family "domain," and it would be useful to also have information from more specific areas of family interaction, the suggestion here is that the teenagers from the autotelic context are automatically processing the contextual information that facilitates optimal experience. They are, like the expert drivers on their way home, not anxiously looking for a landmark or explicitly following a boring map, but enjoying the interaction because signals from the environment keeping the interaction on track have become second nature and automatic. We know from the background questionnaire that the autotelic group endorses items that suggest they are confident they know what their parents expect, they can count on them to be there when needed, and they expect the family to discuss problems and feel good about solutions. These understandings about the family context are the likely result of a repeated activation and feedback system that has been successful in the past; that is, when challenged with a problem the family met it with matching skills, and more often experienced flow.

Additional empirical work needs to be done to substantiate the claim that there is less attention being paid to problems with the structure of the interaction. Toward this end a study is currently under way to analyze the *thoughts* of the adolescents when they are with their parents. This information is being provided by an open-ended ESM question that asks what the adolescents were thinking as they were signaled. For now, if attention was being saved and efficiently focused by the family's rule structure, one would expect to see greater attentional resources or energy available for whatever task is at hand. The present study shows that not only are the adolescents in the autotelic context having smoother relations with their families, they seem to have a reserve of attentional resources and are able to feel more alert, strong, and excited at home.

More important than knowing that the family context seems to be functioning smoothly and successfully is knowing *why* this is the case. A clue might be found by examining the results for the intrinsic motivation composite. Intrinsic motivation showed the strongest differences between the two groups at home ($t = 4.25$, $p < .0001$). The adolescents in the autotelic environment were feeling more in control of their actions, they wished to be doing what they were doing, and they were more involved with it. Part of the economy of attention that is gained in the autotelic context must therefore be attributed to the fact that the symbolic information affecting the consciousness of the adolescents is not being experienced as oppressive to the inborn intrinsic motivation to assimilate, grow, and be self-determined (Piaget 1962; Maslow 1968; Deci & Ryan 1985). Energy is being saved by family rules that incorporate the "flow" of the children while at the same time helping to direct its course. This is a similar idea, though on a smaller scale, to that proposed by Csikszentmihalyi and Massimini (1985), which says that in an evolutionary perspective, flow occurs when there is a good psychological fit or mediation between "extrasomatic" cultural opportunities for action and "intrasomatic" biological predispositions. One simple way that an autotelic context might be accomplishing a "good fit" between the extrasomatic family rules and the intrasomatic adolescent motivation (this radical bifurcation is for heuristic purposes only) is that the abstract rules guiding behavior are presented in a context that also facilitates commitment, warmth, and security. The fact that disciplinary rules are greatly affected by the presence or absence of parental warmth has been noted in a review paper by Becker (1964) that summarized the child-rearing research up to that time. The strongest suggestion of the present study is that it is the implicit phenomenological balance in the five factors of choice, clarity, centering, commitment, and challenge that accomplishes the good fit of the family context to intrinsic motivation and flow. Just as our eyesight functions best within the appropriate parameters of light, so also are there parameters within which our minds work most efficiently (Broadbent 1958; Berlyne 1971). We know from previous ESM studies that a balance of challenges and skills in the foreground of awareness leads to intrinsically motivated flow experiences. The present study applies this same logic to implicit contextual conditions that are relevant for optimal experience.

A third way that higher intrinsic motivation may be resulting from an economical fit between extrasomatic and intrasomatic information is suggested by the biological concept of *neoteny*. Human children are born at the youngest age postconception and the earliest developmental stage in comparison with all other primates. This extreme dependency and delayed somatic development sets up a unique parent–child relationship whereby parents have to put the necessary energy into the instrumental activities of protection and resource management. This averts the need for rigid genetic determinism. There is an interrelation between dependence and autonomy in that greater neoteny leads to an increase in play behavior (freedom at the moment), which leads to a more elaborate development of the cerebral cortex and greater adult freedom and flexibility (Fagen 1981). Since play is considered by many thinkers to be the paradigmatic self-rewarding or autotelic experience (Ellis 1973), by providing an autotelic context parents are also providing a context that facilitates play. Here again an economical fit is found between extrasomatic opportunities and the biological predisposition for neoteny and play.

The quality of experience for the autotelic group is also more optimal at school, where they reported higher affect, cognitive efficiency, intrinsic motivation, and self-concept. These results, which are consistent with the at-home observations, reflect a superior economy of attention, but now outside of the home context. Unless one wishes to conclude that more optimal experience at school leads to more optimal experience at home, the observed advantage must be accounted for as a difference resulting from socialization in the autotelic family context. This socialized difference influences the interpretation and experience of the school environment.

Ryan and Grolnick (1986) have recently concluded that there are individual differences among elementary school children, probably due to long-term socialization differences, that result in different interpretations of classrooms as being conducive to intrinsic motivation. Findings in the present study help to explain how the socializing influence of the family may be affecting moment-to-moment experience at school. Earlier it was said that socialization affects what is experienced in the present as obvious and routine or as problematic (Schutz & Luckmann 1973). Adolescents whose experience at home has been organized by repeated activation and feedback with optimal amounts of choice, clarity, centering, commitment, and challenge, and whose previous contact with adult rule structures at home has generally been experienced as a good fit that facilitates optimal experience and flow, may think it obvious and routine to expect that the school will also provide conditions that fit with one's intrinsic motivation.

The two largest differences on the individual ESM items in school were that teens from the less autotelic families felt less good about themselves and less in control of their actions (see Table 21.3). In terms of their economy of attention, this group may be focusing on contextual problems at school. If boredom or anxiety were the obvious and routine conditions at home, they might be focusing on, for example, the lack of choice or the excess of choice at school. Much additional thought and research are needed to specify what individual differences may be developing over time as a result of constant exposure to one or the other of these contexts under study. Therefore the above observations about how the theorized economy of attention is functioning at school should be considered tentative.

It will be some time before the results of the longitudinal study reveal whether any of the currently observed differences will affect later school achievement. In view of the results, it may be surprising that both of these groups have been excelling at school. For now, the contrast provided by looking at experience with friends while doing relatively passive activities raises some provocative issues concerning how school achievement may be related to the theorized economy of attention. At this point there is no indication that the adolescents from the nonautotelic context enjoy being with their friends any more than the group from the autotelic context. However, the stark contrast between the positive experience they feel with their friends vs. the more negative environments they find at home or at school suggests that there may be more of an incentive for them to spend time with friends in passive leisure than there is for the adolescents who also find autotelic experience at home and in school. This is the insight of a recent study of high achievers (Csikszentmihalyi & Nakamura 1986; Nakamura, Chapter 19). High achievers enjoyed the company of friends, but also were involved with productive activities that provided positive experience. In the absence of clearly autotelic activities in other settings, the low achievers spent significantly more time socializing with friends. The talented group from the nonautotelic context may or may not turn out to be the low achievers. But this group may find it easier to be happy, alert, concentrating, and wishing to be doing their current activity when they are in relatively passive settings like watching television with their friends. Here positive experience is "cheaper" in the sense that it does not require attention or effort to make sense of the situation and to elicit meaningful feedback. This observation is consistent with previous points made about the effect of an autotelic context on the economy of attention.

In sum, observational studies of complex interaction systems like the family and school must rely on a continued specification of theory and continued empirical investigation from numerous angles if the attempt to draw a coherent picture of the processes involved is ever to be successful (Cook & Campbell 1979). The present approach to the investigation of the family – through the impact of the family's rule structure on the subjective experience of children – is a new approach with little previous research to draw on. This initial study has asked broad questions about a general family context before designing more specific questions and controlling for potential variables on which the groups may differ other than the family context. It is therefore to be expected, and it is understood here, that some aspects of the interpretation of this study and the implementation of further studies require additional thought. I have attempted to point out the weakest theoretical links and the most promising avenues for further research. This first look, however, reveals the great influence that a family context can have on the moment-to-moment quality of experience for a child. It also reveals that family contexts should not be viewed along an "objective" dimension like liberal vs. conservative, or permissive vs. authoritarian without taking into account the subjective impact of these contexts on the child's information processing or phenomenology. When moment-to-moment experience is taken into account, the decision to be liberal or conservative, for example, by providing a child with more choice or less choice, cannot be decided a priori to that moment. An autotelic family context is somehow sensitive enough to the child's experience that it is able to adjust and maintain the balance of conditions that facilitate the most rewarding experiences for that child.

22. The future of flow

MIHALY CSIKSZENTMIHALYI

At the end of this volume, it is time to assess the cumulative implications of the assembled evidence. What has been learned about flow in the 10 or so years since the model was first presented? The main conclusions, derived from a variety of different studies, seem rather robust. In the first place, it is clear that the flow experience is recognized as a phenomenological reality by people of all ages, both genders, diverse socioeconomic statuses, and very different cultures, and that it is considered a positive state of consciousness by everyone. Thus, we might conclude that flow is a panhuman, species-specific state of positive psychic functioning.

Second, both the Flow Questionnaires and the Experience Sampling Method point to the fact that flow is generally an *optimal* state. In flow, most of the dimensions of experience reach their positive peaks. The relationship between flow and optimal experience is present both in the short and in the long term; those who are in flow most often tend to have more positive experiences in the rest of their lives.

Third, the evidence suggests that there are large individual differences in the quantity and intensity of flow experienced by different persons. Some people appear to have "autotelic personalities" that make it easier for them to enjoy everyday life, and to transform routine and even threatening situations into challenging opportunities for action. A good start has been made to determine what the traits of such persons are, and how patterns of child-rearing might facilitate their development.

Fourth, there begins to be support for the contention that flow is important to the dynamics of cultural evolution. Both at the micro and at the macro level it is possible to show that order in consciousness provides motivation to repeat the activity that provided the experience of order, thereby replicating differentially those events that make flow possible. If a person enjoys programming computers, for instance, he or she will spend more time at it and will get increasingly more involved in programming, thereby replicating that skill and developing it to higher levels of complexity. At the same time, it seems that apathy, even though far from enjoyable, can also be a powerful motivator. This apparent paradox suggests new lines of conceptualization and research.

Fifth, given the possibility of using the ESM to assess the frequency of flow in everyday life, it has been possible to develop concepts and methods that lend themselves to evaluation and social critique. How much optimal experience is present in various jobs, in school, at home, in leisure? A strong beginning has been made in answering such questions, and the answers are not always what we expected to hear.

The rest of this chapter develops these five central themes in greater detail. And finally, some new questions suggested by these studies are put forth and a few conceptual and praxiological conclusions outlined.

The universality of flow

The main dimensions of flow – intense involvement, deep concentration, clarity of goals and feedback, loss of a sense of time, lack of self-consciousness and transcendence of a sense of self, leading to an autotelic, that is, intrinsically rewarding experience – are recognized in more or less the same form by people the world over. They constitute a "negentropic nucleus," an ordered state of consciousness valued for its own sake. The several cultural groups sampled in Chapter 4, the Japanese (Chapter 6), Koreans (Chapter 8), Alpine mountain farmers (Chapter 12), Australian sailors (Chapter 13), all recognize these parameters of consciousness as fitting descriptions of their own mental states at the times when they are doing what they most wish to be doing. Despite vast linguistic and cultural differences, the experience is perceived and described in similar ways.

Nor do age, gender, or social class make a difference in the perception of flow. The elderly Koreans in Chapter 8 recognize it as well as Japanese youth (Chapter 6), or the American and Italian teenagers described in Chapter 17. In all of the samples, men and women respond similarly to flow. Chapters 7, 12, and 20 specifically focus on the flow experiences of women and show the theoretically predicted relationships. Chapters 7 and 18 deal with differences in social class and occupations and indicate that regardless of status differences people think of flow in the same terms, and value it equally.

In addition to the conclusive similarity in the phenomenological structure of the experience across cultural and demographic boundaries, it appears that the conditions that make the experience happen are also the same. Specifically, a high level of opportunities for action, matched by an equally high level of personal capacities to act, is generally present when the flow experience takes place. This has been documented by the studies using the Flow Questionnaire (Chapters 4 and 12), and by all the chapters in Part IV that have used the ESM. Teengers and adults, men and women, Europeans and Americans, have almost exactly the same reactions to the ebb and flow of their skills in relation to the level of challenges in the environment.

Nor is this optimal experience available only to those fortunate to live a life of easy leisure. Several chapters amply document the fact that the intensity of the flow experience appears to be just as high for farmers who must eke out a precarious existence in the high mountains, for former drug addicts trying to return to a normal life, for students writing a paper, or for people stranded in life-threatening situations. Flow is not a luxury; it is a staple of life.

This uniformity in the *structure* of the experience does not imply a similarity in the *content* of the activities that produce the experience. Cultures differ from each other in the opportunities for action that they make available, and therefore in the forms of flow they make possible. For instance in the highly homogeneous and densely populated Japanese urban settings, one of the main challenges for a young person, especially if he or she is from a lower class family, is simply to be *seen*. It is easy to pass unnoticed, to blend into the crowd. This means that the self of a young person, deprived of information about its existence from the social environment, runs the risk of running out of psychic energy. Therefore one of the unique opportunities for action offered by the motorcycle gangs is *medatsu* – beeing seen, looking conspicuous. The motorcycle run provides a shot of attention to the anonymous youth, thereby contributing a particular form of enjoyment to the flow experience that would not be so enjoyable in a cultural setting where anonymity is not a problem.

Old Korean women enter the flow state when reading the Bible, when knitting, or when cooking an elaborate dinner; the Australian sailors when their boat loses sight of the shore; the young Japanese when their motorcyles begin to rumble in unison. The old Walse mountaineers seem to find it in almost every detail of their daily lives, whereas their children need special leisure activities and entertainments to experience it. These enormous differences in content suggest that every activity including work, child care, and study can produce the focused well-being that is characteristic of flow. If one understands the requirements and structural features of the experience, in theory any activity can be adapted to improve life by making it more enjoyable and meaningful.

But why should flow be a panhuman phenomenon? Why is it so rewarding despite great differences in culture, age, and social condition? These are not idle questions, considering how relatively few experiences are found to be generally rewarding. Universal "needs" such as hunger and sex, whose satisfaction uniformly produces pleasure, are few and far between.

Hunger, sex, the avoidance of pain and of extreme temperatures, are homeostatic mechanisms that propel the organism to action in order to ensure its own survival, and through reproduction, to ensure the survival of the species. When action is taken, pleasure is experienced; pleasure ensures that the organism will be motivated to repeat the behavior necessary to maintain its homeostatic balance. Thus pleasure is a universal experience, basic to the preservation of life, influencing the social structures and institutions of life in every culture and in each epoch.

Flow is not a homeostatic mechanism, but in other respects it very much seems to function like other universal sources of positive rewards, like food or sexuality. The function of flow is not to induce the organism to perform what it needs to survive and to reproduce. Rather, its function seems to be to induce the organism to *grow*. Not in the sense of ontogenetic development, or maturation, but in the sense of fullfilling the potentialities of the organism, and then going beyond even those limits. The universality of flow might be accounted for by the fact that it is a connection evolution has built into our nervous system: Whenever we are fully functioning, involved in a challenging activity that requires all our skills, and more, we feel a sense of great exhilaration. Because of this, we want to repeat the experience. But to feel the same exhilaration again, it is necessary to take on a slightly greater challenge, and to develop slightly greater skills. So the complexity of adaptation increases, propelled forward by the enjoyment it provides. It is through the flow experience that evolution tricks us to evolve further.

Flow and optimal experience

To act as the spearhead of growth, it is not enough for flow to be a *positive* state of consciousness. It should be an *optimal* experience, one of the best states – if not *the* best, then at least on a par with those, homeostatic rewards we call "pleasure." What does the evidence say about the quality of the flow experience?

The development of the Experience Sampling Method has made it possible to answer that question with a precision that would have been impossible even a few years ago. The ESM shows conclusively that if we define flow as those situations in which challenges and skills are both high and in balance, the quality of experience is definitely better than in other situations defined by relatively greater skills (boredom), by a preponderance of challenges (anxiety), or by a lack of both skills and challenges (apathy). Whether one measures the ratio of challenges and skills in terms of a 16-channel model, or in terms of 8- or 4-channel models, the evidence is similar, and in all the samples tested.

If only the four options of a 4-channel model are considered, then all samples show the most positive experiences, on all dimensions, in the quadrant where both challenges and skills are above the individual mean. At this level of resolution one sees a recruitment, a coming together of effortless thinking, feeling, and volition. At this level, the claim that flow is an optimal experience seems clearly vindicated.

When the finer resolution of an 8-channel model is used to inspect the data, some discrepancies from the predicted relationships appear. Flow is still always distinguished by a cluster of experiential dimensions that includes high levels of concentration, alertness, activity, strength, creativity, freedom, and openness. If this is enough to define an experience as "optimal," then the claim can be made that flow is an optimal experience even at this level of analysis. But, contrary to expectation, some of the samples tested did not report being happiest when challenges and skills were perfectly balanced (see Chapters 17 and 18). Among American teenagers, the sense of control, friendliness, cheerfulness, freedom, clarity, satisfaction, motivation, as well as happiness, were higher in situations in which skills were relatively higher than challenges (Chapter 17). Thus if these dimensions are to be included in the definition of what is optimal, it cannot be claimed that flow is always experienced as the best situation on every dimension.

This discrepancy suggests that not everyone is able to achieve that simultaneous recruitment of all dimensions of positive experience that is characteristic of flow – that "negentropic nucleus" of consciousness in which mental effort, happiness, sense of inner strength, and intrinsic motivation are at their peak, harmoniously focused on a difficult set of challenges. Apparently, some people are unable to achieve this congruence, at least in the activities of everyday life. For them the flow experience tends to become split into at least two components: mental effort and inner strength in high-challenge, high-skill contexts; happiness and motivation in situations in which the challenges are relatively fewer. In some leisure activities this split goes even further: When watching television, for instance, people are relatively happy and strongly motivated, although all the other dimensions of experience are extremely low, especially the levels of challenges and skills. In such cases, some of the characteristics of flow are deflected into a situation characterized by apathy. It is important to identify such differences, because they are likely to have important consequences. When the flow experience is split, its motivational force is bound to be reduced. A person who feels strong, active, and concentrated while working, but does not feel either happy or motivated, is likely to devote less energy to his task. At the macro level of analysis, the transmission of cultural values and practices will also be hindered if a sizable number of individuals cannot integrate the flow experience as they are performing their social roles.

The relationship of flow to the quality of experience is manifested in two ways: in the immediate phenomenological moment, and in its long-term consequences. So far we have discussed only the first of these two relationships. When we turn to the second, we find that the frequency of flowlike experiences is related to a better quality of experience in the longer run. Chapter 16 shows that the more time Italian teenagers spend in high-challenge, high-skill contexts, the more happy, cheerful, excited, and satisfied they feel in terms of their overall experiences. The same pattern was found by LeFevre with U.S. adult workers (Chapter 18), and by Wells with working mothers (Chapter 20). These findings suggest that flow not only improves momentary experiences, but helps build a better quality of life in its entirety. In this context another interesting point should be noted. In some of the samples studied, affect (i.e., happy, cheerful, friendly, and sociable) was not the highest during flow; yet in the same groups a long-term relationship between frequency of flow and positive affect was found (e.g., Chapter 18). Thus even if a person might not feel happiest in flow, the fact that he is able to approximate the flow experience often might increase his level of happiness in the rest of life.

One very important relationship between flow and quality of experience is the one that concerns self-esteem. As Wells has shown in Chapter 20, the self-esteem of women changes drastically moment by moment during the day, and it is significantly higher whenever challenges and skills are both higher than average. Women who spend more time in flow also have higher levels of self-esteem in their role as parents. This association between flow and a more positive sense of oneself is currently being replicated with U.S. adolescents in our Chicago laboratory, and with Italian adolescents in Milan. The results confirm overwhelmingly Wells's findings. It seems clear, as claimed in Chapter 2, that the strength of the self depends on the cumulative history of positive feedback one gets in high-challenge, high-skill interactions. It is impossible to develop a strong self by spending most of the time in situations of apathy, boredom, or anxiety.

The autotelic personality

Even though none of the contributions to this volume have dealt with the issue directly, many chapters show large differences in the frequency and the intensity with which people are able to approximate the flow state. Some of these differences might be attributed to situational variables that are more or less conducive to flow, such as more or less challenging jobs, or to overwhelming responsibilities at home. Certainly social role and social structure can greatly facilitate or hinder the individual's access to flow, as argued by, among others, Mitchell, Allison and Duncan, and Macbeth in this volume. And as the evidence in Chapter 12 shows, some traditional farming cultures have succeeded with time in developing a way of life that, like a great "game," makes everyday life challenging and enjoyable.

But even in very comparable situations, individual persons show great differences from each other in how much of their lives they are able to enjoy. This is well illustrated in Chapter 16, where Massimini and Carli present the case studies of Mariarita, a teenager who almost never was in flow, and her classmate Carlo, who reported being in flow one-third of the time. Similarly, Wells found that some of the mothers she studied were in flow only 4 percent of the week of sampling, whereas others were in flow 40 percent of the time. These figures are of course somewhat arbitrary, since they depend on how flow was measured and quantified. For example, if an 8-channel model were to be used instead of a 4-channel one, the definition of what counts as flow would be approximately halved. But whatever measure is used, the conclusion is still abundantly clear: There are large individual differences in the ability to experience flow.

This fact confirms an intuition that was already suggested in the last chapter of *Beyond Boredom and Anxiety* , namely, that in order to improve the quality of life, two complementary strategies are needed: first, to change social conditions so as to make them more conducive to flow; and second, to educate individuals so that they will be able to experience flow regardless of social conditions. Much could be done to improve institutions like school and work, family and urban life. At the same time, even amidst the most enticing opportunities for action some people will continue to stay bored, or feel anxious, unless they have learned to recognize challenges and trust their skills.

What makes some people able to avoid boredom and anxiety? What makes a person able to enjoy opportunities for action that others will ignore? At this point we still do not have much hard evidence on which to base a conclusive answer. The early neurophysiological studies of Dr. Jean Hamilton (1976, 1981) suggest that individuals who can turn boring situations into enjoyable ones process information in a peculiar way. It seems that when they concentrate on a task, their cortical activation level – measuring the mental effort they are expending – actually *decreases* from baseline, instead of increasing, as it normally should. This could be a neurological indication of one of the central components of the phenomenology of flow, a measure of that deep concentration on a limited stimulus field that excludes everything else from consciousness. Perhaps one characteristic that differentiates a person with an autotelic personality is this ability to concentrate more efficiently, with less effort. In contrast, it could be that persons who experience flow more rarely, those who feel more happy and motivated at lower levels of challenges, are those for whom concentration results in an increase of mental effort, which is tiring and exhausting.

Richard Logan in Chapter 10 suggests some other characteristics of the autotelic personality, from a different but complementary point of view. He argues that people who survive solitary ordeals by turning adversity into manageable challenges are individuals who seek to realize the potentialities of their self, and yet are free of the prevailing concern with the self as object. They are people concerned with *realizing* themselves through their thoughts and their actions; but they do not brood about who they are, or identify themselves inappropriately with all the injustices of the world. Extending this pattern to the "ordeal" of everyday life, Logan contends that the narcissistic preoccupation with oneself prevents people from recognizing opportunites and using skills, thereby breeding a lifestyle characterized by boredom and anxiety.

Logan's view is reminiscent of deCharms's (1968) distinction between people who see themselves as *origins*, and those who act as if they were *pawns*. The former believe that they are in control of their actions, whereas the latter believe that they are constantly being pushed around by outside forces. The origins tend to be intrinsically motivated, because they feel a sense of ownership of their actions. Thus everything they do is important because it is a manifestation of their own self that deserves concentration and effort even if nobody else thinks so. The pawns feel rewarded only when they get a valuable recompense for their actions from the outside, because they don't identify with what they do for its own sake. A similar argument has been proposed by Theresa Amabile (1983) to account for the intrinsic motivation of creative people, and by Deci and Ryan (1985) who link the concept of autonomy with intrinsic motivation. And we might recall again Wells's findings in Chapter 20, which suggest relationships of circular causality between flow and self-esteem: While flow experiences seem to strengthen the self, a stronger self might make it easier to experience flow. But why do some persons develop this autotelic personality, grounded in a sense of self-confidence and involvement in the world, whereas others close in on themselves, preoccupied with defending a self that takes fewer and fewer chances to grow?

Kevin Rathunde begins to provide some evidence about the ontogenesis of the autotelic personality in Chapter 21. He shows that teenagers who see their parents as providing choice, clarity, centering, commitment, and challenge in the family context are much more likely to report positive experiences than teenagers who perceive their parents as low on these attributes. A simple conclusion might be that flow is learned in the family. When family interaction is structured so as to make the flow experience more likely, children will develop the skills necessary to turn everyday life situations into enjoyable, growth-producing opportunities. The characteristics of autotelic families as defined by Rathunde overlap, in part, with the criteria of hardiness as described by Kobasa, Maddi, and Kahn (1982), Kobasa, Maddi, and Zola (1983), and by Maddi and Kobasa (1984). They claim that adults who show control, commitment, and a responsiveness to challenges in their lives are healthier, more resistant to stress, and incidentally are also more intrinsically motivated.

It is still too early for a conclusive statement about the autotelic personality. There is no doubt that some people enjoy challenging, growth-producing interactions more than others. It also seems clear that such persons have a better sense of self-esteem, are less preoccupied with themselves, and had the good fortune to grow up in families that taught them how to enjoy life. They might also have a more efficient way of processing information that is either genetically inherited, or developed through practice over time. We need to learn much more about this configuration of traits that suggests, to use Toynbee's phrase, the presence of a "creative minority" that might be responsible to a degree disproportionate to its numbers for the direction in which culture evolves.

Optimal experience and exceptional performance

It takes intrinsic motivation to break through to new levels of complexity in thought or behavior. In general, the social environment does not dispose of sufficient extrinsic rewards to motivate people to spend the huge amounts of psychic energy necessary for mastering a set of complex skills, for confronting new challenges. Thus unless a person enjoys the process, he or she is unlikely to take the risk of crossing an unexplored frontier. Amabile (1983) has argued that creative individuals are highly autotelic, and that concern with extrinsic rewards often interferes with their creativity. A good illustration of how this process works is found in the recent doctoral dissertation of Jean Carney (1986). She scored the projective tests of a group of talented fine art students studied in 1963 by Getzels and Csikszentmihalyi (1976), for content indicating concern for extrinsic and for intrinsic rewards. She found that 20 years after the completion of the tests, almost none of the male artists who had high scores on extrinsic motivation were still producing art. The only ones who did so were the few lucky ones who had been successful right from the beginning. But the great majority of young artists had to struggle for a long time before achieving some recognition. During those lean years, the artists who were extrinsically motivated gradually shifted their commitment from fine art to safer and better remunerated activities; they became contractors, salesmen, or commercial artists. Only those who had started out with a disregard for fame and fortune, and who found their rewards in the making of art itself, persevered long enough to be eventually recognized. To the extent that other fields of creative achievement also provide unpredictable and delayed extrinsic rewards, it makes sense to conclude that an autotelic personality helps to make creativity possible.

Not only creativity, but any skill that requires complex behavior – and hence a great concentration of psychic energy – depends to a large extent on intrinsic motivation. For example, it is unlikely that a person will become a good musician unless he or she enjoys playing music; the skill is so demanding that extrinsic rewards alone could not sustain a person in it for long. Nakamura in Chapter 19 begins to show the divergence between two groups of equally talented young mathematicians: Those who have learned to enjoy doing math continue to improve; those who are either bored or anxious when doing math have stopped developing these particular skills. Here, as in other fields, cognitive abilities do not guarantee success; unless a person likes doing what he or she is good at doing, that skill will not develop.

One detailed view of how flow improves complex achievement is provided by Larson's study of high school students coping with a writing assignment (Chapter 9). Students who were bored by the assignment wrote boring essays, those who were anxious about the assignment wrote essays that were disconnected. The students whose imagination was stirred by the topic, who began to enjoy playing around with the ideas and with the prose, wrote papers that arrested the readers' attention. These findings raise a more general issue: What is the relationship between optimal experience and performance?

Most people are unimpressed by the fact that flow provides an optimal subjective experience, but their interest immediately perks up at any suggestion that it might improve performance. If it could be demonstrated that a fullback played harder if he was in flow, or that an engineer turned in a better product if he was in flow, then they would immediately embrace the concept and make a great deal of it. This, of course, would effectively destroy the autotelic nature of the experience. As soon as the emphasis shifts from the experience per se to what you can accomplish with it, we are back in the realm of everyday life ruled by extrinsic considerations.

Thus, although it is almost certainly true that any performance improves when it provides intrinsic rewards, and that this would be fairly easy to demonstrate (along the lines of the studies reported in Chapters 9 and 19), it is probably better to downplay this connection. At a recent conference in which a group of teachers extolled the importance of intrinsic motivation for learning, a behaviorist on the panel suggested that token economies be introduced in schools to increase intrinsic motivation. After all, he argued, children can be made to do anything with a judicious reinforcement schedule, so they can also be taught to become more intrinsically motivated through appropriate rewards. I must confess that such reasoning boggles my mind. But if the emphasis moves from the experience of flow to the performance it can achieve, similar attempts at perverting the nature of the experience will certainly multiply.

One of the most exciting possibilities of the flow theory concerns its application as a tool for historical interpretation. Thus far psychology has not been of great help to the followers of Clio. Compared to the impact of historical materialism, for instance, psychoanalysis has barely made a ripple in helping explain causation in history. The brief review by Isabella Csikszentmihalyi of how the Jesuit order spread in the 16th and 17th centuries (Chapter 14) provides an alternative perspective on other movements that have left their impact on history. The claim is that, other things being equal, people opt for social arrangements or for idea systems that will make their experience of life more coherent and enjoyable. The flow model provides a conceptual framework for testing this proposition. The perspective is probably most useful in explaining the kinds of changes that are relatively free, that are not constrained by immediate survival pressures. For instance, Kuhn's (1970) description of what motivates paradigm shifts in science is very compatible with our model. He argues that the best way to understand why young scientists begin to reject the ideas of their elders and to seek new ways to represent their field is that the challenges of "normal" science become too tame. Within a well-understood theoretical paradigm the play of ideas becomes stagnant; the excitement of discovery is replaced by routine application. Boredom, the inability to experience flow within the existing set of rules, is perhaps the most powerful impetus for the revision of old theories, a revision that involves the recognition of new challenges, which in turn requires the refinement of new skills.

In Chapter 4, Massimini, Csikszentmihalyi, and Delle Fave begin to show how the theory of optimal experience could help to research the process by which individual decisions add up to produce cultural change. In communities such as the Walse, or the Navajo in Arizona, the struggle for the survival of the culture goes on every day. If young people begin to get bored by the language, the values, or the ways of making a living practiced by their elders, these units of information are not going to be transmitted to the next generation. The same process takes place, in a less obviously visible form, in our culture as well. If drugs provide more enjoyment than work, addictive behavior will be overreproduced in relation to productive activities.

Flow and social justice

One of the basic problems every society must solve is how to motivate people to perform the actions necessary for the maintenance of the social system. A fair distribution of rewards is thus a prerequisite of a well-integrated society. This fact is generally well understood as far as extrinsic rewards are concerned. We agree that property should be protected, that appropriate wages should be paid for labor, that taxes should be as fair as possible. But we seldom ask, how well are intrinsic rewards distributed? Does the average worker, the average housewife get any enjoyment from the activities of everyday life?

A few Utopian political theorists, like Tommaso Campanella in the 17th century, or Jean Jacques Rousseau a hundred years later, had conceived of societies in which the subjective well-being of each citizen was the primary concern. And of course the drafters of the Declaration of Independence went as far as listing "the pursuit of happiness" among the inalienable rights of men, right after life and liberty. In fact, it does not take long to realize that even "life" and "liberty" are not very meaningful unless they allow for the pursuit of happiness. Thus the pursuit of happiness – or, in terms of the present argument, the improvement of the quality of experience – is in many ways the ultimate goal that gives meaning to all other subsidiary goals; it is the "bottom line" of existence.

Even Karl Marx initially became interested in the power differential built into property because he realized that those who lacked economic freedom were less able to control their experiences, and thus their consciousness could be exploited by the owners of the means of production. Paradoxically, historical materialism is based on concern for the quality of experience. But despite these noble precedents, we still know very little about what inequalities in the quality of experience may be lurking in the structures of our society. The census tells us how many people own how much, what the educational level of the country is, and what the health status is of various subgroups of the population. We know much less about how well people are doing in terms of the pursuit of happiness. It is true that the census now includes so-called subjective indicators, which try to assess the degree of satisfaction with different domains of life, and with life as a whole. These measures are still rather coarse, however, and in any case not many politicians have taken them very seriously so far.

The flow model provides a framework for beginning to talk with greater precision about elusive concepts like the "quality of life." Perhaps its most important contribution is to point out that just being satisfied with current conditions cannot be a good indicator of positive experience in the long run. Optimal experience requires increasing challenges and the development of skills apace. Life is meaningful only when people feel that the psychic energy they expend in the course of daily life strengthens their self. Growth must be factored into the equation for a good life.

When the perspective afforded by the flow model is applied to an analysis of the quality of life, the resulting picture turns out to be more complex than expected. On the one hand, the critiques of Mitchell (Chapter 3), Sato (Chapter 6), Allison and Duncan (Chapter 7), and Macbeth (Chapter 13) have a credible ring of authenticity. In one way or another, these authors show how difficult it is to find enjoyment in the situations of everyday life. The opportunities for experience made possible by the technological organization of life are often boring. Having given up on binding ethical rules, chaos threatens from the margins of awareness, resulting in frequent attacks of anxiety. Contemporary consciousness oscillates between anomie and alienation, or anxiety and boredom. The main culprit, according to the critics, is the organization of productive labor: the 9-to-5 grind, the hassles of dead-end jobs. Mitchell suggests that leisure pursuits are one avenue of escape people find into realms of experience that are ordered as well as challenging; Macbeth describes forms of escape that turn into an entire way of life. The Japanese *bosozoku* enact a public symbolic ritual that gives a dramaturgical reality to their desire for meaningful action; whereas the blue-collar working women described by Allison and Duncan retreat into the privacy of their home to savor moments of domestic contentment.

On the other hand, the findings of the Experience Sampling Studies present a different picture. The adult workers studied by LeFevre (Chapter 18), the working mothers that Wells reported on (Chapter 20), were more often in flow at work than in the rest of their lives. The obligatory structure of the high school, resented as it is by teenagers, is still the most consistent provider of flow experiences in the lives of students (Chapters 16, 17, and 19).

How can these differences be reconciled? Are study and work, those ubiquitous demands imposed by social life, a blessing or a curse? One way to account for the divergence is to recognize that when interpreting facts, personal values and assumptions play a primary role. Just as in seeing a glass with water half-way up to the rim it is equally appropriate to say: "That glass is half full" as it is to say: "That glass is half empty," in evaluating the ESM data one might say with equal justification that things are fine, because the obligatory roles of student and worker provide some of the best experiences in people's lives; or one might say that things are in terrible shape, because some of the best experiences in people's lives come from dull jobs and stifling schools.

But the data might be telling us something more profound than that. The relative poverty of experience in free time, the emptiness of most leisure, seems to say that people in our society – or perhaps in all societies – are unprepared to confront free time. When left alone to their own devices most people panic. Unstructured time, those portions of the day when there are no clear demands on psychic energy, are even worse than the time we spend doing alienating labor. We all want to have more free time: But when we get it we don't know what to do with it. Most dimensions of experience deteriorate: People report being more passive, irritable, sad, weak, and so forth. To fill the void in consciousness, people turn on the TV or find some other way of structuring experience vicariously. These passive leisure activities take the worst edge off the threat of chaos, but leave the individual feeling weak and enervated.

Who is to blame for this situation? It is too easy, and probably unfair, to place the blame on "technology," or "capitalism," or that convenient scapegoat, "modern society." After all, the Greeks were already aware that leisure did not come naturally, that it was a difficult art in need of constant cultivation. In more recent times we have assumed that if only people had free time, they would be happy. But free time by itself brings no improvement to the quality of experience. In fact the mind, deprived of external structures for ordering its activity, begins to wander and loses its focus: Randomness prevails in consciousness. The consequence is a deterioration, rather than an improvement in the quality of experience.

In Chapter 12 Massimini and Delle Fave describe people who seem to be working from morning to night, seven days a week, yet flow appears to permeate everything they are doing. In traditional cultures such as the Walse and the Occitans the distinction between work and leisure is blurred. Everything they do is something that needs to be done, that is useful and that has meaning. At the same time, everything they do is done freely and with a view of maximizing the enjoyment of the act. Boredom is avoided by filling up the hours with new challenges, and anxiety is minimized by cultivating skills that help master the environment. For those who have become adapted to this environment, a dull moment is inconceivable. But the fragility of their adaptation is shown by the predicament of the younger generations in these cultures, who appear to have lost their elders' ability to transform the entirety of life into a smooth flow activity. The hope is that perhaps, with time and thought, modern cultures will also sort out which elements of their daily experience aid in producing psychic negentropy and find ways of structuring them into the majority of the activities in their lives.

These considerations suggest that the pursuit of happiness will remain fruitless as long as it is limited to changing the material conditions of existence. No matter how rich and comfortable we get, no matter how much time we are able to free from obligations, the quality of experience is not going to improve one bit unless we learn to invest our psychic energy in ways that will bring intrinsic rewards. From this perspective a good society is one that succeeds in providing a meaningful plan for the investment of psychic energy, an investment that brings enjoyment to every act of daily life, and that allows for the growth of complexity in consciousness for as many of its people as possible. "Equality of opportunity" does not apply only to access to material resources and to power, but also to those opportunities for action that, in conjunction with a person's abilities, make it possible for a person to develop his or her potentialities and to enjoy interaction with the world.

The way of personal growth

Although it is important to keep struggling for the transformation of society – for the development of new values more conducive to a meaningful life, the maximizing of equalities of opportunity, the improvement of jobs and schools, the cultivation of active leisure – it is equally important to begin transforming one's own life along the same lines. It might take a few more thousand years for humanity to realize in the structures of its economic and social institutions the conditions for optimal experience. In the meantime, however, each person can learn to improve the quality of his or her own life, without having to wait for the rest of the world to catch up.

In trying to implement the implications of the flow theory, one of the most difficult things to achieve, either at the conceptual or at the applied level, is a right balance between efforts to change the objective context of experience and efforts to change the subjective interpretation of experience. For example, if one expended effort in trying to change working conditions to bring variety and challenge to boring jobs, one might be exposed to the criticism that this is a waste of time, since it is the subjective construction of the experience that counts. On the other hand, if one were to focus exclusively on the education of consciousness in order to facilitate the flow experience without attempting at the same time to improve external conditions, one would be open to the equally just accusation of a reactionary idealism. And in fact the concept of flow has been occasionally criticized for being too idealistic by materialists, and for being too materialistic by idealists. Often these criticisms are based on misunderstandings, or on too literal and limited interpretations of the dynamics of flow.

One of the most interesting of these criticisms is William Sun's (1987) comparison of the concept of flow and the concept of *Yu* developed in the fourth century B.C. writings of the Taoist thinker Chuang-tzu. *Yu* refers to the right way of following the path, or Tao. Watson (1964) translates it as "wandering"; Crandall (1983) as "walking without touching the ground"; Sun (1987) as "to swim," "to fly," or "to *flow*." In any case, *Yu* is the way Chuang-tzu believes people should live – without concern for external rewards, spontaneously, with full commitment – in short, as a total autotelic experience.

But there is an important difference between *Yu* and flow, in Sun's estimation. He sees the first as a typical Eastern concept, in that it is to be attained entirely by a private effort of consciousness leading to a final liberation of the will, and a transcendence of individuality merging into a superhuman field of energy. In contrast, flow is a typically Western concept in that it hinges on the balancing of external challenges and objective skills. Flow can be only attained, Sun writes, if the external conditions are optimal. And thus, paradoxically, the ancient and mystical *Yu* is a more realistic option than the allegedly pragmatic flow, because it is impossible to reform the world whereas it is possible to reshape consciousness.

As an example of the different approaches to *Yu* and to flow, he cites the well-know parable of Cook Ting from the *Inner Chapters* of the writings of Chuang-tzu. Ting was cook to Lord Hui of Wei:

> Cook Ting was cutting up an ox for Lord Wen-hui. At every touch of his hand, every heave of his shoulder, every move of his

feet, every thrust of his knee – zip! zoop! He slithered the knife along with a zing, and all was in perfect rhythm, as though he were performing the dance of the Mulberry Grove or keeping time to the Ching-shou music. (Watson 1964, p. 46)

Lord Wen-hui is fascinated by how much flow (or *Yu*) his cook gets from his work, and compliments his great skill. But Cook Ting denies that it is a matter of skill: "What I care about is the Way, which goes beyond skill." Then he describes how he achieves his superb performance: a sort of mystical, intuitive understanding of how the ox is put together, which allows Ting to cut it apart with automatic ease: "Perception and understanding have come to a stop and spirit moves where it wants." It is on this example that Sun bases his contrasts with flow: "In this parable, one can see no exciting challenge but peaceful and artistic work of routine" (Sun 1987, p.10). Hence, "only those who enjoy routine work can transform wordly activities into transcendental experience" (p. 12) and "Chuang-tzu only wants to change man's subjective attitude towards worldly life in favor of spiritual playfulness, he never has the extravagant hope of changing objective society in terms of . . . *Yu*" (p. 14).

But how is this transformation of wordly activity into transcendental experience, this spiritual playfulness, to be accomplished? Chuang-tzu offers a very valuable insight, which Sun fails to quote. In fact the paragraph in question is very interesting, for it has given rise to diametrically opposite interpretations. In Watson's translation, it reads as follows:

> However, whenever I come to a complicated place, I size up the difficulties, tell myself to watch out and be careful, keep my eyes on what I'm doing, work very slowly, and move my knife with the greatest of subtley, until – flop! the whole thing comes apart like a clod of earth crumbling to the ground. I stand there holding the knife and look all around me, completely satisfied and reluctant to move on, and then I wipe off the knife and put it away. (Watson 1964, p.47)

Now some earlier scholars take this passage to refer to the working methods of a mediocre carver who does not *Yu* (Waley 1939, p. 73). Presumably Mr. Sun would agree with them. Other more recent ones, like Watson (1964) and like Graham (see Crandall 1983) believe that it refers to Cook Ting's own working methods. In my opinion, the latter reading must be the correct one – not because I know anything about Chinese or about Taoism, but simply from knowledge of the flow experience. It shows that even after all the obvious levels of skill and craft (*chi*) have been left behind, the *Yu* still depends on the discovery of new challenges (the "complicated place" or "difficulties" in the above quotation), and on the development of new skills ("Watch out and be careful, keep my eyes on what I am doing . . . move my knife with the greatest of subtlety").

In other words, the mystical heights of the *Yu* are not attained by some superhuman quantum jump, but simply by the gradual focusing of attention on the opportunities for action in one's environment, which results in a perfection of skills that with time becomes so thoroughly automatic as to seem spontaneous and otherworldly. The performance of a great violinist or of a great mathematician seems equally uncanny, even though it can be explained by the incremental honing of challenges and skills. It is important, however, that Sun has introduced us to Cook Ting: He is certainly an excellent example of how one can find flow in the most unlikely places, in the most humble activities of daily life. And it is also humbling to realize that over 22 centuries ago the dynamics of this experience were so well known.

The point is that the external and the internal approaches to improving the quality of experience are not in opposition to each other. It seems silly to argue which one is *the* right way, when obviously both are necessary. Without concrete challenges, a set of skills, a symbolic discipline, it is impossible to focus attention long enough on a limited stimulus field to begin experiencing flow. Cook Ting may have surpassed the butcher's craft, but without it he would have never started to *Yu*. In other words, the opportunities for action must be there. At the same time, it is also true than no matter how many possibilities the environment offers, one cannot enter flow unless the challenges become personally meaningful, unless they are engaged by one's psychic energy. The rock walls of Yosemite are nothing but grey stone to most people; to the climber, they are an endlessly fascinating delight.

Those who lent their voices to this volume – the West Coast mountaineers, the ocean cruisers, the motorized knights of modern Japan, the farmers of the Alps, the old Koreans, the working mothers of Chicago, the young classical scholars of Milan – and yes, even the Jesuits of centuries ago – have all found ways of joining the dance that Lord Wen-hui witnessed over two thousand years ago. They have found ways to express the potentialities of their being in synchrony with the environment, growing as they learn what is the Self and what is the

Other through patterns of action that relate the two in seamless interaction.

This knowledge must be preserved and increased if human life is to be more than a brief physiological interlude to be endured with a minimum of discomfort. In addition to the people who have found a way to create flow in their lives, there are all too many who have no conception of what they are missing. As the studies of experience in everyday life clearly show, in their hard-won free time most people sink into a state of apathy that brings no joy and leads to no awakening. Drugged by structured information – if not by chemical means – consciousness loses its freedom to initiate action. It becomes what mechanistic psychologists have said all along it was – a passive plaything of outside forces. Ten years after flow first began to be studied systematically, we understand a little better how consciousness can be freed to build a world more suited to its freedom. Let us hope the next decade will be just as fruitful.

References

Adair, J. (1982). *Construction and validation of an instrument designed to assess states of consciousness during movement activity.* Unpublished doctoral dissertation, Temple University.

Adams, D. (1969). Analysis of Life Satisfaction Index. *Journal of Gerontology, 24,* 470–4.

Aebli, H. (1985). Zur Einfuhrung. In M. Csikszentmihalyi, *Das flow-Erlebnis: Jenseits von Angst und Langeweile im Tun Aufgehen.* Stuttgart: Klett-Cotta.

Ainsworth, M. D. S., Bell, S. M., & Stayton, D. J. (1971). Individual differences in strange-situation behavior of one-year-olds. In H. R. Schaffer (Ed.), *The origins of human social relations.* London: Academic Press.

Alloy, L. B., & Abramson, L. Y. (1979). Judgement and contingency in depressed and nondepressed students: sadder but wiser. *Journal of Experimental Psychology, General, 108,* 441–85.

Amabile, T. M. (1983). *The social psychology of creativity.* New York: Springer-Verlag.

Argyle, M. (1987). *The psychology of happiness.* London: Methuen.

Atkinson, R. C., & Shiffrin, R. M. (1968). Human memory: a proposed system and its control processes. In K. Spence & J. Spence (Eds.), *The psychology of learning and motivation* (Vol. 2). New York: Academic Press.

Averill, J. R. (1980). Emotion and anxiety: sociocultural, biological, and psychological determinants. In A. O. Rorty (Ed.), *Explaining emotions* (pp. 37–72). Berkeley: University of California Press.

Bacon, A. W. (1975). Leisure and the alienated worker: a critical assessment of three radical theories of work and leisure. *Journal of Leisure Research, 7* (3), 178–90.

Bakhtin, M. (1968). *Rabelais and his world* (H. Iswosky, Trans.). Cambridge, MA: MIT Press.

Balint, M. (1959). *Thrills and regressions.* London: Hogarth.

Ball, Donald. (1972). What the action is: a cross-cultural approach. *Journal for the Theory of Social Behavior, 2,* 121–43.

Bandura, A. (1977). Self-efficacy: toward a unifying theory of behavioral change. *Psychological Review , 84,* 191–215.

Bandura, A. (1978). The self system in reciprocal determinism. *American Psychologist, 33,* 344–58.

Bandura, A., & Schunk, D. H. (1981). Cultivating competence, self-efficacy, and intrinsic interest through proximal self-motivation. *Journal of Personality and Social Psychology, 41,* 586–98.

384

Bangert, W. V., S.J. (1972). *A history of the society of Jesus*. St. Louis, MO: Institute of Jesuit Sources.

Barakat, H. (1969). Alienation: a process of encounter between utopia and reality. *British Journal of Sociology* , 20, 1–20.

Barthel, M. (1984). *The Jesuits: history and legend of the Society of Jesus* (M. Howson, Trans.). New York: Wm. Morrow.

Barton, A., & Lazarfeld, P. (1969). Qualitative support of theory. In G. McCall & J. Simmons (Eds.), *Issues in participant observations* (pp. 239–244). Boston, MA: Addison-Wesley.

Bauman, R. (1975). Verbal act as performance. *American Anthropologist, 77*, 290–312.

Baumrind, D. (1977). *Socialization determinants of personal agency*. Paper presented at the biennial meetings of the Society for Research in Child Development, New Orleans.

Beach, F. A. (1945). Current concepts of play in animals. *American Naturalist, 79*, 523–41.

Beck, A. T. (1967). *Depression: clinical, experimental, and theoretical aspects*. New York: Harper & Row.

Beck, A. T. (1976). *Cognitive therapy and emotional disorders*. New York: International Universities Press.

Becker, G. (1976). *The economic approach to human behavior*. Chicago: University of Chicago Press.

Becker, W. (1964). Consequences of different kinds of parental discipline. In M. L. Hoffman & L. W. Hoffman (Eds.), *Review of child development research* (Vol.1). New York: Russell Sage Foundation.

Begly, G. C. (1979). *A self-report measure to assess flow in physical activities*. Unpublished M.S. thesis, Pennsylvania State University.

Bekoff, M. (1972). The development of social interaction, play, and metacommunication in mammals: an ethological perspective. *Quarterly Review of Biology, 47* (4), 412–34.

Bekoff, M. (1978). Social play: structure, function, and the evolution of a cooperative social behavior. In G. M. Burghardt & M. Bekoff (Eds.), *The development of behavior: comparative and evolutionary aspects*. New York: Garland Press.

Bem, D. J. (1967). Self-perception: an alternative interpretation of cognitive dissonance phenomena. *Psychological Review, 74*, 183–200.

Bem, D. J. (1972). Self-perception theory. In L. Berkowitz (Ed.), *Advances in experimental and social psychology* (Vol. 6). New York: Academic Press.

Berger, J. L., & Schreyer, R. (1986). *The experiential aspects of recreation*. Logan: Utah State University, Department of Forest Resources.

Berger, P. L., & Luckmann, T. (1967). *The social construction of reality*. Garden City, NY: Anchor Books.

Berger, P. L., Berger, B., & Kellner, H. (1973). *The homeless mind: modernization and consciousness*. Harmondsworth: Penguin.

Berk, S. F. (1980). *Women and household labor*. Beverly Hills, CA: Sage.

Berk, R., & Berk, S. F. (1979). *Labor and leisure at home*. Beverly Hills, CA: Sage.

Berlyne, D. E. (1960). *Conflict, arousal, and curiosity*. New York: McGraw Hill.

Berlyne, D. E. (1966). Exploration and curiosity. *Science, 153*, 25–33.

Berlyne, D. E. (1971). *Aesthetics and psychobiology*. New York: Appleton-Century-Crofts.

Bettelheim, B. (1987). The importance of play. *The Atlantic*, March, pp. 35–46.

Bettelheim, B. (1943). Individual and mass behavior in extreme situations. *Journal of Abnormal and Social Psychology, 38,* 417–52.

Biggart, N. W. (1980). *Authentic experience in a rationalized world: an ethnography of vacation resorts.* Paper presented to the Pacific Sociological Association section on Leisure, Games, and Play, Portland, Oregon.

Bills, R. D., Vance, E. L., & McLean, O. S. (1951). An index of adjustment and values. *Journal of Consulting Psychology, 15,* 257–61.

Blackler, F., & Shimmin, S. (1984). *Applying psychology in organizations.* London: Methuen & Co.

Blauner, R. (1970). Social alienation. In Simon Marcson (Ed.), *Automation, alienation and anomie* (pp. 96–198). New York: Harper and Row.

Bloch, M. (1967). *Land and work in medieval Europe.* Berkeley: University of California Press.

Bloch, P. H. (1986). Product enthusiasm: many questions, a few answers. *Advances in Consumer Research, 6,* 539–43.

Bloch, P. H., & Bruce, G. D. (1984). The leisure experience and consumer products: an investigation of underlying satisfactions. *Journal of Leisure Research, 16* (1), 74–88.

Blumberg, S. H., & Izard, C. E. (1985). Affective and cognitive characteristics of depression in 10- and 11-year-old children. *Journal of Personality and Social Psychology, 49,* 194–202.

Boehmer, H. (1975). *The Jesuits: an historical study.* New York: Gordon Press.

Bowen, E. S. (pseud. of Laura Bohannan). (1954). *Return to laughter.* New York: Harper & Bros.

Boyd, R., & Richerson, P. J. (1985). *Culture and the evolutionary process.* Chicago: University of Chicago Press.

Bratton, R. D., Kinnear, G. K., & Koroluk, G. (1979). Reasons for climbing: a study of the Calgary Section. *The Canadian Alpine Journal, 62,* 55–57.

Broadbent, D. E. (1958). *Perception and communication.* New York: Pergamon Press.

Brodrick, J., S.J. (1947). *The progress of the Jesuits (1556–79).* London: Longmans, Green.

Brodrick, J., S.J. (1971). *The origin of the Jesuits.* Westport, CT: Greenwood Press.

Bronfenbrenner, U. (1961). Toward a theoretical model for the analysis of parent–child relationships in a social context. In J. B. Glidwell (Ed.), *Parental attitudes and child behavior.* Springfield, IL: Charles C. Thomas.

Burhoe, R. W. (1982). Pleasure and reason as adaptations to nature's requirements. *Zygon , 17* (2), 113–31.

Burney, C. (1952). *Solitary confinement.* London: Macmillan.

Butler, R. H., & Alexander, H. M. (1955). Daily patterns of visual exploratory behavior in the monkey. *Journal of Comparative and Physiological Psychology, 48,* 247–9.

Byrd, R. (1938). *Alone.* New York: Putnam.

Cabanac, M. (1971). Physiological role of pleasure. *Science, 173,* 1103–7.

Caillois, R. (1958). *Les jeux et les hommes.* Paris: Gallimard.

Caillois, R. (1961). *Man, play and games.* New York: The Free Press.

Cantril, H. (1965). *The pattern of human concerns.* New Brunswick, NJ: Rutgers University Press.

Carli, M. (1986). Selezione psicologica e qualita dell'esperienza. In F. Massimini & P. Inghilleri (Eds.), *L'esperienza quotidiana* (pp. 285–304). Milan: Franco Angeli.

Carney, J. (1986). *Intrinsic motivation in successful artists from early adulthood to middle age.* Unpublished doctoral dissertation, University of Chicago.
Carrington, P. (1977). *Freedom in meditation.* New York: Doubleday Anchor.
Carver, C. S., & Scheier, M. F. (1981). *Attention and self-regulation: A control theory approach to human behavior.* New York: Springer-Verlag.
Charriere, H. (1970). *Papillon.* New York: Morrow.
Cheska, A. T. (Ed.). (1981). *Play as context.* West Point, NY: Leisure Press.
Chiba, K. (1975). *Bosozoku* [Motorcycle gangs]. Tokyo: Nihon Keizai Shimbunsha.
Chomsky, N. (1965). *Aspects of the theory of syntax.* Cambridge, MA: MIT Press.
Coburn, D. (1975). Job-worker incongruence: consequences for health. *Journal of Health and Social Behavior, 16* (2), 213–25.
Cook, T. D., & Campbell, D. T. (1979). *Quasi-experimentation: design and analysis issues for field settings.* Boston: Houghton Mifflin.
Cooley, C. H. (1912). *Social organization: a study of the larger mind.* New York: Charles Scribner's Sons.
Craik, F., & Lockhart, R. (1972). Levels of processing: a framework for memory research. *Journal of Verbal Learning and Verbal Behavior, 11,* 671–84.
Crandall, M. (1983). On walking without touching the ground: "play" in the *Inner Chapters* of the *Chuang-Tzu.* In V. H. Muir (Ed.), *Experimental essays on Chuang-Tzu* (pp. 101–23). Honolulu: University of Hawaii Press.
Crealock, W. I. B. (1951). *Vagabonding under sail.* New York: David McKay (Paperback 1978).
Crook, J. H. (1980). *The evolution of human consciousness.* New York: Oxford University Press.
Csikszentmihalyi, I. (1968). *The Jesuits and education in Poland, 1565–1773.* Unpublished master's paper, University of Chicago.
Csikszentmihalyi, I. (1986). Il flusso di coscienza in un contesto storico: il caso dei gesuiti. In F. Massimini & P. Inghilleri (Eds.), *L'esperienza quotidiana.* (pp. 181–96). Milan: Franco Angeli.
Csikszentmihalyi, M. (1965). *Artistic problems and their solution: an exploration of creativity in the arts.* Unpublished doctoral dissertation, University of Chicago.
Csikszentmihalyi, M. (1969). The Americanization of rock climbing. *University of Chicago Magazine, 61* (6), 20–7.
Csikszentmihalyi, M. (1974). *Flow: studies in enjoyment.* PHS Grant Report N. RO1HM 22883–02.
Csikszentmihalyi, M. (1975a). Play and intrinsic rewards. *Journal of Humanistic Psychology, 15* (3), 41–63.
Csikszentmihalyi, M. (1975b). *Beyond Boredom and Anxiety.* San Francisco: Jossey-Bass.
Csikszentmihalyi, M. (1978a). Attention and the wholistic approach to behavior. In K. S. Pope & J. L. Singer (Eds.), *The stream of consciousness* (pp. 335–58). New York: Plenum.
Csikszentmihalyi, M. (1978b). Intrinsic rewards and emergent motivation. In M. R. Lepper & D. Greene (Eds.), *The hidden costs of reward.* New York: Erlbaum.
Csikszentmihalyi, M. (1979). The concept of flow. In B. Sutton-Smith (Ed.), *Play and learning* (pp. 335–58). New York: Wiley.
Csikszentmihalyi, M. (1981a). Leisure and socialization. *Social Forces, 60,* 332–40.

Csikszentmihalyi, M. (1981b). Some paradoxes in the definition of play. In A. Cheska (Ed.), *Play as context* (pp. 14–26). New York: Leisure Press.

Csikszentmihalyi, M. (1982a). Towards a psychology of optimal experience. In L. Wheeler (Ed.), *Review of personality and social psychology* (Vol. 2). Beverly Hills, CA: Sage.

Csikszentmihalyi, M. (1982b). Learning, flow, and happiness. In R. Gross (Ed.), *Invitation to life-long learning* (pp.167–87). New York: Fowlett.

Csikszentmihalyi, M. (1982c). Intrinsic motivation and effective teaching: a flow analysis. In J. Bess (Ed.), *Motivating professors to teach effectively* (pp. 15–26). San Francisco: Jossey-Bass.

Csikszentmihalyi, M. (1985a). Emergent motivation and the evolution of the self. In D. Kleiber & M. H. Maehr (Eds.), *Motivation in adulthood* (pp. 93–113). Greenwich, CT: JAI Press.

Csikszentmihalyi, M. (1985b). Reflections on enjoyment. *Perspectives in Biology and Medicine, 28* (4), 469–97.

Csikszentmihalyi, M. (1986). L'Insegnamento e la trasmissione dei memi. In F. Massimini & P. Inghilleri (Eds.), *L'Esperienza quotidiana*. Milano: Franco Angeli.

Csikszentmihalyi, M. (1987a). The flow experience. In M. Eliade (Ed.), *The Encyclopedia of Religion* (Vol. 5, pp. 361–3). New York: Macmillan.

Csikszentmihalyi, M. (1987b). *On the relationship between cultural evolution and human welfare*. Paper presented at the AAAS meetings, Chicago, February.

Csikszentmihalyi, M. (in press). Motivation and creativity: towards a synthesis of structural and energistic approaches to cognition. *New Ideas in Psychology*.

Csikszentmihalyi, M., & Beattie, O. (1979). Life themes: a theoretical and empirical exploration of their origins and effects. *Journal of Humanistic Psychology, 19*, 45–63.

Csikszentmihalyi, M., & Bennett, H. S. (1971). An exploratory model of play. *American Anthropologist, 73* (1), 45–58.

Csikszentmihalyi, M., & Figurski, T. (1982). Self-awareness and aversive experience in everyday life. *Journal of Personality, 50*, 15–28.

Csikszentmihalyi, M., & Graef, R. (1979). Flow and the quality of experience in everyday life. Unpublished manuscript, University of Chicago.

Csikszentmihalyi, M., & Graef, R. (1980). The experience of freedom in daily life. *American Journal of Community Psychology, 8*, 401–14.

Csikszentmihalyi, M., & Larson, R. (1978). Intrinsic rewards in school crime. *Crime and Delinquency, 24*, 322–35.

Csikszentmihalyi, M., & Larson, R. (1984) *Being adolescent: conflict and growth in the teenage years*. New York: Basic Books.

Csikszentmihalyi, M., & Larson, R. (1987). Validity and reliability of the Experience-Sampling Method. *The Journal of Nervous and Mental Disease, 175* (9), 526–36.

Csikszentmihalyi, M., & McCormack, J. (1986). The influence of teachers. *Phi Delta Kappan*, February, 415–19.

Csikszentmihalyi, M., & Massimini, F. (1985). On the psychological selection of bio-cultural information. *New Ideas in Psychology, 3*(2), 115–38.

Csikszentmihalyi, M., & Nakamura, J. (1986). Optimal experience and the uses of talent. Paper presented at the 94th Annual Meeting of the American Psychological Association. Washington, DC, August.

Csikszentmihalyi, M., & Robinson, R. (1986). Culture, time, and the development of talent. In R. J. Sternberg & J. E. Davidson (Eds.), *Conceptions of giftedness* (pp. 264–84). New York: Cambridge University Press.

Csikszentmihalyi, M., & Rochberg-Halton, E. (1981). *The meaning of things: domestic symbols and the self.* New York: Cambridge University Press.

Csikszentmihalyi, M., Larson, R., & Prescott, S. (1977). The ecology of adolescent activity and experience. *Journal of Youth and Adolescence, 6,* 281–94.

Daly, J. A., & Miller, M. D. (1975). The empirical development of an instrument to measure writing apprehension. *Research in the Teaching of English, 9,* 242–9.

Daly, M. (1982). Some caveats about cultural transmission models. *Human Ecology, 10,* 401–8.

Davis, K. (1940). The sociology of parent-youth conflict. *American Sociological Review, 5,* 523–35.

Davis, K. (1988). *Rehearsing the audience.* Urbana, IL: National Council of Teachers of English.

Davis, K., & Moore, W. E. (1945). Some principles of stratification. *American Sociological Review, 10* (2), 242–9.

Davis, L. E., & Cherns, A. B. (1975). *The quality of working life.* New York: The Free Press.

Davis, M. S. (1977). Beyond boredom and anxiety: a review. *Contemporary Sociology, 6* (2), 197–9.

Dawkins, R. (1976). *The selfish gene.* New York: Oxford University Press.

Day, H. I., Berlyne, D. E., & Hunt, D. E. (Eds.). (1971). *Intrinsic motivation: a new direction in education.* New York: Holt.

deCharms, R. (1968). *Personal causation: the internal affective determinants of behavior.* New York: Academic Press.

deCharms, R. (1976). Enhancing motivation: change in the classroom. New York: Irvington.

deCharms, R., & Muir, M. S. (1978). Motivation: social approaches. *Annual Review of Psychology, 29,* 91–113.

Deci, E. L. (1971). Effects of externally mediated rewards on intrinsic motivation. *Journal of Personality and Social Psychology, 18,* 105–15.

Deci, E. L. (1972). Intrinsic motivation, extrinsic reinforcement, and inequity. *Journal of Personality and Social Psychology, 22* (1), 113–20.

Deci, E. L. (1975). *Intrinsic motivation.* New York: Plenum.

Deci, E. L., & Ryan, R. M. (1985). *Intrinsic motivation and self-determination in human behavior.* New York: Plenum Press.

Dember, W. N. (1974). Motivation and the cognitive revolution. *American Psychologist, 29,* 161–8.

Denzin, N. (1978). *The research act.* New York: McGraw-Hill.

Devereux, E. (1970). Socialization in cross-cultural perspective: comparative study of England, Germany, and the United States. In R. Hill & R. Konig (Eds.), *Families in East and West: socialization process and kinship ties* (pp. 72–106). Paris: Mouton.

Devereux, E., Bronfenbrenner, U., & Rogers, R. (1969). Child rearing in England and the United States: a cross-national comparison. *Journal of Marriage and the Family,* May, 257–70.

Diener, E. (1984). Subjective well-being. *Psychological Bulletin, 95,* 542–75.

Diener, E., Horwitz, J., & Emmons, R. A. (1985). Happiness of the very wealthy. *Social Indicators Research, 16,* 263–74.

Dostoyevsky, F. (1957). *The brothers Karamazov* (C. Garnett, Trans.). New York: Signet Classics. (Original work published in 1879–80.)

Dowdall, C. B., & Colangelo, N. (1982). Underachieving gifted students: review and implications. *Gifted Child Quarterly, 26* (4), 179–84.

Dubin, R., Champoux, J., & Porter, L. (1975). Central life interest and organization commitment of blue-collar and clerical workers. *Administration Science Quarterly, 20,* 411–21.

Dumazedier, J. (1985). *Sociologie empirique du loisir. Critique et contre-critique de la civilisation du loisir.* Paris: Editions du Seuil.

Durkheim, E. (1947). *The division of labor in society.* New York: The Free Press. (Original work published in 1893)

Durkheim, E. (1951). *Suicide.* New York: The Free Press. (Original work published in 1897)

Durkheim, E. (1967). *The elementary forms of religious life.* New York: The Free Press. (Original work published in 1912)

Easterbrook, J. (1959). The effect of emotion on cue utilization and the organization of behavior. *Psychological Review, 66,* 183–201.

Eckblad, G. (1981). *Scheme theory: a conceptual framework for cognitive-motivational processes.* London: Academic Press.

Edwards, J., & Klemmack, D. (1973). Correlates of life satisfaction: a re-examination. *Journal of Gerontology, 28,* 492–502.

Egger, G. (1981). *The sport drug.* Sydney: George Allen & Unwin.

Ekman, P. (1972). Universals and cultural differences in facial expressions of emotions. In *Current theory in research on motivation, Nebraska symposium on motivation* (Vol. 19, pp. 207–83). Lincoln: University of Nebraska Press.

Ellis, M. J. (1973). *Why people play.* Englewood Cliffs, NJ: Prentice Hall.

Eysenck, M. W. (1982). *Attention and arousal.* Berlin: Springer Verlag.

Fagen, R. M. (1981). *Animal play behavior.* New York: Oxford University Press.

Fenichel, O. (1951). On the psychology of boredom. In D. Rapaport (Ed.), *Organization and pathology of thought* (pp. 349–61). New York: Columbia University Press.

Festinger, L. (1954). A theory of social comparison processes. *Human Relations, 7,* 117–40.

Feuer, L. (1963). What is alienation? In M. Stein & A. Vidich (Eds.), *Sociology on Trial* (pp. 127–47). Englewood Cliffs, NJ: Prentice-Hall.

Finn, J. D., & Bock, R. D. (1985). *Multivariate VII manual.* Chicago, IL: National Educational Resources.

Fiske, D. W. (1971). *Measuring the concept of personality.* Chicago, IL: Aldine.

Fiske, D. W., & Maddi, S. R. (1961). *Functions of varied experience.* Homewood, IL: The Dorsey Press.

Fortune, R. F. (1963). *Sorcerers of Dobu.* New York: Dutton. (Original work published in 1932)

Foss, M. (1969). *The founding of the Jesuits, 1540.* London: Hamish Hamilton.

Francis, L. (1987). *Chess talk in Washington Park: control in a miniature world.* Paper presented at the meetings of The Anthropological Association for the Study of Play. Montreal, March.

Frankl, V. (1963). *Man's search for meaning.* New York: Washington Square.

Frankl, V. (1978). *The unheard cry for meaning.* New York: Simon & Schuster.

Freedman, D. G. (1979). *Human sociobiology: a holistic approach.* New York: Macmillan/Free Press.

Freedman, D. G. (1984). Village fissioning, human diversity, and ethnocentrism. *Journal of Political Psychology, 5,* 629–34.

French, J. R. P., & Kahn, R. L. (1962). A programmatic approach to studying the industrial environment and mental health. *Journal of Social Issues, 18* (January), 1–47.

Freud, S. (1961). *Civilization and its discontents.* New York: Norton.

Frijda, N. H. (1986). *The emotions.* New York: Cambridge University Press.

Gallina, A. (1986). Essere adolescenti a Milano: una comparazione tra ragazzi e regazze. In F. Massimini & P. Inghilleri (Eds.), *L'esperienza quotidiana* (pp. 273–84). Milan: Franco Angeli.

Ganss, G. E., S.J. (1970). *The constitutions of the Society of Jesus.* St. Louis, MO: The Institute of Jesuit Sources.

Garvey, C. (1977). *Play.* Cambridge, MA: Harvard University Press.

Gerth, H. H., & Mills, C. W. (Eds.). (1946). *From Max Weber.* New York: Oxford University Press.

Getzels, J. W., & Csikszentmihalyi, M. (1976). *The creative vision: a longitudinal study of problem finding in art.* New York: Wiley Interscience.

Getzels, J. W., & Jackson, P. W. (1962). *Creativity and intelligence: explorations with gifted students.* New York: Wiley.

Gibaud-Wallston, J., & Wandersman, L. P. (1978). *Development and utility of the parenting sense of competence scale.* Paper presented at the annual meetings of the American Psychological Association, Toronto, August.

Giddens, A. (1971). *Capitalism and modern social theory.* London: Cambridge University Press.

Glaser, B., & Strauss, A. (1967). *The discovery of grounded theory.* Chicago: Aldine.

Glaser, D. (1978). *Crime in our changing society.* New York: Holt, Rinehart and Winston.

Goffman, E. (1967). *Interaction ritual.* New York: Doubleday Anchor Books.

Goffman, E. (1974). *Frame analysis.* New York: Harper & Row.

Gottfried, A. E. (1985). Academic intrinsic motivation in elementary and junior high school students. *Journal of Educational Psychology, 77* (6), 631–45.

Graef, R. (1978). *An analysis of the person by situation interaction through repeated measures.* Unpublished doctoral dissertation, University of Chicago.

Graham, A. C. (1983). Notes on the composition of Chuang-Tzu. Quoted in M. Crandall, On walking without touching the ground, pp. 101–23, in V. H. Muir, *Experimental essays on the Chuang-Tzu.* Honolulu: University of Hawaii Press.

Gray, H. R. (1977). *Enjoyment dimensions of favorite leisure activities of middle- and old-aged adults based on the flow model.* Unpublished doctoral dissertation, Pennsylvania State University.

Grazia, S. de. (1962). *Of time, work, and leisure.* Garden City, NY: Doubleday.

Greene, D., & Lepper, M. R. (1974). Effects of extrinsic rewards on children's subsequent interests. *Child Development, 45,* 1141–5.

Griffith, B. (1979). *Blue water: a guide to self-reliant sailboat cruising.* Boston: Sail Books.

Guttmann, A. (1978). *From ritual to record.* New York: Columbia University Press.

Hamilton, J. A. (1976). Attention and intrinsic rewards in the control of psychophysiological states. *Psychotherapy and Psychosomatics, 27,* 54–61.

Hamilton, J. A. (1981). Attention, personality, and self-regulation of mood: absorbing interest and boredom. In B. A. Maher (Ed.), *Progress in experimental personality research, 10,* 282–315.

Hamilton, J. A., Holcomb, H. H., & De la Pena, A. (1977). Selective attention and eye movements while viewing reversible figures. *Perceptual and Motor Skills, 44,* 639–44.

Hamilton, M. (1982). Symptoms and assessment of depression. In E. S. Paykel (Ed.), *Handbook of affective disorders.* New York: Guilford Press.

Hannerz, U. (1969). *Soulside.* New York: Columbia University Press.

Harlow, H. F. (1953). Mice, monkeys, men, and motives. *Psychological Review,* *60,* 23–32.

Harris, D. V. (1972). Stress-seeking and sport involvement. In D. V. Harris (Ed.), *Women and sport: a national research conference* (pp. 71–89). Pennsylvania State University, HPER series 2.

Harris, J. C., & Park, R. J. (Eds.). (1983). *Play, games, and sports.* Champaign, IL: Human Kinesics.

Harrison, A., & Minor, J. (1978). Interrole conflict, coping strategies, and role satisfaction among black working women. *Journal of Marriage and the Family,* *40,* 799–805.

Harrison, A., & Minor, J. (1982). Interrole conflict, coping strategies, and role satisfaction among single and married employed mothers. *Psychology of Women Quarterly, 6* (3), 354–60.

Hasher, L., & Zacks, R. T. (1979). Automatic and effortful processes in memory. *Journal of Experimental Psychology: General, 108,* 356–88.

Havighurst, R., & Albrecht, R. (1953). *Older People.* New York: Longman & Green.

Hebb, D. O. (1955). Drive and the CNS. *Psychological Review* (July), 243–52.

Hebb, D. O. (1966). *The organization of behavior.* New York: Wiley & Sons.

Heider, F. (1958). *The psychology of interpersonal relations.* New York: Wiley.

Herzberg, F. (1966). *Work and the nature of man.* Cleveland, OH: World.

Hesse, S. (1979). Women working: historical trends. In K. Feinstein (Ed.), *Working women and families* (pp. 35–62). Beverly Hills, CA: Sage.

Hilgard, E. (1980). The trilogy of mind: cognition, affection, and conation. *Journal of the History of the Behavioral Sciences, 16,* 107–17.

Hilliard, D. C.(1987). *Risk, control, and competition: Structure and experience in recreational settings.* Paper presented at the meetings of The Anthropological Association for the Study of Play. Montreal, March.

Hiscock, E. C. (1968). *Atlantic cruise in Wanderer III.* London: Oxford University Press.

Hoffman, J. E., Nelson, B., & Houck, M. R. (1983). The role of attentional resources in automatic detection. *Cognitive Psychology, 51,* 379–410.

Hogan, T. (1980). Students' interests in writing activities. *Research in the Teaching of English, 14,* 119–26.

Hollingshead, A. B. (1957). *Two factor index of social position.* New Haven, CT: August B. Hollingshead.

Hollis, C. (1968). *A history of the Society of Jesus.* London: Weidenfeld and Nicolson.

Homusho [Ministry of Justice]. (1983). *Showa 58 Nendo Hanzai Hakusho* [1983 White Paper on Crime]. Tokyo: Okurasho Insatsukyoku.

Hormuth, S. E. (1986). The sampling of experiences in situ. *Journal of Personality, 54* (1), 262–93.

Hoyt, D. R., Karser, M. A., Perters, G. R., & Babchuck, N. (1980). Life satisfaction and activity theory: a multidimensional approach. *Journal of Gerontology, 35,* 935–41.

Huizinga, J. (1970). *Homo ludens: a study of the play element in culture.* New York: Harper & Row. (Original work published in 1939)

Hunt, J. McV. (1965). Intrinsic motivation and its role in psychological development. In D. Levine (Ed.), *Nebraska Symposium on Motivation* (Vol. 12, pp. 189–282). Lincoln: University of Nebraska Press.

Ingham, R. (1986). Psychological contributions to the study of leisure – Part one. *Leisure Studies, 5,* 255–79.

Inghilleri, P. (1986). La teoria del flusso di coscienza: esperienza ottimale e sviluppo del se. In F. Massimini & P. Inghilleri (Eds.), *L'esperienza quotidiana* (pp. 85–106). Milan: Franco Angeli.

Iso-Ahola, S. E. (1979). Basic definitions of leisure. *Journal of Leisure Research, 11* (11), 28–39.

Iso-Ahola, S. E. (1980). *The social psychology of leisure and recreation.* Dubuque, IO: Wm. C. Brown.

Izard, C. E. (1971). *The face of emotion.* New York: Appleton-Century-Crofts.

Izard, C. E. (1977). *Human emotions.* New York: Plenum.

Izard, C. E., Kagan, J., & Zajonc, R. B. (1984). *Emotions, cognition, and behavior.* New York: Cambridge University Press.

Jackson, G. (1973). *Surviving the long night.* New York: Vanguard.

James, W. (1890). *Principles of psychology: Vol. 1.* New York: Henry Holt.

Jenkins, T. M. (1979). Perfume in the ozone. *Summit* (June-July), 20–1, 24–5, 29–30.

Johnson, F. (Ed.). (1973). *Alienation.* New York: Seminar Press.

Kabanoff, B. (1980). Work and nonwork: a review of models, methods, and findings. *Psychological Bulletin, 88* (1), 60–77.

Kabanoff, B., & Obrien, G. (1982). Relationship between work and leisure attributes across occupational and sex groups in Australia. *Australian Journal of Psychology, 34* (2), 165–82.

Kahneman, D. (1973). *Attention and effort.* Englewood Cliffs, NJ: Prentice-Hall.

Kando, T., & Summers, W. (1971). The impact of work on leisure. *Pacific Sociological Review, 14* (July), 310–27.

Kaneto, Y. (1981). *Shonen no Boryoku* [Violence of Adolescents]. Tokyo: Tachibana Shobo.

Kant, I. (1978). *Anthropology* (V. L. Dowdell, Trans.). Carbondale, IL: Southern Illinois University Press. (Original work published 1798)

Karasek, R. A. (1979). Job demands, job decision, latitude and mental strain: implications for job redesign. *Administrative Science Quarterly, 24,* 285–308.

Keisatsucho [National Police Agency]. (1981). *Showa 56 Nendo Keisatsu Hakusho* [1981 white paper on the police]. Tokyo: Okurasho Insatskyoku.

Keisatsucho [National Police Agency]. (1983). *Showa 58 Nendo Keisatsu Hakusho* [1983 white paper on the police]. Tokyo: Okurasho Insatsukyoku.

Keisatsucho [National Police Agency]. (1984). *Showa 59 Nendo Keisatsu Hakusho* [1984 white paper on the police]. Tokyo: Okurasho Insatsukyoku.

Kelley, H. H. (1967). Attribution theory in social psychology. In D. Levine (Ed.), *Nebraska symposium on motivation* (Vol. 15). Lincoln: University of Nebraska Press.

Kelley, H. H. (1973). The processes of causal attribution. *American Psychologist, 28,* 107–28.

Kelly, J. R. (1982). *Leisure.* Englewood Cliffs, NJ: Prentice-Hall.

Kelly, J. R. (1986). *Freedom to be: a new sociology of leisure.* New York: Macmillan.

Kikuchi, K. (1981). Bosozoku ni tsuiteno Ichi Kosatsu [A treatise on motorcycle gangs]. *Katei Saibansho Geppo,* July,106–25.

Kleiber, D. A. (1980). The meaning of power in sport. *International Journal of Sport Psychology, 11* (1), 34–41.

Kleiber, D. A. (1981). Searching for enjoyment in children's sports. *The Physical Educator 38,* 86–93.

Kleiber, D. A. (1985). Developmental premises for adult involvement in adolescent leisure. *World Leisure and Recreation, 27* (6), 10–14.

Kleiber, D. A. (1986). Motivational reorientation in adulthood and the resources of leisure. In D. Kleiber & M. Maehr (Eds.), *Motivation and adulthood*. Greenwich, CT: JAI Press.

Kleiber, D. A., & Barnett, L. A. (1980). Leisure in childhood. *Young Children*, July, 47–53.

Knapp, M. R. J. (1976). Predicting the dimensions of life satisfaction. *Journal of Gerontology, 31*, 595–604.

Knox-Johnston, R. (1969). *A world of my own*. London: Cassell.

Kobasa, S. C., Maddi, S. R., & Kahn, S. (1982). Hardiness and health: a prospective study. *Journal of Personality and Social Psychology, 42* , 168–77.

Kobasa, S. C., Maddi, S. R., & Zola, M. A. (1983). Type A and hardiness. *Journal of Behavioral Medicine, 6*, 41–51.

Koh, D., Sakauye, K., Koh, D., & Murata, A. (1981). *Assessing and enhancing the adaptive capabilities of elderly immigrants from Asia: a methodological note*. Unpublished manuscript, University of Illinois Medical Center.

Kohut, H. (1978). *The search for the self*. New York: International Universities Press.

Kubey, R., & Csikszentmihalyi, M. (In press). *Mirror of the mind*.

Kuhn, T. S. (1970). *The structure of scientific revolutions* (2d. ed.). Chicago: University of Chicago Press.

Langer, S. (1957). *Philosophy in a new key*. Cambridge, MA: Harvard University Press.

Larson, R. (1978). Thirty years of research on the subjective well-being of older Americans. *Journal of Gerontology, 33*, 109–24.

Larson, R., & Csikszentmihalyi, M. (1982). The praxis of autonomous learning. Unpublished manuscript, University of Chicago.

Larson, R., & Csikszentmihalyi, M. (1983). The Experience Sampling Method. In H. T. Reis (Ed.), *Naturalistic approaches to studying social interaction (New Directions for Methodology of Social and Behavioral Science, No. 15)*. San Francisco, CA: Jossey-Bass.

Larson, R., Csikszentmihalyi, M., & Graef, R. (1980). Mood variability and the psychosocial adjustment of adolescents. *Journal of Youth and Adolescence, 9*, 469–90.

Larson, R., Hecker, B., & Norem, J. (1985). Students' experience with research projects: pains, enjoyment and success. *The High School Journal*, Oct.-Nov., 61–9.

Lasch, C. (1978). *The culture of narcissism*. New York: W. W. Norton.

Leary, J. P. (1977). White guy's stories of the night street. *Journal of the Folklore Institute, 14*, 59–71.

Leeper, R. W. (1975). Some needed developments in the motivational theory of emotions. In E. Levine (Ed.), *Nebraska symposium on motivation* (Vol. 13). Lincoln: University of Nebraska Press.

Le Guay, L. (1975). *Sailing free*. Sydney: Ure Smith.

Lepper, M. R., & Greene, D. (1975). Turning play into work: effects of adult surveillance and extrinsic rewards on children's intrinsic motivation. *Journal of Personality and Social Psychology, 31* (3), 479–86.

Lepper, M. R., & Greene, D. (Eds.). (1978). *The hidden costs of reward: new perspectives on the psychology of human motivation*. Hillsdale, NJ: Lawrence Erlbaum.

Lepper, M. R., Greene, D., & Nisbett, R. E. (1973). Undermining children's intrinsic interest with extrinsic reward: a test of the "overjustification" hypothesis. *Journal of Personality and Social Psychology, 28* (1), 129–37.

Lester, J. (1983). Wrestling with the self on Mt. Everest. *Journal of Humanistic Psychology, 23* (2), 31–41.

Levi-Strauss, C. (1966). *The savage mind.* Chicago: University of Chicago Press.

Lewinsohn, P. M., & Libet, J. (1972). Pleasant events, activity schedules, and depression. *Journal of Abnormal Psychology, 79,* 291–5.

Lewis, D. (1967). *Daughters of the wind.* London: Gollancz.

Lewis, D. (1969). *Children of three oceans.* London: Collins.

Lewis, D. (1977). *Ice bird.* New York: Fontana.

Liberman, A. M., Mattingly, I. G., & Turvey, M. T. (1972). Language codes and memory codes. In A. W. Melton & E. Martin (Eds.), *Coding processes in human memory.* New York: John Wiley.

Lindbergh, C. (1953). *The Spirit of St. Louis.* New York: Scribner.

Linder, S. (1970). *The harried leisure class.* New York: Columbia University Press.

Lloyd, J., & Barenblatt, L. (1984). Intrinsic intellectuality: its relation to social class, intelligence, and achievement. *Journal of Personality and Social Psychology, 46* (3), 646–54.

Lohman, N. (1977). Correlations of life satisfaction, morale and adjustment measures. *Journal of Gerontology, 32,* 73–5.

Lunn, A. (1957). *A century of mountaineering.* London: George Allen & Unwin.

Lyman, S. M., & Scott, M. B. (1970). Accounts. In S. M. Lyman & M. B. Scott (Eds.), *A sociology of the absurd* (pp. 111–43). New York: Appleton-Century-Crofts.

Maccoby, E. E. (1980). *Social development: psychological growth and the parent-child relationship.* San Diego, CA: Harcourt Brace Jovanovich.

MacPhillamy, D. J., & Lewinsohn, P. M. (1974). Depression as a function of levels of desired and obtained pleasure. *Journal of Abnormal Psychology, 83,* 651–7.

Maddi, S. R., & Kobasa, S. C. (1984). *The hardy executive: health under stress.* Homewood, IL: Dow-Jones.

Main, M. (1973). *Play, exploration and competence as related to child-adult attachment.* Unpublished doctoral dissertation, Johns Hopkins University.

Malik, S. (1985). *Crime and leisure time in the Kingdom of Saudi Arabia.* Rijadh: Ministry of the Interior, Publications of the Center for Crime Research.

Malone, T. W. (1980). *What makes things fun to learn? A study of intrinsically motivating computer games.* Palo Alto, CA: Xerox Research Center, Cognitive and Instructional Science Series.

Mandler, G. (1975). *Man and emotion.* New York: Wiley.

Mann, Z. B. (1978). *Fair winds and far places.* Minneapolis, MN: Dillon Press.

Mannell, R. C. (1979). A conceptual and experimental basis for research in the psychology of leisure. *Society and Leisure, 2,* 179–96.

Mannell, R. C., & Bradley, W. (1986). Does greater freedom always lead to greater leisure? Testing the person × environment model of freedom and leisure. *Journal of Leisure Research, 18,* 4.

Mansfield, P. (1982). Women and work. *Health Education, 13* (5), 5–8.

Marx, K. (1956). *Karl Marx: selected writings in sociology and social philosophy* (T. B. Bottomore & Maximilien Rubel, Eds.). London: Watts.

Maslow, A. (1965). Humanistic science and transcendent experience. *Journal of Humanistic Psychology, 5* (2), 219–27.

Maslow, A. (1968). *Toward a psychology of being.* New York: Van Nostrand.

Massimini, F. (1979a). *I presupposti teoretici e osservativi del paradigma della selezione culturale. Primo contributo: Il doppio sistema ereditario.* Milan: Ghedini.

Massimini, F. (1979b). *I presupposti teoretici e osservativi del paradigma della selezione culturale. Secondo contributo: Le comunita ed emergenza del secondo sistema ereditaria.* Milan: Ghedini.

Massimini, F. (1982). Individuo e ambiente: I papua Kapauku della Nuova Guinea occidentale. In F. Perussia (Ed.), *Psicologia ed ecologia.* (pp. 27–154). Milan: Franco Angeli.

Massimini, F. (1986). Reply to the commentaries by Freedman, Martin and Milgram, Ryan and Deci, and Stettner. *New Ideas in Psychology,* Vol. 2.

Massimini, F., & Calegari, C. (1979). *Il contesto normativo sociale: Teoria e metodo di analisi.* Milan: F. Angeli Editore.

Massimini, F., & Carli, M. (1986). La selezione psicologica umana tra biologia e cultura. In F. Massimini & P. Inghilleri (Eds.), *L'esperienza quotidiana* (pp. 65–84). Milan: Franco Angeli.

Massimini, F., & Inghilleri, P. (1986). *L'Esperienza quotidiana: teoria e metodo d'analisi.* Milan: Franco Angeli.

Massimini, F., Csikszentmihalyi, M., & Carli, M. (1987). The monitoring of optimal experience: a tool for psychiatric rehabilitation. *Journal of Nervous and Mental Disease, 175* (9), 545–9.

Massimini, F., Csikszentmihalyi, M., & Delle Fave, A. (1986). Selezione psicologica e flusso di coscienza. In F. Massimini & P. Inghilleri (Eds.), *L'esperienza quotidiana* (pp. 133–80). Milan: Franco Angeli.

Matas, L., Arend, R. A., & Sroufe, L. A. (1978). Continuity of adaptation in the second year: the relationship between quality of attachment and later competence. *Child Development, 49,* 547–56.

Matza, D. (1964). *Delinquency and drift.* New York: Wiley.

Mayers, P. (1978). *Flow in adolescence and its relation to the school experience.* Unpublished doctoral dissertation, University of Chicago.

Mead, G. H. (1938). *The philosophy of the act* (C. W. Morris, Ed.). Chicago: University of Chicago Press.

Mead, G. H. (1970). *Mind, self and society* (C. W. Morris, Ed.). Chicago: University of Chicago Press. (Original work published 1934)

Mermod, M. (1973). *The voyage of the Geneve* (J. Hoare, Trans.). London: John Murray Ltd. (First published in French 1968)

Merton, R. K. (1938). Social structure and anomie. *American Sociological Review,* 3 (October), 672–82.

Merton, R. K. (1957). *Social theory and social structure.* Glencoe, IL: The Free Press.

Miller, G. A. (1956). The magical number seven, plus or minus two: some limits on our capacity to process information. *Psychological Review, 63,* 81–97.

Mitchell, R. G., Jr. (1983). *Mountain experience: the psychology and sociology of adventure.* Chicago: University of Chicago Press.

Moitessier, B. (1971). *The long way* (W. Rodarmor, Trans.). England: Granada.

Murdock, G. P. (1967). *Ethnographic atlas.* Pittsburgh: University of Pittsburgh Press.

Murphy, G. E., Simons, A. D., Wetzel, R. D., & Lustman, P. J. (1984). Cognitive therapy and pharmacotherapy: singly and together in the treatment of depression. *Archives of General Psychiatry, 41,* 33–41.

Nagayama, Y., et al. (1981). *Bosozoku Mondai ni kansuru Chosa Hokokusha* [Report on motorcycle gang problem]. Osaka: Osaka Bosozoku Mondai Kenkyukai.

Nakabe, H. (Ed.) (1979). *Bosozoku Hyakunin no Shissoo* [The run of 100 motorcycle gangs]. Tokyo: Daisan Shokan.

Neisser, U. (1967). *Cognitive psychology*. New York: Appleton-Century-Crofts.

Neisser, U., Hirst, W., & Spelke, E. S. (1981). Limited capacity theories and the notion of automaticity: reply to Lucas and Bub. *Journal of Experimental Psychology: General, 110* (4), 499–500.

Neugarten, B., Havighurst, R., & Tobin, S. S. (1961). The measurement of life satisfaction. *Journal of Gerontology, 16,* 134–43.

Neulinger, J. (1981a). *The psychology of leisure*. Springfield, IL: Charles Thomas.

Neulinger, J. (1981b). *To leisure*. Boston: Allyn & Bacon.

Neulinger, J., & Raps, C. (1972). Leisure attitudes of an intellectual elite. *Journal of Leisure Research, 4* (3), 192–207.

Nietzsche, F. (1964). *Thus spake Zarathustra* (R. J. Hollingdale, Trans.). New York: Penguin. (Original work published in 1885)

Noe, F. (1971). Autonomous spheres of leisure activity for industrial executive and the blue collarite. *Journal of Leisure Research, 3* (4), 220–49.

Norman, D. A. (1976). *Memory and attention*. New York: Wiley.

Nusbaum, H. C., & Schwab, E. C. (Eds.). (1986). The role of attention and active processing in speech perception. In *Pattern recognition by humans and machines* (Vol. 1, pp. 113–57). New York: Academic Press.

Nussbaum, F. L. (1953). *The triumph of science and reason, 1660–1685*. New York: Harper and Brothers.

Oakley, A. (1980). Reflections on the study of household labor. In S. Berk (Ed.), *Women and household labor*. Beverly Hills, CA: Sage.

Ogg, D. (1960). *Europe in the seventeenth century*. New York: Collier Books.

Olson, D., Bell, R., & Porter, J. (1982). *Family adaptability and cohesion evaluation scales II*. St. Paul: University of Minnesota Publications, Family Social Science Department.

Omark, D. R., Strayer, F. F., & Freedman, D. G. (1980). *Dominance relations*. New York: Garland Press.

Orme, J. E. (1969). *Time, experience, and behavior*. London: Iliffe Books.

Pardey, L., & Pardey, L. (1982). *The self-sufficient sailor*. New York: Norton.

Parker, S. (1971). *The future of work and leisure*. New York: Praeger.

Parsons, T. (1951). *The social system*. Glencoe, IL: The Free Press.

Pearson, K. (1979). *Surfing subcultures*. St. Lucia, Aust.: Queensland University Press.

Peplau, L. A., & Perlman, D. (Eds.). (1982). *Loneliness: a sourcebook of research and theory* . New York: Wiley Interscience.

Pfeiffer, E. (1976). *Multidimensional functional assessment: the OARS methodology*. Durham, NC: Duke University Center of the Study of Aging and Human Development.

Piaget, J. (1951). *Play, dreams and imitation in childhood*. Routledge & Kegan Paul.

Piaget, J. (1962). *Play, dreams and imitation in childhood*. New York: W. W. Norton.

Piaget, J. (1981). *Intelligence and affectivity* (T. A. Brown & C. E. Kaegi, Trans.). Palo Alto, CA: Annual Reviews.

Pirsig, R. (1977). Cruising blues and their cure. *Esquire, 87* (5), 65–8.

Plihal, J. E. (1982). *Intrinsic rewards in teaching*. Unpublished doctoral dissertation, University of Chicago.

Pope, K. S., & Singer, J. L. (1978). *The stream of consciousness*. New York: Plenum.

Popper, K. R. (1965). *The logic of scientific discovery*. New York: Harper Torchbooks.

Progen, J. L. (1978). *A description of stimulus seeking in sport according to flow theory*. Unpublished M.A. thesis, University of North Carolina.

Pryor, M., & Reeves, J. (1982). Male and female patterns of work opportunity structure to life satisfaction. *International Journal of Women's Studies, 5* (3), 215–26.

Raph, J. B., Goldberg, M. L., & Passow, A. H. (1966). *Bright underachievers.* New York: Teachers College Press.

Rathunde, K. (1987). *Optimal experience and family context of talented adolescents.* Unpublished manuscript, University of Chicago.

Redfield, R. (1953). *The primitive world and its transformations.* Ithaca, NY: Cornell University Press.

Renfrew, C. (1986). Varna and the emergence of wealth in prehistoric Europe. In A. Appadurai (Ed.), *The social life of things* (pp.141–68). New York: Cambridge University Press.

Ridley, F. A. (1938). *The Jesuits: a study in counter-revolution.* London: Secker and Warburg.

Robinson, R. E. (1986). Sex differences and mathematics achievement: aspects of the daily experience of giftedness in adolescence. In F. Massimini & P. Inghilleri (Eds.), *L'esperienza quotidiana* (pp. 417–36). Milan: Franco Angeli.

Rosenberg, M. (1965). *Society and the adolescent self-image.* Princeton, NJ: Princeton University Press.

Rosenberg, M. (1979). *Conceiving the self.* New York: Basic Books.

Roth, H. (1972). *Two on a big ocean.* New York: Macmillan.

Ryan, R. M., & Grolnick, W. S. (1986). Origins and pawns in the classroom: self-report and projective assessments of individual differences in children's perceptions. *Journal of Personality and Social Psychology, 50,* 550–8.

Sahlins, M. (1972). *Stone age economics.* Chicago: Aldine Press.

Samdahl, D. M. (1986). *The self and social freedom: a paradigm of leisure.* Unpublished doctoral dissertation, University of Illinois.

Sato, I. (1984). *Bosozoku no Esunograhi* [An ethnography of motorcycle gangs]. Tokyo: Keiso Shobo.

Saunders, M. (1975). *The Walkabouts.* London: Victor Gollancz.

Schacht, R. (Ed.). (1970). *Alienation.* Garden City, NY: Doubleday.

Schlucter, W. (1979). The paradox of rationalization: on the relation of ethics and the world. In G. Roth & W. Schlucter (Eds.), *Max Weber's vision of history* (pp. 11–64). Berkeley: University of California Press.

Schneider, W., & Shiffrin, R. M. (1977). Controlled and automatic human information processing: I. Detection, search, and attention. *Psychological Review, 84,* 1–66.

Schutz, A., & Luckmann, T. (1973). *The structures of the life-world .* Evanston, IL: Northwestern University Press.

Schwartzman, H. S. (1978). *Transformations.* New York: Plenum.

Scott, M. D. (1965). The social sources of alienation. In I. Horowitz (Ed.), *The New Sociology* (pp. 239–52). New York: Oxford University Press.

Seeman, M. (1959). On the meaning of alienation. *American Sociological Review, 24,* 783–91.

Seligman, M. E. P. (1975). *Helplessness: on depression, development, and death.* San Francisco, CA: Freedman.

Seligman, M. E. P., Peterson, C., Kaslow, N. J., Tannenbaum, R. L., Alloy, L. B., & Abramson, L. Y. (1984). Attributional style and depressive symptoms among children. *Journal of Abnormal Psychology, 93,* 235–38.

Shiffrin, R. M. (1976). Capacity limitation in information processing, attention, and memory. In W. K. Estes (Ed.), *Handbook of learning and cognitive processes.* Hillsdale, NJ: Erlbaum.

Shiffrin, R. M., & Schneider, W. (1977). Controlled and automatic human information processing: II. Perceptual learning, automatic attending, and a general theory. *Psychological Review, 84*, 127–90.

Simon, H. A. (1969). *Sciences of the artificial.* Boston: MIT Press.

Simpson, I., & Mutran, E. (1981). Women's social consciousness: sex or worker identity. In R. Simpson & I. Simpson (Ed.), *Research in the sociology of work* (pp. 335–50). Greenwich, CT: JAI Press.

Singer, J. L. (1984). *The human personality.* New York: Harcourt Brace Jovanovich.

Slocum, J. (1900). *Sailing alone around the world* (1900) and *The voyage of the "Liberdade"* (1895). London: The Reprint Society, 1949.

Smith, A. (1980). *An inquiry into the wealth of nations.* London: Methuen. (Original work published in 1776)

Smith, P. K. (1982). Does play matter? Functional and evolutionary aspects of animal and human play. *The Behavioral and Brain Sciences, 5*, 139–84.

Smith, R. (1981). Boredom: a review. *Human Factors, 23*, 239–340.

Solzhenitsyn, A. (1976). *The Gulag Archipelago.* New York: Harper & Row.

Spence, J. D. (1984). *The Memory Palace of Matteo Ricci.* New York: Viking Penguin.

Spreitzer, E., & Snyder, E. (1974). Work orientation, meaning of leisure and mental health. *Journal of Leisure Research, 6* (3), 207–19.

Sternberg, R. J. (1984). Mechanisms of cognitive development: a componential approach. In R. J. Sternberg (Ed.), *Mechanisms of cognitive development.* New York: W. H. Freeman.

Sun, W. (1987). *Flow and Yu: comparison of Csikszentmihalyi's theory and Chuangtzu's philosophy.* Paper presented at the meetings of The Anthropological Association for the Study of Play. Montreal, March.

Sutton-Smith, B. (1971). Play, games and controls. In J. P. Scott & S. F. Scott (Eds.), *Social control and social change* (pp. 73–102). Chicago: University of Chicago Press.

Sutton-Smith, B. (Ed.). (1979). *Play and learning.* New York: Garden Press.

Sutton-Smith, B., & Kelley-Byrne, D. (1984). *The masks of play.* New York: Leisure Press.

Sutton-Smith, B., & Roberts, J. M. (1963). Game involvement in adults. *Journal of Social Psychology, 60*, 15–30.

Tamura, M., & Mugishima, F. (1975). Bosozoku no Jittai Bunseki [The present state of motorcycle gangs]. *Kagaku Keisatsu Kenkyujo Hokoku, 16*, 38–72.

Taniguchi, M. (1982). Bosozoku [Motorcycle gangs]. In K. Kikuchi & M. Horiuchi (Eds.), *Asobigata Hiko* [Playlike delinquency] (pp. 124–33). Tokyo: Gakuji Shuppan.

Tannenbaum, A. J. (1983). *Gifted children: psychological and educational perspectives.* New York: Macmillan.

Taylor, C. (1979). Interpretation and the sciences of man. In P. Rabinow & W. Sullivan (Eds.), *Interpretive social science: a reader.* Berkeley: University of California Press.

Taylor, F. W. (1923). *Principles of scientific management.* New York: Harper.

Tazelaar, J., & Bussiere, J. (1977). *To challenge a distant sea.* Chicago: Henry Regnery.

Textor, R. B. (1967). *A cross-cultural summary.* New Haven, CT: Human Relations Area Files Press.

Thackray, R. I. (1981). The stress of boredom and monotony: a consideration of the evidence. *Psychosomatic Medicine, 43*, 165–76.

Thomas, W. I., & Thomas, D. S. (1928). *The child in America.* New York: Alfred A. Knopf.

Thompson, F. (1913). *Saint Ignatius Loyola*. J. H. Pollen, S. J., Ed. London: Burnes & Oates.

Tomkins, S. S. (1962). *Affect, imagery and consciousness*, Vol. 1: *The positive affects*. New York: Springer Verlag.

Tomkins, S. S. (1963). *Affect, imagery and consciousness*, Vol. 2: *The negative affects*. New York: Springer Verlag.

Toscano, M. (1986). Scuola e vita quotidiana: un caso di selezione culturale. In F. Massimini & P. Inghilleri (Eds.), *L'esperienza quotidiana* (pp. 305–18). Milan: Franco Angeli.

Treisman, A. M., & Gelade, G. (1980). A feature integration theory of attention. *Cognitive Psychology, 12*, 97–136.

Treisman, A. M., & Schmidt, H. (1982). Illusory conjunctions in the perception of objects. *Cognitive Psychology, 14*, 107–41.

Turkle, S. (1984). *The second self: computers and the human spirit*. New York: Simon & Schuster.

Turner, V. (1969). *The ritual process*. New York: Aldine.

Turner, V. (1974a). *Dramas, fields, and metaphors*. Ithaca, NY: Cornell University Press.

Turner, V. (1974b). Liminal to liminoid in play, flow, and ritual: an essay in comparative symbology. *Rice University Studies, 60* (3), 53–92.

Turner, V. (1982). *From ritual to theatre: the human seriousness of play*. New York: Performing Arts Journal Publication.

Ueno, J. (1980a). *Dokyumento Bosozoku I* [Documents, motorcycle gangs Part I]. Tokyo: Futami Shobo.

Ueno, J. (1980b). *Dokyumento Bosozoku II* [Documents, motorcycle gangs Part II]. Tokyo: Futami Shobo.

Ueno, J. (1980c). *Dokyumento Bosozoku III* [Documents, motorcycle gangs Part III]. Tokyo: Futami Shobo.

Uexkull, J. von (1957). *Instinctive behaviour*. London: Methuen.

Waley, A. (1939). *Three ways of thought in ancient China*. London: G. Allen & Unwin.

Walshok, M. (1979). Occupational values and family roles: women in blue-collar and service occupations. In K. Feinstein (Ed.), *Working women and families* (pp. 63–83). Beverly Hills, CA: Sage.

Watson, B. (1964). Translation of *Chuang Tzu, basic writings*. New York: Columbia University Press.

Weber, M. (1922). Die protestantische Ethik und der Geist des Kapitalismus. In I. C. B. Mohr (Ed.), *Gesammelte Aufsatze zur Religions-Sociologie*. Tubingen.

Weber, M. (1930). *The Protestant ethic and the spirit of capitalism*. London: Allen and Unwin.

Wells, A. (1985). *Variations in self-esteem in the daily life of mothers: theoretical and methodological issues*. Unpublished doctoral dissertation, University of Chicago.

Wells, A. (1986). Variazioni nell'autostima delle madri nei diversi contesti quotidiani: influenza della presenza dei figli. In F. Massimini & P. Inghilleri (Eds.), *L'esperienza quotidiana* (pp. 369–90). Milan: Franco Angeli.

White, R. C. (1955). Social class differences in the use of leisure. *American Journal of Sociology, 61*, 145–50.

White, R. W. (1959). Motivation reconsidered: the concept of competence. *Psychological Review, 66*, 297–333.

Whitmore, J. R. (1980). *Giftedness, conflict, and underachievement*. Boston: Allyn & Bacon.

Wicklund, R. A. (1975). Objective self-awareness. In L. Berkowitz (Ed.), *Advances in experimental social psychology,* 8 (pp. 233–75). New York: Academic Press.

Widmeyer, W. N. (Ed.). (1978). *Physical activity and the social sciences.* Waterloo, Ont.: University of Waterloo.

Wilensky, H. (1960). Work, careers, and social integration. *International Social Science Journal, 12* (Fall), 543–60.

Willis, P. (1978). *Profane culture.* London: Routledge and Kegan Paul.

Wilson, E. O. (1975). *Sociobiology: the new synthesis.* Boston, MA: Belknap Press.

Wilson, R. N. (1981). The courage to be leisured. *Social Forces, 60,* 282–303.

Winnicott, D. W. (1951). *Collected papers.* New York: Basic Books.

Wolfe, T. (1979). *The right stuff.* New York: Farrar, Straus, & Giroux.

Wylie, R. C. (1979). *The self-concept: theory and research on selected topics* (Vol.2, 2d ed.). Lincoln: University of Nebraska Press.

Zajonc, R. B. (1984). On the primacy of emotion. *American Psychologist, 39,* 117–23.

Zelizer, B. (1987). Media, event, performance: journalists in flow. Paper presented at the meetings of The Anthropolical Association for the Study of Play. Montreal, March.

Zilli, M. G. (1971). Reasons why the gifted adolescent underachieves and some of the implications of guidance and counseling to this problem. *Gifted Child Quarterly, 15* (5) 279–92.

Name index

Subject index

achievement, scholastic, 319, 320, 362; and flow, 322–6; and use of time, 321–2; in math, defined, 321

activation, 265, 307, 311, 351; and achievement, 324–5; and family context, 352–5, 357; and flow, 316, 318; and frequency of flow, 312; cross-cultural differences in, 292; measured by ESM, 253, 309, 310, 323

affect, 265, 311, 351; and family context, 352–3, 357, and flow, 312, 316, 317, 369; cross-cultural differences in, 292; measured by ESM, 253, 268, 309, 323

age differences, 188, 194, 197, 201, 253, 364; in adolescence, 151, 288; in old age, 138–49, 199, 201, 202; in the enjoyment of studying, 305; in the enjoyment of work, 201, 203, 204, 206

alienation, 10, 37–41, 43, 49, 53, 207, 215, 216, 263, 345, 377, 378; and flow, 40

anomie, 10, 37, 38, 39, 42–3; and flow, 40

antiflow, see flow experience

anxiety, 22, 30, 31, 36, 45, 88, 114, 164, 261, 371; activities associated with, 265, 267, 278–9; and achievement, 322–5, 374; and autotelic family, 345, 348, 351, 358, 362; and culture, 186, 233; and self-esteem, 330, 333, 335, 340; as antiflow, 87, 275, 282, 285–6, 377; as obstacle to creative writing, 150, 152–7, 162,

165; cross-cultural differences in, 289–92, 305; examples of, 282, 283; frequency of, 289, 311, 316; in school, 264; in work, 188, 202; measured by ESM, 261–3, 270–1, 277, 332, 368; quality of experience in, 272, 276, 286, 291, 311, 313–14

apathy, 138, 157, 365, 383; activities associated with, 279; and achievement, 322–5; and job satisfaction, 337; and leisure, 317; and self-esteem, 333; cross-cultural differences in, 289–93, 295–6, 299, 305; examples of, 281–4; frequency of, 289, 311, 316; measured by ESM, 261–3, 270, 275, 285, 332, 368; quality of experience in, 272, 276, 286, 291, 298, 311, 313–14, 317, 369

arousal: measured by ESM, 270, 281–2, 290, 300–1; see also optimal arousal

attention: and flow, 30, 32, 33, 72, 98–9, 122, 163, 176, 259; and consciousness, 17–19, 22; and family context, 343–6, 358; and psychic entropy, 22, 154, 157, 159, 162, 184; as psychic energy, 19, 21, 39, 346, 359; as selective mechanism in evolution, 61, 65; attraction of, 108–9, 116, 240, 247; centering, focusing, or investing of, 62, 85, 90, 109, 162–3, 175–6, 185, 199, 280, 282, 287, 299, 343, 382; control of, 163, 165, 186, 206, 238; economy of, 358, 360, 361, 362, 363; in Jesuit spiritual exercises, 237, 239;

mountain climbing, 5, 46–59, 77, 101,
106, 110, 115, 116, 163, 179, 194,
205, 217, 266, 307, 382
music: listening to, 277, 278, 279,
281, 282, 283, 322, 356

natural settings: use of in flow and
ESM studies, 10–11, 15
nature: and cruising, 227, 229, 230; as
source of flow, 187, 198, 199, 203,
216, 222; logic of, 219
negentropy: psychic, 24, 27, 29, 33,
66, 150, 260, 283, 284, 365, 368,
379; systemic, 351, 352, 353, 357
neoteny, 361
nonflow, see flow experience

occupation: its effects on flow, 46–59,
118–37, 206, 209, 263, 308, 313–28,
365; of mothers, 336
optimal arousal, 5, 44, 164, 167, 344
optimal experience, 24, 29, 31, 60, 68,
69, 74, 75, 279, 282, 283, 284, 364,
367–70; age differences in, 188, 197,
201; and achievement, 323, 373–6;
and family context, 264, 342–63;
and history, 192; and life choices,
212; and lifestyle, 213; and self-esteem, 327–41; class differences in,
87, 121–7, 207–8, 316; cultural differences in, 66–81, 89, 194, 197,
305; gender differences in, 87, 89;
in productive activities, 199, 204,
208, 209, 210, 277, 280, 307–18;
measurement of, 195, 268–87, 368;
of traditional farmers, 198, 201,
203, 378, 379; studying as, 302, 354;
see also autotelic experience; enjoyment; flow experience; negentropy,
psychic
ordeals, 90–1, 172–80, 251, 371
order, 191, 267, 283, 353; Jesuit, 232,
234–5, 237–8, 245; restoration of,
278–81; see also negentropy

personality, see autotelic personality
play, 5, 45, 52–7, 59, 94, 104, 113,
116, 344, 346, 361, 381; anthropology of, 9; as metaphor for life, 172;
of ideas, 159, 375
pleasure, 24–5, 29, 34, 63, 206, 368;
its role in evolution, 61, 64–5, 367

potency, see activation
progress, 189
psychic energy, 19, 21, 39, 360, 366,
377; and creativity, 150, 157, 171;
and evolution, 29, 61; and productive goals, 209, 263, 284, 286, 326,
373, 379; control of, 87, 206; in flow
experience, 33, 34, 163; structuring
of, 235, 237, 247, 321, 345, 378; see
also attention
psychic entropy, see entropy, psychic
psychology: and history, 232, 266,
375; humanistic, 216, 287; limitations of current approaches, 15–17,
383; of Jesuit order, 238
psychopathology, 13, 15, 23, 87, 93

quality of life, 377; see also optimal
experience

rationalization: of life, 49–53, 206; of
leisure and sports, 53–7, 206; of society, 50, 52–4, 58, 194; of work,
50, 52, 57–8
reading, 317; as flow activity, 69, 75,
76, 79, 132, 276, 279; as part of creative writing, 158, 165
relaxation: and achievement, 326;
measured by ESM, 270, 290, 300,
301
religion, 240, 244, 245; and flow, 9,
60, 62, 75, 76, 78, 85, 141; as flow,
232–48; survival of, 65
rewards, intrinsic: see intrinsic
motivation
risk, 46, 373; in cruising, 217, 226,
227; in motorcycle riding, 93, 96,
100, 101, 115, 116; random, 227
ritual, 9, 54, 65, 76, 78, 91, 92, 177,
377; of Jesuits, 236
rock climbing, see mountain climbing
roles, 37, 38, 52, 58, 113, 116, 210,
236, 281, 369, 370, 378; uncertainty
in, 42, 112; of women, 119
rules, 50, 65, 93, 101, 102, 112, 113,
190, 265, 343, 347; and anomie, 42;
clarity of, 345, 346, 358, 360, 363;
cultural, 186, 232, 233, 343; importance of, 32, 163, 345, 359; in cruising, 229; of religious orders, 235,
238, 246, 247; transgression of, 56